HOW TO THRIVE AT COLLEGE

Finding Your Path at CSU

CHARLESTON SOUTHERN UNIVERSITY

Kendall Hunt
publishing company

Cover design by Jonathan Merkling. © Kendall Hunt Publishing Company
Cover photos © Charleston Southern University

Kendall Hunt
publishing company

www.kendallhunt.com
Send all inquiries to:
4050 Westmark Drive
Dubuque, IA 52004-1840

Copyright © 2017 by Kendall Hunt Publishing Company

PAK ISBN: 978-1-5249-8380-2
Text alone ISBN: 978-1-5249-8381-9

All rights reserved. No part of this publication may be reproduced, stored in a retrieval system, or transmitted, in any form or by any means, electronic, mechanical, photocopying, recording, or otherwise, without the prior written permission of the copyright owner.

Published in the United States of America

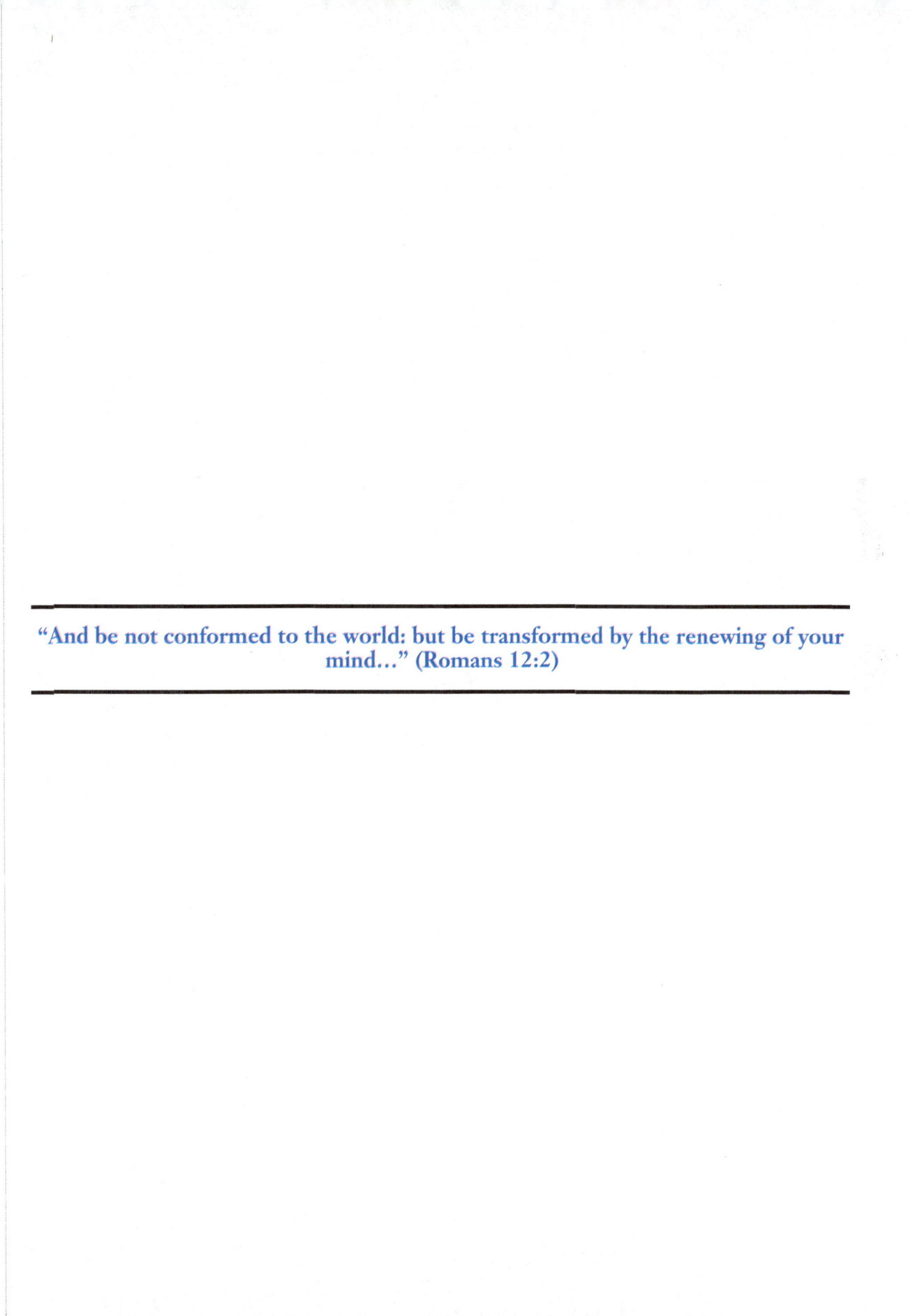

"And be not conformed to the world: but be transformed by the renewing of your mind…" (Romans 12:2)

Contents

Preface   ix

Introduction   1

MISSION, VISION, AND CORE VALUES OF
CHARLESTON SOUTHERN UNIVERSITY   3

THE HISTORY OF CSU   6

CSU: THEN AND NOW   9

Key Reflections: If our purpose is to glorify God by showing who He is to those around us, it is imperative that we understand clearly how God wants us to accomplish that purpose. *How does CSU's mission of integrating faith in learning, leading and serving demonstrate a desire to serve God's purpose for this university?*

Chapter 1: Touching All the Bases   21

CSU FAITH INTEGRATION (THE GREATEST COMMANDMENT)   45

Key Reflections: Successful students are **involved, interactive, resourceful,** and **reflective**. *How can these same abilities apply to the way you demonstrate God's love when interacting with your professors? Your peers? Which of the four characteristics of successful students do you need to work on most right now? How do you plan to improve in this area?*

Chapter 2: Deep Learning   51

CSU FAITH INTEGRATION (LOVE, OBEDIENCE, AND WORSHIP, GETTING TO KNOW HIM)   85

Key Reflections: Deep learning goes beyond surface-level memorization. It's connecting new ideas to ideas that have already been learned. *How do think your current personal worldview could impact the time you invest in showing your love for the people and things in your life? In your schoolwork, what practices can you incorporate to ensure you are focusing on deep learning instead of memorization?*

Chapter 3: Test-Taking Skills and Strategies   91

CSU FAITH INTEGRATION (LOVE DECLARED, AS YOU LOVE YOURSELF)   114

Key Reflections: Effective performance on college exams requires spending time applying effective strategies in advance of the test, during the test, and after test results are returned. *How can the time you spend engaging with God's Word impact the way you see God working in your life? How might you adjust some of your test-taking strategies based on the information discussed in Chapter 3?*

Chapter 4: Three Key Academic Success and Lifelong Learning Skills   121

CSU FAITH INTEGRATION (THE NEW COMMANDMENT, LOVE ONE ANOTHER, AS I HAVE LOVED YOU)   146

Key Reflections: Research skills enable you to locate, evaluate, and integrate information, while writing and speaking skills enable you to comprehend, communicate, and demonstrate your mastery of that information to others. Higher-level thinking involves reflecting on knowledge acquired and taking it to a higher level—by performing additional mental action on it—such as evaluating its validity, integrating it with other ideas, or applying it to solve problems.

In what ways do you think the life of Christ is a good standard to use for learning how to love God and follow his commandment to love others? Which skill (research, writing, or speaking) do you need to improve the most? What are you going to do to start working on improving this skill now? Which form of higher-level thinking have you used in your studies the most so far this term? Which form of higher-level thinking do you need to practice more?

Chapter 5: Diversity   153
CSU Faith Integration (Love and Forgiveness, It's Your Attitude, Effective Speaking)   186

Key Reflections: Intellectual ability is only one form of human intelligence. Social and emotional intelligence are equally, if not more, important for living a successful, healthy, and happy life. Diversity refers to the variety of groups that comprise the human species. Humans differ from one another in multiple ways, including physical features, religious beliefs, mental and physical abilities, national origins, social backgrounds, gender, and other ways.

Key Reflections: God's justice is rooted in His love; God's forgiveness toward us is based on Christ accepting the judgment for our unloving actions. *How do you think stereotypes and prejudices affect our willingness to forgive wrongs done to us by others? What "Strategies for Overcoming Stereotypes and Prejudices" will you put into practice? How will this help you grow as a student and individual?*

Chapter 6: Health and Wellness   191
CSU Faith Integration (Truth and Grace, Love in Action)   213

Key Reflections: Our physical wellness is largely a reflection of the way we eat, our level of physical activity, the nature of the relationships we keep, and the ways in which we spend our time. *Which dimension of wellness do you need to work on the most? What can you do to improve in that dimension of wellness? How do you think the way in which you (personally) live your life is a reflection of your relationship with God?*

Chapter 7: Time Management   217
CSU Faith Integration (In Times of Loss, At All Times)   233

Key Reflections: Effective goal-setting gets you going, but effective time management gets things done. The enemy of effective time management is procrastination. There are multiple effective strategies for beating the procrastination habit. *How do you plan to ensure that your time-spending habits are aligned with your educational goals and priorities?*

Key Reflections: "By this we know love, because He laid down His life for us. And we also ought to lay down our lives for the brethren. But whoever has this world's goods, and sees his brother in need, and shuts up his heart from him, how does the love of God abide in him?" 1 John 3:16–17

We should have our ears open to hearing when those around us are in need. *Using the talents and blessings God has given you, what are some ways that you could fit some time into your schedule to meet the needs of others?*

Chapter 8: Educational Planning and Academic Decision-Making   243
CSU Faith Integration (Putting Love Into Practice, How to Love God)   270

Key Reflections: Studies show that the vast majority of students entering college are uncertain about their academic specialization. Most students do not reach a final decision about their major before starting college. Your college experience opens career doors for you, but it's your attitude, initiative, and effort that enable you to step through those doors and into a successful career. *Of the four awareness steps for career planning, at which step are you currently?*

Key Reflection: "But the fruit of the Spirit is love, joy, peace, longsuffering, kindness, goodness, faithfulness, gentleness, self-control. Against such there is no law. And those who are Christ's have crucified the flesh with its passions and desires. If we live in the Spirit, let us also walk in the Spirit." Galatians 5: 19–25

God has equipped each of us with special skills, talents, and yearnings. *What do you think are your unique skills and talents? How could you use these to show God's love to others?*

Chapter 9: Goal Setting and Motivation   285
CSU Faith Integration (Your Decision)   297

Key Reflections: Set SMART goals that are challenging and realistic. Use effective strategies to maintain motivation. Possess: an Internal Locus of Control, Self-Efficacy, Grit, and a Growth Mindset. Goal-setting is the key that gets us going and motivation is the fuel that keeps us going until we cross the finish line.

Specifically, how can you display patience and perseverance to ensure you can accomplish your goals? What goals are you willing to set to show God's love to others?

Preface

Individuals come to college to gather knowledge, find their purpose, and earn a degree.

As you are soon to discover, the first year in college will be a pivotal period of academic, social, and emotional development for you and your peers. The freshman year and your first semester, in particular, are considered a transitional stage of adjustment from the high school setting to college life. The table below compares some key differences you are likely to experience right away.

\multicolumn{3}{c}{**High School Versus College**}		
Characteristic	High School Model	College Model
Setting for Learning	Most learning occurs *in class*. Students may study outside class as little as one to two hours a week.	Most learning occurs *outside of class*. On average, Students will need to study about two hours outside of class for each hour spent in class.
Schedule	Students attend class back-to back for about 6 hours each day; *30–35 per week.*	The student creates his or her own schedule. Classes do not meet every day. There may be many unscheduled hours between classes. Class times vary throughout the day and evening. The student spends only *12–18 hours per week in class.*
Role of the Instructor	Teachers are directive and nurturing.	Professors are caring, but expect the student to be independent and to take personal responsibility for learning.
Office Hours	Teachers do not keep office hours. Instead, they answer questions and offer help to students *in class.*	Professors schedule regular office hours for the purpose of meeting with students *individually* when extra help is needed.
Reading Requirements	The student seldom needs to read anything more than once—and *sometimes listening in class is enough.*	The amount of reading assigned by professors may be large. The student must review class notes and text material *regularly.* Preparation for exams typically requires *multiple* reviews of all course materials. "Cramming" the night before an exam does little to no good.

Presentation of Material	Teachers present the material at a *slower pace*, and the presentation is designed to support the textbook.	Professors present the material at a *more rapid pace* and their presentation is designed to *supplement* the text. Professors expect you to study the book on your own and then they will add to or explain it.
Frequency of Testing	There is *frequent testing*. Therefore, the student is required to master only a small amount of the total course material for any single exam.	*Testing is less frequent*—sometimes just a midterm and final. Therefore, the student must be prepared to demonstrate mastery of a much larger amount of material for a single exam.
Extra Credit	High school grades may be derived not only from exams but also from other assignments. Consistently good homework grades or *extra credit assignments might be used to compensate for poor performance on exams and raise your course grade.*	College grades are usually derived from exams and major papers or projects. Typically, there is *limited opportunity (or none) to earn extra credit points toward the semester grade.*

Charleston Southern's **GNED 101 Freshman Seminar** course is intentionally designed to serve as a foundation on which the remainder of your college courses and experiences are built. This course will focus on those academic and non-academic components that will impact you during your freshman year—and influence your success through college and beyond.

Your approach to this class and your entire learning involvement here will be influenced by the framework of your ***personal worldview***—how you think, evaluate, and experience everything in the world around you.

A key focus of Charleston Southern University is the integration of faith with learning, leading and serving. We believe that intellect, faith, and love of serving God must function synergistically to empower students fully. This focus is derived from the most important principle given to the Church; Jesus replied:

> "Love the Lord your God with all your heart and with all your soul and with all your mind." This is the first and greatest commandment (Matt. 22:37–38).

We want our students to love truth and pursue it freely. We endeavor to show them that learning can strengthen and extend their faith. 2 Timothy 3:16 tells us—

> "All Scripture is inspired by God and is useful to teach us what is true and to make us realize what is wrong in our lives. It corrects us when we are wrong and teaches us to do what is right."

Not only does all truth belong to God, but the spiritual battle for the modern world we live in is taking place in a sophisticated and secular marketplace that requires well trained and well informed minds to engage in the struggle (Harris, R. A., 2014).

At CSU, we believe that a ***biblical worldview***, faith, and activities of the student should be deeply connected within the learning experience, and curriculum design should provide a structure for students to explore the Christian faith in relation to course materials.

> We are told to do no less than ready our minds: "Always be prepared to give an answer to everyone who asks you to give the reason for the hope that you have" (1 Peter 3:15b).

It is our desire that your CSU educational experience will inspire you to seek truth from a biblical worldview, discover God's calling for your life, and deem you equipped to further the kingdom of God by learning, leading and serving, *wherever your future takes you.*

The design of this text is an anthology of best practices for college success, interwoven with practical applications for pursuing a life that honors and glorifies God.

College Success Skills

On campus, new students must try to make sense of the clear and unspoken expectations, rituals, and norms of the higher education culture—a process that can be simultaneously exhilarating, overwhelming and alienating. Not surprisingly, students often struggle with balancing the demands of work, family, and school—on top of having difficulty grasping what is expected of them in a given class or on a given assignment (Jehangir, 2010). **How to Thrive at College: Finding your path at CSU** will provide many college success tools and tips to support and inspire students through to graduation.

Faith Integration

The New Commandment is a term used in Christianity to describe Jesus's commandment to "love one another." Jesus gave these final instructions to his disciples after the Last Supper had ended, and after Judas Iscariot had departed in John 13:30. Jesus was preparing his disciples for the time when he would leave them. Just as he had loved them while with them, likewise they were to, henceforth, stand in for Jesus—*in their love and care for one another.*

Written by a professor with experience as a pastor and NASA researcher, James Klemaszewski's ***The New Commandment*** explains with clarity what it means to be a Christian who follows God and shows *His love*. Filled with and based upon scripture, it provides practical applications to illustrate God's love and how to show it…*His way*. Readers will understand how to successfully fulfill God's purpose for them, live fulfilled lives and, ultimately, how to glorify Him.

In **How to Thrive at College: Finding your path at CSU,** you will learn about the best practices for succeeding in college and what it means to honor God through your relationships. It is our desire that you will discover the value of applying the biblical principles and lifelong success skills introduced here with your pursuit of building Relationships and glorifying God—*in College and beyond.*

REFERENCES

Harris, R. A., 2014. Faithful mind, thoughtful faith: Integrating faith and learning. VirtualSalt Publishing, Trustin, CA

Jehangir, R. (2010). Stories as knowledge: Bringing the lived experience of first-generation college students into the academy. Urban Education, 45(4), 533–553. doi:10.1177/0042085910372352

Introduction

It's official; you are now a Charleston Southern University Buccaneer! You have chosen a university that is like none other. What makes CSU special? Our mission, vision, and culture are unique to higher education. Our mission of *Promoting Academic Excellence in a Christian Environment* is the overarching framework that gives structure to everything we do. The founders of this university were guided by biblical inspiration found in Matthew 28:19-20:

Our institutional goals, including **Faith Integration**, **Academic Excellence**, and **Student Engagement and Success** are purposed to fulfill CSU's vision to be a Christian university nationally recognized for **integrating faith in learning, leading, and serving**. As a student at CSU, learning, leading, and serving will become the pillars of your entire educational experience.

> Go ye therefore, and teach all nations, baptizing them in the name of the Father, and of the Son, and of the Holy Ghost: Teaching them to observe all things whatsoever I have commanded you: and, lo, I am with you always, even unto the end of the world.

From *Thriving in College and Beyond: Research-Based Strategies for Academic Success and Personal Development*, Fourth Edition by Joseph B. Cuseo, Aaron Thompson, Michele Campagna, and Viki S. Fecas. Copyright © 2016 Kendall Hunt Publishing Company. Reprinted by permission.

All photos in this section are © Charleston Southern University

BIBLICAL WORLDVIEW

Do you have a worldview? The answer is *"yes"* even if you are not familiar with the term. A worldview is the framework from which we view reality and make sense of life and the world around us. Whether conscious or subconscious, every person has some type of worldview. A personal worldview is a combination of all you believe to be true, and what you believe becomes the driving force behind every emotion, decision, and action. Therefore, it affects your response to every area of life: from philosophy to science, theology and anthropology to economics, law and politics to art and social order—*everything*. In the tradition of our mission to integrate the Christian faith in learning, leading, and serving, CSU programming, both inside and outside the classroom, is framed by a **biblical worldview**. Someone with a *biblical worldview* believes his or her primary reason for existence is to love and serve God. The faculty, staff, and coaches at CSU are practicing Christians, each making a statement of faith as a condition of employment with the university.

On the other hand, our students are not required to make a statement of faith as a condition of their matriculation to the university. This means that you will be interacting daily with students who may have a different religious or cultural background than your own—*a different worldview*. We at CSU embrace this diversity as a distinctive facet of our campus culture. Your college experience is intended to be a holistic learning experience and part of that process will be to practice and prepare to connect and collaborate with individuals who are different than you. We encourage you to embrace this opportunity!

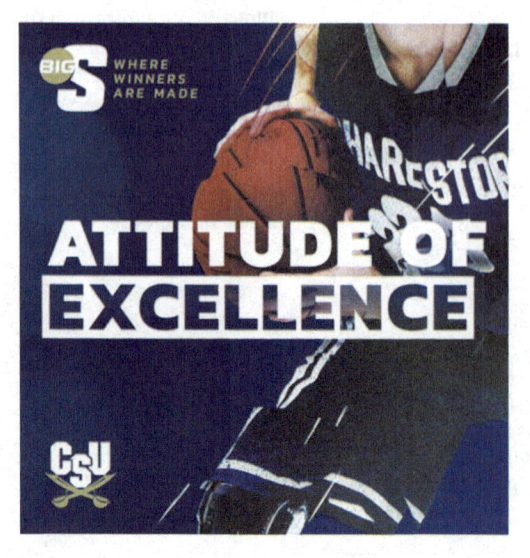

All CSU students will be presented with the Gospel of Christ, both directly and indirectly—from the required Christian Studies core classes and Chapel testimonials to the concrete and abstract influences that shape the lens of disciplinary studies across our curriculum. Small group bible study, mission trips, community service, corporate worship at ELEVATE, and weekly on-campus church service are other areas where you can let your light shine. This is how we at CSU integrate faith in learning, leading, and serving.

MISSION AND VISION

MISSION

Promoting Academic Excellence in a Christian Environment

VISION

To be a Christian university nationally recognized for integrating faith in learning, leading, and serving

> *Learning*: 2 Corinthians 10:5 We demolish arguments and every pretension that sets itself up against the knowledge of God, and we take captive every thought to make it obedient to Christ.
>
> *Leading*: Colossians 3:17 And whatever you do, whether in word or deed, do it all in the name of the Lord Jesus, giving thanks to God the Father through him.
>
> *Serving*: Ephesians 2:10 For we are God's workmanship, created in Christ Jesus to do good works, which God prepared in advance for us to do.

INSTITUTIONAL GOALS

> *Faith Integration:* Strengthen the culture of the university by making biblical faith a priority

Academic Excellence: Assure excellence in academic programs to maximize student learning

Student Engagement and Success: Increase student satisfaction, retention, graduation rates, and employment opportunities

Regional, National, and International Reputation: Promote academic and student success regionally, nationally, and internationally

Faculty, Staff, and Coaches Development: Provide for the personal and professional development of faculty, staff, and coaches

Enrollment: Grow enrollment by expanding academic programs and employing a variety of delivery methods

Athletics: Improve the competitive status of CSU's Division I athletic program

Resource Development: Generate sufficient financial resources to accomplish the university's goals and objectives

Financial Stewardship: Maximize the university's financial and physical resources

CORE VALUES
SCRIPTURE
II Timothy 3:16 "All Scripture is given by inspiration of God and is profitable for doctrine, for reproof, for correction, for instruction in righteousness." The Bible is the inerrant and infallible record of God's revelation to humanity, and it is the only sufficient source of appeal on matters relating to the Christian faith.

GOD
Genesis 1:1 "In the beginning, God created the heavens and the earth." John 1:3 "All things were made by him; and without him was not anything made that was made." There is one and only one living and true God. The historical account of Genesis decrees that He is the personal and direct Creator of all that exists, including the first human beings Adam and Eve. To Him, we owe the highest love, reverence, and obedience.

JESUS CHRIST
John 14:6 "Jesus saith unto them, I am the way, the truth, and the life: no man cometh unto the Father, but by me." God made provision through Christ for the redemption of sinful humanity by His substitutionary atonement on the cross, and He alone is sufficient as Savior.

SALVATION
John 3:16 "For God so loved the world, that he gave his only begotten Son, that whosoever believeth in him should not perish, but have everlasting life." Salvation involves God's gracious redemption of individuals

and is offered freely to all who accept Jesus Christ as personal Lord and Savior by repentance and faith.

LIFE OF THE BELIEVER

Romans 12:2 "And do not be conformed to this world, but be transformed by the renewing of your mind, that you may prove what is that good and acceptable and perfect will of God." Christians are to be consistent with Scripture in their character and conduct.

DIVERSITY

Genesis 1:27 "God created man in His own image, in the image of God He created him; male and female He created them." Because all people are made in God's divine image, they possess full dignity and are worthy of respect. Matthew 22:39 "You shall love your neighbor as yourself." Jesus' command for us to love others as ourselves extends to all people. Revelation 7:9 "After these things I looked, and behold, a great multitude which no one could number, all nations, tribes, peoples, and tongues, standing before the throne and before the Lamb . . ." Charleston Southern University defines diversity as people groups varying in ethnic makeup, cultural background, age, language, educational and professional experience, ability, veteran, and/or socioeconomic status. Our commitment to diversity is biblically informed; therefore, the university engages and supports diversity-related matters as they are clearly defined in Scripture.

EDUCATION

Deuteronomy 6:6-7a ". . . these words which I command you today shall be in your heart. You shall teach them diligently to your children . . ." Matthew 28:19-20 ". . . make disciples of all the nations . . . teaching them to observe all things that I have commanded you . . ." Christianity is the faith of enlightenment and intelligence . . . All sound learning is, therefore, a part of our Christian heritage. The new birth opens all human faculties and creates a thirst for knowledge. Moreover, the cause of education in the Kingdom of Christ is coordinate with the causes of missions and general benevolence, and should receive along with these the liberal support of the churches. An adequate system of Christian education is necessary to a complete spiritual program for Christ's people.

EVANGELISM AND MISSIONS

Acts 1:8 "But ye shall receive power, after that the Holy Ghost is come upon you; and ye shall be witnesses unto me both in Jerusalem, and in all Judea, and in Samaria, and unto the uttermost part of the earth." It is the privilege and duty of every Christian to share the Gospel of Christ personally and by all other methods in harmony with the Gospel.

-Adapted from THE BAPTIST FAITH AND MESSAGE, Southern Baptist Convention, 2000

HISTORY of CSU

Charleston Southern University, formerly Baptist College at Charleston, is one of the largest accredited, private universities in South Carolina. Affiliated with the South Carolina Baptist Convention, the university offers 48 undergraduate degrees and 8 graduate degree programs and enrolls 3,600 students. The university has graduated more than 18,000 students in its 50-year history.

The urgent need for another college in the Lowcountry became a matter of active and organized consideration in 1954. South Carolina Baptists made its establishment a matter of official deliberation at a meeting of the General Board in September 1955.

After considerable study by official education committees, both locally and convention wide, the Capital Needs Committee of the State Convention brought a recommendation which initiated efforts to begin seeking both a site and funds for the establishment of a college. The South Carolina Baptist Convention agreed to support the plan, and more than 70,000 individuals made contributions ranging from $1 to $20,000.

Former Charleston mayor, J. Palmer Gaillard Jr., was instrumental in helping supporters acquire 500 acres of land 16 miles from the city limits of Charleston, at the northeast intersection of Interstate 26 and Highway 78. In 1964, trustees were elected by the South Carolina Baptist Convention.

Dr. John A. Hamrick, pastor of First Baptist Church of Charleston and founder of First Baptist Church School, was elected the first president of the university by the Board of Trustees in November 1964. The first semester of Charleston Southern University was in the fall of 1965, in buildings of the First Baptist Church of North Charleston. Administrative offices were located in the First Baptist Church of Charleston. Professors from The Citadel and the Medical University offered to serve as part-time professors to supplement the small faculty. The old St. John Hotel, now The Mills House Hotel, offered to rent rooms to house students.

By September 1966, buildings on the campus were ready, and the university's second year began amid construction, landscaping and the physical development of the campus. By the third year, a 60-member faculty was in place, and majors were offered in 17 academic areas. In 1969, the founding class graduated, and by 1971 the school gained accreditation.

In 1984, Dr. Jairy C. Hunter Jr. became the second president of Charleston Southern University. The Graduate Studies Program in Education became accredited in 1986. It was expanded to include concentrations in elementary and secondary education beginning with the 1988 spring term. The School of Business began to offer a Master of Business Administration degree in 1990. In 1993, the School of Education began offering a Master of Education in Educational Administration, a Master of Science in Criminal Justice, Physicians Assistant Program and Doctor of Education.

In 2018, Dr. Dondi E. Costin, the former Air Force Chief of Chaplains, became the third president of Charleston Southern University, and we can't wait to see what new programs and opportunities are around the corner for CSU!

The university has grown from an initial student body of 588. There are now many significant campus buildings to provide for the needs of the university. From its beginning, the university has sought to provide not only excellent academic opportunities, but has also, in all its planning, held to the ideal of the development of the total individual. Employment of personnel deeply committed to assisting each individual student to attain his maximum potential within a Christian environment has made this institution distinctive.

OUR TIMELINE IN HISTORY

1955	Official deliberation held at the South Carolina Baptist Convention General Board regarding the establishment of a college in the Low country
1964	Dr. John A. Hamrick elected first president of the Baptist College at Charleston
1965	First semester held in the fall
1966	Buildings on campus ready to receive students
1969	Founding class graduated
1971	School gained accreditation
1972	Strom Thurmond Student Center dedicated
1975	Athletic teams moved to NCAA Division I
1984	Dr. Jairy C. Hunter Jr. elected second president of the Baptist College at Charleston

Introduction

1984	Lightsey Chapel dedicated
1986	Graduate Studies Program in Education became accredited
1990	The School of Business began to offer a Master of Business Administration
1990	University achieved university status
1990	Baptist College at Charleston renamed **Charleston Southern University**
1991	Hunter Reception Center dedicated
1995	School of Nursing dedicated
1997	Study Abroad Program launched
1999	Master of Science in Criminal Justice added as a graduate offering
2000	The Brewer Center, Whitfield Stadium Center, and Whittington Hall open
2001	Bagwell-Settle Track dedicated
2003	University builds first Habitat for Humanity house
2004	Teaching and Learning Program in Ghana nationally recognized
2005	Science Building Officially Opened
2006	L. Mendel Rivers Library renovated and Java City added
2007	Wyndham by Wingate Inn opens
2007	Air Force ROTC Detachment 772 nationally recognized
2009	Dr. Hunter's service honored with highest state civilian award: The Order of the Palmetto
2009	Master of Science in Nursing Education added
2013	Whitfield Center for Christian Leadership opens and Nursing Building expansion opens
2014	Chick-fil-A Express opens, and Hunter Reception Center expanded and renamed the Jairy C. and Carolyn K. Hunter Center, in recognition of Dr. and Mrs. Hunter's 30 years of service to CSU
2014	CSU celebrates its 50th Anniversary
2015	Charleston Southern recognized as College of Distinction
2016	CSU breaks ground on Singleton Baseball Complex
2017	CSU launched the ELI Program
2018	Dr. Dondi E. Costin becomes the 3rd president of CSU

Introduction

THEN...	NOW...
In fall 1965, first classes held at First Baptist Church in North Charleston, SC with 500 full-time and part-time students, a small group of faculty and approximately 150 resident students who were boarded at the St. John Hotel on Meeting Street (downtown Charleston). In fall 1968, the Baptist College had a headcount of 1,449 and 1,147 full-time students.	Current enrollment is 3,673 with students representing 26 of the United States and 21 countries. Full-time faculty of 165 and additional adjunct faculty sustain our academic curriculum. Current housing facilities are overflowing and construction of additional dormitory space is soon to break ground. The university's strategic plan includes the goal of 4,000 students by the year 2020.
In 1965–66, the curriculum included these undergraduate majors: religion, music, biology, physical education, physics/math, business, English, and foreign languages.	The University currently offer 48 undergraduate degree programs and 5 certificate programs within the following areas: • School of Business • School of Education • School of Christian Studies • College of Nursing • College of Health Sciences • College of Science and Mathematics • College of Humanities and Social Sciences

Introduction

School athletics began in 1965–66 competing under the NAIA conference in men's track and field, cross country, and basketball. The first basketball team was known as the "wandering buccaneers" because of no practice facilities of their own. Early administration wanted a mascot to be the *Christians* or the *Crusaders*. The students did not. "Their first game was held at College of Charleston because they had no gym. Students showed up wearing eye patches, bandanas, and earrings. They were waving swords and holding signs that said **BUCCANEERS**. And ever since that fateful night downtown Charleston in 1965, we've been the Buccaneers." (Cutlass)	The school joined the Big South Conference in 1983 as club football, then moved to NCAA Division III status in 1990. All sports, including football are now NCAA Division I-AA status. • Current Men's teams: Football, Basketball, Baseball, Cross Country, Golf, and Track and Field (indoor and outdoor) • Current Women's teams: Basketball, Soccer, Softball, Cross Country, Track and Field (indoor and outdoor), Volleyball, Golf, and Tennis *Bucky the Buccaneer lives on as our faithful Mascot!*
In May 1960, the founding class graduated 158 students. First graduation held in Lightsey Chapel Auditorium, May 1985.	For many years, graduation ceremonies were held in the Lightsey Chapel. Graduating classes have swelled to overflow this traditional venue requiring a relocation to the North Charleston Coliseum. A record of 676 undergraduate and graduate degrees was awarded in the 2015–16 academic year.
In September 1966, the college moved to its present campus site and contained a small handful of buildings: a classroom building that also housed the library (present day Norris and Wingo Halls); a science administration building that also housed the student center and dining hall (present day Ashby and Jones Halls); and temporary housing facilities in trailers for 360 students and housing staff.	During Dr. Hunter's tenure as president, many new buildings have been added to the campus: Lightsey Chapel, Jairy C. & Carolyn K. Hunter Center, Derry Patterson Wingo Nursing building, Whitfield Stadium enter, Brewer Center, Whittington Hall, the Science Building, Wingate by Wyndham hotel, Whitfield Center for Christian Leadership, the Health Sciences Building, along with renovations to several existing buildings.
In 1971, the Baptist College achieves accreditation by the Southern Association of Colleges and Schools (SACS) as a liberal arts/general baccalaureate degree institution.	Most recent SACS reaffirmation in 2016 resulted in zero recommendations. Other areas CSU currently holds special accreditation include: • Commission on Accreditation of Athletic Training Education • International Assembly for Collegiate Business Education • Council for the Accreditation of Educator Preparation • National Association of Schools of Music • American Music Therapy Association • Accrediting Commission for Education in Nursing • Computing Accreditation Commission of ABET
Founded as the Baptist College at Charleston	In 1990, the college gained University status and its name changed to *Charleston Southern University*.

Dr. John A. Hambrick was the college's first President, serving from 1964 to 1983. Dr. Jairy C. Hunter came on board in 1984 as the second president of the school and served until 2018.	Dr. Dondi E. Costin became the 3rd president of Charleston Southern University and serves to present day.
First Master's degrees awarded in 1985—with three students.	Currently offering 10 graduate degree programs: • Athletic Training • Business: MBA, Leadership, Organizational Management, Human Resource Management • Computer Science • Criminal Justice • Education • Christian Studies • Nursing • Physician's Assistant Program
In 1997, six students participated in CSU's first study abroad program in Spain.	Study abroad for experiential education can take you anywhere! Meet with the Director of the Office of International Programs to discuss opportunities. 2018-19 students will launched our ELI (Experiential Learning Initiative) Program that provides enriched educational opportunities via internships, practicums, clinicals, field courses, and other real-world application of classroom theory.
In 2009, the Evening College revamped and expanded to College of Distance and Continuing Education.	The University currently offers 16 online programs: • Healthcare Management • Hospitality and Tourism Management • Human Resource Management • Organizational Management • Project Management • Completion degree in Computer Systems and Information Science • Master of Science in Analytics
	• Master of Science in Organizational Leadership • Master of Arts in Christian Studies • Master of Science in Computer Science • Master of Science in Organizational Management • Master of Science in Project Management • Master of Business Administration • Master of Science in Nursing • Master of Science in Supply Chain Management • Master of Science in Criminal Justice • Doctor of Education

12 Introduction

ARIAL VIEW OF CAMPUS

CSU ALMA MATER

Hail to thee, O Charleston Southern:
Fount of God's great truth and knowledge.
We thy children all sing praises ever more to thee.
Source of inspiration, beacon of salvation;
Honor, Courage, Faith and Justice
These thou hast taught us day by day.
Hail to thee O Charleston Southern,
Alma Mater Hail!

UNIVERSITY MASCOT
BUCKY THE BUCCANEER

OFFICIAL SCHOOL COLORS
Blue (**Pantone 295**) and Gold (**Pantone 7503**)

CLUBS AND ORGANIZATIONS

ACADEMIC CLUBS AND ORGANIZATIONS

Alpha Nu Omega Student Nursing Association

Alpha Sigma Theta American Criminal Justice Association

Enactus International organization for Business students

Future Teacher's Society teacher education candidates

Health Promotions Club promotes health and wellness to students

Market Economics Society dedicated to the study and development of economic knowledge

Music Therapy Club students hear from professionals in the field, share clinical ideas and learn more about obtaining a career in music therapy

Psychology Club brings educational speakers to meetings to inform students of job opportunities, graduate programs, and nonprofit agencies

Spanish Club learns about Spanish and Hispanic culture

ACADEMIC HONOR SOCIETIES

Alpha Chi is a coeducational society whose purpose is to promote academic excellence and exemplary character among college and university students and to honor those who achieve such distinction.

Alpha Kappa Delta is the International Sociology Honor Society.

Alpha Phi Sigma is the National Criminal Justice Honor Society and recognizes academic excellence of undergraduate and graduate students of criminal justice.

Alpha Sigma Lambda Honor Society is dedicated to recognize the special achievements of adult professionals who accomplish academic excellence while facing competing interests of home and work.

Beta Beta Beta (Tri Beta) is a society for students, particularly undergraduates, dedicated to improve the understanding and appreciation of biological study and extending boundaries of human knowledge through scientific research.

Sigma Beta Delta is an international honor society recognizing scholarship and achievement in business and promoting personal and professional improvement and a life distinguished by honorable service.

Sigma Delta Pi the National Collegiate Hispanic Honor Society

Sigma Tau Delta the international English Honor Society

Sigma Theta Tau the Nursing Honor Society

BOARD OF STUDENT ORGANIZATIONS

The Board of Student Organizations (BSOs) exists to oversee all clubs and organizations at Charleston Southern University. They work directly with the Student Activities Office and the Student Government Association. Our executive board seeks to bring unity to student organizations, to provide opportunities to service campus and the surrounding community, and to enhance school spirit.

CAMPUS MINISTRIES

Baptist Collegiate Ministries (BCMs) ministers to the campus by conducting evangelistic outreach projects, Bible studies, and discipleship and missions opportunities for students

Fellowship of Christian Athletes (FCAs) seeks to impact the world for Jesus Christ through the influence of athletes and coaches. At CSU, every athletic team is provided a chaplain, and each coach is invited to meet weekly for Coaches Bible Study.

One Accord Gospel Choir a choral group of about 70 voices, leads worship several times a year on campus as well as around the state. The group meets in the Brewer Center on Wednesday nights for Bible study, corporate worship, and rehearsal.

Young Life Charleston provides an accepting community to be a part of while exploring or deepening your faith.

CAMPUS MEDIA

Sefer is the student literary magazine, featuring poetry, prose, and photography created by current CSU students. The staff is advised by Charleston Southern University's English department.

SERVICE CLUBS AND ORGANIZATIONS

African American Society promotes a finer appreciation of the African American contribution to American life, a better understanding of the African heritage of black Americans and participates in activities to encourage harmony among all people that will result in better understanding of society.

Alpha Delta Pi Sorority chapter at Charleston Southern University was installed in December 2014 as the first NPC sorority on campus. The sisters of ADPi are committed to sisterhood, values and ethics, high academic standards, and social responsibility. Their national philanthropy is The Ronald McDonald House Charities.

Alpha Kappa Alpha Sorority, Inc. was the FIRST black Greek letter sorority. Alpha Kappa Alpha's mission is to cultivate and encourage high scholastic and ethical standards, to promote unity and friendship among college women, to study and help alleviate problems concerning girls and women in order to improve their social stature, to maintain a progressive interest in college life, and to be of "Service to All Mankind."

The *BSOs* exists to oversee all clubs and organizations at Charleston Southern University. They work directly with the Student Activities Office and the Student Government Association.

The *Campus Activities Board* is a student-run organization that plans events for students. The board meets weekly and opens its doors to new members each semester.

College Republicans is the nation's oldest, largest, and most active youth political organization. College Republicans are the grassroots arm of the Republican Party.

Delta Sigma Theta Sorority, Inc. through sisterhood, scholarship, and service the Nu Sigma Chapter of Delta Sigma Theta Sorority, Inc. is always geared toward success.

Kappa Alpha Psi Fraternity was founded in 1911 at Indiana University. Locally, the organization was founded in 2001 (Omicron Mu Chapter). Its fundamental purpose of the fraternity is achievement in every field of human endeavor.

Phi Beta Sigma is a service fraternity that promotes the idea of brotherhood, scholarship, and service.

Psi Delta Phi service sorority seeks to show Christian love, to be effective witnesses, to be women of God, to promote unity and friendship, to encourage high ethical standards, to be of service to all mankind, to be God's lighthouse shining out His love and power, and to glorify Jesus Christ.

Psi Kappa Phi is a Christian service fraternity seeking to further the Kingdom of God and to serve all mankind by cultivating and exchanging Christian love, promoting unity and friendship, instilling strong ethical standards, and encouraging high scholastic achievement among the brotherhood.

Sigma Gamma Rho Sorority, Inc. is a service organization that thrives on the principles of scholarship, service, and sisterhood. Sigma Gamma Rho enhances the quality of life for women and their families in the United States and globally through community service.

Student Government Association (SGA) serves as an effective self-government, to ensure continuous exchange of ideas and opinions between the students and administration, to promote a widespread interest in student affairs, to further the activities of student life, to develop a greater spirit of progressive citizenship, to assume the fullest responsibilities and powers of self-government consistent with the policies of the administration of CSU to promote the general welfare, and to protect the rights of the students.

Student Veterans of America enhance the lives of veteran students and their family. Through academic support and tutoring as well as comradery, we strive to make CSU a great school for veterans.

Zeta Phi Beta Sorority, Inc. fosters the principles of scholarship, service, sisterly love and finer womanhood. As a community-conscious, action-oriented organization, they aim to also integrate faith in learning, leading, and serving.

Introduction

Welcome to College

Possible Classroom Exercises & Out-of Class Assignments

The following exercises/assignments may be used in conjunction with content covered in the Introduction.

Future-Life Scenarios

1. *Best-Case Scenario*

    Ask your students to consider the benefits of a college education and write a short paper in which they project themselves into the future and imagine what type of life they would be enjoying as college graduates. Ask them to include the aspects of their life that relate to each of the seven categories of college benefits.

2. *Worst-Case Scenario*

    Use the same steps as in the previous assignment, but ask students to imagine what their life might be like without a college education and a college degree.

Reviewing the College/University Mission Statement
(In-Class Exercise)

Steps:
1. Distribute copies of your College/University Catalog or Bulletin.
2. Ask your class to find the Mission Statement.
3. Have your students write a reflection statement or short paper in response to the following question: "What does the mission statement mean to me?" (Or, "What does it have to do with me?")

Here are some illustrative comments made by students who engaged in this exercise:

"It means that I have a great opportunity."

"It means that all the resources I need to survive in life are offered but it is up to me to take advantage of them."

"It means that if I play my cards right and keep myself on track, I will be able to follow my dreams because that's what my college is here to help us to do."

(Courtesy of Dr. Ariane Schauer, Marymount College, California.)

This exercise may also be adapted to educate students about different missions pursued by different types of postsecondary institutions (e.g., research universities, comprehensive state universities, liberal arts colleges, and community colleges). This will also give you the opportunity to articulate the distinctive advantages of your particular type of college or university so that students can immediately begin to capitalize on its distinctive advantages—for example, the multitude of resources available at a large research university; the accessibility to professors at a small liberal arts college; and the diversity of students and emphasis on teaching at a community college.

Campus pride could be further enhanced with some discussion of your particular college's unique history and distinctive programs.

Alumni Success Stories

Ask graduates of your college to visit your class and to describe how they have benefited from their college experience, both professionally and personally. If you don't know or have access to any alums, ask your Alumni Relations Office for recommendations.

CHAPTER 1

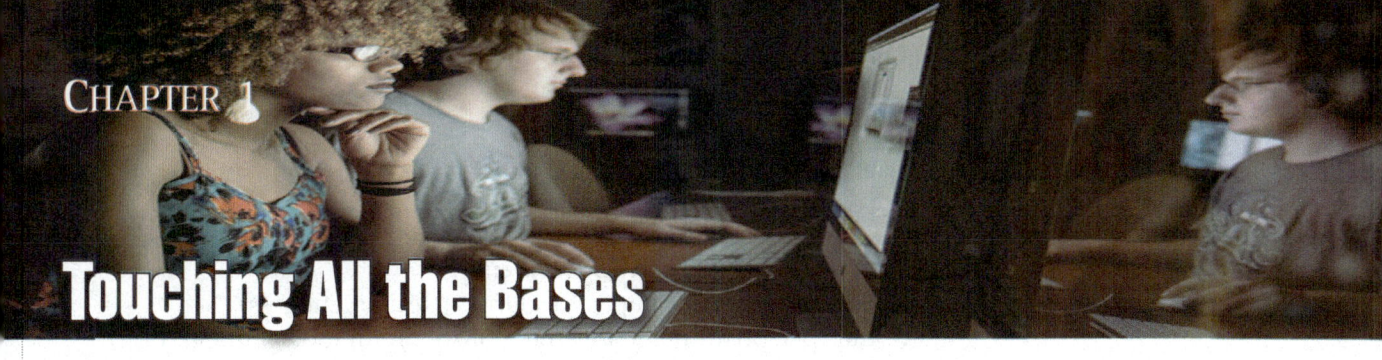

Touching All the Bases

USING POWERFUL PRINCIPLES OF STUDENT SUCCESS AND KEY CAMPUS RESOURCES

Chapter Preview

This chapter focuses on the "big picture"—the most powerful principles you can implement to promote your own success and the key campus resources you can use to help you succeed. It describes *what* these key principles and resources are, *why* they're effective, and *how* to capitalize on them.

Learning Goal

Alert you to the most powerful strategies and resources that you can use immediately to get off to a fast start in college and use continually to achieve excellence throughout your college experience.

Integrate Your Faith

Successful students are involved, interactive, resourceful, and reflective. How can these same abilities apply to the way you demonstrate God's love when interacting with your professors? Your peers?

Ignite Your Thinking

Reflection 1.1

1. In what three major ways do you think college will differ from high school?

2. What three personal characteristics, qualities, or strategies do you think will be most important for college success?

From *Thriving in College and Beyond: Research-Based Strategies for Academic Success and Personal Development*, Fourth Edition by Joseph B. Cuseo, Aaron Thompson, Michele Campagna, and Viki S. Fecas. Copyright © 2016 Kendall Hunt Publishing Company. Reprinted by permission.

Powerful Principles of College Success

Research points to four powerful principles of college success:

1. Active Involvement (Engagement)
2. Capitalizing on Campus Resources (Resourcefulness)
3. Interpersonal Interaction and Collaboration (Social Integration)
4. Reflection and Self-Awareness (Mindfulness)

(Sources: Astin, 1993; Barber, King, & Baxter Magolda, 2013; Kuh, et al., 2005; Light, 2001; Pascarella & Terenzini, 1991, 2005; Tinto, 1993.)

These four principles are presented in the opening chapter of this book because they represent the foundational basis for all success strategies discussed throughout the book.

Touching the First Base of College Success: Active Involvement (Engagement)

Research indicates that active involvement may be the most powerful principle of human learning and college success (Astin, 1993; Kuh, et al., 2005). To succeed in college, you can't be a passive spectator; you need to be an active player.

Active involvement includes the following key components:

- The amount of *time* you devote to the college experience—inside and outside the classroom
- The degree of *effort or energy* (mental and physical) you invest in the learning process.

Think of something you do with intensity, passion, and commitment. If you were to approach college in the same way, you would be faithfully

> "Tell me and I'll listen. Show me and I'll understand. Involve me and I'll learn."
> —Teton Lakota Indian saying

FIGURE 1.1: The Diamond of College Success

```
           Capitalizing on Campus Resources
                  (Resourcefulness)

   Interpersonal                          Active Involvement
Interaction and Collaboration   COLLEGE      (Engagement)
   (Social Integration)         SUCCESS

           Reflection and Self-Awareness
                  (Mindfulness)
```

©Kendall Hunt Publishing Company

implementing the principle of active involvement. Here's how you can apply both key components of active involvement—time and energy—to the major learning challenges you'll face in college.

Time in Class

Not surprisingly, the total amount of time you spend on learning is associated with how much you learn and how deeply you learn. This association leads to a straightforward recommendation: Attend all your classes in all your courses. It may be tempting to skip or cut classes because college professors are less likely to monitor your attendance or take roll than high school teachers. However, don't let this new freedom fool you into thinking that missing classes will not affect your course grades. Over the past 75 years, numerous studies have shown a direct relationship between class attendance and course grades—as one goes up or down, so does the other (Credé, Roch, & Kieszczynka, 2010; Launius, 1997; Shimoff & Catania, 2001; Tagliacollo, Volpato, & Pereira, 2010). **Figure 1.2** depicts the results of a study conducted at the City Colleges of Chicago, which shows the relationship between students' class attendance during the first five weeks of the term and their final course grades.

> "My biggest recommendation: GO TO CLASS. I learned this the hard way my first semester. You'll be surprised what you pick up just by being there. I wish someone would have informed me of this before I started school."
>
> —Advice to new students from a college sophomore

FIGURE 1.2: Relationship between Class Attendance Rate and Course Final Grades

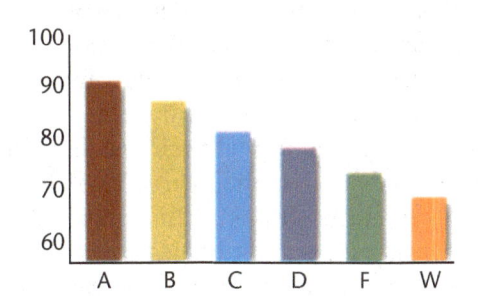

©Kendall Hunt Publishing Company

Note

Look at going to class like going to work. If you miss work days, it lowers your pay; if you miss classes, it lowers your grades.

> "Eighty percent of success is showing up."
>
> —Woody Allen, Oscar & Golden Globe winning film director, writer, and author

Reflection 1.2

During your senior year in high school, about how many hours per week did you spend on schoolwork outside of class?

Time Spent on Coursework Outside of Class

In college, you will spend much less time sitting in class than you did in high school; however, you will be expected to spend much more time working on your courses outside of class. Less than 40% of beginning college students report having studied six or more hours per week during their final year in high school (Pryor, et al., 2012) and only one-third expect to spend more than 20 hours per week preparing for class in college (National Survey of Student Engagement, 2009).

Unfortunately, less than 10% of beginning college students say they will study at least two hours out of class for every hour spent in class—which is what most college faculty believe is necessary to do well in college (Kuh, 2005). This has to change if college students are to earn good grades. Just as successful athletes need to put in time and effort to improve their physical performance, successful students need to do the same to improve their academic performance. Studies repeatedly show that the more time college students spend on academic work outside of class, the higher grades they earn in their college courses (National Survey of Student Engagement, 2009). In one study of more than 25,000 college students it was found that the percentage of students receiving "A" grades was almost three times higher for students who spent 40 or more hours per week on academic work than it was for students who spent between 20 and 40 hours. For students who spent 20 or fewer hours per week on academic work, the percentage of them receiving a grade of "C" or below was almost twice as high as it was for students who spent 40 or more hours on academic work (Pace, 1990, 1995).

If you need further motivation to achieve good grades, keep in mind that higher grades earned in college translates into career success after college. Research on college graduates indicates that the higher their grades were in college, the higher: (a) their starting salary, (b) the status (prestige) of their first job, and (c) their career mobility (ability to change jobs or move into different positions). This relationship between higher college grades and greater career advantages exists for students at all types of colleges and universities—regardless of the reputation or prestige of the institution the students attended (Pascarella & Terenzini, 1991, 2005). In other words, how well students do in college matters more to their career success than where they went to college.

> "I thought I would get a better education if the school had a really good reputation. Now, I think one's education depends on how much effort you put into it."
>
> —First-year college student

Active Involvement in the Learning Process

College success will require that you work harder (put in more time than high school) and smarter (learn more strategically and effectively). Probably the most powerful principle of effective learning is active involvement (engagement); there's simply no such thing as "passive learning." You can ensure you're actively involved in the learning process by engaging in some form of *action* on what you're learning, such as the actions listed below.

- *Writing.* For example, when reading, take notes on what you're reading rather than passively highlighting sentences.

- *Speaking.* For example, rather than studying silently, explain what you're learning to a study-group partner.
- *Organizing.* For example, create an outline, diagram, or concept map that pulls together the ideas you're learning.

Active Listening and Note-Taking in Class

You will find that many college professors rely heavily on the lecture method—they profess their knowledge by speaking for long stretches of time and expect students to listen and take notes on the knowledge they dispense. This method of instruction places great demands on your ability to listen actively and take notes that are both accurate and complete. Research consistently shows that most test questions on college exams come from professors' lectures and students who take better class notes get better grades (Brown, 1988; Cuseo, et al., 2013; Kiewra, 2000).

The best way to apply the principle of active involvement during a class lecture is to engage in the physical action of writing notes. Writing down what your instructor is saying in class "forces" you to pay closer attention to what is being said and reinforces your retention of what was said. By taking notes, you not only hear the information (auditory memory), you also see it on paper (visual memory) and feel it in the muscles of your hand as you write it (motor memory).

> "I never had a class before where the teacher just stands up and talks to you. He says something and you're writing it down, but then he says something else."
>
> —First-year college student (Erickson, Peters, & Strommer, 2006)

Note

Your role in the college classroom is not that of a passive spectator or an absorbent sponge who sits back and soaks up information through osmosis. Instead, it's like being an aggressive detective or investigative reporter on a search-and-record mission. Your job is to actively search for information by picking your instructor's brain, picking out the instructor's key points, and recording your "pickings" in your notebook.

> "All genuine learning is active, not passive. It is a process in which the student is the main agent, not the teacher."
>
> —Mortimer Adler, American professor of philosophy and educational theorist

Box 1.1 contains a summary of top strategies for classroom listening and note-taking that you can put into action right now.

Box 1.1

Top Tips for Active Listening and Note-Taking in the College Classroom

One task that you'll be expected to perform during the very first week of college is taking notes in class. Studies show that professors' lecture notes are the number one source of test questions (and test answers) on college exams. You can improve the quality of your note-taking and your course grades by using the following strategies.

1. **Get to every class.** Whether or not your instructors take roll, you're responsible for all material covered in class. Remember that a full load of college courses (15 units) only requires that you be in class about 13 hours per week. If you consider your class work to

Box 1.1 *(continued)*

be a full-time job, any job that requires you to show up for only 13 hours a week is a pretty sweet deal; it's a deal that supplies you with much more educational freedom than you had in high school. To miss classes in college when you're required to spend so little time in class per week is an abuse of this educational freedom. It's also an abuse of the money that you, your family, and taxpaying American citizens are paying to support your college education.

2. **Get to every class on time.** During the first few minutes of a class session, instructors often share valuable information—such as important reminders, reviews, and previews.

3. **Get organized.** Bring the right equipment to class. Get a separate notebook for each class, write your name on it, date each class session, and store all class handouts in it.

4. **Get in the right position.**
   - The ideal place to sit in class is at the front and center of the room—where you're in the best position to hear and see what's going on.
   - The ideal posture to adopt is sitting upright and leaning forward—because your body influences your mind; if your body is in an alert and ready position, your mind is likely to follow.
   - The ideal social position to occupy in class is near motivated classmates who will not distract you, but motivate you to listen actively and take notes aggressively.

Note *These attention-focusing strategies are particularly important in large classes where you're likely to feel more anonymous, less accountable, and less engaged.*

5. **Get in the right frame of mind.** Come to class with the attitude that you're there to pick your instructor's brain, pick up answers to test questions, and pick up points to elevate your course grade.

6. **Get it down (in writing).** Actively look, listen, and record important points at all times in class. Pay special attention to whatever information instructors put in writing, whether it appears on the board, on a slide, or in a handout.

7. **Don't let go of your pen (or keyboard).** When in doubt, write it out (or type it out); it's better to have it and not need it than to need it and not have it.

Note *Most college professors don't write all important information on the board for you; instead, they expect you to listen carefully and write it down yourself.*

8. **Finish strong.** During the last few minutes of class, instructors often share valuable information, such as timely reminders, reviews, and previews.

9. **Stick around.** When class ends, don't bolt out of the room; instead, hang out for a few moments and quickly review your notes (by yourself or with a classmate). This quick end-of-class review will help your brain retain the information it just received. If you detect any gaps or confusing points in your notes, try to consult with your instructor immediately after class.

Reflection 1.3

Do you feel prepared to do the type of note-taking required in college classes? What adjustments or changes will you need to make in your previous classroom learning habits to meet the challenge?

Finish class with a rush of attention, not a rush out the door!

Active Class Participation

You can implement the principle of active involvement in the college classroom by not only taking notes in class, but also by being an engaged participant who comes to class well prepared (e.g., having done the assigned reading), asks relevant questions, and contributes thoughtful comments during class discussions. Class participation increases your ability to stay alert and attentive in class, and it sends a clear message to your instructors that you are a motivated student who wants to learn. Class participation is also likely to account for a portion of your grade in many courses, so your attentiveness and involvement in class can have a direct, positive effect on your college grades.

Active Reading

Note-taking not only promotes active listening in class, it also promotes active reading out of class. Taking notes on what you're reading (or on information you've highlighted while reading) keeps you actively involved in the reading process because it requires more mental and physical energy than merely reading the material or passively highlighting sentences.

College professors also expect you to relate or connect what they talk about in class to the reading they've assigned. Thus, it's important to start developing good reading habits now. You can do so by using the top tips suggested in **Box 1.2**.

Box 1.2

Top Tips for Strengthening Textbook Reading Comprehension and Retention

1. **Get the textbooks required for your courses as soon as possible and get your reading assignments done on time.** Information from reading assignments ranks right behind lecture notes as a source of test questions on college exams. Many professors deliver their lectures with the expectation that you've done the assigned reading and assume you can build on that knowledge to understand their lectures. If you haven't done the reading, you'll have more difficulty following what your instructor is saying in class. Thus, by not doing the assigned reading you pay a double penalty: you miss information found in the reading that's not covered in class which will likely appear on exams, and you miss understanding ideas presented in class that build on the reading.

Box 1.2 (continued)

> I recommend that you read the first chapters right away because college professors get started promptly with assigning certain readings. Classes in college move very fast because, unlike high school, you do not attend class five times a week but two or three times a week."
>
> —Advice to new college students from a first-year student

2. **Read with the right equipment.**
   - Bring a writing tool (pen, pencil, or keyboard) to record important information and a storage space (notebook or computer) in which you can save and later retrieve information acquired from your reading for later use on tests and assignments.
   - Have a dictionary nearby to quickly find the meaning of unfamiliar words that may interfere with your ability to comprehend what you're reading. Looking up definitions of unfamiliar words helps you understand what you're reading and also builds your vocabulary. A strong vocabulary will improve your reading comprehension in all college courses, as well as your performance on standardized tests, such as those required for admission to graduate and professional schools.
   - Check the back of your textbook for a glossary (list) of key terms included in the book. Each college subject and academic discipline has its own special language, and decoding it is often the key to understanding the concepts covered in the course. The glossary that appears at the end of your textbook is more than an ancillary add-on; it's a valuable tool that you can use to improve your comprehension of course concepts. Consider making a photocopy of the glossary at the back of your textbook so you can access it easily while you're reading—without having to repeatedly stop, hold your place, and go to the back of the text to find it.

3. **Get in the right position.** Sit upright and have light coming from behind you, over the side of your body opposite your writing hand. This will reduce the distracting and fatiguing effects of glare and shadows.

4. **Get a sneak preview.** Approach the chapter by first reading its boldface headings and any chapter outline, summary, or end-of-chapter questions that may be provided. This will supply you with a mental map of the chapter's important ideas before you start your trip through it. Getting an overview of the chapter will help you keep track of its major ideas (the "big picture") and reduce your risk of getting lost in all the smaller details you encounter along the way.

5. **Finish each of your reading sessions with a short review.** Rather than using the last few minutes of a reading session to cover a few more pages, end it with a review of what you've highlighted or noted as important information. Since most forgetting takes place immediately after you stop processing (taking in) information and start doing something else, it's best to use your last minutes of reading time to "lock in" the most important information you've just read.

Note *When reading, your goal should be to discover or uncover the most important ideas, so the final step in the reading process should be to review (and lock in) the most important ideas you've discovered.*

Touching the Second Base of College Success: Capitalizing on Campus Resources (Resourcefulness)

Successful people are *resourceful*; they seek out and take advantage of resources to help them reach their goals. Your campus is chock full of resources that have been intentionally designed to support your quest for educational and personal success. Studies show that students who utilize campus resources report higher levels of satisfaction with college and get more out of the college experience (Pascarella & Terenzini, 1991, 2005).

> "Do not be a PCP (Parking Lot → Classroom → Parking Lot) student. The time you spend on campus will be a sound investment in your academic and professional success."
>
> —Drew Appleby, professor of psychology

Note
Capitalizing on campus services is not only valuable, it's also "free"; the cost of these services has already been covered by your college tuition. By investing time and energy in campus resources, you maximize the return on your financial investment in college—you get a bigger bang for your buck.

Utilizing campus resources is a natural extension of the principle of active involvement. Successful students are *involved* students, both inside and outside the classroom. Out-of-class involvement includes involvement with campus resources. The first step toward making effective use of campus resources is becoming aware of the full range of resources available to you and what they can do for you. Listed below are key campus services that are likely to be available to you and what they can do for you.

Learning Center

This campus resource is designed to strengthen your academic performance. The individual and group tutoring provided here will help you master difficult course concepts and assignments, and the people working here are professionally trained to help you learn *how to learn*. Just as professors are experts in the subjects they teach: learning resource professionals are experts in the process of learning. They are professionals who can equip you with effective learning strategies that can be used in all courses, as well as specific strategies for dealing with the demands of certain courses and teaching styles. You're also likely to find trained peer tutors in this center who can often help you understand concepts better than more experienced professionals because they're closer to you in age and experience.

> "Where I learn the material best is tutoring because they go over it and if you have questions, you can ask. They have time for you or will make time for you."
>
> —First-year college student

Studies show that college students who capitalize on academic support services outside the classroom achieve higher grades and are more likely to complete their college degree, particularly if they begin their involvement with these support services during their first year of college (Bailey, 2009; Cuseo, 2003). Students who seek and receive assistance from the Learning Center also show significant improvement in academic self-efficacy—that is, they develop a stronger sense of personal control over their academic performance and higher expectations for academic success (Smith, Walter, & Hoey, 1992).

> "At colleges where I've taught, we found that the grade point average of students who used the Learning Center was higher than the college average, and honors students were more likely to use the center than other students."
>
> —Joe Cuseo, professor of psychology and lead author of this text

Despite the powerful advantages associated with student use of academic support services, these services are typically underused by college students—especially by students who need them the most (Cuseo, 2003; Walter & Smith, 1990). Unfortunately, some college students believe that seeking academic help is admitting they're not smart, self-sufficient, or able to succeed on their own. Don't buy into this myth. In high school, students may only go to an office on campus if they're required to (e.g., if they forgot to do something or did something wrong). In college, students go to campus offices to enhance their success by taking advantage of the services and support they provide.

Note

Using academic support services doesn't mean you're helpless, need remedial repair work, or require academic life support because you're on the verge of flunking out. Instead, it's a sign that you're a motivated and resourceful student who is striving for academic excellence.

Writing Center

Many college campuses offer specialized support for students seeking to improve their writing skills. At CSU, the Writing Center is the place on campus where you can receive assistance at any stage of the writing process, whether it be collecting and organizing your ideas, composing your first draft, or proofreading your final draft. Since writing is an academic skill that you'll use throughout your college experience, if you improve your writing skills, you're likely to improve your overall academic performance. Thus, the Writing Center can be one of your most valuable campus resources.

Reflection 1.4

How much writing did you typically do in your high school courses?

How much confidence do you have in your writing skills right now?

Disability Services

If you have a physical or learning disability that's interfering with your performance in college, or you think you may have such a disability, Disability Services is the campus resource to consult for assistance and support. Programs and services typically provided by this office include:

- Assessment for learning disabilities;
- Verification of eligibility for disability support services;
- Authorization of academic accommodations for students with disabilities; and
- Specialized counseling, advising, and tutoring.

College Library

The L. Mendel Rivers Library is your campus resource for finding information and completing research assignments (e.g., term papers and group projects). Librarians are professional educators who provide instruction outside the classroom; you can learn from them just as you can learn from faculty inside the classroom. They can help you develop research skills for accessing, retrieving, and evaluating information. These are lifelong learning skills that promote your educational success at all stages of the college experience as well as your professional and personal success beyond college.

> The next best thing to knowing something is knowing where to find it."
>
> —Dr. Samuel Johnson, English literary figure and original author of the Dictionary of the English Language (1747)

Academic Advisement

All CSU students with a declared major are assigned to a faculty academic advisor who is a professor teaching in that discipline. Studies show that students who develop clear educational and career goals are more likely to persist in college and complete their college degree (Braxton, Hirschy, & McClendon, 2011; Kuh, et al., 2011; Lotkowski, Robbins, & Noeth, 2004). Research also indicates that most beginning college students need help clarifying their educational goals, deciding on a major, and identifying career options (Cuseo, 2005; Tinto, 2012). As a first-year college student, being undecided or uncertain about your educational and career goals is nothing to be embarrassed about. However, you should start thinking about your future now. Connect early and often with an academic advisor to help you clarify your educational goals and choose a field of study that best complements your interests, talents, and values.

Student Services

This is your campus resource for involvement in student life outside the classroom, including student clubs and organizations, recreational programs, leadership activities, and volunteer experiences. Research consistently shows that experiential learning outside the classroom contributes as much to your personal development and career success as class work (Kuh, 1995; Kuh, et al., 1994; Pascarella & Terenzini, 2005). This is one reason why most campuses no longer refer to out-of-class experiences as "*extra* curricular" activities; instead they are referred to as "*co*-curricular" experiences—which conveys the message they're equally important as classroom-based learning. Studies show that students who become actively involved in campus life are more likely to:

- Enjoy their college experience;
- Graduate from college; and
- Develop leadership skills that enhance career performance beyond college (Astin, 1993).

> **Note**
> *Co-curricular experiences are also resume-building experiences, and campus professionals with whom you interact regularly while participating in co-curricular activities (e.g., director of student activities or dean of students) can be valuable resources for personal references and letters of recommendation.*

Devoting some out-of-class time to co-curricular experiences should not interfere with your academic performance. Keep in mind that in college you'll be spending much less time in the classroom than you did in high school. As mentioned previously, a full load of college courses (15 units) requires that you be in class for about 13 hours per week. This can leave you with sufficient time to become involved in learning experiences on or off campus. Research indicates that students' academic performance and progress to degree completion aren't impaired if they spend 20 or fewer hours on co-curricular and part-time work experiences (Advisory Committee on Student Financial Assistance, 2008). In fact, they earn higher grades than students who don't get involved in any out-of-class activities (Pascarella, 2001; Pascarella & Terenzini, 2005).

> "Just a [long] list of club memberships is meaningless; it's a fake front. Remember that quality, not quantity, is what counts."
> —Lauren Pope, former director of the National Bureau for College Placement

Financial Aid Office

If you have questions concerning how to obtain assistance in paying for college, the staff in this office can guide you through the application process. The paperwork needed to apply for and secure financial aid can sometimes be confusing or overwhelming. Don't let the process of applying for financial aid intimidate you or prevent you from seeking financial aid because professional financial aid counselors can walk you through the process. They can also help you find:

- Part-time employment on campus through a work—study program;
- Low-interest student loans; and
- Grants and scholarships.

If you have any doubt about whether you're using the most effective plan for financing your college education, make an appointment to see a professional in your Financial Aid Office right now.

The Career Center

Research indicates that students are more likely to stay in college and graduate when they have some sense of how their present academic experience relates to their future career goals (Braxton, et al., 2011; Kuh, et al., 2011; Tinto, 1993). Studies also show that most new students are uncertain about what career they will pursue (Gordon & Steele, 2003). So, if you're uncertain about your future career, welcome to a club to which many other first-year students belong.

The Career Development Center is the place to go for help in finding a meaningful connection between your current college experience and your future career goals. Here's where you'll find such services as personal career counseling, workshops on career exploration and development, and career fairs where you'll be able to meet professionals working in different fields. Although it may seem like your career is light years away, the process of exploring, planning, and preparing for career success should begin now—in your first year of college.

Counseling Center

Here's where you can get ideas and strategies for managing college stress, gaining greater self-awareness, and reaching your full potential. Personal counselors are professionals who do more than just help students maintain mental health; they also develop students' emotional intelligence, interpersonal skills, and personal growth.

Touching the Third Base of College Success: Interpersonal Interaction and Collaboration (Social Integration)

Students who become socially integrated or connected with other members of the college community are more likely to complete their first year of college and go on to complete their college degree (Pascarella & Terenzini, 2005; Tinto, 1993). (For effective ways to make interpersonal connections with key members of your college community, see **Box 1.3**.)

Box 1.3

Social Integration: Making Connections with Members of Your College Community

Listed below are top tips for making key social connections in college. Start developing these relationships right now so you can build a base of social support to help you succeed during the critical first year of college.

- Connect with a student development professional you may have met during orientation.
- Join a college club, student organization, campus committee, intramural team, or volunteer service group whose members share the same personal or career interests as you. If you can't find a club or organization you were hoping to join, consider starting it on your own. For example, if you're an English major, consider starting a Writing Club or a Book Club.
- Connect with a peer leader who has been trained to assist new students (e.g., orientation week leader, peer tutor, or peer mentor).
- Connect with classmates and team up with them to take notes, complete reading assignments, study for exams, or take classes together. Look especially to team up with a peer who may be in more than one class with you.

Box 1.3 *(continued)*

- Connect with peers who live near you or who commute to school from the same community in which you live. If your schedules are similar, consider carpooling together.
- Connect with faculty members—particularly in a field that you're considering as a major. Visit them during office hours, converse briefly with them after class, or communicate with them via e-mail.
- Connect with an academic advisor to discuss and develop your educational plans.
- Connect with academic support professionals in your college's Learning Center for personalized academic assistance or tutoring related to any course in which you'd like to improve your performance or achieve academic excellence.
- Connect with a college librarian to get early assistance or a head start on any research project that you've been assigned.
- Connect with a personal counselor or campus minister to discuss college adjustment or personal challenges you may be experiencing.

Reflection 1.5

How likely is it that you will join this club or organization?

Four particular forms of interpersonal interaction have been found to promote student learning and motivation in college:

1. Student—faculty interaction,
2. Student—advisor interaction,
3. Student—mentor interaction, and
4. Student—student (peer) interaction.

Strategies for capitalizing on each of these key forms of interaction are provided below.

Interacting with Faculty Members

College success is strongly influenced by the frequency and quality of student—faculty interaction *outside the classroom*. Out-of-class contact with faculty is associated with the following positive outcomes for college students:

- Improved academic performance;
- Increased critical thinking skills;
- Greater satisfaction with the college experience;
- Increased likelihood of completing a college degree; and
- Stronger desire to pursue education beyond a four-year degree (Astin, 1993; Pascarella & Terenzini, 1991, 2005).

These positive outcomes are so powerful and widespread that we encourage you to immediately begin making connections with your professors outside of class time. Here are some of the easiest ways to do so.

1. **Seek contact with your instructors right after class.** If something covered in class captures your interest, approach your instructor to discuss it further. You could ask a quick question about something you weren't sure you understood, or have a short conversation about how the material covered in class really hit home for you or connected with something you learned in another course. Interacting briefly with instructors after class can help them get to know you as an individual and help you gain the confidence to approach them during office hours.

2. **Connect with course instructors during their office hours.** One of the most important pieces of information you'll find on a course syllabus is your instructor's office hours. College professors specifically reserve times in their weekly schedule to be available to students in their office. (Make note of them and make an earnest attempt to capitalize on them.) Try to visit the office of each of your instructors at least once, preferably early in the term, when quality time is easier to find. Don't wait until later in the term when major exams and assignments start piling up. Even if your early contact with instructors is only for a few minutes, it can be a valuable icebreaker that helps them get to know you as a person and helps you feel more comfortable interacting with them in the future.

   Making office visits *with other classmates* is an effective way to get additional assistance in preparing for exams and completing assignments—for the following reasons:

   - You're more likely to feel comfortable about venturing onto your instructor's "turf" in the company of peers than entering this unfamiliar territory on your own. As the old expression goes, "There's safety in numbers."
   - When you make an office visit as a team, the information shared by the instructor is heard by more than one person; your teammates may pick up some useful information that you may have missed, misinterpreted, or forgotten to write down (and vice versa).
   - You save time for your instructors by allowing them to help more than one student at a time. This means they won't have to engage in as many "repeat performances" for individual students seeking help at separate times.
   - You send a message to the instructor that you're a motivated student who's serious about the course, because you've taken the time—ahead of time—to connect with your peers and prepare for the office visit.

> "[In high school] the teacher knows your name. But in college they don't know your name; they might see your face, but it means nothing to them unless you make yourself known."
>
> —First-year college student

> "I wish that I would have taken advantage of professors' open-door policies when I had questions, because actually understanding what I was doing, instead of guessing, would have saved me a lot of stress and re-doing what I did wrong the first time."
>
> —College sophomore

> "Two heads are better than one, not because either is infallible, but because they are unlikely to go wrong in the same direction."
>
> —C.S. Lewis, English novelist and essayist

3. **Connect with your instructors through e-mail.** Electronic communication is another effective tool for experiencing the benefits of student—faculty interaction outside the classroom, particularly if your professor's office hours conflict with your class schedule, work responsibilities, or family commitments. If you're a commuter student who doesn't live on campus, or if you're an adult student juggling family and work commitments along with your academic schedule, e-mail communication may be an especially effective and efficient way to interact with faculty. E-mail may also be a good way to initially communicate with instructors and build self-confidence to eventually seek out face-to-face interaction with them. In one national survey, almost half of college students reported that e-mail enabled them to communicate their ideas with professors on subjects they would not have discussed in person (Pew Internet & American Life Project, 2002). However, if you miss class, don't use e-mail to ask such questions as:

- Did I miss anything important in class today?
- Could you send me your PowerPoint slides from the class I missed?

Also, when using e-mail to communicate with your instructors, be sure to:

- Include your full name in the message.
- Mention the class or course in which you're enrolled.
- Use complete sentences, correct grammar, and avoid informal "hip" expressions (e.g., "yo," "whatup").
- Spell check and proofread your message before sending it.
- Include your full contact information. (If you're communicating via Facebook, watch your screen name; for example, names like "Sexsea" or "Studly" wouldn't be appropriate.)
- Give your instructor time to reply. (Don't expect an immediate response, particularly if you send your message in the evening or on a weekend.)

Lastly, when you're *in class*, use personal technology responsibly and sensitively by adhering to the guidelines provided in **Box 1.4**.

Box 1.4

Guidelines for Civil and Responsible Use of Personal Technology in the College Classroom

Behavior that interferes with the right of others to learn or teach in the classroom is referred to as *classroom incivility*. Listed below are forms of classroom incivility that involve student use of personal technology. Be sure to avoid them.

Using Cell Phones

Keeping a cell phone on in class is a clear form of classroom incivility because it can interfere with the right of others to learn. In a study of college

Box 1.4 (continued)

students who heard a cell phone ringing during class and were later tested on information presented in class, they scored approximately 25% lower for information that was presented at the time the cell phone rang. This drop in performance was found even if the material was covered by the professor just prior to the cell phone ringing and if it was projected on a slide while the phone rang. The study also showed that students' attention to information presented in class is significantly reduced when classmates frantically search through handbags or pockets to find and silence a ringing (or vibrating) phone (Shelton, et al., 2009). These findings clearly suggest that cell phone use in class disrupts the learning process and the civil thing to do is:

- Turn your cell phone off before entering class, or keep it out of the classroom altogether. (You can use *studiousapp.com* to automatically silence your phone at times of the day when you're in class.) In rare cases where you may need to leave class to respond to an emergency, ask your instructor for permission in advance.
- Don't check your cell phone during the class period by turning it off and on.
- Don't look at your cell phone at any time during an exam because your instructor may suspect that you're looking up answers to test questions.

> "The right to do something does not mean that doing it is right."
> —William Safire, American author, journalist, and presidential speech writer

Text Messaging

Although this form of electronic communication is silent, it still can distract or disturb your classmates. It's also discourteous or disrespectful to instructors when you put your head down and turn your attention away from them while they're speaking in class. The bottom line: Be sensitive to your classmates and your instructor—don't text in class!

Surfing the Web

Although this can be done without creating distracting sounds, it still can create visual distractions. Unless you're taking class notes on it, keep your laptop closed to avoid distracting your classmates and raising your instructors' suspicion that you're a disinterested or disrespectful student.

Final Note: In addition to technological incivilities, other discourteous classroom behaviors include personal grooming, holding side conversations, and doing homework for other classes. Even if your attendance is perfect, "little things" you do in class that reflect inattention or disinterest can send a strong message to your instructors that you're an unmotivated or discourteous student.

Reflection 1.6

Have you observed any recent examples of classroom incivility that you thought were particularly distracting or discourteous? What was the uncivil behavior and what consequences did it have on others?

Interacting with Academic Advisors

If you need some help understanding college policies and procedures, or navigating the bureaucratic maze of course options and course requirements, an academic advisor is the person to see. Advisors also serve as key referral agents who can direct you to, and connect you with, key campus support services that best meet your educational needs and career goals.

Your academic advisor should be someone whom you feel comfortable speaking with, someone who knows your name, and someone who's familiar with your personal interests and abilities. Give advisors the opportunity to get to know you personally, and seek their input on courses, majors, and any academic difficulties you may be experiencing.

Note

Advisors can be much more than course schedulers; they can be mentors. Unlike your course instructors—who may change from term to term—your academic advisor may be the one professional on campus with whom you have regular contact and a continuous relationship throughout your college experience.

Reflection 1.7

Do you have a personally assigned advisor?

If yes, do you know who this person is and where he or she can be found?

If you don't have a personally assigned advisor, where will you go if you have questions about your class schedule or educational plans?

Interacting with a Mentor

A mentor may be described as an experienced guide who takes a personal interest in you and helps you progress toward your goals. For example, in the movie *Star Wars*, Yoda served as a mentor for Luke Skywalker. Research demonstrates that when first-year college students have a mentor, they feel more valued and are better able to stay on track until they complete their degree (Campbell & Campbell, 1997; Crisp & Cruz, 2009; Komarraju, Musulkin, & Bhattacharya, 2010). A mentor can help you anticipate issues, resolve problems, and be someone with whom you can share your struggles as well as your success stories and personal accomplishments. Keep an eye out for a person on campus with whom you can develop this type of relationship. A variety of people have the potential to be a mentor for you, including:

- Your instructor in a first-year seminar or experience course
- Your academic advisor
- Faculty member in your major field of interest
- Peer mentor or peer leader
- Academic support professional (e.g., professional working in the Learning Center)

- Career counselor
- Personal counselor
- Student development professional (e.g., the director of student life or residential life)
- Campus minister or chaplain
- Financial aid counselor
- Professionals working in a career you're interested in pursuing

Reflection 1.8

Think about your first interactions with faculty, staff, and administrators on campus. Did you meet anyone who took interest in you and who might be a potential mentor for you?

Interaction with Peers (Student–Student Interaction)

Your peers can be more than competitors or a source of negative peer pressure; they can also be collaborators, a source of positive social influence, and a resource for college success. Peer support is important at any stage of the college experience, but it's especially valuable during the first term of college. It's at this stage when new students have a strong need for belongingness and social acceptance because they're in the midst of a major life transition. As a new student, it may be useful to view your first-year experience through the lens of psychologist Abraham Maslow's hierarchy of human needs (see **Figure 1.3**). According to Maslow, humans only reach their full potential and achieve peak performance after their more basic emotional and social needs have been met (e.g., needs for personal safety, social acceptance, and self-esteem). Making early connections with your peers helps you meet these basic human needs, provides you with a base of social support that eases your integration into the college community, and prepares you to move up to higher levels of the need hierarchy (e.g., achieving academic excellence and reaching your educational goals).

Getting involved with campus organizations or activities is one way to connect with other students. Also, try to interact with experienced students who have spent more time at college than you. Sophomores, juniors, and seniors can be valuable social resources for a new student. In particular, seek out contact with students who have been selected and trained as peer mentors or peer leaders.

Research clearly demonstrates that college students learn as much from peers as they do from instructors and textbooks (Astin, 1993; Pascarella, 2006). One study of more than 25,000 college students revealed that when peers interact with one another while learning, they achieve higher levels of academic performance and are more likely to persist to degree completion (Astin, 1993).

FIGURE 1.3: Abraham Maslow's Hierarchy of Needs

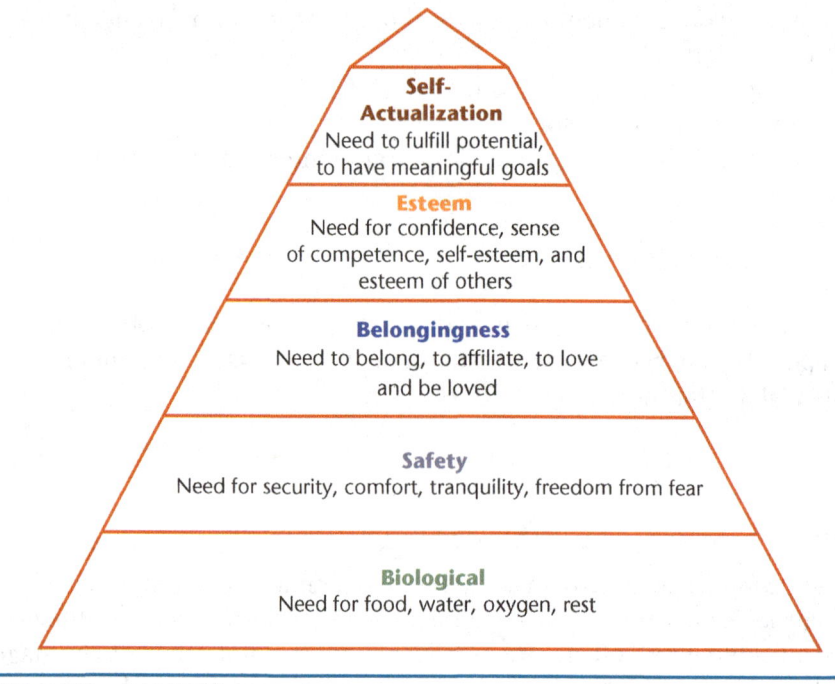

Self-Actualization
Need to fulfill potential, to have meaningful goals

Esteem
Need for confidence, sense of competence, self-esteem, and esteem of others

Belongingness
Need to belong, to affiliate, to love and be loved

Safety
Need for security, comfort, tranquility, freedom from fear

Biological
Need for food, water, oxygen, rest

©Kendall Hunt Publishing Company

> "Surround yourself with only people who are going to lift you higher."
> —Oprah Winfrey, actress and talk-show host

Be observant—keep an eye out for peers who are successful. Start building your social support network by surrounding yourself with success-seeking and success-achieving students. Learn from them, emulate their productive habits and strategies, and use them as a social resource to promote your own success.

Reflection 1.9

Think about classmates in courses you're taking this term. Would you be willing to ask any of them if they'd like to form a learning team? Why?

Self-Awareness

In addition to reflecting on what you're learning, it's also important to reflect on yourself. This process is known as *introspection*—it involves turning inward to gain deeper self-awareness and understanding of who you are, what you're doing, and where you're going. Two forms of self-awareness are particularly important for success in college: (a) self-monitoring and (b) self-assessment.

Self-Monitoring

One characteristic of successful learners is that they self-monitor (check themselves) while learning to remain aware of:

- Whether they're using effective learning strategies (e.g., if they're giving their undivided attention to what they're learning)
- Whether they're truly comprehending what they are learning (e.g., if they're understanding it at a deep level or memorizing it at a surface level)
- How they're regulating or adjusting their learning strategies to meet the demands of different academic tasks and subjects (e.g., if they're reading technical material in a science textbook, they read at a slower rate and check their understanding more frequently than when reading a novel) (Weinstein, Acee, & Jung, 2011).

You can begin to establish good self-monitoring habits by getting in the routine of periodically pausing to reflect on the strategies you're using to learn and how you "do" college. For instance, you can ask yourself the following questions:

- Am I listening attentively to what my instructor is saying in class?
- Am I comprehending what I'm reading outside of class?
- Am I effectively using campus resources designed to support my success?
- Am I interacting with campus professionals who can contribute to my current success and future development?
- Am I interacting and collaborating with peers who can support (not sabotage) my learning and development?
- Am I effectively implementing college success strategies (such as those identified in this book)?

> "We learn neither by thinking nor by doing; we learn by thinking about what we are doing."
>
> —George Stoddard, Professor Emeritus, University of Iowa

Note

Successful students and successful people are mindful—*they watch what they're doing and remain aware of whether they're doing it effectively and to the best of their ability.*

Chapter Summary and Highlights

The key ideas contained in this chapter are summarized in the following self-assessment checklist of success-promoting principles and practices.

A Checklist of Success-Promoting Principles and Practices

1. **Active Involvement (Engagement)**
   Inside the classroom, I will:
   - ☐ *Get to class*. I'll treat it like a job and be there on all days I'm expected to.
   - ☐ *Get involved in class*. I'll come prepared, listen actively, take notes, and participate.

Outside the classroom, I will:
- ☐ *Read actively.* I'll take notes while I read to increase attention and retention.
- ☐ *Double up.* I'll spend twice as much time on academic work outside of class as I spend in class. If I'm a full-time student, I'll make it a full-time job and put in a 40-hour workweek (with occasional "overtime" as need).

2. **Capitalizing on Campus Resources (Resourcefulness)**
   I will capitalize on academic and student support services available to me, such as the:
   - ☐ Learning Center
   - ☐ Writing Center
   - ☐ College Library
   - ☐ Student Services
   - ☐ Financial Aid Office
   - ☐ Counseling Center
   - ☐ Career Services

3. **Interpersonal Interaction and Collaboration (Social Integration)**
   I will interact and collaborate with the following members of my college community:
   - ☐ **Peers.** I'll join student clubs and participate in campus organizations.
   - ☐ **Faculty members.** I'll connect with my course instructors and other faculty members after class, in their offices, or via e-mail.
   - ☐ **Academic advisors.** I'll see an advisor for more than course registration, and I'll find an advisor whom I can relate to and develop an ongoing relationship.
   - ☐ **Mentors.** I'll try to find someone on campus who can serve as an experienced guide and role model for me.

4. **Reflection and Self-Awareness (Mindfulness)**
   I will engage in:
   - ☐ **Reflection.** I'll step back from what I'm learning, review it, and connect it to what I already know.
   - ☐ **Self-Monitoring.** I'll maintain self-awareness of how I'm learning in college and if I'm using effective strategies.
   - ☐ **Self-Assessment.** I'll reflect on and evaluate my personal interests, talents, learning styles, and learning habits.

In short, successful students are:

- **Involved.** They *get into* it by investing time and effort in the college experience;
- **Interactive.** They *team up* for it by interacting and collaborating with others;

- **Resourceful.** They *get help* with it by capitalizing on their surrounding resources; and
- **Reflective.** They *step back* from it to think about their performance and themselves.

References

Advisory Committee on Student Financial Assistance. (2008, September). *Apply to succeed: Ensuring community college students benefit from need-based financial aid*. Washington, DC: Author. Retrieved from https://www2.ed.gov/about/bdscomm/list/acsfa/applytosucceed.pdf.

Astin, A. W. (1993). *What matters in college?* San Francisco: Jossey-Bass.

Bailey, G. (2009). *University of North Carolina, Greensboro application for NADE certification, tutoring program*. NADE Certification Council Archives. Searcy, AR: Harding University.

Barber, J. P., King, P. M., & Baxter Magolda, M. B. (2013). Long strides on the journey toward self-authorship: Substantial developmental shifts in college students' meaning making. *The Journal of Higher Education, 84*(6), 866–999.

Braxton, J. M., Hirschy, A. S., & McClendon, S. A. (2011). *Understanding and reducing college student departure*. ASHE-ERIC Higher Education Report, Volume 30, Number 3.

Brown, R. D. (1988). Self-quiz on testing and grading issues. *Teaching at UNL (University of Nebraska—Lincoln), 10*(2), 1–3.

Campbell, T. A., & Campbell, D. E. (1997, December). Faculty/student mentor program: Effects on academic performance and retention. *Research in Higher Education, 38*, 727–742.

Credé, M., Roch, S. G., & Kieszczynka, U. M. (2010). Class attendance in college: A meta-analytic review of the relationship of class attendance with grades and student characteristics. *Review of Educational Research, 80*(2), 272–295.

Crisp, G., & Cruz, I. (2009). Mentoring college students: A critical review of the literature between 1990 and 2007. *Research in Higher Education, 50*, 525–545.

Cuseo, J. B. (2003). Comprehensive academic support for students during the first year of college. In G. L. Kramer, et al. (Eds.), *Student academic services: An integrated approach* (pp. 271–310). San Francisco: Jossey-Bass.

Cuseo, J. B. (2005). "Decided," "undecided," and "in transition": Implications for academic advisement, career counseling, and student retention. In R. S. Feldman (Ed.), *Improving the first year of college: Research and practice* (pp. 27–50). Mahwah, NJ: Lawrence Erlbaum.

Cuseo, J. B., Thompson, A., Campagna, M., & Fecas, V. S. (2013). *Thriving in college & beyond: Research-based strategies for academic success and personal development* (3rd ed.). Dubuque, IA: Kendall Hunt.

Erickson, B. L., Peters, C. B., & Strommer, D. W. (2006). *Teaching first-year college students*. San Francisco: Jossey-Bass.

Gordon, V. N., & Steele, G. E. (2003). Undecided first-year students: A 25-year longitudinal study. *Journal of the First-Year Experience and Students in Transition, 15*(1), 19–38.

Kiewra, K. A. (2000). Fish giver or fishing teacher? The lure of strategy instruction. *Teaching at UNL (University of Nebraska—Lincoln), 22*(3), 1–3.

Komarraju, M., Musulkin, S., & Bhattacharya, G. (2010). Role of student–faculty interactions in developing college students' academic self-concept, motivation, and achievement. *Journal of College Student Development, 51*(3), 332–342.

Kuh, G. D. (1995). The other curriculum: Out-of-class experiences associated with student learning and personal development. *Journal of Higher Education, 66*(2), 123–153.

Kuh, G. D. (2005). Student engagement in the first year of college. In M. L. Upcraft, J. N. Gardner, B. O. Barefoot & Associates (Eds.), *Challenging and supporting the first-year student: A handbook for improving the first year of college* (pp. 86–107). San Francisco: Jossey-Bass.

Kuh, G. D., Douglas, K. B., Lund, J. P., & Ramin-Gyurnek, J. (1994). *Student learning outside the classroom: Transcending artificial boundaries*. ASHE-ERIC Higher Education Report No. 8. Washington, DC: George Washington University, School of Education and Human Development.

Kuh, et al. (2005). *What matters to student success: A review of the literature*. National Postsecondary Education Cooperative.

Kuh, G. D., Kinzie, J., Buckley, J. A., Bridges, B. K., & Hayek, J. C. (2011). *Piecing together the student success puzzle: Research, propositions, and recommendations*. ASHE Higher Education Report (Vol. 116). John Wiley & Sons.

Launius, M. H. (1997). College student attendance: Attitudes and academic performance. *College Student Journal, 31*(1), 86–93.

Light, R. J. (2001). *Making the most of college: Students speak their minds*. Cambridge, MA: Harvard University Press.

Lotkowski, V. A., Robbins, S. B., & Noeth, R. J. (2004). *The role of academic and non-academic factors in improving student retention*. ACT Policy Report. Retrieved from https://www.act.org/research/policymakers/pdf/college_retention.pdf.

National Survey of Student Engagement. (2009). *NSSE Annual Results 2009. Assessment for improvement: Tracking student engagement over time*. Bloomington, IN: Author.

Pace, C. (1990). *The undergraduates: A report of their activities*. Los Angeles: University of California, Center for the Study of Evaluation.

Pace, C. (1995, May). *From good processes to good products: Relating good practices in undergraduate education to student achievement*. Paper presented at the meeting of the Association for Institutional Research, Boston.

Pascarella, E. T. (2001, November/December). Cognitive growth in college: Surprising and reassuring findings from the National Study of Student Learning. *Change*, 21–27.

Pascarella, E. T. (2006). How college affects students: Ten directions for future research. *Journal of College Student Development, 57*(5), 508–520.

Pascarella, E., & Terenzini, P. (1991). *How college affects students: Findings and insights from twenty years of research*. San Francisco: Jossey-Bass.

Pascarella, E., & Terenzini, P. (2005). *How college affects students: A third decade of research* (Vol. 2). San Francisco: Jossey-Bass.

Pew Internet & American Life Project. (2002). *The Internet goes to college: How students are living in the future with today's technology*. Retrieved from http://www.pewinternet.org/files/old-media/Files/Reports/2002/PIP_College_Report.pdf.

Pryor, J. H., De Angelo, L., Palucki-Blake, B., Hurtado, S., & Tran, S. (2012) *The American freshman: National norms fall 2011*. Los Angeles: Higher Education Research Institute, UCLA.

Shelton, J. T., Elliot, E. M., Eaves, S. D., & Exner, A. L. (2009). The distracting effects of a ringing cell phone: An investigation of the laboratory and the classroom setting. *Journal of Environmental Psychology*, (March). Retrieved from http://news-info.wustl.edu/news/page/normal/14225.html.

Shimoff, E., & Catania, C. A. (2001). Effects of recording attendance on grades in Introductory Psychology. *Teaching of Psychology, 23*(3), 192–195.

Smith, J. B., Walter, T. L., & Hoey, G. (1992). Support programs and student self-efficacy: Do first-year students know when they need help? *Journal of the Freshman Year Experience, 4*(2), 41–67.

Tagliacollo, V. A., Volpato, G. L., & Pereira, A., Jr. (2010). Association of student position in classroom and school performance. *Educational Research, 1*(6), 198–201.

Tinto, V. (1993). *Leaving college: Rethinking the causes and cures of student attrition* (2nd ed.). Chicago: University of Chicago Press.

Tinto, V. (2012). *Completing college: Rethinking institutional action*. Chicago: The University of Chicago Press.

Walter, T. L., & Smith, J. (1990, April). *Self-assessment and academic support: Do students know they need help?* Paper presented at the annual Freshman Year Experience Conference, Austin, Texas.

Weinstein, C. E., Acee, T. W., & Jung, J. (2011). Self-regulation and learning strategies. New *Directions for Teaching and Learning, 126*, 45–53.

Chapter 1 Exercises

1.1 Reality Bite

Alone and Disconnected: Feeling like Calling It Quits

Josephine is a first-year student in her second week of college. She doesn't feel like she's fitting in with other students on her campus. She also feels a little guilty about the time she's taking time away from family and friends back home, and she fears that her ties with them will be weakened or broken if she continues spending so much time at school and on schoolwork. Josephine is feeling so torn between college, her family, and her old friends that she's beginning to have second thoughts about returning to college next term.

Reflection and Discussion Questions

1. What would you say to Josephine that might persuade or motivate her to stay in college?
2. What could Josephine do to get more connected with her college community and feel less disconnected from her family and hometown friends?
3. What could Josephine do for herself right now to minimize the conflict she's experiencing between her commitment to college and her commitment to family and high school friends?
4. Can you relate to Josephine's situation? If yes, in what way? If no, why not?

1.2 Birds of a Different Feather: High School vs. College

The following list identifies 12 key differences between high school and college. Rate each difference on a scale from 1 to 4 in terms of how aware you were of this difference when you began college:

   1 = totally unaware

   2 = not fully aware

   3 = somewhat aware

   4 = totally aware.

a) In high school, teachers often re-teach material in class that students were assigned to read.

b) In college, professors often don't cover the same material in class that appears in assigned reading, yet information from the assigned reading still appears on exams.

   Awareness Rating _____

> "In college, if you don't go to class, that's up to you. Your professor doesn't care really if you pass or fail."
>
> —First-year student

a) In high school, teachers often take class time to remind students of assignments and their due dates.
b) In college, professors list their assignments and due dates on the course syllabus and expect students to keep track of them on their own.

Awareness Rating _____

a) In high school, students spend most of their learning time in class; they spend much less time studying outside of class than they spend learning in class.
b) In college, students typically spend no more than 15 hours per week in class and are expected to spend at least twice as much time studying out of class for every hour they spend in class.

Awareness Rating _____

a) In high school, tests are given frequently and cover limited amounts of material.
b) In college, exams are given less frequently (e.g., midterm and final) and tend to cover large amounts of material.

Awareness Rating _____

a) In high school, make-up tests and extra credit opportunities are often available to students.
b) In college, if an exam or assignment is missed, rarely do students have a chance to make it up or recapture lost points through extra credit work.

> In high school, they're like, 'Okay, well, I'll give you another day to do it.' In college, you have to do it that day . . . teachers are like, 'If you don't do it, that's your problem."
> —First-year student

Awareness Rating _____

a) A grade of "D" in high school is still passing.
b) In college, students go to campus offices to enhance their success by taking advantage of the support services provided in these offices.

Awareness Rating _____

1.3 Syllabus Review

Review the syllabus (course outline) for all classes you're enrolled in this term, and answer the following questions.

Self-Assessment Questions

1. Is the overall workload what you expected? Are you surprised by the amount of work required in any particular course(s)?
2. At this point in the term, what do you see as your most challenging or demanding course or courses? Why?
3. Do you think you can handle the total workload required by the full set of courses you're enrolled in this term?
4. What adjustments or changes do you think you'll make to your previous learning and study habits to accommodate your academic workload this term?

1.4 Creating a Master List of Resources on Your Campus

1. Your final product will be a list that includes the following:

Campus Support Service	Type of Support Provided	Contact Person	Campus Location
_____	_____	_____	_____
_____	_____	_____	_____
_____	_____	_____	_____
_____	_____	_____	_____

etc.

Touching all the Bases:
Using Powerful Student-Success Principles & Key Campus Resources

Name: _____

Possible Classroom Exercises & Out-of Class Assignments

In addition to, or instead of the exercises included at the end of the chapter, the following may be used as exercises/assignments relating to content covered in Chapter 1.

Class Discussion Questions

The following questions may be used to stimulate class discussion of issues covered in this chapter.

Question #1. What do you think are the specific qualities or characteristics of *successful college students*?

Student responses to these questions are likely to coincide with and reinforce the four core principles of success outlined in chapter 1, namely, successful students and successful people are:

(a) *active*—they take charge and get involved,
(b) *resourceful*—they capitalize on available resources,
(c) *interactive*—they interact and collaborate with others, and
(d) *reflective*—they are self-aware, i.e., they "watch themselves" to be sure they're actually doing what it takes to be successful.

Question #2. How will the academic experience in college differ from *high school*?

Student responses to this discussion question may be used as a lead-in to their completing Exercise 1.3 at the end of the chapter.

Student discussion of these two questions can take place as a large group (whole class), in small "buzz groups," or in any of the following collaborative learning formats. Given the research indicating a sense of belongingness and social acceptance are important needs for new college students, it may be a good idea to utilize small-group learning experiences as much as possible in the FYE course, particularly early in the term, to connect students with their peers—especially if your class includes a significant number of commuter students—who are less likely to make these connections outside the classroom.

"Pairs Compare"

1. Students *pair-up* to generate ideas.
2. Each pair of students *joins another pair* to compare the ideas they have in common and the ideas that are unique to each pair.

"Think-Pair-Share"

1. Give students a specified period of time in class to *think and write down their ideas individually* about the question that has been presented to them.
2. Students pair-up with a neighboring student to discuss their thoughts, listening carefully to their partner's ideas so that they can jointly construct a composite response that builds on their individual thoughts.
3. Students then *share their pair's thoughts* with the *whole class*.

"Think-Pair-Square"

1. Students first think *alone* about the question.
2. Students *pair*-up with a nearby student to discuss their thoughts.
3. *Two pairs join together* to form a "*square*" (4-member team) to discuss or integrate their ideas.

One key academic task that college students are expected to perform in their first week of college are taking lecture notes. You can help students get in the habit of performing this academic task early and effectively by directing them to the note-taking strategies summarized in Box 1.1. Described below are some in-class exercises that might be used to help students develop effective early habits with respect to this important academic responsibility.

Commercials for Campus Resources
Steps:

1. As an extension of Exercise 1.5 (p. 000), have students form small (3-4 member) teams and ask each team to assume the role of researching a different campus resource.
2. Have the teams present their research to the class in the form of a commercial designed to advertise or "sell" the campus resource—i.e., persuade the class to "consume" its services.

Note: A third step could be added after the teams' presentations, whereby the class is broken into small groups and are given a minute to come up with a key question about the resource to ask the presenting team.

CHAPTER 2

Deep Learning

STRATEGIC NOTE-TAKING, READING, AND STUDYING

Chapter Preview

This chapter helps you apply research on human learning and the human brain to become a more effective and efficient learner. It takes you through three key stages of the learning process—from the first stage of acquiring information through lectures and readings, to the second stage of studying and retaining the information you've acquired, through the final stage of retrieving (recalling) the information you studied. The ultimate goal of this chapter is to supply you with a set of powerful strategies that makes your learning *deep* (not surface-level memorization), *durable* (long-lasting), and *retrievable* (accessible to you when you need it).

Learning Goal

Develop a repertoire of effective strategies for studying smarter, learning deeply, and retaining longer what you have learned.

Integrate Your Faith

How do think your current personal worldview could impact the time you invest in showing your love for the people and things in your life?

Ignite Your Thinking

Reflection 2.1

What would you say is the key difference between learning and memorizing?

From *Thriving in College and Beyond: Research-Based Strategies for Academic Success and Personal Development*, Fourth Edition by Joseph B. Cuseo, Aaron Thompson, Michele Campagna, and Viki S. Fecas. Copyright © 2016 Kendall Hunt Publishing Company. Reprinted by permission.

51

Learning is the fundamental mission of all colleges and universities. One of the major goals of a college education is to help students become independent, self-directed learners. Learning doesn't stop after college graduation; it's a lifelong process that is essential for success in the 21st century. The ongoing information technology revolution, coupled with global interdependence, is creating a greater need for effective learning skills that can be used throughout life in different and cultural and occupational contexts. Today's employers value job applicants who have "learned how to learn" and will continue to be "lifelong learners" (SECFHE, 2006).

What Is Deep Learning?

When students learn deeply, they dive below the surface of shallow memorization; they go further by building mental bridges between what they're trying to learn and what they already know (Piaget, 1978; Vygotsky, 1978). Knowledge isn't acquired by simply pouring information into the brain as if it were an empty jar. It's a matter of attaching or connecting new ideas to ideas that are already stored in the brain. When this happens, facts are transformed into *concepts*—networks of connected or interrelated ideas. In fact, when something is learned deeply, the human brain actually makes a physical (neurological) connection between separate nerve cells (LeDoux, 2002). (See **Figure 2.1**.)

FIGURE 2.1: Network of Brain Cells

Deep learning involves making connections between what you're trying to learn and what you already know. When you learn something deeply, it's stored in the brain as a link in an interconnected network of brain cells.

©Jurgen Ziewe/Shutterstock.com

Studies suggest that most college students don't engage in deep learning (Arum & Roksa, 2011; Kuh, 2005; Nathan, 2005). They may show up for class most of the time, cram for their exams, and get their assignments done right before they're due. These learning strategies may enable students to survive college, but not thrive in college and achieve academic excellence.

Stages in the Learning and Memory Process

Learning deeply and retaining what you've learned is a process that involves three key stages:

1. **Sensory input (perception).** Taking information into the brain;
2. **Memory formation (storage).** Transforming that information into knowledge and storing it in the brain; and
3. **Memory recall (retrieval).** Bringing that knowledge back to mind when you need it.

These three stages are summarized visually in **Figure 2.2**. These stages of the learning and memory process are similar to the way information is processed by a computer: (1) information is entered onto the screen (input), (2) that information is saved in a memory file (storage), and (3) the saved information is recalled and used when it's needed (retrieval). This three-stage process can serve as a framework for using the two major routes through which knowledge is acquired in college: from lectures and readings.

FIGURE 2.2: **Key Stages in the Learning and Memory Process**

Stage 1		Stage 2	Stage 3
Sensory Perception → Attention → Working Memory →		Memory Storage →	Retrieval
Hearing (lectures) Seeing (readings)	(Studying)	(Long-Term Memory)	(Test-Taking)

©Kendall Hunt Publishing Company

Effective Lecture-Listening and Note-Taking Strategies

The importance of developing effective listening skills in the college classroom was highlighted in a classic study of more than 400 students who were given a listening test at the start of their college experience. At the end of their first year in college, 49% of those students who scored low on the listening test were on academic probation—compared to only 4.4% of students who scored high on the listening test. On the other hand, 68.5% of students who scored high on the listening test were eligible for the honors program at the end of their first year—compared to only 4.17% of those students who had low listening test scores (Conaway, 1982).

Reflection 2.2

Do you think writing notes in class helps or hinders your ability to pay attention to and learn from your instructors' lectures?

Why?

Studies show that information delivered during lectures is the number one source of test questions (and answers) on college exams (Brown, 1988; Kuhn, 1988). When lecture information isn't recorded in students' notes and appears on a test, it has only a 5% chance of being recalled (Kiewra, et al., 2000). Students who write notes during lectures achieve higher course grades than students who just listen to lectures (Kiewra, 1985, 2005), and students with a more complete set of lecture notes are more likely to demonstrate higher levels of overall academic achievement (Johnstone & Su, 1994; Kiewra & DuBois, 1998).

Contrary to a popular belief that writing while listening interferes with the ability to listen, students report that taking notes actually increases their attention and concentration in class (Hartley, 1998; Hartley & Marshall, 1974). Studies also show that when students write down information that's presented to them, they're more likely to remember the most important aspects of that information when tested later (Bligh, 2000). One study discovered that students with grade point averages (GPAs) of 2.53 or higher record more information in their notes and retain a larger percentage of the most important information than do students with GPAs of less than 2.53 (Einstein, Morris, & Smith, 1985). These findings aren't surprising when you consider that *hearing* information, *writing* it, and then *seeing* it after it's been written produces three different memory traces (tracks) in the brain, thus tripling your chances of remembering it.

Furthermore, when notes are taken, you're left with a written record of lecture information that can be studied later to improve your test performance. In contrast, if you take few or no notes, you're left with little or no information to study for upcoming exams. As previously noted, the majority of questions on professors' exams come from information contained in their lectures. So, come to class with the attitude that your instructors are dispensing answers to test questions as they speak and your job is to pick out and record these answers so you can pick up points on the next exam.

Note
Points your professors make in class that make it into your notes turn into points earned on your exams (and higher grades in your courses).

You can get the most out of lectures by employing effective strategies at three key times: *before*, *during*, and *after* class.

Pre-Lecture Strategies: What to Do *Before* Class

1. **Check your syllabus to see where you are in the course and determine how the upcoming class fits into the total course picture.** By checking the course syllabus before individual class sessions you'll see how each part (class) relates to the whole (course). This strategy capitalizes on the brain's natural tendency to seek larger patterns and see the "big picture." The human brain is naturally inclined to connect parts into a meaningful whole (Caine & Caine, 2011). It looks for patterns and connections rather than isolated bits and pieces of information (Jensen, 2008). In **Figure 2.3**, notice how your brain naturally ties together and fills in the missing information to perceive a whole pattern that is meaningful.

FIGURE 2.3: **Triangle Illusion**

You perceive a white triangle in the middle of this figure. However, if you use three fingers to cover up the three corners of the white triangle that fall outside the other (background) triangle, the white triangle suddenly disappears. What your brain does is take these corners as starting points and fills in the rest of the information on its own to create a complete or whole pattern that has meaning to you. (Also, notice how you perceive the background triangle as a complete triangle, even though parts of its three sides are missing.)

©Kendall Hunt Publishing Company

2. **Get to class early so that you can review your notes from the previous class session and from any reading assignments relating to the day's lecture topic.** Research indicates that when students review information related to an upcoming lecture topic, they take more accurate and complete lecture notes (Jairam & Kiewra, 2009; Kiewra, 2005). Thus, a good way to improve your ability to learn from lectures is to review your notes from the previous class session and read textbook information related to the lecture topic—*before* hearing the lecture. Reviewing previously learned information activates your prior knowledge, enabling you to connect lecture material to what you already know—a powerful way to promote deep learning (Bruner, 1990; Piaget, 1978; Vygotky, 1978).

3. **Adopt a seating location that maximizes attention and minimizes distraction.** Many years of research show that students who sit in the front and center of class tend to earn higher exam scores and course grades (Tagliacollo, Volpato, & Pereira, 2010; Benedict & Hoag, 2004; Rennels & Chaudhair, 1988). These results have been found

> "I like to sit up front so I am not distracted by others and I don't have to look around people's heads to see the chalkboard."
>
> —*First-year college student*

> "I tend to sit at the very front of my classrooms. It helps me focus and take notes better. It also eliminates distractions."
>
> —*First-year college student*

even when students are assigned seats by their instructor, so it's not just a matter of more motivated and studious students sitting in the front of the room. Instead, the better academic performance achieved by students sitting front and center stems from learning advantages associated with this seating location.

Front-and-center seating benefits your academic performance by improving your vision of material written on the board or screen and your ability to hear the instructor's lectures. In addition, sitting in the front means you don't have to peer over or around the heads of other students. This results in more direct eye contact with the instructor, which increases your focus of attention, reduces your sense of anonymity, and increases your level of involvement in class.

Lastly, sitting in the front of class can also reduce your level of anxiety about speaking in class because you will not have numerous classmates sitting in front of you turning around to look at you when you speak.

The *bottom line*: When you enter a classroom, get in the habit of heading for a seat in the front and center of class. In large classes, it's even more important to get "up close and personal" with your instructors—not only to improve your attention, note-taking, and class participation—but also to improve your instructors' ability to remember who you are and how well you performed in class. This will work to your advantage when you ask your instructors for letters of recommendation.

4. **Sit by people who will enable (not disable) your ability to listen and learn.** Intentionally sit near classmates who will not distract you or interfere with the quality of your note-taking. The human attention span has a limited capacity; we can give all or part of our attention to whatever task we're performing. Actively listening to and taking notes on lecture information is a demanding task that demands undivided attention.

Note

When you enter class, you have a choice about where you're going to sit. Choose wisely by selecting a location that will maximize your attentiveness to the instructor and your effectiveness as a note-taker.

© Kendall Hunt Publishing Company.

The evolution of student attention from the back to the front of class.

Reflection 2.3

When you enter a classroom, where do you usually sit?

Why do you sit there? Is it a conscious choice or more like an automatic habit?

Do you think that the seat you usually choose places you in the best possible position for listening and learning in the classroom?

---

5. **Adopt a seating posture that screams attention.** Sitting upright and leaning forward increases attention because these signs of physical alertness reach the brain and stimulate mental alertness. If your body is in an alert and ready position, your mind picks up these physical cues and follows your body's lead. Baseball players get into a ready position before a pitch is delivered to ready themselves to catch batted balls; similarly, learners who assume a ready position in the classroom put themselves in a better position to catch ideas batted around in class. Studies show that when humans are mentally alert and ready to learn, a greater amount of C-kinase (a brain chemical) is released at the connection point between brain cells, which increases the likelihood that neurological (learning) connections are formed between them (Howard, 2014).

   Another advantage to being attentive in class is that it sends a clear message to your instructor that you're a courteous and conscientious student. This can influence your instructor's perception and evaluation of your academic performance; if at the end of the course you're on the border between a higher and lower grade, you're more likely to get the benefit of the doubt.

Listening and Note-Taking Strategies: What to Do *During* Class

1. **Give lectures your undivided attention.** As previously noted, research shows that in all subject areas, the majority of test questions appearing on college exams come from the professor's lectures and students who take better class notes get better course grades (Brown, 1988; Cuseo, et al., 2013; Kiewra, 2000). Studies also show that the more time students spend surfing the web or using Facebook during lectures, the lower their test scores. These results hold true for all students, regardless of how they scored on college admissions tests (Ravizza, Hambrick, & Fenn, 2014).

   Remember that like all humans, not all professors are created equal. You'll have some that are more dynamic and easier to pay attention to than others. It's the less dynamic ones that will tempt you to lose attention and stop taking notes. Don't let the less engaging or less entertaining professors lower your course grades. Instead, view them as a challenge; step up your focus of attention, continue taking notes to keep yourself engaged, and leave the course with the satisfaction of earning a good grade.

2. **Take your own notes in class.** Don't rely on someone else to take notes for you. Taking notes in your own words focuses your attention and ensures the notes you take make sense to you. Research indicates that students who record and review their own notes on information presented to them earn higher scores on memory tests for that information than do students who review notes taken by others (Jairam & Kiewra, 2009; Kiewra, 2005). Taking your own notes in your own words makes them *meaningful to you*. While it's a good idea to collaborate with classmates to compare notes for completeness and accuracy, or to pick up points you may have missed, you shouldn't rely on someone else to do your note-taking for you.

3. **Be alert to cues for the most important information contained in lectures.** Since the human attention span is limited, it's impossible to attend to and make note of everything. Thus, we need to use our attention *selectively* to detect and select information that matters most. Here are some strategies for identifying and recording the most important information delivered by professors during lectures:

    - Pay particular attention to information your instructors put *in print*—on the board, on a slide, or in a handout. If your instructor has taken the time and energy to write it out or type it out, this is usually a good clue that the information is important and you'll likely see it again—on an exam.
    - Pay special attention to information presented during the *first and last few minutes of class*. Instructors are most likely to provide valuable reminders, reviews, and previews at the start and end of a class session.
    - Look for *verbal and nonverbal cues* that signal the instructor is delivering important information. Don't just tune in when your professors are writing something down and tune out at other times. It's been found that students record almost 90% of material written on the board, but less than 50% of important ideas that professors state but don't write on the board (Johnstone & Su, 1994; Locke, 1977; Titsworth & Kiewra, 2004). So, don't fall into the reflex-like routine of just taking notes when you see your instructor writing notes. Instead, listen actively to ideas you *hear* your instructor saying and take notes on these ideas as well. **Box 2.1** contains strategies for detecting clues to important information that professors are delivering orally in class.

Box 2.1

Detecting When Instructors Are Delivering Important Information during Lectures

Look for *verbal* cues, such as:
- Phrases signaling important information (e.g., "The point here is . . ." or "What's most significant about this is . . .").
- Information that's repeated or rephrased in a different way (e.g., "In other words, . . .", or "To put it another way . . .").
- Stated information that's followed by a question to check understanding (e.g., "Is that clear?" "Do you follow that?" "Does that make sense?" or "Are you with me?").

Watch for *vocal (tone of voice)* cues, such as:
- Information delivered in a louder tone or at a higher pitch than usual—which may indicate excitement or emphasis.
- Information delivered at a slower rate or with more pauses than usual—which may be your instructor's way of giving you more time to write down these important ideas.

Keep an eye out for *nonverbal* cues, such as:
- Information delivered by your instructor with more than the usual:
  a) Facial expressiveness (e.g., raised or furrowed eyebrows);
  b) Body movement (e.g., gesticulation and animation);
  c) Eye contact (e.g., looking directly and intently at the faces of students to see if they're following or understanding what's being said).
- Your instructor moving closer to the students (e.g., moving away from the podium or blackboard).
- Your instructor orienting his or her body directly toward the class (i.e., both shoulders directly or squarely facing the class).

---

4. **Keep taking notes even if you don't immediately understand what your instructor is saying.** If you are uncertain or confused about the material being presented, don't stop taking notes. Having notes on that material will at least leave you with a record to review later—when you have more time to think about it and make sense of it. If you still don't understand it after taking time to review it, seek clarification from your instructor, a classmate, or your textbook.

5. **Take organized notes.** If your instructor continues to make points relating to the same idea, take notes on that idea within the same paragraph. When the instructor shifts to a new idea, skip a few lines and shift to a new paragraph. Be alert to phrases that your instructor may use to signal a shift to a new or different idea (e.g., "Let's turn to . . ." or "In addition to . . ."). Use these phrases as cues for taking notes in paragraph form.

    By recording different ideas in different paragraphs, the organizational quality of your notes improves as will your comprehension and retention of them. Be sure to leave extra space between paragraphs (ideas) to give yourself room to add information that you may have initially missed, or to later translate the professor's words into your own words.

Another popular strategy for taking organized notes is the *Cornell Note-Taking System*. This system is summarized in **Box 2.2**.

Box 2.2

The Cornell Note-Taking System

1. On the page on which you're taking notes, draw a horizontal line about 2 inches from the bottom edge of the paper.
2. If there's no vertical line on the left side of the page, draw one line about 2½ inches from the left edge of the paper (as shown in the scaled-down illustration here).
3. When your instructor is lecturing, use the large space to the right of the vertical line (area A) to record your notes.
4. After a lecture, use the space at the bottom of the page (area B) to summarize the main points you recorded on that page.
5. Use the column of space on the left side of the page (area C) to write questions that are answered in the notes on the right.
6. Quiz yourself by looking at the questions listed in the left margin while covering the answers to them that are found in your class notes on the right.

Note: You can use this note-taking and note-review method on your own, or you could team up with two or more students and do it collaboratively.

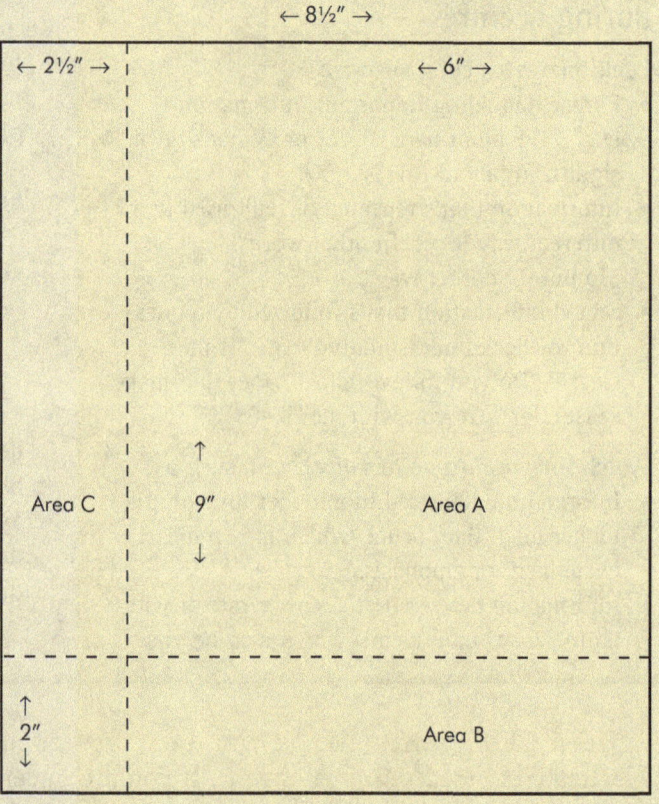

©Kendall Hunt Publishing Company

Post-Lecture Strategies: What to Do *After* Class

1. **As soon as class ends, quickly check your notes for missing information or incomplete thoughts.** Information delivered during a lecture is likely to be fresh in your mind immediately after class. A quick check of your notes at this time will allow you to take advantage of your short-term memory. By reviewing and reflecting on your notes, you can help move that information into long-term memory before forgetting takes place. This quick review can be done alone or, better yet, with a motivated classmate. If you both have gaps in your notes, check them out with your instructor before he or she leaves the classroom. Even though

it may be weeks before you'll be tested on the material, the quicker you pick up missed points and clear up sources of confusion, the better; it will help you understand upcoming material—especially upcoming material that builds on previously covered material. Catching confusion early in the game also enables you to avoid the mad last-minute rush of students seeking help from the instructor just before test time. You want to reserve the critical time just before exams to study notes you know are complete and accurate, rather than rushing around trying to find missing information and seeking last-minute help on concepts presented weeks earlier.

Reflection 2.4

Do you tend to stick around a few minutes after class sessions end to review your notes and clear up missing information or confusing points?

If you don't, why not?

---

2. **Before the next class session meets, reflect on and review your notes to make sense of them.** Your professors will often lecture on information that you may have little prior knowledge about, so it's unrealistic to expect that you will understand everything that's being said the first time you hear it. Instead, set aside time to reflect on and review your notes as soon as possible after class has ended. During this review process, take notes on your notes by:
   - Translating technical information into your own words to make it more meaningful to you; and
   - Reorganizing your notes to get ideas related to the same point in the same place.

Studies show that students who organize their lecture notes into meaningful categories demonstrate superior recall of that information on memory tests—compared to students who simply review the notes they took in class (Howe, 1970; Kiewra, 2005).

Note

Effective note taking is a two-stage process: Stage 1 involves actively taking notes in class and stage 2 takes places after class—when you take time to reflect on your notes and process them more deeply.

Strategic Reading

Expect to do more reading in college than you did in high school and be ready to be held accountable for the reading you're assigned. Information from assigned readings ranks right behind information from lectures as a source of test questions on college exams (Brown, 1988; Cuseo, et al., 2013). There is strong evidence that completing and comprehending assigned readings is associated with higher course grades (Sappington, Kinsey, & Munsayac, 2002). You're likely to find exam questions relating to reading assignments that your professors didn't talk much about in class (or even mention in class). College professors often expect you to relate or connect their lectures with material they've assigned you to read. Furthermore, professors often deliver class lectures with the assumption that students have done the assigned reading, so if you haven't done it, you're more likely to have difficulty following what your instructor is saying in class. Thus, you should not only do the assigned reading but also do it according to the schedule the instructor has established. By completing assigned reading in a timely manner, you will (a) be better positioned to understand class lectures, (b) acquire information that's likely to appear on exams but not covered in class, and (c) improve the quality of your participation in class.

The following research-based strategies can be used to improve your reading comprehension and retention.

Pre-Reading Strategies: What to Do *Before* Reading

1. **Before jumping into your assigned reading, first see how it fits into the overall organizational structure of the book and course.** You can do this efficiently by taking a quick look at the book's table of contents to see where the chapter you're about to read is placed in the overall sequence of chapters. Look especially at its relationship to the chapters that immediately precede and follow it. This strategy will give you a sense of how the particular part you're focusing on connects with the bigger picture. Research shows that if students have advanced knowledge about how material they're about to learn is organized—if they see how its parts relate to the whole *before* they start learning the specific parts—they're better able to comprehend and retain the material (Ausubel, Novak, & Hanesian 1978; Chen & Hirumi, 2009). Thus, the first step toward improving reading comprehension and retention of a book chapter is to see how it relates to the book as a whole.

Reflection 2.5

When you open a textbook to read a chapter, how do you start the reading process? What's the first thing you do?

2. **Preview the chapter by first reading its boldface headings and any chapter outline, objectives, summary, or end-of-chapter questions that may be included.** Before tackling the chapter's specific content, get in the habit of previewing what's in the chapter to get a general sense of its overall organization. If you dive into the specific details first, you may

lose sight of how the smaller details relate to the larger picture. Since the brain's natural tendency is to perceive and comprehend whole patterns rather than isolated bits of information, start by seeing how the parts of the chapter relate to the whole. Just as looking at the whole picture of a completed jigsaw puzzle beforehand helps you connect its parts, so too does getting a picture of the whole chapter before reading its parts.

3. **Take a moment to think about what you may already know that relates to the main topic of the chapter.** This strategy will activate the areas of your brain where your prior knowledge about that topic is stored, thereby preparing it to make meaningful connections with the material you're about to read.

Strategies to Do *During* the Reading Process

1. **Read selectively to locate the most important information.** Effective reading begins with a plan for identifying what should be noted and remembered. Here are three key strategies you can use while reading to help you determine what information you should focus on and retain.

    - **Use boldface or dark-print headings and subheadings as cues for identifying important information.** These headings organize the chapter's major points; you can use them as "traffic" signs to direct you to the most important information in the chapter. Better yet, turn the headings into questions and read to find answers to them. This question-and-answer routine ensures that you read actively and with a purpose. (You can set up this strategy while previewing the chapter by placing a question mark after each heading contained in the chapter.) Creating and answering questions while reading also keeps you motivated because the questions stimulate curiosity and a desire to find answers to them (Walter, Knudsvig, & Smith, 2003). Another advantage of posing and answering questions about what you're reading is that it's an effective way to prepare for exams—you're practicing exactly what you'll be expected to do on exams—answering questions.

    - **Pay close attention to information that's *italicized*, underlined, CAPITALIZED, or bulleted.** These features call attention to key terms that must be understood and built on before you can proceed to understand higher-level concepts covered later in the reading. Don't simply highlight these words because their special appearance suggests they're important. Read these terms carefully and be sure you understand them before you continue reading.

    - **Pay special attention to the first and last sentences in each paragraph.** These sentences provide an important introduction and conclusion to the key point contained in the paragraph. It's a good idea to reread the first and last sentences of each paragraph before you move on to the next paragraph, particularly when reading material that's cumulative (builds on previously covered material), such as science and math.

Note

Your goal when reading is not just to cover the assigned pages, but to uncover the most important ideas contained on those pages.

2. **Take written notes on important information you find in your reading.** A good way to stop and think deeply about key ideas in your reading is to take notes on those ideas in your own words. Research shows that the common student practice of just highlighting the text (the author's words) is not a particularly effective strategy (Dunlosky, et al., 2013). Highlighting is a passive learning process, whereas note-taking actively engages you in the reading process and enables you to transform the text into your own words. Don't slip into the habit of using your textbook simply as a coloring book in which the artistic process of highlighting information in spectacular, kaleidoscopic colors distracts you from the more important process of learning actively and thinking deeply about what you're reading. Highlighting is okay as long it's not the only thing you do while reading; take time to make notes on the material you've highlighted—in your own words—to ensure that you reflect on it and make it personally meaningful. Taking notes on information delivered during lectures will improve your performance on exams; taking notes on your reading assignments will do the same.

> "I would advise you to read with a pen in your hand, and enter in a little book of short hints of what you find that is curious, or that might be useful; for this will be the best method of imprinting such particulars in your memory, where they will be ready."
>
> —Benjamin Franklin, 18th-century inventor, newspaper writer, and cosigner of the Declaration of Independence

> "I had the worst study habits and the lowest grades. Then I found out what I was doing wrong. I had been highlighting with a black magic marker."
>
> —Jeff Altman, American comedian

©Kendall Hunt Publishing Company

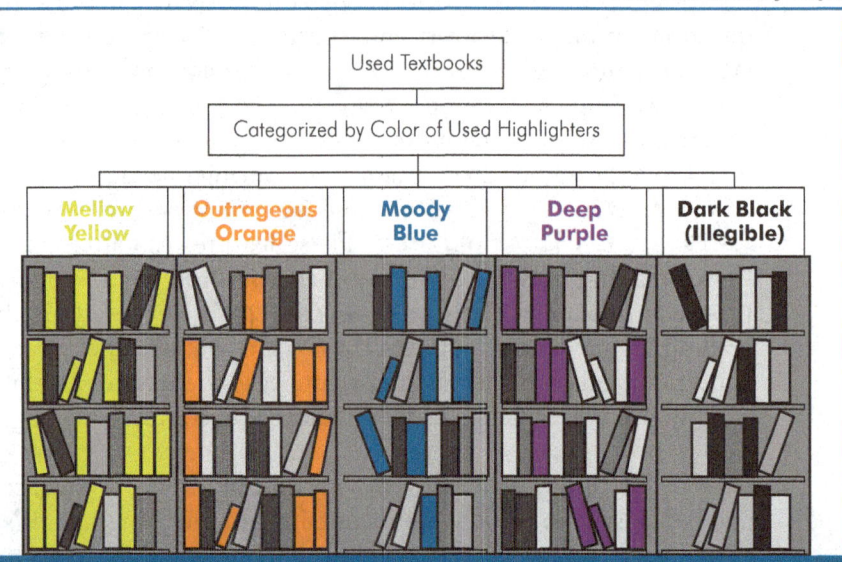

Highlighting textbooks in psychedelic colors is a very popular reading strategy among college students, but it's a less effective strategy for producing deep learning than taking written notes on what you read.

When you transform what someone else has written into your own words, you're implementing a powerful principle of deep learning: relating what you're trying to learn to what you already know (Demmert & Towner, 2003). A good time for pausing and writing a brief summary of what you've read in your own words is when you encounter a boldface heading because it indicates you're about to encounter a new topic; this is the ideal time to deepen your knowledge of what you just finished reading and use that knowledge to help you understand what's coming next.

Reflection 2.6

When reading a textbook, do you usually have the following tools on hand?

Highlighter:	yes	no
Pen or pencil:	yes	no
Notebook:	yes	no
Class notes:	yes	no
Dictionary:	yes	no
Glossary:	yes	no

If you don't usually have one or more of the above tools on hand while reading, which one(s) do you plan to have on hand in the future?

---

3. **Make use of visual aids that accompany the written text.** Don't fall into the trap of thinking that visual aids can or should be skipped because they're merely supplemental or ornamental. Visual aids, such as charts, graphs, diagrams, and concept maps, are powerful learning and memory tools for a couple of reasons: (a) they enable you to "see" the information in addition to reading (hearing) it, and (b) they pull together separate ideas into a unified snapshot.

   Visual aids also improve learning and memory of written material by delivering information to the brain through a different sensory modality. In addition, periodically pausing to view visual aids adds variety and a change of pace to the reading process. Breaking up sustained periods of reading with a change of pace and different sensory input helps maintain your interest and attention (Malmberg & Murname, 2002; Murname & Shiffrin, 1991).

4. **Regulate or adjust your reading speed to the type of subject matter you're reading.** As you know, academic subjects vary in terms of their level of technicality and complexity. Reading material in a math or science textbook requires reading at a slower rate with more frequent pauses to check for understanding than reading a novel or a short story.

Post-Reading Strategies: What to Do *After* Reading

1. **End your reading sessions with a short review of the key information you've highlighted and taken notes on.** Rather than ending your reading session by trying to cover a few more pages, reserve the last five minutes to review the key ideas you already covered. Most forgetting of information takes place immediately after we stop focusing on the information and turn our attention to another task (Averell & Heathcote, 2011; Baddeley, 1999). By taking a few minutes at the end of a reading session to review the most important information you've just read, you help your brain "lock" that information into long-term memory before getting involved with another task.

The graph in **Figure 2.4** represents the results of a classic experiment that tested how well information is recalled at various times after it was originally learned. As you can see on the far left of the graph, most forgetting occurs soon after information has been taken in (e.g., after 20 minutes, more than 60% of it was forgotten). The results of this classic study have been confirmed multiple times (Schacter, 2001) and they underscore the importance of reviewing key information acquired through reading *immediately* after you've read it. By doing so, your memory for that information improves dramatically because you're intercepting the human "forgetting curve" at its steepest point of memory loss—just after information has been taken in.

FIGURE 2.4: The Forgetting Curve

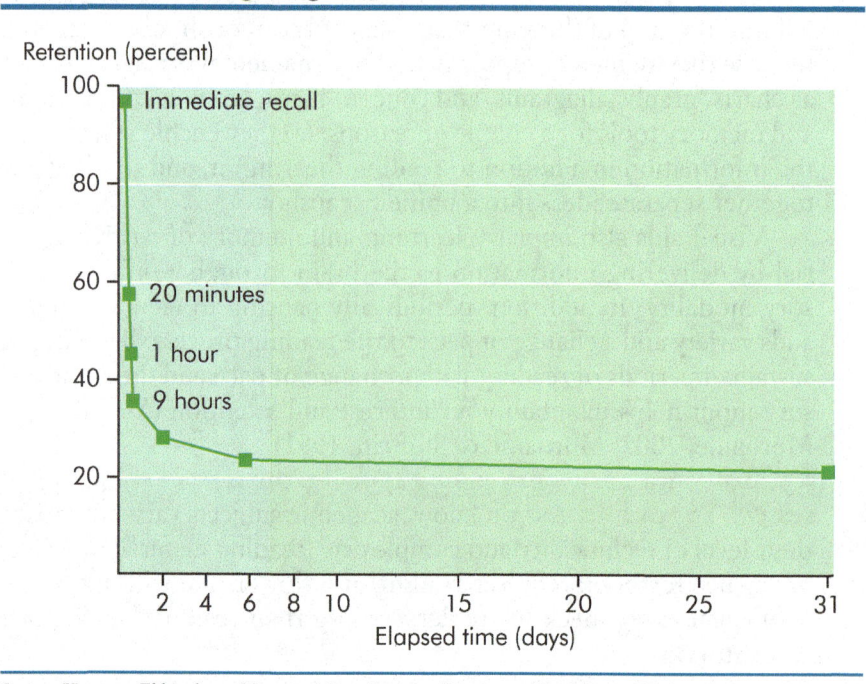

Source: Hermann Ebbinghaus, *Memory: A Contribution to Experimental Psychology*, 1885–1913.

2. **After completing a reading assignment, if you're still confused about an important idea or concept contained in the reading, go to another source.** The problem may not be you—it may be the way the author has presented or explained it. You may be able to clear up your confusion by simply consulting another source or resource, such as those listed below.
   - **Look at how another book explains it.** Not all textbooks are created equal; some do a better job of explaining certain concepts than others. Check to see whether your library or campus bookstore has other texts dealing with the same subject as your course. A different book may be able to explain a hard-to-understand concept much better than your assigned textbook.
   - **Seek help from your instructor.** If you completed the reading assignment and made every effort to understand a particular concept but still can't grasp it, most instructors should be willing to assist you.
   - **Seek help from learning assistance professionals or peer tutors in your Learning Center (Academic Support Center).** This is your key campus resource for help with reading assignments, particularly if your instructor is unavailable or unwilling to provide assistance.

Box 2.3

SQ3R: A Method for Improving Reading Comprehension and Retention

A popular system for organizing and remembering key reading strategies, such as those discussed in this chapter, is the *SQ3R* system. SQ3R is an acronym for five steps that can be taken to increase textbook reading comprehension and retention, particularly when reading highly technical or complex material. The following sequences of steps comprise this method:

1. Survey
2. Question
3. Read
4. Recite
5. Review

S = Survey: Get a preview and overview of what you're about to read.

1. Use the chapter's title to activate your thoughts about the subject and get your mind ready to receive information related to it.
2. Read the introduction, chapter objectives, and chapter summary to become familiar with the author's purpose, goals, and key points.
3. Note the boldface headings and subheadings to get a sense of the chapter's organization before you begin reading. This supplies you with a mental structure or framework for making sense of the information you're about to read.
4. Take note of any graphics—such as charts, maps, and diagrams; they provide valuable visual support and reinforcement for the material you're reading.
5. Pay special attention to reading aids (e.g., italics and boldface font); use them to identify, understand, and remember key concepts.

Q = Question: Stay active and curious.

As you read, use boldface headings to formulate questions and read to find answers to those questions. When your mind is actively searching for answers, it becomes more engaged in the learning

Box 2.3 (continued)

process. As you read, add any questions of your own that come to mind.

R = Read: Find answers to questions you've created.

Read one section at a time—with your questions in mind—and search for answers to these questions.

R = Recite: Rehearse your answers.

After you complete reading each section, recall the questions you asked and see if you can answer them from memory. If not, look at the questions again and practice your answers until you can recall them without looking. Don't move onto the next section until you're able to answer all questions in the section you've just completed.

R = Review: Look back and get a second view of the whole picture.

Once you've finished the chapter, review all the questions you've created for different parts or sections. See whether you can still answer them without looking. If not, go back and refresh your memory.

Reflection 2.7

Rate yourself in terms of how frequently you use the following reading strategies, using the following scale:

4 = always, 3 = sometimes, 2 = rarely, 1 = never

1.	I read chapter outlines and summaries before I start reading the chapter content.	4 3 2 1
2.	I preview a chapter's boldface headings and subheadings before I begin to read the chapter.	4 3 2 1
3.	I adjust my reading speed to the type of subject I am reading.	4 3 2 1
4.	I look up the meaning of unfamiliar words and unknown terms that I come across before I continue reading.	4 3 2 1
5.	I take written notes on information I read.	4 3 2 1
6.	I use the visual aids included in my textbooks.	4 3 2 1
7.	I finish my reading sessions with a review of important information that I noted or highlighted.	4 3 2 1

Strategic Studying: Learning More Deeply and Remembering Longer

Studying isn't a short sprint that takes place just before test time. Instead, it's more like a long-distance run that takes place over time. Studying the night before an exam should be the last step in a sequence of test-preparation steps that take place well before test time, which include: (a) taking accurate and complete notes in class, (b) doing the assigned reading, and (c) seeking help from professors or peers along the way for any concepts that are unclear or confusing. After these steps have been taken, you are then well-positioned to study the material you've acquired and learn it deeply.

Described below is a series of study strategies you can use to promote deep and durable (long-lasting) learning.

Give Studying Your Undivided Attention

The human attention span has limited capacity—we have only so much of it available to us at any point in time and we can give all or part of it to whatever task(s) we're working on. As the phrase "paying attention" suggests, it's like paying money; we only have so much of it to spend. Thus, if attention while studying is spent on other activities at the same time (e.g., watching TV or messaging friends), there's a deduction in the amount of attention paid to studying. In other words, studying doesn't receive our undivided attention.

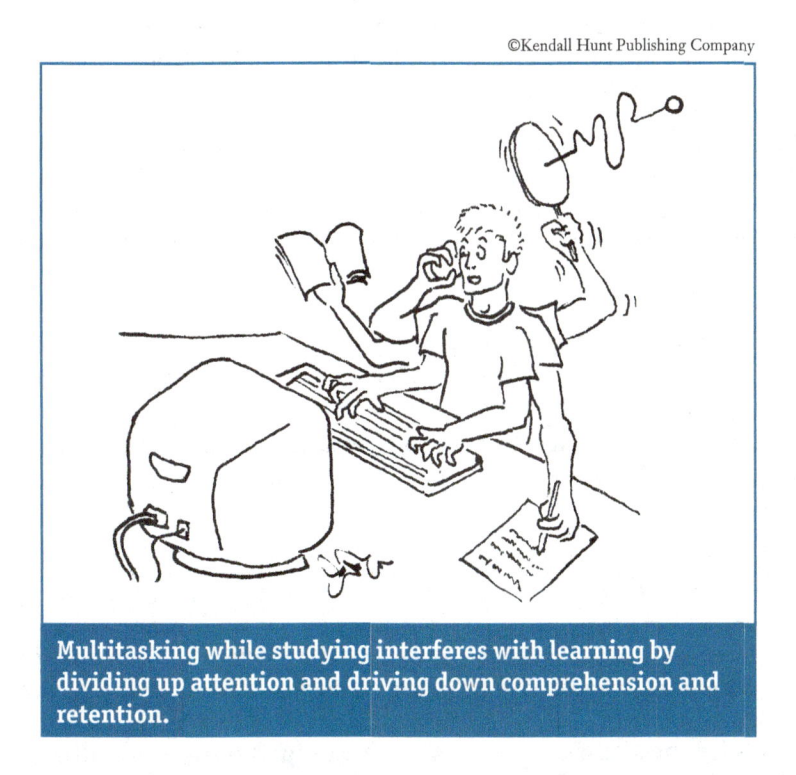

©Kendall Hunt Publishing Company

Multitasking while studying interferes with learning by dividing up attention and driving down comprehension and retention.

Studies show that when people multitask they don't pay equal attention to all tasks at the same time; instead, they divide their attention by shifting it back and forth between tasks (Howard, 2014). Their performance on the task that demands the most concentration or deepest

> "You can do several things at once, but only if they are easy and undemanding. You are probably safe carrying on a conversation with a passenger while driving on an empty highway [but] you could not compute the product of 17 x 24 while making a left turn into dense traffic, and you certainly should not try."
>
> —Daniel Kahneman, professor emeritus of Psychology, and author of Thinking Fast and Slow

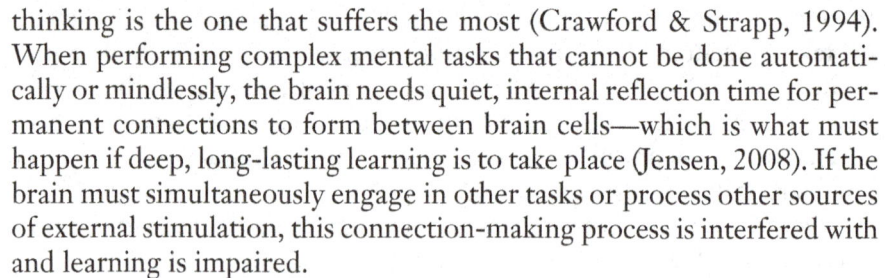

thinking is the one that suffers the most (Crawford & Strapp, 1994). When performing complex mental tasks that cannot be done automatically or mindlessly, the brain needs quiet, internal reflection time for permanent connections to form between brain cells—which is what must happen if deep, long-lasting learning is to take place (Jensen, 2008). If the brain must simultaneously engage in other tasks or process other sources of external stimulation, this connection-making process is interfered with and learning is impaired.

So, give study time your undivided attention by unplugging all your electronic accessories. You can even use apps to help you do so (e.g., to silence your phone). Another strategy would be to set aside a short time block of time to check electronic messages after you've completed a longer block of study time (e.g., as a study break); this allows you to use social media as a reward *after* putting in a stretch of focused study time. Just don't do both at the *same* time.

Make Meaningful Associations

Deep learning doesn't take place by simply absorbing information like a sponge—in exactly the same, prepackaged form as you received it from a textbook or lecture. Instead, deep learning involves actively translating the information you receive into a form that makes sense to you (Biggs & Tang, 2007; Mayer, 2002).

> "When you have to do work, and you're getting it. It's linking what I already know to what I didn't know."
>
> —Student's description of a "good class"

Note
Deep learning is not about teachers transmitting information to students; it's about students transforming *that information into* knowledge *that's meaningful to them.*

The brain's natural learning tendency is to translate unfamiliar information into a familiar form that makes sense and has personal meaning. This is illustrated in the experience.

You can experience the brain's natural inclination for meaning-making by reading the following passage, which once appeared anonymously online.

> *Aoccdrnig to rscheearch at Cmabridge Uinverstisy, it deos't mattaer in what order the ltteers in a word are, the only iprmoetnt thing is that the frist and lsat ltteer be at the rghit pclae. The rset can be a total mses and you can still raed it wouthit a porbelm. This is bcusae the human mind deos not raed ervey lteter by istlef, but the word as a wlohe. Amzanig huh?*

Notice how easily you made meaning out of unfamiliar, misspelled words by naturally transforming them into familiar, meaningful words—which were already stored in your brain. Whenever you're learning something new, capitalize on the brain's natural tendency to find meaning by trying to connect what you're trying to understand to what you already know.

Learning the specialized terminology associated with different academic disciplines may seem like learning a foreign language for a student with little or no experience with these terms. However, before you start brutally beating these terms into your brain through sheer repetition, try to find meaning in them. One way to do so is by looking up the term's word root in the dictionary or by identifying its prefix or suffix, which may give away the term's meaning. For instance, suppose you're taking a biology course and studying the autonomic nervous system—the part of the nervous system that operates without conscious awareness or voluntary control (e.g., your heart and lungs). The meaning of this biological term is found in its prefix "auto," meaning self-controlling or "automatic" (e.g., automatic transmission). Once you find meaning in a term, you can learn it faster and retain it longer than by memorizing it through sheer repetition.

If looking up an academic term's root, prefix, or suffix doesn't reveal its meaning, see if you can make it meaningful to you in some other way. Suppose you looked up the root of the term "artery" and nothing about the origins of this term helped you understand its meaning or purpose. You could create your own meaning for this term by taking its first letter (a), and have it stand for "away"—to help you remember that arteries carry blood away from the heart. By so doing, you take a meaningless term and make it personally meaningful and memorable.

Another way you can make learning meaningful is by *comparing and contrasting* what you're learning with what you already know. When you're studying, get in the habit of asking yourself the following questions:

a) How is this idea similar or comparable to something that I've already learned? (Compare)
b) How is this idea different from what I've already learned? (Contrast)

Research indicates that this simple strategy is one of the most powerful ways to promote learning of academic information (Marzano, Pickering, & Pollock, 2001). When you ask yourself the question, "How is this similar to and different from concepts I already know?" you make the learning process more meaningful and relevant because you're relating what you're trying to learn to what you already know or have already experienced.

Note
When learning, go for meaning first, memorization last. If you can connect what you're trying to learn to what you already know, the deeper you'll learn it and the longer you'll remember it.

Integrate Information from Lectures and Readings

Connect ideas from your lecture notes and reading assignments that relate to the same concept. Get them in the same place by recording them on the same index card under the same category heading. Index cards can be

> "The extent to which we remember a new experience has more to do with how it relates to existing memories than with how many times or how recently we have experienced it."
>
> —Morton Hunt, The Universe Within: A New Science Explores the Human Mind

used like a portable file cabinet, whereby each card functions like the hub of a wheel, around which individual pieces of related information can be attached like spokes. In contrast, when ideas pertaining to the same point or concept are spread all over the place, they're more likely to take that form in your mind—leaving them mentally disconnected and leaving you more confused or overwhelmed (and stressed out).

Note
Deep learners ask questions like: How can this specific piece of information be categorized or classified into a larger concept? How does this particular idea relate to or "fit into" something bigger?

Distribute Study Time across Separate Study Sessions

Learning deeply depends not only on *how* you learn (your method), but *when* you learn (your timing). Equally important as how much time you spend studying is how you distribute or spread out your study time. Research consistently shows that for students of all abilities and ages, distributing study time across several shorter sessions results in deeper learning and longer retention than channeling all study time into one long session (Brown, Roediger, & McDaniel, 2014; Carey, 2014; Dunlosky, et al., 2013). Distributed practice improves your learning and memory in two major ways:

- It minimizes loss of attention due to fatigue or boredom.
- It reduces mental interference by giving the brain some downtime to cool down and lock in information it has received before being interrupted by the need to deal with additional information (Malmberg & Murnane, 2002; Murname & Shiffrin, 1991). Memory works like a muscle: after it's been exercised, if given some "cool down" time before it's exerted again, it builds greater strength—that is, stronger memory for what it previously learned (Carey, 2014). On the other hand, if the brain's downtime is interfered with by the arrival of additional information, it gets overloaded and its capacity for handling information becomes impaired. That's what cramming does—it overloads the brain with lots of information in a limited period of time. In contrast, distributed study does just the opposite—it uses shorter sessions with downtime between sessions—giving the brain time to slow down and retain the information it's previously processed (studied) and more time to move that information from short-term to long-term memory (Willis, 2006).

Distributed study is also less stressful and more motivating than cramming. You're more likely to start studying when you know you won't be doing it for a long stretch of time (or lose any sleep doing it). It's also easier to sustain attention for tasks that are done for a shorter period of time.

Although cramming just before exams is better than not studying at all, it's far less effective than studying that's spread out across time. Instead of frantically cramming total study time into one long session ("massed

> "Hurriedly jam-packing a brain is akin to speed-packing a cheap suitcase—it holds its new load for a while, then most everything falls out."
> —Benedict Carey, author, *How We Learn: Throw Out the Rule Book and Unlock Your Brain's Potential*

practice"), use *distributed practice*—"distribute" or space out your study time over several shorter sessions.

Reflection 2.8

Are you more likely to study in advance of exams or cram just before exams?

How do you think most students would answer this question?

Use the "Part-to-Whole" Study Method

A natural extension of distributed practice is the part-to-whole method. This method involves breaking up the material you need to learn into smaller parts and studying those parts in separate sessions in advance of the exam; then you use your last study session just before the exam to review (restudy) the parts you previously studied in separate sessions. Thus, your last session isn't a cram session or even a study session; it's a review session.

Research shows that students of all ability levels learn material in college courses more effectively when it's studied in small units and when progression to the next unit takes place only after the previous unit has been mastered or understood (Pascarella & Terenzini, 1991, 2005).

Don't buy into the myth that studying in advance is a waste of time because you'll forget it all by test time. (Procrastinators often use this argument to rationalize their habit of putting off studying until the very last moment, which forces them to cram frantically the night before exams.) Even if you aren't able to recall what you previously studied when you look at it again closer to test time, research shows that once you start reviewing it, you can relearn it in a fraction of the time it took the first time. Since it takes much less time to relearn the material because the brain still has a memory trace for information studied in the earlier sessions (Kintsch, 1994), it proves you didn't completely forget it and that studying it in advance wasn't a waste of time. Another key advantage of breaking material you're learning into smaller parts and studying those parts in advance of major exams is that it allows you to check your understanding of the part you studied before moving on to learning the next part. This is a particularly important advantage in courses where learning the next unit of material builds on your understanding the previous unit (e.g., math and science).

Capitalize on the Power of Visual Learning

The human brain consists of two hemispheres (half spheres)—left and right (see **Figure 2.5**). Each of these hemispheres specializes in a different type of learning. The left hemisphere specializes in verbal learning;

FIGURE 2.5:

The human brain is comprised of two half spheres (hemispheres): the left hemisphere specializes in verbal learning, and the right hemisphere specializes in visual learning.

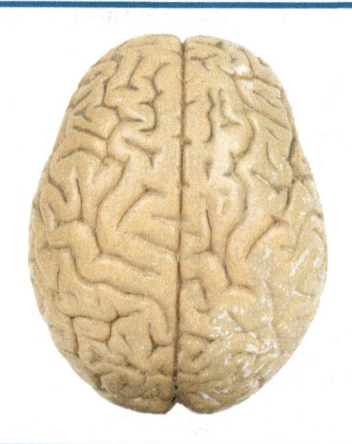

©JupiterImages Corporation.

it deals primarily with words. In contrast, the right hemisphere specializes in visual–spatial learning; it deals primarily with perceiving images, patterns, and objects that occupy physical place or space. If you involve both hemispheres of the brain while studying, two different memory traces are recorded—one in each major hemisphere (half) of the brain. This process of laying down dual memory traces (verbal and visual) is referred to as *dual coding* (Paivio, 1990). Since two memory traces are better than one, dual coding results in deeper learning and longer retention.

To capitalize on the advantage of dual coding, be sure to use all the visual aids available to you, including those found in your textbook and those provided by your instructor in class. You can also create your own visual aids by representing what you're learning in the form of pictures, symbols, or concept maps—such as flowcharts, timelines, spider webs, wheels with hubs and spokes, or branching tree diagrams. (See **Figure 2.6** for an example of a concept map.) When you transform material you're learning into a visual pattern, you're putting it into a form that's compatible with the brain's tendency to store information in neurological networks (Willis, 2006). Drawing also keeps you actively engaged in the process of learning, and by representing verbal information in visual form, you double the number of memory traces recorded in your brain. As the old saying goes, "A picture is worth a thousand words."

Note

Don't forget that drawings and visual illustrations can be more than just forms of artistic expression; they can also be powerful learning tools—you can draw to learn!

FIGURE 2.6: Concept Map for the Human Nervous System

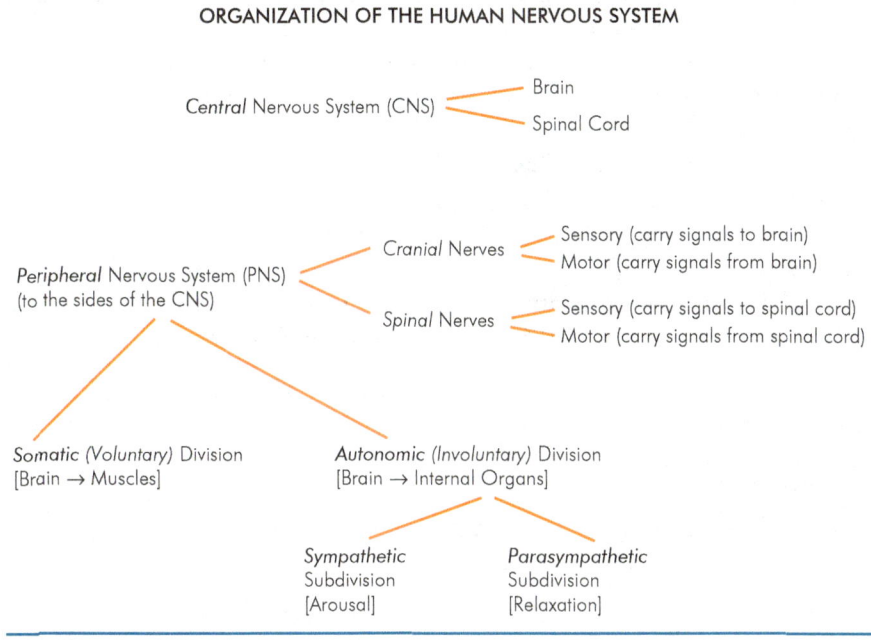

ORGANIZATION OF THE HUMAN NERVOUS SYSTEM

Central Nervous System (CNS)
— Brain
— Spinal Cord

Peripheral Nervous System (PNS) (to the sides of the CNS)
— *Cranial* Nerves
  — Sensory (carry signals to brain)
  — Motor (carry signals from brain)
— *Spinal* Nerves
  — Sensory (carry signals to spinal cord)
  — Motor (carry signals from spinal cord)

Somatic (Voluntary) Division [Brain → Muscles]

Autonomic (Involuntary) Division [Brain → Internal Organs]
— *Sympathetic* Subdivision [Arousal]
— *Parasympathetic* Subdivision [Relaxation]

©Kendall Hunt Publishing Company

Build Variety into the Study Process

Infusing variety and change of pace into your study routine can increase your motivation to study and your concentration while studying. Here are some practical strategies for doing so.

Mix it up: periodically shift the type of academic tasks you perform during a study session. Changing the nature of the academic work you do while studying increases your alertness and concentration by reducing *habituation*—attention loss that occurs after repeatedly engaging in the same type of mental task (Thompson, 2009). You can combat attention loss due to habituation by varying the type of tasks you perform during a study session. For instance, you can shift periodically among tasks that involve reading, writing by hand, typing on a keyboard, reviewing, reciting, and solving problems. Similar to how athletes benefit from mixing different types of drills into their workouts (e.g., separate drills for building strength, speed, and endurance), studies of human learning show that "interleaving" (mixing) different academic subjects or academic skills while studying results in deeper learning and stronger memory (Brown, Roediger, & McDaniel, 2014; Carey, 2014).

Study in different places. In addition to spreading out your studying at different times, it's also a good idea to spread it out in different places. Studying in different locations provides different environmental contexts for learning; this reduces the amount of mental interference that normally builds up when all information is studied in the same place. The great public speakers in ancient Greece and Rome used this method of changing places to remember long speeches by walking through different rooms while rehearsing their speech, learning each major part of their speech in a different room (Higbee, 2001).

Although it's useful to have set times for studying so that you get into a regular work routine, this doesn't mean you learn best by always studying in the same place. Periodically changing the academic tasks you perform while studying, as well as the environment in which you perform them, has been found to improve attention to (and retention of) what you're studying (Carey, 2014; Druckman & Bjork, 1994).

Break up long study sessions with short study breaks that involve physical activity (e.g., a short jog or brisk walk). Study breaks that include physical activity refresh the mind by giving it a rest from studying. Physical activity also stimulates the mind by increasing blood flow to your brain—helping you retain what you've studied and regain concentration for what you'll study next.

Learn with and through a variety of senses. When memory is formed in the brain, different sensory aspects of it are stored in different areas. For example, if your brain receives auditory input (e.g., hearing your own words or the words of others), visual input (viewing images, maps, or charts), and motor input (movement made when writing, drawing, or manipulating), that inputted information reaches your brain through multiple sensory modalities and is better retained because it: (a) creates more interconnections in areas of the brain where that information is stored, and (b) provides multiple cues for retrieving (recalling) the information (Willis, 2006; Shams & Seitz, 2011; Zull, 2002). Different forms of sensory input are stored as multiple neurological tracks in different parts of the brain, which deepens learning and strengthens memory.

Don't forget that movement is also a sensory channel. When you move, your brain receives kinesthetic stimulation—the sensations generated by your muscles. Memory traces for movement are commonly stored in an area of your brain (the cerebellum) that plays a major role for all types of learning (Middleton & Strick, 1994; Jensen, 2005). Thus, incorporating movement into the process of learning improves your ability to retain what you're studying by adding a motor (muscle) memory trace of it to your brain. You can use movement to help you learn and retain academic information by using your body to act out what you're studying or symbolize it with your hands (Kagan & Kagan, 1998). Suppose you're trying to remember five points about something (e.g., five consequences of the Civil War). When you're studying these points, count them on your fingers as you try to recall each of them.

(Complete Exercise 2.5 at the end of this chapter. If your results on the "My PEPs Learning Style Inventory" indicate that you have kinesthetic

> "I have to *hear* it, *see* it, *write* it, and *talk* about it."
> —First-year college student responding to the question: "How do you learn best?"

> "When I have to remember something, it's better for me to do something with my hands so I could physically see it happening."
> —First-year college student

and tactile preferences, such learning-through-movement activities may be particularly effective ways to strengthen your learning.)

Also, remember that talking involves muscle movement of your lips and tongue. Thus, speaking aloud when you're studying, either to a friend or to yourself, can improve memory by supplying kinesthetic stimulation to your brain (in addition to the auditory stimulation your brain receives from hearing what you're saying).

Figure 2.7 shows a map of the outer surface of the human brain; you can see how different parts of the brain are specialized to receive input from different sensory modalities. When multiple sensory modalities are used while learning, multiple memory traces of what you're studying are recorded in separate areas of the brain, resulting in deeper learning and stronger memory for what's been studied.

FIGURE 2.7: A Map of the Functions Performed by the Outer Surface of the Human Brain

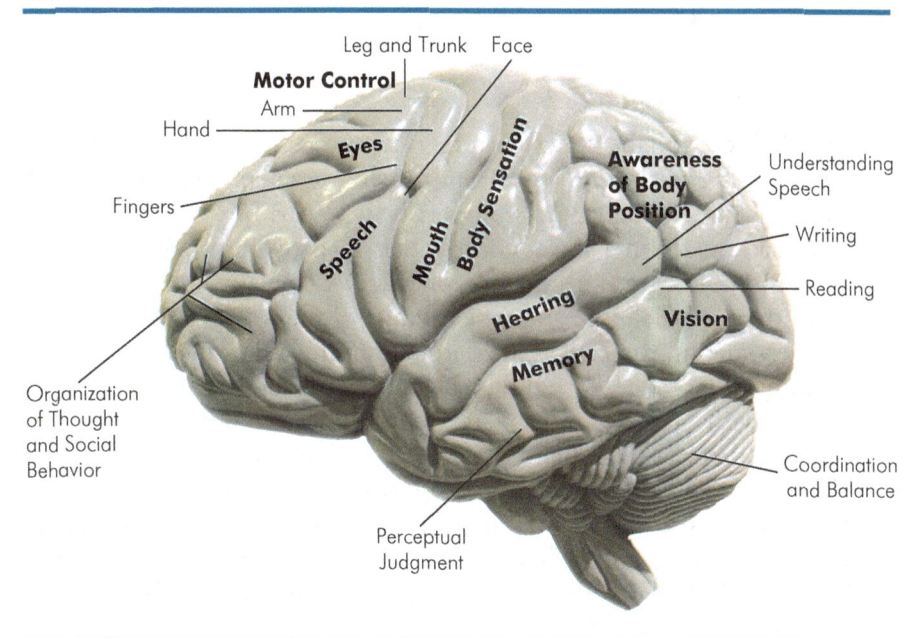

Brain image modified from ©David Huntley/Shutterstock.com

Learn with Emotion

Neural connections run between the emotional and memory centers of the brain (Zull, 1998). Thus, the emotions we're experiencing while learning can affect how deeply we learn. Research indicates that emotional intensity, excitement, and enthusiasm strengthen memory of academic information just as they do for memory of life events and personal experiences. When we're emotionally excited about what we're learning, adrenaline is released and is carried through the bloodstream to the brain. Once adrenaline reaches the brain, it increases blood flow and glucose production, which stimulates learning and strengthens memory (LeDoux, 1998; Rosenfield, 1988). Thus, if you become passionate and enthused about what you're learning, you're more likely to learn it deeply and remember it longer (Howard, 2014; Minninger, 1984).

One way to do this is by keeping in mind the importance or significance of what you're learning. For instance, if you're learning about photosynthesis, remind yourself that you're not just learning a chemical reaction, you're learning about the driving force that underlies all plant life on the planet. If you don't know why the concept you're studying is significant, find out—do a computer search, talk it over with your instructor, or ask an advanced student majoring in the field.

Note

Make learning a "total body experience." Put your whole self into it—your mind, your body, and your heart.

Learn Collaboratively

Simply defined, collaborative learning is the process of two or more people working *interdependently* to advance each other's success—as opposed to working independently or competitively. Learning is strengthened when it takes place in a social context that involves interpersonal interaction. As scholars put it, human knowledge is "socially constructed" or built up through dialogue and an exchange of ideas; conversations with others become internalized as ideas in your mind and influence your way of thinking (Bruffee, 1993). Thus, by having frequent, intelligent conversations with others, you broaden your knowledge base, deepen your learning, and elevate the quality of your thinking.

Research from kindergarten through college shows that students who learn collaboratively in teams experience significant gains in both academic performance and interpersonal skills (Cross, Barkley, & Major, 2005; Gilles & Adrian, 2003; Johnson, Johnson, & Smith, 1998). In one national study that involved in-depth interviews with more than 1,600 college students, it was discovered that almost all students who struggled academically had one particular study habit in common: they always studied alone (Light, 2001).

To maximize the power of collaboration, use the following pair of guidelines to choose teammates who will enhance the quality and productivity of your learning team:

1. Observe your classmates with an eye toward identifying potentially good teammates. Look for motivated students who will actively contribute to your team's success (rather than those whom you suspect may just be hitchhikers looking for a free ride).

2. Don't team up exclusively with peers who are familiar with or similar to you in terms of their personal characteristics, backgrounds, and experiences. This familiarity can actually interfere with your team's performance by turning your learning team into a social group or gab-fest that gets off track and onto topics that have nothing to do with studying (e.g., what you did last weekend or what you're planning to do next weekend). Instead, include teammates who differ from you with respect to such characteristics as: age, gender, race or ethnicity, and cultural or geographical background. Such variety brings different life experiences, styles of thinking strategies and learning styles to your team, which enriches your team's diversity and learning capacity.

Note

Capitalize on the advantages of collaborating with peers of varied backgrounds and lifestyles. Studies show that we learn more from people who are different from us than from people similar to us (Pascarella, 2001; Thompson & Cuseo, 2014).

Keep in mind that collaborative learning can be much more than just forming study groups the night before an exam. You can team up with classmates more regularly to work on a variety of academic tasks, such as those listed below.

Note-Taking Teams. Immediately after class sessions end, take a couple of minutes to team up with other students to compare and share notes. Since listening and note-taking are demanding tasks, it's likely that a classmate will pick up an important point you missed and vice versa. By teaming up *immediately after class*, if you and your teammates find missing or confusing information, quickly consult with the instructor before leaving the room.

Reading Teams. After completing reading assignments, team up with classmates to compare your highlighting and margin notes. See what you both identified as the most important material to be studied for upcoming exams.

Writing Teams. Students can provide each other with feedback to revise and improve their own writing. Studies show that when peers assess each other's writing, the quality of their individual writing gets better and they develop a more positive attitude about the writing process (Topping, 1998). You can form peer-writing teams to help at any or all of the following stages in the writing process:

1. Topic selection and refinement: to help one another come up with a list of possible topics and subtopics to write about;
2. Pre-writing: to clarify your writing purpose and audience;
3. First draft: to improve your general writing style and tone; and
4. Final draft: to proofread, detect, and correct clerical errors before submitting your written work.

Library Research Teams. Many first-year students are unfamiliar with the process of using a college or university library to conduct academic research. Some experience "library anxiety" and avoid even stepping foot into the library, particularly if it's a large and intimidating place (Malvasi, Rudowsky, & Valencia, 2009). Forming library research teams is an effective way to develop a social support group that can make library research less intimidating by converting it from a solitary experience done alone to a collaborative venture done as a team. Working together with peers on any research task can reduce anxiety, create collective energy, and result in a final product that's superior to what could have been produced by a single person working independently.

Note

It's perfectly acceptable and ethical to team up with others to search for information and share resources. This isn't cheating or plagiarizing—as long as your final product is completed individually and what you turn into the instructor represents your own work.

Study Teams. When seniors at Harvard University were interviewed, nearly every one of them who had participated in study groups considered the experience to be crucial to their academic progress and success (Light, 1990, 1992, 2001).

Additional research on study groups indicates that they are effective only if each member has done the required course work in advance of team meetings—for example, if all teammates attended class consistently and completed required readings (Light, 2001). To fully capitalize and maximize the power of study teams, each team member should study individually *before* studying with the group and come to the group prepared with answers and ideas to share with teammates, as well as specific questions or points of confusion about which they hope to receive help from other members of the team. This ensures that all team members are individually accountable for their own learning and equally responsible for contributing to their teammates' learning.

> "I would suggest students get to know [each] other and get together in groups to study or at least review class material. I find it is easier to ask your classmates with whom you are comfortable 'dumb' questions."
>
> —Advice to first-year students from a college sophomore (Walsh, 2005)

Note

Don't forget that team learning goes beyond late-night study groups. Students could and should form learning teams in advance of exams to help each other with other academic tasks—such as note-taking, reading, writing, and library research.

Test-Review Teams. After receiving your results on course examinations (and assignments) you can collaborate with peers to review your performance as a team. When you compare your answers to the answers of other students, you're better able to identify what you did well and where you lost points. By seeing the answers of teammates who received maximum credit on certain questions, you get a clearer picture of what went wrong and what you can do to get it right next time.

Reflection 2.9

Think about the students in your classes this term. Are there classmates who would be good candidates to connect with and form learning teams?

Chapter Summary and Highlights

This chapter identified key principles of human learning and supplied specific strategies for learning effectively in college and throughout life. Deep learning goes beyond surface-level memorization. It's connecting new ideas to ideas that have already been learned. Deep learners build mental bridges between what they're trying to learn and what they already know.

Information delivered during lectures is the information that's most likely to appear as items on college exams. Students who don't take good lecture notes have a slim chance of recalling the information at test time. Thus, effective note taking is critical to successful academic performance in college.

Information from reading assignments is the second most common source of test questions on college exams. Professors often don't discuss information in class that's contained in assigned reading. Thus, doing the assigned reading, and doing it in a way that maximizes comprehension and retention, is essential for academic success in college.

Learning from lectures requires active involvement (e.g., actively taking notes while listening to lectures) as does learning from reading (e.g., actively taking notes while reading). Active involvement during the learning process engages your attention and enables information to enter the brain. Reflection on what you have learned keeps it in the brain by locking it into memory. Self-awareness also promotes deep learning. By reflecting on whether you truly understand what you're studying, you become a more self-aware learner and a more successful student.

Cramming total study time into one long session ("massed practice") immediately before exams doesn't promote deep learning or long-term retention. Research consistently shows that *distributed practice*, whereby study time is "distributed" or spread out over several shorter sessions, is more effective—particularly if the last study session just before an exam is used to review (restudy) the parts that were previously studied in separate sessions. Learning is also deepened by engaging as many senses as possible during the learning process.

Lastly, deep learning is enhanced when done *collaboratively*. Research from kindergarten through college shows that students who learn in teams experience significant gains in both academic performance and interpersonal skills.

Learning More through the World Wide Web: Internet-Based Resources

For additional information on learning deeply and strategically, see the following websites:

Strategic Learning & Study Strategies:
http://www.dartmouth.edu/~acskills/success/

http://www.isu.edu/success/strategies/handouts.shtml

Brain-Based Learning:
http://www.brainrules.net/the-rules

Learning Math and Overcoming Math Anxiety:
www.mathacademy.com/pr/minitext/anxiety

www.onlinemathlearning.com/math-mnemonics.html

References

Arum, R., & Roska, J. (2011). *Academically adrift: Limited learning on college campuses*. Chicago: The University of Chicago Press.

Ausubel, D., Novak, J., & Hanesian, H. (1978). *Educational psychology: A cognitive view* (2nd ed.). New York: Holt, Rinehart & Winston.

Averell, L., & Heathcote, A. (2011). The form of the forgetting curve and the fate of memories. *Journal of Mathematical Psychology, 55*(1): 25–35.

Baddeley, A. D. (1999). *Essentials of human memory*. Hove: Psychology.

Benedict, M. E., & Hoag, J. (2004). Seating location in large lectures: Are seating preferences or location related to course performance? *Journal of Economics Education, 35,* 215–231.

Biggs, J., & Tang, C. (2007). *Teaching for quality learning at university* (3rd ed.) Buckingham: SRHE and Open University Press.

Bligh, D. A. (2000). *What's the use of lectures?* San Francisco: Jossey Bass.

Brown, R. D. (1988). Self-quiz on testing and grading issues. *Teaching at UNL (University of Nebraska—Lincoln), 10*(2), 1–3.

Brown, P. C., Roediger III, H. L., & McDaniel, M. A. (2014). *Make it stick: The science of successful learning*. Cambridge, MA: The Belknap Press of Harvard University Press.

Bruffee, K. A. (1993). *Collaborative learning: Higher education, interdependence, and the authority of knowledge*. Baltimore: Johns Hopkins University Press.

Bruner, J. (1990). *Acts of meaning*. Cambridge, MA: Harvard University Press.

Caine, R., & Caine, G. (2011). *Natural learning for a connected world: Education, technology and the human brain*. New York: Teachers College Press.

Carey, B. (2014). *How we learn*. London: Random House.

Chen, B., & Hirumi, A. (2009). Effects of advance organizers on learning for differentiated learners in a fully web-based course. *International Journal of Instructional Technology & Distance Learning*. Retrieved from http://itdl.org/Journal/Jun_09/article01.htm.

Conaway, M. S. (1982). Listening: Learning tool and retention agent. In A. S. Algier & K. W. Algier (Eds.), *Improving reading and study skills* (pp. 51–63). San Francisco: Jossey-Bass.

Crawford, H. J., & Strapp, C. M. (1994). Effects of vocal and instrumental music on visuospatial and verbal performance as moderated by studying preference and personality. *Personality and Individual Differences, 16*(2), 237–245.

Cross, K. P., Barkley, E. F., & Major, C. H. (2005). *Collaborative learning techniques: A handbook for college faculty*. San Francisco: Jossey-Bass.

Cuseo, J. B., Thompson, A., Campagna, M., & Fecas, V. S. (2013). *Thriving in college & beyond: Research-based strategies for academic success and personal development* (3rd ed.). Dubuque, IA: Kendall Hunt.

Demmert, W. G., Jr., & Towner, J. C. (2003). *A review of the research literature on the influences of culturally based education on the academic performance of Native American students. Retrieved from the Northwest Regional Educational Laboratory, Portland, Oregon, website http://www.nrel.org/indianaed/cbe.pdf.

Druckman, D., & Bjork, R. A. (Eds.). (1994). *Learning, remembering, believing: Enhancing human performance.* Washington, DC: National Academies Press.

Dunlosky, J., Rawson, K. A., Marsh, E. J., Nathan, M. J., & Willingham, D. T. (2013). Improving students' learning with effective learning techniques: Promising directions from cognitive and educational psychology. *Psychological Science in the Public Interest, 14*(1), 4–58.

Einstein, G. O., Morris, J., & Smith, S. (1985). Note-taking, individual differences, and memory for lecture information. *Journal of Educational Psychology, 77*(5), 522–532.

Gilles, R. M., & Adrian, F. (2003). *Cooperative learning: The social and intellectual outcomes of learning in groups.* London: Farmer Press.

Hartley, J. (1998). *Learning and studying: a research perspective.* London: Routledge.

Hartley, J., & Marshall, S. (1974). On notes and note taking. *Universities Quarterly, 28,* 225–235.

Higbee, K. L. (2001). *Your memory: How it works and how to improve it.* New York: Marlowe.

Howard, P. J. (2014). *The owner's manual for the brain: Everyday applications of mind-brain research* (4th ed.). New York: HarperCollins.

Howe, M. J. (1970). Note-taking strategy, review, and long-term retention of verbal information. *Journal of Educational Psychology, 63,* 285.

Jairam, D., & Kiewra, K. A. (2009). An investigation of the SOAR study method. *Journal of Advanced Academics* (August), 602–629.

Jensen, E. (2005). *Teaching with the brain in mind* (2nd ed.). Alexandria, VA: ASCD.

Jensen, E. (2008). *Brain-based learning.* Thousand Oaks, CA: Corwin Press.

Johnson, D., Johnson, R., & Smith, K. (1998). Cooperative learning returns to college: What evidence is there that it works? *Change, 30,* 26–35.

Johnstone, A. H., & Su, W. Y. (1994). Lectures: a learning experience? *Education in Chemistry, 31*(1), 65–76, 79.

Kagan, S., & Kagan, M. (1998). *Multiple intelligences: The complete MI book.* San Clemente, CA: Kagan Cooperative Learning.

Kiewra, K. A. (1985). Students' note-taking behaviors and the efficacy of providing the instructor's notes for review. *Contemporary Educational Psychology, 10,* 378–386.

Kiewra, K. A. (2000). Fish giver or fishing teacher? The lure of strategy instruction. *Teaching at UNL (University of Nebraska—Lincoln), 22*(3), 1–3.

Kiewra, K. A. (2005). *Learn how to study and SOAR to success.* Upper Saddle River, NJ: Pearson Prentice Hall.

Kiewra, K. A., & DuBois, N. F. (1998). *Learning to learn: Making the transition from student to lifelong learner.* Needham Heights, MA: Allyn and Bacon.

Kiewra, K. A., Hart, K., Scoular, J., Stephen, M., Sterup, G., & Tyler, B. (2000). Fish giver or fishing teacher? The lure of strategy instruction. *Teaching at UNL (University of Nebraska—Lincoln), 22*(3).

Kintsch, W. (1994). Text comprehension, memory, and learning. *American Psychologist, 49,* 294–303.

Kuh, G. D. (2005). Student engagement in the first year of college. In M. L. Upcraft, J. N. Gardner, B. O. Barefoot & Associates (Eds.), *Challenging and supporting the first-year student: A handbook for improving the first year of college* (pp. 86–107). San Francisco: Jossey-Bass.

Kuhn, L. (1988). What should we tell students about answer changing? *Research Serving Teaching, 1*(8).

LeDoux, J. (1998). *The emotional brain: The mysterious underpinnings of emotional life.* New York: Simon & Schuster.

LeDoux, J. (2002). *Synaptic self: How our brains become who we are.* New York: Penguin Books.

Light, R. L. (1990). *The Harvard assessment seminars.* Cambridge, MA: Harvard University Press.

Light, R. L. (1992). *The Harvard assessment seminars, second report.* Cambridge, MA: Harvard University Press.

Light, R. J. (2001). *Making the most of college: Students speak their minds.* Cambridge, MA: Harvard University Press.

Locke, E. (1977). An empirical study of lecture note-taking among college students. *Journal of Educational Research, 77,* 93–99.

Malmberg, K. J., & Murnane, K. (2002). List composition and the word-frequency effect for recognition memory. *Journal of Experimental Psychology: Learning, Memory, and Cognition, 28,* 616–630.

Malvasi, M., Rudowsky, C., & Valencia, J. M. (2009). *Library Rx: Measuring and treating library anxiety, a research study.* Chicago: Association of College and Research Libraries.

Marzano, R. J., Pickering, D. J., & Pollock, J. (2001). *Classroom instruction that works: Research-based strategies for increasing student achievement.* Alexandria, VA: Association for Supervision and Curriculum Development.

Mayer, R. E. (2002). Rote versus meaningful learning. *Theory into Practice, 41*(4), 226–232.

Middleton, F., & Strick, P. (1994). Anatomical evidence for cerebellar and basal ganglia involvement in higher brain function. *Science, 226*(5184), 458–461.

Minninger, J. (1984). *Total recall: How to boost your memory power.* Emmaus, PA: Rodale.

Murname, K., & Shiffrin, R. M. (1991). Interference and the representation of events in memory. *Journal of Experimental Psychology: Learning, Memory, & Cognition, 17,* 855–874.

Nathan, R. (2005). *My freshman year: What a professor learned by becoming a student.* Ithaca, New York: Cornell University Press.

Paivio, A. (1990). *Mental representations: A dual coding approach.* New York: Oxford University Press.

Pascarella, E. T. (2001, November/December). Cognitive growth in college: Surprising and reassuring findings from the National Study of Student Learning. *Change,* 21–27.

Pascarella, E., & Terenzini, P. (1991). *How college affects students: Findings and insights from twenty years of research.* San Francisco: Jossey-Bass.

Pascarella, E., & Terenzini, P. (2005). *How college affects students: A third decade of research* (Vol. 2). San Francisco: Jossey-Bass.

Piaget, J. (1978). *Success and understanding.* Cambridge, MA: Harvard University Press.

Ravizza, S. M., Hambrick, D. Z.. & Fenn, K. M. (2014). Non-academic internet use in the classroom is negatively related to classroom learning regardless of intellectual ability. *Computers & Education, 78,* 109–114.

Rennels, M. R., & Chaudhair, R. B. (1988). Eye-contact and grade distribution. *Perceptual and Motor Skills, 67* (October), 627–632.

Rosenfield, I. (1988). *The invention of memory: A new view of the brain.* New York: Basic Books.

Sappington, J., Kinsey, K., & Munsayac, K. (2002). Two studies of reading compliance among college students. *Teaching of Psychology, 29*(4), 272–274.

Schacter, D. L. (2001). *The seven sins of memory: how the mind forgets and remembers.* Boston: Houghton Mifflin.

SECFHE. (2006). *A national dialogue: The Secretary of Education's Commission on the future of higher education.* (U.S. Department of Education Boards and Commissions: A Draft Panel Report). Retrieved from http://www.ed.gov/about/bdscomm/list/hiedfuture/reports/0809-draft.pdf.

Shams, W., & Seitz, K. (2011). Influences of multisensory experience on subsequent unisensory processing. *Frontiers in Perception Science, 2*(264), 1–9.

Tagliacollo, V. A., Volpato, G. L., & Pereira, A., Jr. (2010). Association of student position in classroom and school performance. *Educational Research, 1*(6), 198–201.

Thompson, A., & Cuseo, J. (2014). *Diversity and the college experience.* Dubuque, IA: Kendall Hunt.

Thompson, R. F. (2009). Habituation: A history. *Neurobiology of Learning and Memory, 92*(2), 127–134.

Titsworth, S., & Kiewra, K. A. (2004). Organizational lecture cues and student notetaking. *Contemporary Educational Psychology, 29,* 447–461.

Topping, K. (1998). Peer assessment between students in colleges and universities. *Review of Educational Research, 68*(3), 249–276.

Vygotsky, L. S. (1978). Internalization of higher cognitive functions. In M. Cole, V. John-Steiner, S. Scribner, & E. Souberman (Eds. & Trans.), *Mind in society: The development of higher psychological processes* (pp. 52–57). Cambridge, MA: Harvard University Press.

Walsh, K. (2005). *Suggestions from more experienced classmates.* Retrieved from http://www.uni.edu/walsh/introtips.html.

Walter, T. W., Knudsvig, G. M., & Smith, D. E. P. (2003). *Critical thinking: Building the basics* (2nd ed.). Belmont, CA: Wadsworth.

Willis, J. (2006). *Research-based strategies to ignite student learning: Insights from a neurologist and classroom teacher.* Alexandria, VA: ASCD.

Zull, J. E. (1998). The brain, the body, learning, and teaching. *The National Teaching & Learning Forum, 7*(3), 1–5.

Zull, J. E. (2002). *The art of changing the brain: Enriching the practice of teaching by exploring the biology of learning.* Sterling, VA: Stylus.

Chapter 2 Exercises

2.1 Quote Reflections

Review the sidebar quotes contained in this chapter and select two that were especially meaningful or inspirational to you.

For each quote, provide a three- to five- sentence explanation why you chose it.

2.2 Reality Bite

Too Fast, Too Frustrating: A Note-Taking Nightmare

Susan Scribe is a first-year student majoring in journalism. She's currently enrolled in an introductory course that is required for her major (Introduction to Mass Media). The instructor in this course lectures at a rapid rate and uses vocabulary that goes right over her head. Since she cannot get all her instructor's words down on paper and cannot understand half the words she does manage to write down, she becomes frustrated and stops taking notes. She wants to do well in this course because it's the first course in her major, but she's afraid she'll fail it because her class notes are so pitiful.

Reflection and Discussion Questions

1. Can you relate to this case personally, or do know any students who are in the same boat as Susan?
2. What would you recommend that Susan do at this point? Why?

2.3 Self-Assessment of Learning Habits

Look back at the ratings you gave yourself for effective note-taking, reading, and studying. Add up your total score for these three sets of learning strategies (the maximum score for each set is 28):

Note Taking = _____

Reading = _____

Studying = _____

Total Learning Strategy Score = _____

Self-Assessment Questions

1. In which learning strategy area did you score lowest?
2. Do you think the area in which you scored lowest has anything to do with your lowest course grade at this point in the term?

3. Of the seven strategies listed under the area you scored lowest, which could you immediately put into practice to improve your performance in the course you're having most difficulty with this term?

4. What's the likelihood that you will put the preceding strategies into practice this term?

2.4 Consulting with a Learning Specialist

Make an appointment to visit your Learning Center or Academic Support Center on campus to discuss the results of your note-taking, reading, and studying self-assessment in Exercise 2.3 (or any other learning self-assessment you may have taken). Ask for recommendations about how you can improve your learning habits in your lowest score area. Following your visit, answer the following questions.

Learning Resource Center Reflection

1. Who did you meet with in the Learning Center?
2. What steps were recommended to you for improving your academic performance?
3. How likely is it that you will take the steps mentioned in the previous question?
    a) definitely
    b) probably
    c) possibly
    d) unlikely

    Why?
4. Do you plan to see a learning specialist again? (If yes, why? If no, why not?)

2.5 Learning Style Assessment

Take the *My PEPs Learning Style Inventory* that accompanies this textbook.

What do the results suggest are your strongest learning styles?

For which classes would the suggestions offered be most helpful to you this semester?

Incredible Shrinking Notes

Name: _____

A fun 3-step process helps students "boil down" note taking.

Students will:
- Listen an article
- Fill a 3- x 5-inch sticky note or index card with important facts from the reading selection.
- Narrow down those notes to the important notes that fit on a medium-size (approximately 3- x 3-inch) sticky note or card.
- Narrow down those notes to the *most important* notes that will fit on a small (approximately 1- x 2-inch) sticky note or card.

Materials Needed
- three "sticky notes" or index cards in three different sizes—approximately 3- x 5 inches, 3 x 3 inches, and 1 x 2 inches—for each student
- An article you will read

Lesson Plan

About the Lesson
This lesson uses an article as the starting point for note-taking exercises.

The Lesson
This activity can be used as a listening activity.

To begin, give each student a sticky note or index card roughly 3- x 5-inches in size.

Display a sample of the largest sticky note or card. Share with students that this activity is going to include three brief writing assignments; each successive assignment will require them to write less. Emphasize that for the purpose of this assignment, it is important that students' write in the same size for all three assignments. The reason for that rule will become clear as the activity proceeds. You might demonstrate the "ideal" size writing on the largest sticky note or card. See the sample text box below.

Read aloud the chosen article. During the first reading, students should not take notes. Instruct them to listen carefully, consider all the details in the selection, and think about the details they think are most important or significant.

Then tell students you are going to read the passage again. This time, students should jot down notes on a 3- x 5-inch sticky note or index card. They should fill the card with their notes. (Remind them that they should pay close attention to the size of their writing.)

Next, provide students with a sticky note or card of medium size. (See Materials Needed above.) Tell them their job is to study the notes on their large card and eliminate some of the less important information. They then should fill up the medium-size card with notes from the large card that they think are most important. (Remind them to pay close attention to the size of their writing.)

Finally, provide students with the smallest sticky note or index card. Now, students really have to make careful judgments about the most important information to transfer from the medium-size card to the small card.

In the end, students should have notes that express the *most important* facts or themes found in the reading selection.

Emphasize to students that this lesson in note taking is intended to help them see that note taking is about scaling down information to the most important details. Students can also employ this strategy as they study for unit tests. They can read through their notes; "boil down" those notes to key facts, ideas, and themes; and write those key ideas in the margins of their notebooks. The key ideas are the ideas that represent the themes worth reviewing for the upcoming unit test. To study for that test, students might simply review their margin notes and practice supplying supporting information for each key idea.

Assessment

Read aloud a news story from today's newspaper and have students write the key idea(s) on a small sticky note or index card. Students also might employ the three-card strategy used in this lesson to "boil down" the news story to its main idea/ideas.

Lesson Plan Source

Education World

Submitted By

Gary Hopkins

Adapted from: http://www.educationworld.com/a_lesson/03/lp322-02.shtml

SQ3R Reading and Study Skill System
SURVEY—gather the necessary information to focus and prepare goals.
1. *Read the title* to help your mind prepare to receive the subject at hand.
2. *Read the introduction and/or summary* in order to get familiar with the purposes of the chapter and focus on the author's statement of the most important points.

3. *Notice each boldface heading and subheading* in order to organize your mind before you begin to read. It will help you create a structure for the information to come.
4. *Notice any graphics* such as charts, maps, diagrams, etc. They are there to help you, don't ignore them.
5. *Notice reading aids* such as italics, bold face print, chapter objectives, and chapter reviews. They are included to help you sort, understand, and remember.

QUESTION—focus on the material.

When your mind is actively searching for answers to questions, it becomes engaged in learning. As you read through, use the boldface headings to formulate questions you think will be answered in that particular section. The better the questions you come up with, the better your understanding of the material is likely to be. As you continue to read, you can continue to add as many questions as you'd like.

READ—to answer the question(s).

Read one section at a time, keeping your questions in mind, and search for the answers. Always keep an eye out for new questions that need to be asked.

RECITE—train your mind to concentrate and retain the information it is taking in through reading.

After you read each section, take a moment to recall the questions you asked, and see if you can answer them from memory. If not, look back again as often as you need too until you can rehearse them without looking. Don't move on to the next section until you can! If you highlight information in your text book do it during this step of the SQ3R reading system.

REVIEW—begin building memory and improving your mental organization.

Once you have finished the chapter, review by once again asking yourself the questions you created from the headings. See if you can still answer them all without looking. If not, go back and refresh your memory, then try again!

FYE SQ3R Worksheet

Name _____ Section _____

Survey: *Record important titles and subtitles from work.*

_____
_____
_____
_____
_____
_____

Question: *Write "Who, What, When, Where, and Why" questions from main topics.*

_____
_____
_____
_____
_____
_____

Read: *To answer the questions.*

Recite: *Record key facts and phrases to answer each question.*

_____
_____
_____
_____
_____
_____
_____
_____

Review: *Review highlighted information to move information from short term to long term memory.*

CHAPTER 3

Test-Taking Skills and Strategies

WHAT TO DO BEFORE, DURING, AND AFTER EXAMS

Chapter Preview

This chapter supplies you with a systematic set of strategies for improving your performance on different types of tests, including multiple-choice and essay exams. It identifies strategies that can be used before, during, and after exams, as well as practical tips for becoming more "test wise" and less "test anxious."

Learning Goal

Acquire effective strategies to improve your performance on multiple-choice, true–false, and essay tests.

Integrate Your Faith

How can the time you spend engaging with God's Word impact the way you see God working in your life?

Ignite Your Thinking

Reflection 3.1

On which of the following types of tests do you tend to perform better?

a) Multiple-choice tests

b) Essay tests

Why?

Learning in college courses typically takes place in a three-stage process: (1) acquiring information from lectures and readings; (2) studying that information and storing it in your brain as knowledge; and (3) demonstrating

From *Thriving in College and Beyond: Research-Based Strategies for Academic Success and Personal Development*, Fourth Edition by Joseph B. Cuseo, Aaron Thompson, Michele Campagna, and Viki S. Fecas. Copyright © 2016 Kendall Hunt Publishing Company. Reprinted by permission.

that knowledge on exams. The following sections of this chapter contain strategies relating primarily to the third stage of this learning process and they are divided into three categories:

- Strategies to use *in advance* of a test,
- Strategies to use *during* a test, and
- Strategies to use *after* test results are returned.

Pre-Test Strategies: What to Do *in Advance* of Exams

Your ability to remember material on an exam that you studied prior to the exam depends not only on how long and how well you studied, but also on the type of exam questions used to test your memory (Roediger, 2008). You may be able to remember what you've studied if you're tested in one format (e.g., multiple-choice) but not if tested in a different format (e.g., essay). Thus, the type of questions that will appear on an upcoming exam should influence the type of study strategies you use to prepare for the exam. Test questions can be classified into the following two major categories, depending on the type of memory required to answer them.

1. *Recognition* test questions ask you to select or choose the correct answer from choices that are provided for you. Falling into this category are multiple-choice, true—false, and matching questions. These test questions don't require you to supply or produce the correct answer on your own; instead, you're asked to recognize or pick out the correct answer—similar to picking out the "correct" criminal from a lineup of potential suspects.
2. *Recall* test questions require you to retrieve information you've studied and reproduce it on your own. As the word "recall" implies, you have to re-call ("call back") information and supply it yourself—as opposed to picking it out from information supplied for you. Recall test questions include essay and short-answer questions that require you to provide your own answer—in writing.

Since recognition test questions (e.g., multiple-choice or true—false) ask you to recognize or pick out the correct answer from answers provided for you, reading your class notes and textbook highlights and identifying key information may be an effective study strategy—because it matches the type of mental activity you'll be performing on the exam—reading test questions and identifying correct answers provided to you.

On the other hand, recall test questions, such as essay questions, require you to retrieve information and generate your own answers. They don't involve answer recognition; they require answer *production*—you produce the answer in writing. If you study for essay tests by just looking over your class notes and reviewing your reading highlights, you're using a study strategy that doesn't align with or match what you'll be expected to do on the test itself, which is to supply the correct information yourself. To prepare for essay-test questions, you need to practice *retrieval*—recalling the information on your own—without looking at it.

Two essay-test preparation strategies that ensure you engage in memory retrieval are: (1) recitation and (2) creation of retrieval cues. Each of these strategies is described below.

Recitation

Stating aloud the information we want to remember—without looking at that information—is a memory-improvement strategy known as *recitation*. Memory is strengthened substantially when we reproduce on our own what we're trying to remember, instead of simply looking it over or rereading it (Roediger & Karpicke, 2006). Research consistently indicates that this type of self-testing may be the most powerful of all test preparation strategies (Carey, 2014). Recitation strengthens memory and better prepares you for essay tests because it:

- Requires *more mental effort* to dig out (retrieve) the answer on its own, which strengthens memory for the answer and allows the brain to practice exactly what it's expected to do on essay tests.
- Gives you clear *feedback* about whether or not you know the material. If you can't retrieve and recite it without looking at it, you know for sure that you won't be able to recall it at test time and need to study it further. You can provide yourself with this feedback by putting the question on one side of an index card and the answer on the flip side. If you find yourself flipping over the index card to look at the answer in order to remember it, this shows you can't retrieve the information on your own and you need to study it further. (To create electronic flash cards, see: www.studystack.com or studyblue.com)
- Encourages you to *use your own words*. If you can paraphrase it—rephrase what you're studying in your own words—it's a good indication you really understand it; and if you really understand it, you're more likely to recall it at test time.

Recitation can be done silently, by speaking aloud, or by writing out what you're trying to recall. Speaking aloud or writing out what you're reciting are particularly effective essay-test preparation strategies because they involve physical activity, which ensures that you're actively involved and engaged in the learning process.

(Check the results of your "My PEPs Learning Style Inventory." How does the recitation technique match up with your auditory preference? What recommendations would work best for you?)

Creating Retrieval Cues

Suppose you're trying to remember the name of a person you know; you know you know it, but just can't recall it. If a friend gives you a clue (e.g., the first letter of the person's name or a name that rhymes with it), it's likely to suddenly trigger your memory of that person's name. What your friend did was provide a retrieval cue. A *retrieval cue* is a type of memory reminder (like a string tied around your finger) that brings back to mind what you've temporarily forgotten.

Research shows that students who can't remember previously studied information are better able to recall that information if they're given a retrieval cue. In a classic study, students studied a long list of items, some of which were animals (e.g., giraffe, coyote, and turkey). After they finished studying, students were given a blank sheet of paper and asked to write down the names of those animals. None of the students were able to recall all of the animals that appeared on the list they previously studied. However, when the word "animals" was written on top of the answer sheet to provide students with a retrieval cue, they were able to recall many of the animals they had forgotten (Tulving, 1983). Research findings such as these suggest that category names can serve as powerful retrieval cues. By taking pieces of information you need to recall on an essaytest and organizing it into categories, you can then use the category names as retrieval cues at test time. Retrieval cues work because memories are stored in the brain as part of an interconnected network. So, if you're able to recall one piece or segment of the network (the retrieval cue), it can trigger recall of other pieces of information linked to it in the same network (Willingham, 2009).

Reflection 3.2

Think about items of information you need to remember in a course you're taking this term. Group these items into a category that can be used as a retrieval cue to help you remember them.

1. What's the course?

2. What's the category you've created as a retrieval cue?

3. What items of information would this retrieval cue help you recall?

Another strategy for creating retrieval cues is to come up with your own catchword or catchphrase to "catch" or batch together all related ideas you're trying to remember. Acronyms can serve as catchwords, with each letter acting as a retrieval cue for a batch of related ideas. For instance, suppose you're studying for an essaytest in abnormal psychology that will include questions testing your knowledge of different forms of mental illness. You could create the acronym SCOT as a retrieval cue to help you remember to include the following key elements of mental illness in your essay answers: Symptoms (S), Causes (C), Outcomes (O), and Therapies (T).

Strategies to Use *Immediately Before* a Test

1. **Before the exam, take a brisk walk or light jog.** Physical activity increases mental alertness by increasing oxygen flow to the brain; it also decreases tension by increasing the brain's production of emotionally "mellowing" brain chemicals (e.g., serotonin and endorphins).
2. **Come fully armed with all the test-taking tools you need.** In addition to the basic supplies (e.g., no. 2 pencil, pen, blue book, Scantron, calculator, etc.), bring backup equipment in case you experience equipment failure (e.g., an extra pen in case your first one runs out of ink or extra pencils in case your original one breaks).
3. **Get to the classroom as early as possible.** Arriving early allows you to take a few minutes to get into a relaxed pretest state of mind by thinking positive thoughts, taking slow, deep breaths, and stretching your muscles.

    (Take a look at the "structure preference" results from your "My PEPs Learning Style Inventory." What do they suggest you do when starting an exam?)

4. **Sit in the same seat you normally occupy in class.** Research indicates that memory is improved when information is recalled in the same place where it was originally received or reviewed (Sprenger, 1999). Thus, taking a test in the same place where you heard the information delivered will likely improve your test performance.

    Studies also show that when students take a test on material in the same environment where they studied the material, they tend to remember more of it at test time than do students who study the material in one place and take a test on that material in a different place (Smith & Vela, 2001). While it's unlikely you will be able to do all your studying in the same room where your test will be taken, it may be possible to do a short, final review session in your classroom or in an empty classroom with similar features. This should strengthen your memory because the physical features of the room become associated with the material you're trying to remember. Seeing these features again at test time can help trigger your memory of that material.

    A classic, fascinating study supporting this recommendation was once conducted on a group of deep sea divers. Some divers learned a list of words on a beach, while the others learned the list underwater. They were later tested for their memory of the words. Half the divers who learned the words on the beach remained there to take the test; the other half were tested underwater. Half the divers who

> "Avoid flipping through notes (cramming) immediately before a test. Instead, do some breathing exercises and think about something other than the test."
>
> —*Advice to first-year students from a college sophomore*

studied the words underwater took the test in the same place; the other half took the test on the beach. The results showed that the divers who took the test in the same place where they learned the list recalled 40% more of the items than the divers who did their learning and testing in different places (Godden & Baddeley, 1975). This study provides strong evidence that memory is strengthened when studying and testing takes place in the same location.

Other intriguing studies have shown that if students are exposed to a certain aroma while they're studying (e.g., the smell of chocolate) and are later exposed to that same smell during a memory test for what they studied, they display better memory for the information they studied (Schab & Crowder, 2014). One possible, practical application of this finding to improve your memory during a test is to put on a particular cologne or perfume while studying, and put in on again on the day of the test. This may improve your memory for the information you studied by matching the scent of your study environment with the scent of your test environment. Although this strategy may seem silly, keep in mind that the area of the human brain where humans perceive smell has connections with the brain's memory centers (Jensen, 2005). These neurological connections probably explain why people often report that certain smells can trigger long-ago memories (e.g., the smell of a summer breeze triggering memories of summer games played during childhood).

Since smell is related to memory, you may be able to use smell as a retrieval cue to stimulate recall for information you've studied. In so doing, you may improve your performance on essay tests.

Box 3.1

Nutritional Strategies for Strengthening Academic Performance

Is there a "brain food" that can enhance our test performance? Can we "eat to learn" or "eat to remember"? Some animal studies suggest that memory can be improved by consumption of foods containing lecithin—a substance that helps the brain produce acetylcholine—a chemical that plays an important role in the formation of memories (Ueda, et al., 2011; Ulus & Wurtman, 1977). Fish contains high amounts of lecithin, which may explain why fish is sometimes referred to as "brain food."

Despite the results of some animal studies, not enough human research evidence is available to conclude that consuming certain foods will dramatically increase our ability to retain information or knowledge. However, the following nutritional strategies can improve mental performance on days when our knowledge is tested.

1. **Eat breakfast on the day of the exam.** Studies show that when students eat a nutritious breakfast on the day they are tested, they achieve higher test scores (Phillips, 2005; Schroll, 2006). Breakfast on the day of an exam should include grains, such as whole wheat toast, whole grain cereal, oatmeal, or bran, because those foods contain complex carbohydrates that deliver a steady stream of energy to the body throughout the day. These complex

Box 3.1 *(continued)*

carbohydrates also help your brain produce a steady stream of serotonin—a brain chemical that reduces tension and anxiety.

> " *No man can be wise on an empty stomach."*
> —George Eliot, 19th-century English novelist

2. **Make the meal you eat before an exam a light meal.** The meal you consume nearest test time should not be a large one because it will elevate your blood sugar to a high level, causing large amounts of insulin must be released into the bloodstream to reduce the blood sugar level. This draws blood sugar away from the brain, causing mental fatigue.

3. **If you need an energy boost prior to an exam, eat a piece of fruit rather than a candy bar.** Candy bars are processed sweets that infuse synthetic sugar into the bloodstream, which provides a short and sudden burst of energy. That's the good news; the bad news is that this short-term rush of blood sugar and sudden jolt of energy can also increase bodily tension followed by a sharp drop in energy and feelings of sluggishness (Haas, 1994; Thayer, 1997). The key is to find a food that elevates energy without elevating tension and sustains this energy level over an extended period of time. The best nutritional option for producing such a steady, sustained state of higher energy is *natural* sugar contained organically in a piece of fruit, not processed sugar artificially slipped into a candy bar.

4. **Avoid consuming caffeine before an exam.** Although caffeine increases alertness, it's a stimulant that elevates bodily tension and nervousness. These are feelings you don't want to experience during a test, particularly if you're prone to test anxiety. Also, caffeine is a diuretic, which means it will increase your urge to urinate. You certainly want to avoid this urge during an exam—when you're confined to a classroom and can't afford to take time to tend to urological needs (or be distracted by them).

©Kendall Hunt Publishing Company

Consuming large doses of caffeine or other stimulants before exams is likely to increase your alertness, but it's also likely to increase your level of stress and test anxiety.

Strategies to Use *During* Exams

1. **As soon as you receive a copy of the test, write down any hard-to-remember terms, formulas, and equations and any memory-retrieval cues you may have created before you start the exam.** This will help ensure you don't forget this important information when you start focusing your attention on the test itself.

2. **First answer questions you know well and carry the most points.** Before automatically attacking the first question that appears on test, take a moment to check out the overall layout of the test and note the questions that are worth the most points and the questions you're best prepared to answer. Tackle these questions first. Put a checkmark next to questions whose answers you're unsure of and come back to them later—after you've answered the questions you're sure of—to ensure you get these points added to your total test score before you run out of test time.

3. **If you experience "memory block" for information you know, use the following strategies to unlock it.**
   - Mentally put yourself back in the environment in which you studied. Recreate the situation by mentally picturing the place where you first heard or saw the information and where you studied it—including sights, sounds, smells, and time of day. This memory-improvement strategy is referred to as *guided retrieval*, and research supports its effectiveness for recalling information of any kind, including information recalled by eyewitnesses to a crime (Glenberg, 1997; Glenberg-Robertson, 1998).
   - Think of any idea or piece of information that relates to the information you can't remember. Studies show that when students forget information they studied, they're more likely to suddenly remember that information if they first recall a piece related to it in some way (Reed, 2013). This strategy works because related pieces of information are typically stored in the same area of the brain—as part of an interconnected neural network.
   - Take your mind off the question by turning to another question. This frees your subconscious to focus on the forgotten information, which can suddenly trigger your conscious memory of it. Moving on to other test questions also allows you to find information included in later test questions that may enable you to recall information related to the earlier question that you previously forgot.
   - Before turning in your test, carefully review and double-check your answers. This is the critical last step in the test-taking process. Sometimes the performance pressure and anxiety associated with test taking can cause students to overlook details, misread instructions, unintentionally skip questions, or make absent-minded mistakes. So take time to look over your answers and check for any mindless mistakes you may have made. Avoid the temptation to immediately cut out of class after answering the

last test question because you're pooped out or stressed out. When you think about the amount of time and effort you put into preparing for the exam, it's foolish not to take a little more time to detect and correct any silly mistakes you may make that could cost you points and lower your test score.

Reflection 3.3

I'm most likely to experience memory block during exams in the following subjects:

During tests, when I experience memory block, I usually . . .

Strategies for Answering Multiple-Choice Test Questions

You're likely to encounter multiple-choice questions on college tests (particularly in large classes), on certification or licensing exams for particular professions (e.g., nursing and teaching), as well as on admissions tests for graduate school (e.g., master's and doctoral degree programs) and professional school (e.g., law school and medical school). Since you're likely to take multiple-choice tests frequently in college and beyond, this section of the text is devoted to a detailed discussion of strategies for taking such tests. These strategies are also applicable to *true—false* questions, which are really essentially multiple-choice questions with two choices: true or false.

1. **Read all choices listed and use a *process-of-elimination* approach.** Search for the correct answer by first eliminating choices that are clearly wrong; continue to do so until you're left with one choice that

©Kendall Hunt Publishing Company

To be or not to be?
(a) Orange Julius
(b) Julius Erving ("Dr. J.")
(c) Julius Caesar
(d) Caesar Salad
(e) Casarean Section

A **process-of-elimination** approach is an effective test-taking strategy to use when answering difficult multiple-choice questions.

represents the best option. Keep in mind that the correct answer is often the one that has the highest probability or likelihood of being true; it doesn't have to be absolutely true—just truer than all the other choices listed.

2. **For a choice to be correct, the *entire statement* must be true.** If any part of the statement is inaccurate or false, eliminate it because it's an incorrect answer.

3. **Use *test-wise* strategies when you cannot narrow down your choice to one answer.** Your first strategy on any multiple-choice question should be to choose an answer based on your knowledge of the material, not by guessing the correct answer based on how the question is worded. However, if you've relied on your knowledge, used the process-of-elimination strategy to eliminate clearly wrong choices, and you're still left with two or more answers that appear to be correct, then you should turn to being *test wise*—use the wording or placement of the test question itself to increase your chances of selecting the correct answer (Flippo & Caverly, 2009). Here are three test-wise strategies you can use for multiple-choice questions when more than one choice appears to be correct:

   - **Pick the answer that contains qualifying words.** Correct answers are more likely to contain modifying words such as "usually," "probably," "often," "likely," "sometimes," "perhaps," or "may." Knowledge often doesn't come neatly packaged as absolute or unqualified truths, so choices are more likely to be false if they make broad generalizations or contain words such as "always," "every," "never," "only," "must," and "completely."
   - **Pick the longest answer.** True statements often require more words to make them true.
   - **Pick a middle answer rather than the first or last answer.** If you've narrowed down the correct answer to either "a" or "c," your best bet may be to go with "c." Similarly, if you've narrowed your choices to "b" or "d," go with "b." Studies show that instructors have a tendency to place the correct answer in the middle, rather than as the first or last choice (Miller, Linn, & Gronlund, 2012)—perhaps because they think the correct answer will be too obvious or stand out if it's placed at the top or bottom of the list.

4. **Check to be sure that your answers are aligned with the right questions.** When looking over your test before turning it in, search carefully for questions you may have skipped and intended to go back to later. Sometimes you may skip a test question on a multiple-choice test and forget to skip the number of that question on the answer form. This will throw off all your other answers by one space or line and result in a disastrous "domino effect" of wrong answers that can do major damage to your total test score. To prevent this from happening, check the alignment of all your answers to be sure there are no blank spaces on your column of answers and that your order of answers line up with the order or test questions.

5. **Don't feel that you must remain locked into your first answer.** When reviewing your answers on multiple-choice and true–false tests, don't be afraid to change an answer after you've given it more thought. Don't buy into the common belief that your first answer is always your best answer. There have been numerous studies on the topic of changing answers on multiple-choice and true–false tests, dating all the way back to 1928 (Higham & Gerrard, 2005). These studies consistently show that most changed test answers go from being incorrect to correct, resulting in improved test scores (Bauer, Kopp, & Fischer, 2007; Prinsell, Ramsey, & Ramsey, 1994). In one study of more than 1,500 students' midterm exams in an introductory psychology course, it was discovered that when students changed answers, 75% of the time they changed from an incorrect to correct answer (Kruger, Wirtz, & Miller, 2005). These results probably reflect the fact that students often catch mistakes when reading the question again or when they find some information later in the test that causes them to reconsider (and correct) their first answer to an earlier test question.

If you have good reason to think an answer change should be made, don't be afraid to make it. The only exception to this general rule is when you find yourself changing many of your original answers; this may indicate that you were not well prepared for the exam and are just doing a lot of guessing and second-guessing.

Reflection 3.4

On multiple-choice exams, do you ever change your original choice?

If you do make changes, what's your usual reason for doing so?

Strategies for Answering Essay Questions

Along with multiple-choice questions, essay questions are among the most common types of test questions on college exams. The following strategies are recommended for strengthening your performance on essay questions.

1. **Look for "mental action" verbs in the question that point to the type of thinking your instructor expects you to demonstrate in your answer.** Box 3.2 contains a list of thinking verbs you're likely to see in essay questions and the type of mental action typically called for by each of these verbs. As you read this list, place a check mark next to the verbs that represent a type of thinking you've rarely or never been asked to do in the past.

> **Box 3.2**

Mental Action Verbs Commonly Found in Essay-Test Questions

Analyze. Break the topic down into its key parts and evaluate the parts in terms of their accuracy, strengths, and weaknesses.

Compare. Identify the similarities and differences between major concepts.

Contrast. Identify the differences between ideas, particularly sharp differences and clashing viewpoints.

Describe. Provide details (e.g., who, what, where, and when).

Discuss. Analyze (break apart) and evaluate the parts (e.g., strengths and weaknesses).

Document. Support your judgment and conclusions with scholarly references or research evidence.

Explain. Provide reasons that answer the questions "why?" and "how?"

> I keep six honest serving men. They taught me all I knew. Their names are what and why and how and when and where and who."
> —Rudyard Kipling, "The Elephant's Child," The Just-So Stories

Illustrate. Supply concrete examples or specific instances.

Interpret. Draw your own conclusion and explain why you came to that conclusion.

Support. Back up your ideas with logical reasoning, persuasive arguments, or statistical evidence.

2. **Make an outline of your key ideas before you start writing sentences.** First, do a quick "information dump" by jotting down the main points you plan to make in your essay answer in outline form. Outlines are effective for several reasons:
   - **An outline ensures you don't forget to include your most powerful points.** The points listed in your outline serve as memory-retrieval cues that help you remember the "big picture" before getting lost in all the details.
   - **An outline earns you points by improving your answer's organizational quality.** In addition to reminding you of the points you need to make, an outline gives you a plan for ordering your ideas in a sequence that flows smoothly from beginning to middle to end. One factor instructors consider when awarding points for an essay answer is how well that answer is organized. An outline will make your answer's organization clearer and more coherent to the reader, which will increase the amount of points you're awarded.
   - **An outline helps reduce test anxiety.** By organizing your points ahead of time, you can focus on expressing (writing) those points without the added stress of figuring out what you're going to say at the same time you're trying to figure out *how* to say it.

- **An outline can add points to answers you don't have time to complete.** If you run out of test time before writing out your full answer to an essay question, an outline shows your instructor what you planned to include in your written answer. The outline itself is likely to earn you some points because it demonstrates your knowledge of the major points called for by the question.

Exhibit 1

Identical twins
Adoption
Parents/family tree
6/6

1. There are several different studies that scientists conduct, but one study that they conduct is to find out how genetics can influence human behavior in <u>identical twins</u>. Since they are identical, they will most likely end up very similar in behavior because of their identical genetic makeup. Although environment has some impact, genetics are still a huge factor and they will, more likely than not, behave similarly. Another type of study is with <u>parents and their family trees</u>. Looking at a subject's family tree will explain why a certain person is bipolar or depressed. It is most likely caused by a gene in the family tree, even if it was last seen decades ago. Lastly, another study is with adopted children. If an <u>adopted child</u> acts a certain way that is unique to that child, and researchers find the parents' family tree, they will most likely see similar behavior in the parents and siblings as well.

No freewill
No afterlife

6/6

2. The monistic view of the mind-brain relationship is so strongly opposed and criticized because there is a belief or assumption that <u>free will</u> is taken away from people. For example, if a person commits a horrendous crime, it can be argued "monistically" that the chemicals in the brain were the reason, and that a person cannot think for themselves to act otherwise. This view limits responsibility.

   Another reason that this view is opposed is because it has been said that <u>there is no afterlife</u>. If the mind and brain are one and the same, and there is <u>NO</u> difference, then once the brain is dead and is no longer functioning, so is the mind. Thus, it cannot continue to live beyond what we know today as life. <u>And</u> this goes against many religions, which is why this reason, in particular, is heavily opposed.

A college sophomore's answers to short essay questions that demonstrate effective use of bulleted lists or short outlines (in the side margin) to ensure recall of key points.

---

3. **Get directly to the point on each question.** Avoid elaborate introductions that take up your test time (and your instructor's grading time) but don't earn you any points. An answer that begins with the statement "This is an interesting question that we had a great discussion on in class . . ." is pointless because it doesn't add points to your test score. Timed essay tests often leave you pressed for time; don't

waste that time on flowery introductions that contribute nothing to your test grade.

One effective way to get directly to the point on essay questions is to include part of the question in the first sentence of your answer. For example, suppose the test question asks you to, "Argue for or against capital punishment by explaining how it will or will not reduce the nation's homicide rate." Your first sentence could be, "Capital punishment will not reduce the homicide rate for the following reasons . . ." Thus, your first sentence becomes your thesis statement—it points you directly to the major points you're going to make in your answer and earns immediate points for your answer.

4. **Answer essay questions with as much detail as possible.** Don't assume that your instructor already knows what you're talking about or will be bored by details. Instead, take the approach that you're writing to someone who knows little or nothing about the subject—as if you're an expert teacher who is explaining it from scratch.

Note

As a general rule, it's better to over-explain than under-explain your answers to essay questions.

5. **Support your points with evidence—facts, statistics, quotes, or examples.** When you're answering essay questions, take on the mindset of a lawyer: make your case by presenting concrete evidence (exhibit A, exhibit B, etc.).

6. **Leave space between your answers to each essay question.** This strategy will enable you to easily add information to your original answer if you recall something later in the test that you would like to include.

7. **Proofread your answers for spelling and grammar.** Before turning in your test, proofread what you've written and correct any spelling or grammatical errors you find. Catching and correcting clerical errors will improve your test score. Even if your instructor doesn't explicitly state that grammar and spelling count toward your grade, these mechanical mistakes are still likely to influence your professor's overall evaluation of your written work.

8. **Neatness counts.** Many years of research indicate that neatly written essays are scored higher than sloppy ones, even if the answers are essentially the same (Huck & Bounds, 1972; Hughes, et al., 1983; Pai, et al., 2010). These findings aren't surprising when you consider that grading essay answers is a time-consuming, labor-intensive task that requires your instructor to plod through multiple answers written by students with multiple styles of handwriting—ranging from crystal clear to quasi-cryptic. If you make your instructor's job a little easier by writing as clearly as possible and cleaning up any sloppy markings before turning in your test, you're likely to earn more points for your answers.

Reflection 3.5

What do you usually do with tests and assignments after they're returned to you? Why?

Post-Test Strategies: What to Do *After* Receiving Your Test Results

Successful test performance involves both forethought (preparation before the test) and afterthought (reflection after the test). Often, when students get a test back, they check to see what grade they got, then stuff it in a binder or toss it into the nearest wastebasket. Don't fall prey to this unproductive habit; instead, use your test results as feedback to improve your future performance. Reflect on your results and ask yourself: How can I learn from this? How can I put it to use to correct my mistakes and repeat my successes? Remember: A test score isn't an end result; it may tell you where you are now, but it doesn't tell you where you'll end up. Use your results as a means to another end—a higher score on the next test.

> "When you make a mistake, there are only three things you should do about it: admit it; learn from it; and don't repeat it."
> —Paul "Bear" Bryant, legendary college football coach

Note

If you do poorly on an exam, don't get bitter—get better. View your mistakes in terms of what they can do for *you, not* to *you. A poor test performance can be turned into a productive learning experience, particularly if it occurs early in the course when you're still learning the rules of the game. You can use your test results as a valuable source of feedback for improving your future performance and final course grade.*

In the movie and record industry, if the first cut isn't successful, additional "takes" ("take two," "take three," etc.) are made until it's done right. Successful students do the same thing: If they make a mistake on "take one," they stick with it and continue working to improve their performance on the next take.

©Lightspring/Shutterstock.com

In the movies, a clipboard is used to signal the next take (shooting) if the previous take was unsuccessful. Take the same approach to your test performances. If you make a mistake, consider it "take one," learn from it, and approach the next take with the mindset that you're going to improve your previous performance.

> "A man who has committed a mistake and doesn't correct it is committing another mistake."
> —Confucius, ancient Chinese philosopher and educator

Listed below are strategies you can use to transform your test results into performance-enhancing feedback.

1. **When you get a test back, determine where you gained points and lost points.** Pinpoint what went right so you do it again, and troubleshoot what went wrong so you don't make the same mistake again. On test questions where you lost points, use the strategies summarized in **Box 3.3** to pinpoint the source of the problem.

Box 3.3

Strategies for Pinpointing the Source of Lost Points on Exams

On test questions where you lost points, identify the stage in the learning process where the breakdown occurred by asking yourself the following questions.

- **Did I have the information I needed to answer the question correctly?** If you didn't have the information needed to answer the question, where should you have acquired it in the first place? Was it information presented in class that didn't get into your notes? If yes, consider adopting strategies for improving your classroom listening and note-taking. If the missing information was contained in your assigned reading, check whether you're using effective reading strategies.
- **Did I have the information but didn't study it because I didn't think it was important?** If you didn't expect the information to appear on the test, review the strategies for detecting the most important information delivered during class lectures and in reading assignments.
- **Did I study it, but didn't retain it?** Not remembering information you studied may mean one of three things:
    a) You didn't learn it deeply and didn't lay down a strong enough memory trace in your brain for you to recall it at test time. This suggests you need to put in more study time or use a different study strategy to learn it more deeply.
    b) You may have tried to cram in too much study time just before the exam and may have not given your brain time enough to "digest" (consolidate) the information and store it in long-term memory. The solution may be to distribute your study time more evenly in advance of the next exam and take advantage of the "part-to-whole" study method.
    c) You studied hard and didn't cram, but you may need to study smarter or more strategically.
- **Did I study the material but didn't really understand it or learn it deeply?** This suggests you may need to self-monitor your comprehension more carefully while studying to track whether you're truly understanding the material and moving beyond "shallow" or "surface" learning.
- **Did I know the material but lost points due to careless test-taking mistakes?** If this happened, the solution may simply be to take more time to review your test after completing it and check for absentminded errors before turning it in. Or, your careless errors may have resulted from test anxiety that interfered with your concentration and memory.

2. **Get feedback from your instructor.** Start by noting any written comments your instructor made on your exam; keep these comments in mind when you prepare for the next exam. You can seek additional feedback by making an appointment to speak with your instructor during office hours. Come to the appointment with a positive mindset about improving your next test performance, not complaining about your last test grade.
3. **Seek feedback from professionals in your Learning Center or Academic Support Center.** Tutors and other learning support professionals can also be excellent sources of feedback about adjustments you can make in your test preparation and test-taking strategies. Ask these professionals to take a look at your tests and seek their advice about how to improve your test performance.
4. **Seek feedback from your classmates.** Your peers can also be a valuable source of information on how to improve your performance. You can review your test with other students in class, particularly with students who did well. Their test answers can provide you with models of what type of work your instructor expects on exams. You might also consider asking successful students what they did to be successful, such as how they prepared for the test and what they did during the test.

Teaming up after tests and assignments *early in the term* is especially effective because it enables you to get a better idea of what the instructor will expect from students throughout the remainder of the course. You can use this information as early feedback to diagnose your initial mistakes, improve your next performance, and raise your overall course grade—while there's still plenty of time in the term to do so. (See **Box 3.4** for a summary of the type of feedback you should seek from others to best strengthen your academic performance.)

Reflection 3.6

How would you rate your general level of test anxiety during exams? (Circle one.)

                high   moderate   low

What types of tests or subjects tend to produce the most test stress or anxiety for you?

Why?

Box 3.4

Key Features of Performance-Enhancing Feedback

When asking for feedback from others on your academic performance, seek feedback that has the following performance-improvement features:

- Effective feedback is *specific*. Seek feedback that identifies precisely what you should do to improve your performance and how you should go about doing it. After a test, seek feedback that provides you with more than information about what your grade is, or why you lost points. Seek specific information about what particular adjustments you can make to improve your next performance.

- Effective feedback is *prompt*. After receiving your grade on a test or assignment, *immediately* review your performance and seek feedback as soon as possible. This is the time when you're likely most motivated to find out what you got right and wrong, and it's also the time when you're most likely to retain the feedback you receive.

- Performance-enhancing feedback is *proactive*. Seek feedback *early* in the learning process. Be sure to ask for feedback at the start of the term. This will leave you with plenty of time and opportunity to use the feedback throughout the term to accumulate points and earn a higher final grade.

Strategies for Reducing Test Anxiety

High levels of anxiety can interfere with the ability to recall information that's been studied and increases the risk of making careless concentration-related errors on exams—such as, overlooking key words in test questions (Fernández-Castillo & Caurcel, 2014; Tobias, 1993). Studies also show that students who experience high levels of test anxiety are more likely to use ineffective "surface"-level study practices that rely on memorization, rather than more effective "deep-learning" strategies that involve seeking meaning and understanding (Biggs & Tang, 2007; Ramsden, 2003). The strategies listed below can help you recognize and minimize test anxiety.

1. **Understand what test anxiety is and what it's not.** Don't confuse anxiety with stress. Stress is a physical reaction that prepares your body for action by arousing and energizing it; this heightened level of arousal and energy can actually strengthen your performance. In fact, to be totally stress-free during an exam may mean that you're too laid back and could care less about how well you're doing. Peak levels of performance—whether academic or athletic—are not achieved by completely eliminating stress. Research shows that experiencing a *moderate* level of stress (neither too high nor too low) during exams and other performance-testing situations serves to maximize alertness, concentration, and memory (Sapolsky, 2004). The key is to keep stress at a manageable level so you can capitalize on its capacity to get you pumped up or psyched up, but prevent it from reaching a level where you become stressed out or psyched out.

If you often experience the following physical and psychological symptoms during tests, it probably means your stress level is too high and may be accurately called *test anxiety*.

- You feel bodily symptoms of tension during the test, such as pounding heartbeat, rapid pulse, muscle tension, sweating, or a queasy stomach.
- You have difficulty concentrating or maintaining your focus of attention while answering test questions.
- Negative thoughts and feelings rush through your head, such as fear of failure or self-putdowns (e.g., "I always mess up on exams.")
- You rush through the test just to get it over with and get rid of the uncomfortable feelings you're experiencing.
- Even though you studied and know the material, you go blank during the exam and forget much of what you studied. However, after turning in the exam and leaving the test situation, you're often able to remember the information you were unable to recall during the exam.

2. **Use effective test preparation strategies prior to the exam.** Test anxiety research indicates that college students who prepare well for exams and use effective study strategies prior to exams—such as those discussed in Chapter 5—experience less test anxiety during exams (Cassady & Johnson, 2002). Studies also show that there is a strong relationship between test anxiety and procrastination—that is, students who put off studying to the very last minute are more likely to report higher levels of test anxiety (Carden, Bryant, & Moss, 2004). The high level of pretest tension caused by last minute rushing to prepare for an exam often carries over to the test itself, resulting in higher levels of tension during the exam. Furthermore, late night cramming deprives the brain of stress-relieving dream (REM) sleep (Voelker, 2004), causing the sleep-deprived student to experience higher levels of anxiety the following day—the day of the test.

3. **Stay focused on the test in front of you, not the students around you.** Don't spend valuable test time looking at what others are doing and wondering whether they're doing better than you are. If you came to the test well prepared and still find the test difficult, it's very likely that other students are finding it difficult too. If you happen to notice that other students are finishing before you do, don't assume they breezed through the test or that they're smarter than you. Their faster finish may simply reflect the fact that they didn't know many of the answers and decided to give up and get out, rather than prolong the agony.

4. **During the exam, concentrate on the here and now.** Devote your attention fully to answering the test question that you're currently working on; don't spend time thinking (and worrying) about the test's outcome or what your grade will be.

5. **Focus on the answers you're getting right and the points you're earning, rather than worrying about what you're getting wrong and how many points you're losing.** Our thoughts can influence our emotions (Ellis, 2004), and positive emotions—such as those associated with optimism and a sense of accomplishment—can improve mental performance by enhancing the brain's ability to process, store, and retrieve information (Fredrickson & Branigan, 2005). One way to maintain a positive mindset is to keep in mind that college exams are often designed to be more difficult than high school tests, so it's less likely that students will get 90% to 100% of the total points. You can still achieve a good grade on a college exam without having to achieve a near-perfect test score.

6. **Don't forget that it's just a test, not a measure of your intelligence, academic ability, or self-worth.** No single exam can measure your true intellectual capacity or academic talent. In fact, the test grade you receive may not be a true indicator of how much you've actually learned. A low test grade also doesn't mean you're not capable of doing better work or destined to end up with a poor grade in the course—particularly if you adopt a "growth mindset" that views mistakes as learning opportunities.

7. **If you continue to experience test anxiety after trying to overcome it on your own, seek assistance from a professional in your Learning (Academic Support) Center or the Counseling Center.** You can try to overcome test anxiety (or any other personal issue) through the use of self-help strategies. However, if the problem persists after you've done your best to overcome it, there's no need to keep struggling on your own; instead, it's probably time to seek help from others. This doesn't mean you're weak or incompetent; it means you have the emotional intelligence and resourcefulness to realize your limitations and capitalize on the support networks available to you.

Chapter Summary and Highlights

Effective performance on college exams involves strategies used in advance of the test, during the test, and after test results are returned. Good test performance starts with good test preparation and awareness of the type of test questions you will be expected to answer (e.g., multiple-choice or essay). Test questions can be classified into two major categories, depending on the type of memory required to answer them: (1) *recognition* questions and (2) *recall* questions. Each of these types of questions tests your knowledge and memory in a different way.

Recognition test questions ask you to select or choose the correct answer from choices provided for you. Falling into this category are multiple-choice, true–false, and matching questions. These test questions don't require you to supply or produce the correct answer on your own; instead, you recognize or pick out the correct answer. Since recognition test questions ask you to recognize or select the correct answer from among answers provided for you, reviewing your class notes and textbook highlights may be an effective study strategy for multiple-choice and true—false test questions because it matches the type of mental activity you'll be asked to perform on the exam—which is to read test questions and look for the correct answer.

Recall test questions, on the other hand, require you to retrieve information you've studied and reproduce it on your own. This means you have to recall (re-call or "call back") the information you studied and supply it yourself. Recall test questions include essay and short answer questions; these questions don't involve answer recognition, but answer *production*—you produce the answer in writing. Studying for these types of test questions require *retrieval*—such as reciting the information without looking at it.

Effective test performance not only involves effective test-preparation strategies, but also effective test-taking strategies. For multiple-choice tests, effective test-taking strategies include using a *process-of-elimination* approach to weed out incorrect answers before identifying the best option, and *test-wise* strategies that use the wording of test questions to increase the likelihood of choosing the correct answer (e.g., choosing the longest answer and eliminating answers that contain absolute truths or broad generalizations).

Lastly, effective test performance involves carefully reviewing test results and using them as feedback to improve your future performance and final course grade. When test results are returned, determine where you earned and lost points. Pinpoint what went right so you continue doing it, and troubleshoot what went wrong so you prevent it from happening again.

Learning More through the World Wide Web: Internet-Based Resources

For additional information on strategic test-taking and managing test anxiety, see the following websites:

Test-Taking Strategies:
https://miamioh.edu/student-life/rinella-learning-center/academic-counseling/self-help/test-taking/index.html

https://www.stmarys-ca.edu/academics/academic-resources-support/student-academic-support-services/tutorial-academic-skills-8

Overcoming Test Anxiety:
http://www.studygs.net/tstprp8.htm

http://www.sic.edu/files/uploads/group/34/PDF/TestAnxiety.pdf

References

Bauer, D., Kopp, V., & Fischer, M. R. (2007). Answer changing in multiple choice assessment: change that answer when in doubt—and spread the word! *BMC Medical Education, 7,* 28–32.

Biggs, J., & Tang, C. (2007). *Teaching for quality learning at university* (3rd ed.) Buckingham: SRHE and Open University Press.

Carden, R., Bryant, C., & Moss, R. (2004). Locus of control, test anxiety, academic procrastination, and achievement among college students. *Psychological Reports, 95*(2), 581–582.

Carey, B. (2014). *How we learn.* London: Random House.

Cassady, J. C., & Johnson, R. E. (2002). Cognitive test anxiety and academic performance. *Contemporary Educational Psychology, 27*(2), 270–295.

Ellis, A. (2004). *Rational emotive behavior therapy: It works for me—It can work for you.* Amherst, NY: Prometheus Books.

Fernández-Castillo, A., & Caurcel, M. J. (2014). State test-anxiety, selective attention and concentration in university students. *International Journal of Psychology, 50*(4), 265–271.

Flippo, R. F., & Caverly, D. C. (2009). *Handbook of college reading and study strategy research* (2nd ed.). New York: Lawrence Erlbaum Associates.

Fredrickson, B. L., & Branigan, C. (2005). Positive emotions broaden the scope of attention and thought-action repertoires. *Cognition & Emotion, 19,* 313–332.

Glenberg, A. M. (1997). What memory is for. *Behavioral and Brain Sciences, 20,* 1–55.

Glenberg, A. M., Schroeder, J. L., & Robertson, D. A. (1998). Averting the gaze disengages the environment and facilitates remembering. *Memory & Cognition, 26*(4), 651–658.

Godden, D., & Baddeley, A. (1975). Context dependent memory in two natural environments. *British Journal of Psychology, 66*(3), 325–331.

Haas, R. (1994). *Eat smart, think smart.* New York: HarperCollins.

Higham, P. A., & Gerrard, C. (2005). Not all errors are created equal: Metacognition and changing answers on multiple-choice tests. *Canadian Journal of Experimental Psychology/Revue canadienne de psychologie expérimentale, 59*(1), 28.

Huck, S., & Bounds, W. (1972). Essay grades: An interaction between graders' handwriting clarity and the neatness of examination papers. *American Educational Research Journal, 9*(2), 279–283.

Hughes, D. C., Keeling, B., & Tuck, B. F. (1983). Effects of achievement expectations and handwriting quality on scoring essays. *Journal of Educational Measurement, 20*(1), 65–70.

Jensen, E. (2005). *Teaching with the brain in mind* (2nd ed.). Alexandria, VA: Association for Supervision and Curriculum Development.

Kruger, J., Wirtz, D., & Miller, D. (2005). Counter-factual thinking and the first instinct fallacy. *Journal of Personality and Social Psychology, 88,* 725–735.

Miller, M. D., Linn, R. L., & Gronlund, N. E. (2012). *Measurement and assessment in teaching* (7th ed.). Englewood Cliffs, NJ: Pearson.

National Resource Center for the First-Year Experience and Students in Transition. (2004). *The 2003 Your First College Year (YFCY) Survey.* Columbia, SC: Author.

Pai, M. R., Sanji, N., Pai, P. G. & Kotian, S. (2010). Comparative assessment in pharmacology multiple choice questions versus essay with focus on gender differences. *Journal of Clinical and Diagnostic Research* [serial online], *4*(3), 2515–2520.

Phillips, G. W. (2005). Does eating breakfast affect the performance of college students on biology exams? *Bioscene, 30*(4), 15–19.

Prinsell, C. P., Ramsey, P. H., & Ramsey, P. P. (1994). Score gains, attitudes, and behaviour changes due to answer-changing instruction. *Journal of Educational Measurement, 31,* 327–337.

Ramsden, P. (2003). *Learning to teach in higher education* (2nd ed.). London: RoutledgeFalmer.

Reed, S. K. (2013). *Cognition: Theory and applications* (3rd ed.). Belmont, CA: Wadsworth/Cengage.

Roediger, III, H. L. (2008). Relativity of remembering: Why the laws of memory vanished. *Annual Review of Psychology, 59*, 225–254.

Roediger, III, H. L., & Karpicke, J. (2006). The power of testing memory: Basic research and implications for educational practice. *Perspectives on Psychological Science, 1*(3), 181–210.

Sapolsky, R. (2004). *Why zebras don't get ulcers*. New York: W. H. Freeman.

Schab, F. R., & Crowder, R. G. (2014). *Memory for odors*. New York: Psychology Press.

Schroll, R. M. (2006). Effects of breakfast on memory retention of students at the college level. *Saint Martin's University Biology Journal, 1*, 35–50.

Smith, S., & Vela, E. (2001). Environmental context-dependent memory: A review and meta-analysis. *Psychonomic Bulletin & Review, 8*(2), 203–220.

Sprenger, M. (1999). *Learning and memory: The brain in action*. Alexandria, VA: Association for Supervision and Curriculum Development.

Thayer, R. E. (1997). *The origin of everyday moods: Managing energy, tension, and stress*. New York: Oxford University Press.

Tobias, S. (1993). *Overcoming math anxiety*. New York: W.W. Norton.

Tulving, E. (1983). *Elements of episodic memory*. Oxford: Clarendon Press/Oxford University Press.

Ueda, Y., Wang, M. F., Irei, A. V., Sarukura, N., Sakai, T., & Hsu, T. F. (2011). Effect of dietary lipids on longevity and memory in SAMP8 mice. *Journal of Nutritional Science Vitaminol, 57*(1), 36–41.

Ulus, I. H., Scally, M. C., & Wurtman, R. C. (1977). Choline potentiates the dinduction of adrenal tyrosine hydroxylase by reserpine, probably by enhancing the release of acetylcholine. *Life Sci, 21*, 145–148.

Voelker, R. (2004). Stress, sleep loss, and substance abuse create potent recipe for college depression. *Journal of the American Medical Association, 291*, 2177–2179.

Willingham, D. B. (2009). *Cognition: The thinking animal*. Upper Saddle River, NJ: Pearson.

Chapter 3 Exercises

3.1 Quote Reflections

Review the sidebar quotes contained in this chapter and select two that were especially meaningful or inspirational to you.

For each quote, provide a three- to five-sentence explanation why you chose it.

3.2 Reality Bite

Bad Feedback: Shocking Midterm Grades

Fred has enjoyed his first weeks on campus. He has met lots of people and really likes being in college. He's also very pleased to discover that, unlike high school, his college schedule doesn't require him to be in class for five to six hours per day. That's the good news. The bad news is that unlike high school, where his grades were all As and Bs, Fred's first midterm grades in college are three Cs, one D, and one F. He's stunned and a bit depressed by his midterm grades because he thought he was doing well. Since he never received grades this low in high school, he's beginning to think that he's not college material and may flunk out.

Reflection Questions

1. What factors may have caused or contributed to Fred's bad start?
2. What are Fred's options at this point?
3. What do you recommend Fred do right now to get his grades up and avoid being placed on academic probation?
4. What might Fred do in the future to prevent this midterm setback from happening again?

3.3 Self-Assessment of Test-Taking Habits and Strategies

Rate yourself in terms of how frequently you use these test-taking strategies according to the following scale:

4 = always, 3 = sometimes, 2 = rarely, 1 = never

1.	I take tests in the same seat I usually sit in to take class notes.	4	3	2	1
2.	I answer easier test questions first.	4	3	2	1
3.	I use a process-of-elimination approach on multiple-choice questions to eliminate choices until I find one that is correct or appears to be the most accurate option.	4	3	2	1
4.	Before answering essay questions, I look for key action words indicating what type of thinking I should display in my answer (e.g., "analyze," "compare").	4	3	2	1

5. On essay questions, I outline or map out the major ideas I'll include in my answer before I start writing sentences. 4 3 2 1

6. I look for information included on the test that may help me answer difficult questions or that may help me remember information I've forgotten. 4 3 2 1

7. I leave extra space between my answers to essay questions in case I want to come back and add more information later. 4 3 2 1

8. I carefully review my work, double-checking for errors and skipped questions before turning in my tests. 4 3 2 1

Self-Assessment Reflections

Which of the above strategies do you already use?

Of the ones you don't use, which one are you *most* likely to implement and *least* likely to implement? Why?

3.4 Midterm Self-Evaluation

At this point in the term, you may be experiencing the "midterm crunch"—a wave of midterm exams and due dates for assignments. This is a good time to step back and assess your academic progress.

Using the form below, list the courses you're taking this term and the grades you are currently receiving in each of these courses. If you don't know what your grade is, take a few minutes to check your syllabus for your instructor's grading policy and add up your scores on completed tests and assignments; this should give you at least a rough idea of where you stand in your courses. If you're having difficulty determining your grade in a course, even after checking your course syllabus and returned tests or assignments, ask your instructor how you could estimate your current grade.

	Course No.	Course Title	Grade
1.			
2.			
3.			
4.			
5.			

Reflection Questions

1. Were these the grades you *expected*? If not, were they better or worse than you anticipated?
2. Were these the grades you were *hoping* for? Are you pleased or disappointed?
3. Do you see any patterns in your performance that suggest what you're doing well and what you need to improve?
4. If you had to pinpoint one action you could immediately take to improve your lowest course grades, what would it be?

3.5 Calculating Your Midterm Grade Point Average

Use the information below to calculate what your grade point average (GPA) would be if your current course grades turn out to be your final grades for the term.

How to Compute Your Grade Point Average (GPA)

Most colleges and universities use a grading scale ranging from 0 to 4 to calculate a student's grade point average (GPA) or QPA (quality point average). Some schools use a grading system that involves only letters (A, B, etc.), while other institutions use letters as well as pluses and minuses (A-, B+, etc.). Check you college catalog or student handbook to determine what grading system is used at your campus.

The typical point value (points earned) by different letter grades are listed below.

Grade = Point Value

A = 4.0
A- = 3.7
B+ = 3.3
B = 3.0
B- = 2.7
C+ = 2.3
C = 2.0
C- = 1.7
D+ = 1.3
D = 1.0
D- = .7
F = 0

1. **Calculate the grade points you're earning in each of your courses this term by multiplying the course's number of units (credits) by the point value of the grade you're now earning in the course.** For instance, if you have a grade of B in a three-unit course, that course is earning you 9 grade points; if you have a grade of A in a two-unit course, that course is earning you 8 grade points.

2. **Calculate your grade point average by using the following formula:**

$$\text{GRADE POINT AVERAGE (GPA)} = \frac{\text{Total Number of Grade Points for all Courses}}{\text{Divided by Total Number of Course Units}}$$

For instance, see the fictitious example below:

Course	Units	×	Grade	=	Grade Points
Roots of Rock 'n' Roll	3	×	C (2)	=	6
Daydreaming Analysis	3	×	A (4)	=	12
Surfing Strategies	1	×	A (4)	=	4
Wilderness Survival	4	×	B (3)	=	12
Sitcom Analysis	2	×	D (1)	=	2
Love and Romance	3	×	A (4)	=	12
	16				48

$$\text{GPA} = \frac{48}{16} = 3.0$$

Reflection Questions

1. What is your GPA at this point in the term?

2. At the start of this term, was this the GPA you expected to attain? If there is a gap between the GPA you expected to achieve and the GPA you now have, what do you think accounts for this discrepancy?

3. Do you think your actual GPA at the end of the term will be higher or lower than it is now? Why?

Note: It's very typical for GPAs to be lower in college than they were in high school, particularly during the first year of college. Here are the results of one study that compared students' high school GPAs with their GPAs after their first year of college:

- A total of 29% of beginning college students had GPAs of 3.75 or higher in high school, but only 17% had GPAs that high at the end of their first year of college.

- A total of 46% had high school GPAs between 3.25 and 3.74, but only 32% had GPAs that high after the first year of college (National Resource Center for the First-Year Experience and Students in Transition, 2004).

FYE-My Test Taking Strategies

Name: _____
Section: _____

Respond to the 3 questions below on your own. Once you have completed the worksheet, pair with your neighbor and combine your best strategies. Share with the group.

My 5 most effective strategies **before** taking a test:

1.
2.
3.
4.
5.

My 5 most effective strategies **during** a test:

1.
2.
3.
4.
5.

My 5 most effective strategies **after** a test:

1.
2.
3.
4.
5.

Adapted from: University of South Carolina 2012 Faculty Resource Manual 2.0 University 101 Programs

Chapter 3 Test-Taking Skills and Strategies

This is a timed test and you have <u>5 minutes</u> to complete it!

1. Read everything carefully before doing anything.
2. Write your name in the section provided for the date.
3. Circle the word "name" in sentence two.
4. If you have followed directions carefully to this point, call out "I have."
5. Draw five small squares in the lower right-hand corner.
6. Draw a smiley face in the upper right-hand corner.
7. In your normal speaking voice, count from ten to one backwards.
8. Put a circle around each number on this page.
9. Write your favorite color in the right-hand margin on this page.
10. Put a circle completely around the sentence in number seven.
11. On the bottom of this page, multiply 70 by 30.
12. Clap your hands three times.
13. Draw a rectangle around the word "smiley" in sentence six.
14. Write today's date in the section provided for your name.
15. Do only what's asked of you in step 2. Then sit quietly and wait for everyone else to show you how good they are at following directions.

What did you just learn about following directions? How will this help you the next time you have to take a test?

_____

_____

_____

_____

CHAPTER 4

Three Key Academic Success and Lifelong Learning Skills

INFORMATION LITERACY, WRITING, AND SPEAKING

Chapter Preview

Research, writing, and speaking effectively are flexible, transferable skills that can be applied to improve performance across all majors, all careers, and throughout life. In this chapter, you will acquire strategies to research and evaluate information, write papers and reports, and use writing as a learning and thinking tool. You will also learn how to make effective oral presentations, overcome speech anxiety, and gain self-confidence about speaking in public.

Learning Goal

Acquire skills for accessing and referencing ideas obtained through scholarly research, as well as strategies for effectively communicating your own ideas through writing and speaking.

Integrate Your Faith

We need to research and evaluate how God has demonstrated His love for us, so that we can use it as a model for how we are to love one another.

Ignite Your Thinking

Reflection 4.1

What would you say is the difference between acquiring factual knowledge and learning a transferable skill?

The Importance of Research and Communication Skills

We're now living in the "information" and "communication" age; more information is being produced, reproduced, and communicated in today's world than at any other time in human history (Cairncross, 2001; Friedman, 2005).

From *Thriving in College and Beyond: Research-Based Strategies for Academic Success and Personal Development*, Fourth Edition by Joseph B. Cuseo, Aaron Thompson, Michele Campagna, and Viki S. Fecas. Copyright © 2016 Kendall Hunt Publishing Company. Reprinted by permission.

> "Employers are far more interested in the prospect's ability to think and to think clearly, to write and speak well, and how (s)he works with others than in his major or the name of the school (s) he went to. Several college investigating teams found that these were the qualities on which all kinds of employers, government and private, base their decisions."
>
> —*Lauren Pope, author,* Looking Beyond the Ivy League

> "Information literacy is knowing how, where, and why to get information. You can quickly and easily find information on anything. You have no fear of something you don't know, because you know you can easily find information about it."
>
> —*First-year college student*

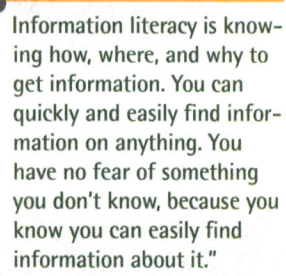

Because information is being generated and disseminated at such a rapid rate, "information literacy"—the ability to search for, locate, and evaluate information for relevance and accuracy—has become an essential 21st-century skill for managing and making sense of the overload of information currently available to us. Oral and written communication skills have also become increasingly important for career success in today's work world. College graduates with well-developed communication skills have a clear advantage in today's job market (AAC&U, 2013; National Association of Colleges & Employers, 2014). If you dedicate yourself to improving your information literacy, writing, and speaking skills, you'll improve both your academic performance in college and your career performance beyond college.

Information Literacy: Research Strategies for Locating and Evaluating Information

In addition to writing assignments relating to course readings and class lectures, you're likely to be assigned research reports that require you to locate and evaluate information on your own. As noted in Chapter 2, one of the major goals of a college education is to empower students to become self-reliant, lifelong learners. One key characteristic of a self-reliant, lifelong learner is *information literacy*—the ability to locate, evaluate, and use information (National Forum on Information Literacy, 2015). When you become information literate, you become a critical consumer of information who knows where and how to find credible information whenever you need it.

Described below is a six-step process for locating, evaluating, and using information to write research papers and reports in college (and beyond). This process can also be used to research information for oral presentations and group projects.

1. Define Your Research Topic or Question

The first step in the information search process is to be sure you've selected a research topic that's acceptable to your instructor, and a topic that's neither: (a) too *narrow*, leaving you with an insufficient amount of information to write about; or (b) too *broad*, leaving you with too much information to cover. If you have any doubts about your topic's acceptability or scope, before going any further, seek feedback from your instructor or from a professional in your college library.

Note

Librarians are information literacy experts and educators. Be sure to capitalize on the one-on-one instructional support they can provide for you outside the classroom.

2. Identify Resources for Locating Information

Two major resources are available to you for locating information:

- Print resources—such as, card catalogs, published indexes, and guidebooks; and

- Online resources—such as, online card catalogs, Internet search engines, and electronic databases.

Before beginning the information search process, be sure you know what sources your instructor requires or prefers.

Different information search tools are likely to generate different types of information; therefore, it's best to rely on more than one search tool. See **Box 4.1** for a summary of key information search tools and terms.

Box 4.1

Key Information Search Tools and Terms

As you read the following list of terms, place a check mark next to each term you're familiar with, and a plus sign next to those you've use before.

Abstract: a concise summary of the source's content, usually appearing at the beginning of an article; this information can help you decide quickly whether the source is relevant to your research topic.

Catalog: a library database containing information about what information sources the library owns and where they're located. Most catalogs are now in electronic form and can be searched by typing in a topic heading, author, or keyword.

Citation: a reference to an information source (e.g., book, article, or web page) that provides enough information to allow the reader to retrieve the source. Citations used in a college research paper must be presented in a standard format, such as APA or MLA format.

Database: a collection of data (information) that's been organized to make it easily accessible and retrievable. A database may include:

a) *reference citations*—such as, author, date, and publication source,
b) *abstracts*—summary of the contents of a scholarly article,
c) *full-length documents*, or
d) a combination of (a), (b), and (c).

Descriptor (a.k.a. Subject Heading): a key word or phrase in the index of a database (card or catalog) describing the subjects or content areas found within it, enabling you to quickly locate sources relevant to your research topic. For example, "emotional disorders" may be a descriptor for a psychology database that enables you to find information related to anxiety and depression. (Some descriptors or subject headings are accompanied by suggestions for using different search words to explore the topic you're investigating.)

Index: an alphabetical listing of topics contained in a database.

Keyword: a word used to search multiple databases that matches the search word to information found in different databases. A keyword is very specific; information relating to your topic that doesn't exactly match the key word isn't likely to be retrieved. For example, if the key word is "college," it may not supply you with potentially useful sources that have "university" instead of "college" in their titles.

Search Engine: a computer-run program that allows you to search for information across the entire Internet or at a particular website. For regularly updated summaries of different electronic search engines, how they work, and the type of information they generate, check: "search enginewatch.com/reports" and "researchbuzz.com."

Search Thesaurus: a list of words or phrases with similar meaning, allowing you to identify which of these words or phrases to use as key words,

Box 4.1 *(continued)*

descriptors, or subject headings in the database. This feature enables you to choose the best search terms before beginning the search process.

Subscription Database: a database that can only be accessed with a paid subscription. You may be able to access many of these databases at no personal cost because your college or university library has subscribed to them.

URL (Uniform Resource Locator): an Internet address consisting of a series of letters and/or numbers that pinpoints the exact location of an information resource (e.g., http://www.thrivingincollege.com).

Wildcard: a symbol, such as an asterisk (*), question mark (?), or exclamation point (!), that can be used to substitute different letters into a search word or phrase, allowing an electronic search to be performed on all variations of the word represented by the symbol. For example, an asterisk at the end of the key word, *econom**, may be used to search all information sources containing the words "economy," "economical," or "economist."

Source: Hacker & Fister (2014)

For a more extensive glossary of Internet terms, see: Matisse's Glossary of Internet Terms at http://www.matisse.net/files/glossary.html.

Reflection 4.2

Look back at the terms listed in **Box 4.1**. What terms were already familiar to you? Which of these tools have you used before?

When you locate a source, your first step is to evaluate its relevance to your paper's topic. One strategy for efficiently determining the relevance of a source is to ask if it will help you answer at least one or more of the following questions about your topic: Who? What? When? Where? Why? How?

3. Evaluate the Credibility and Quality of Your Sources

The primary purpose of searching for sources is to seek *documentation*—references you will use to support or confirm your conclusions. Since sources of information can vary widely in terms of their accuracy and quality, you need to think critically and make sound judgments to determine which of them are valid and reputable. The Internet has made this judgment process more challenging because most of its posted information is "self-published" and not subjected to the same quality control measures as information published in professional journals and books—which go public only after they're reviewed by a neutral panel of experts and carefully edited by professional editors. Listed below are criteria you can use to critically evaluate the sources you locate.

Credibility: Is the source written by an authority or expert in the field (e.g., someone with an advanced educational degree or professional experience relating to the topic)? For example, if your topic relates to an international issue, a highly credible source would be an author who has an advanced degree in international relations, or extensive professional experience in international affairs.

Scholarly: Does the information appear in a scholarly publication that's been reviewed by a panel or board of impartial experts in the field? Scholarly publications are written in a formal style that include references to other published sources, and they're "peer reviewed" or "peer refereed," meaning that they've been evaluated and approved for publication by other experts in the field. Professional journals are peer reviewed (e.g., *New England Journal of Medicine*) but not popular magazines (e.g., *Newsweek*) or popular websites (e.g., Wikipedia.org). Subscription databases accessible through your college or university library are more likely to contain peer-reviewed sources than free databases available to you on the world wide web. You may, however, use websites like "Google Scholar" (scholar.google.com) to find some scholarly sources that can be accessed for free.

Note

Wikipedia isn't considered to be a scholarly source, but you can track down scholarly references mentioned at this site, read them, and cite them in your report.

Currency: Has the source been published or posted recently? In certain fields of study, such as science and technology, recent references may be strongly preferred because new data is generated rapidly in these fields and information can become quickly outdated. In other fields, such as history and philosophy, older references may be viewed as classics, and citing them is perfectly acceptable. If you're not sure if current references are strongly preferred, check with your instructor before you begin the search process.

Objectivity: Is the author likely to be impartial or unbiased toward the subject? Consider how the professional position or personal background of authors may influence their ideas or their interpretation of evidence. Scholars should be impartial and objective in their pursuit of truth; they should not be in a position to gain fiscally, personally, or politically by drawing a certain conclusion about their topic of investigation. You should always be skeptical about the objectivity of web-based information sources whose address ends with ".com" because these are "com"mercial sites whose primary purpose is to sell products and make money, not to educate the public and engage in the objective pursuit of truth. To assess the objectivity of websites, always ask yourself why the site was created, what its objective or purpose is, and who sponsors it.

Even scientific research may lack objectivity. For instance, if you find an article on climate change written by scientists who work for or with an industry that risks incurring costs or losing revenue by switching to a more ecologically efficient source of energy, it would be reasonable to suspect that these researchers have a conflict of interest and may be biased toward reaching a conclusion that will benefit their employer (and themselves). When evaluating an article, ask yourself the following questions to check for bias: (a) Is the author a member of a special interest group or organization that could affect the article's objectivity? (b) Does the author consider alternative or opposing viewpoints, and deal with those viewpoints fairly? (c) Does the author use words that convey rationality and objectivity, or are they characterized by emotionality and an inflammatory tone?

If you think an article may lack complete objectivity, but still find that it's well written and contains good information or arguments, you can cite it in your paper. However, be sure you demonstrate critical thinking by noting that its conclusions may have been biased by the author's background or position.

4. Include a Sufficient Quantity and Variety of Sources

The quality of your research will be judged on the credibility of your sources as well as their number and variety.

Have you cited a sufficient number of references? As a general rule, it's better to include a larger than smaller set of references because it provides your paper with a broader base of support and a wider range of perspectives. In addition, using multiple sources allows you to demonstrate the higher-level thinking skill of synthesis—the ability to integrate information from numerous sources.

Have you used different *types* of sources? For some research reports, the variety of references cited may be as important as their sheer quantity. You can intentionally vary your sources by drawing on different types of references, such as:

- Books
- Scholarly journals—written by professionals and research scholars in the field
- News magazine and newspaper articles—written by journalists
- Course readings and class notes
- Personal interviews and personal experiences.

You can also vary your references by using both (a) *primary* sources—firsthand information or original documents (e.g., research experiments or novels), and (b) *secondary* sources—publications that build on or respond to primary sources (e.g., textbook or newspaper articles that critically review a novel or movie).

Lastly, you can vary your references by blending older, classic sources with newer, cutting-edge references. This combination will enable you to demonstrate how certain ideas have changed or evolved over time.

5. Use Your Sources as Stepping Stones to Your Own Ideas and Conclusions

It's your name that appears on the front cover of your research report, so it should be something more than an accumulation or amalgamation of other peoples' ideas. Simply collecting and compiling the ideas of others will result in a final product that reads more like a high school book report than a college research paper. Look at your sources as raw material you shape into a finished product that has your stamp on it. Don't just report or describe information drawn from other sources; instead, react to the information you cite, interpret it, and use it as evidence to support your own interpretations and conclusions.

6. Cite Your Sources with Integrity

College students with integrity don't cheat on exams and then rationalize that their cheating is acceptable because "others are doing it," nor do they plagiarize the work of others and pawn it off as their own. By accurately citing and referencing your sources, you demonstrate intellectual honesty by giving credit where credit is due. You credit others whose ideas you've borrowed and you credit yourself for the careful research you've done.

When should sources be cited? Simply put: You must cite anything included in your paper that was obtained from a source other than yourself. This includes other people's words, ideas, statistics, research findings, and visual work (e.g., diagrams, pictures, or drawings). There's only one exception to this rule: Information that's *common knowledge*—that is, information most people already know does not have to be cited. Common knowledge includes things like well-known facts (e.g., the earth is the third planet from the sun) and familiar dates (e.g., the Declaration of Independence was signed in 1776).

The Internet has given us easy access to an extraordinary amount of information and has made research much easier—that's the good news. The bad news is that it has also made proper citation more challenging. Determining the true "owner" or original author of posted information isn't as clear cut as it is for published books and articles. If you can't find the name of an author, at least cite the website, the date of the posted information (if available), and the date you accessed or downloaded it. If you have any doubt about an online source, print it out and check it out with your instructor or a professional librarian.

> "When a student violates an academic integrity policy, no one wins, even if the person gets away with it. It isn't right to cheat and it is an insult to everyone who put the effort in and did the work. I learned my lesson and have no intention of ever cheating again."
>
> —First-year college student's reflection on an academic integrity violation

Note

As a general rule, if you're unsure about whether a source should be cited, it's better to cite it and risk being corrected for over-citing than it is to run the risk of being accused of plagiarism—a serious violation of academic integrity that can have grave consequences. (See **Box 4.2** *for specific details about what constitutes or defines plagiarism and specific ways to avoid it.)*

Where and how should sources be cited? Your sources should be cited in two places: (a) the *body* of your paper, and (b) the *reference section* at the end of your paper (also known as a "bibliography" or "works cited" section). How your sources should be cited depends on the referencing style of the particular academic field or discipline in which you are writing your paper, so be sure you know the citation style your instructor prefers. It's likely you will be expected to use either (or both) of two referencing styles in college:

- *MLA* style—the style adopted by the Modern Language Association—which is commonly used in the Humanities and Fine Arts (e.g., English and Music); or
- *APA* style—the style adopted by the American Psychological Association—which is most commonly used in the Social and Natural Sciences (e.g., Sociology and Anthropology), and is the style used in this book.

You may be asked to use other styles in advanced courses in specialized fields, such as *The Chicago Manual of Style* for papers in history, or the Council of Biology Editors (CBE) style for papers in the biological sciences. Software programs are now available that automatically format references according to a particular citation style, such as CiteFast (www.citefast.com) and EasyBib (www.easybib.com). If you use these programs, be sure to proofread the results because they can sometimes generate inaccurate or incomplete citations (Hacker & Fister, 2014).

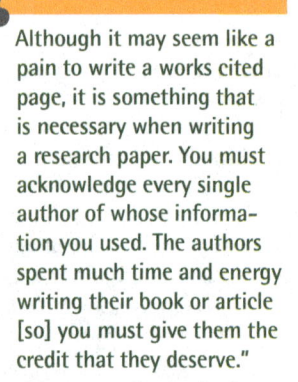

> "Although it may seem like a pain to write a works cited page, it is something that is necessary when writing a research paper. You must acknowledge every single author of whose information you used. The authors spent much time and energy writing their book or article [so] you must give them the credit that they deserve."
>
> —First-year student's reflection on a plagiarism violation

Reflection 4.3

Prior to college, did you write papers that required citation of references? If yes, do you know what referencing style you used?

Box 4.2

Plagiarism: A Violation of Academic Integrity

What Exactly Is Plagiarism?

Plagiarism is a violation of academic integrity that involves intentional or unintentional use of someone else's work without acknowledging it, which gives the reader the impression that it's your own work.

Common Forms of Plagiarism

1. Paying someone, or paying a service, for a paper and turning it in as your own work.
2. Submitting an entire paper, or portion thereof, that was written by someone else.
3. Copying sections of someone else's work and inserting it into your own work.

Box 4.2 (continued)

4. Cutting paragraphs from separate sources and pasting them into the body of your own paper.
5. Paraphrasing or rewording someone else's words or ideas without citing that person as a source. (Good strategies for paraphrasing without plagiarizing may be found at: http://www.upenn.edu/academicintegrity/ai_paraphrasing.html.)
6. Placing someone else's exact words in the body of your paper and not placing quotation marks around them.
7. Failing to cite the source of factual information in your paper that's not common knowledge.

Good examples of different forms of plagiarism may be found at: http://www.princeton.edu/pr/pub/integrity/pages/plagiarism/

Final Notes:

- If you include information in your paper and just list its source in your reference (works cited) section—without citing the source in the *body* of your paper—this still qualifies as plagiarism.
- Be sure only to include sources in your reference section that you actually used and cited in the body of your paper. Although including sources in your reference section that aren't cited in your paper isn't technically a form of plagiarism, it may be viewed as being deceitful because you're "padding" your reference section, giving the reader the impression that you incorporated more sources into your paper than you actually did.

Sources: Academic Integrity at Princeton (2011); Purdue University Online Writing Lab (2015)

Reflection 4.4

Reflect back at the different forms of plagiarism described in **Box 4.2**. Were there any you were surprised to see, or didn't realize was a form of plagiarism?

Writing Skills and Strategies

The Power of Writing

Writing is a versatile academic skill that can be used to strengthen your performance across the curriculum, including general education courses and courses in your major. It's the primary route through which you will communicate your knowledge and the quality of your thinking. No matter how many great ideas you have in your head, if you can't get those ideas out of your head and onto paper, you'll never receive full credit for them in college courses that will require you to write. Improving your writing will not only improve your written communication skills, it will enable you to better demonstrate your knowledge and elevate your course grades.

In addition to strengthening your academic performance in college, your ability to write clearly, concisely, and persuasively will promote your

> "Want one more reason for developing strong writing skills? *Money.* Good writing skills are consistently one of the most sought-after skills by employers."
>
> —Karen Brooks, career development specialist and author, *You Majored in What? Mapping Your Path From Chaos to Career*

professional success beyond college. When college alumni were asked about what professional skills they were using in the workplace, more than 90% of them ranked "need to write effectively" as a skill that was of "great importance" to their current work (Worth, cited in Light, 2001). In fact, the letter of application (cover letter) you write to apply for employment positions after college graduation is likely to be the first impression you'll make on a potential employer. Thus, a well-written letter of application may be your first step toward converting your college degree into your first career position.

Note
Strengthening your writing skills will strengthen your academic performance throughout college and your professional performance throughout all stages of your career.

Writing Papers and Reports

Studies show that only a small percentage of high school students engage in writing assignments that are as lengthy and challenging as those required in college. Most high school writing assignments involve summaries or descriptive reports, whereas in college, students are expected to engage in expository (persuasive) writing that requires them to express ideas and prove a point by supporting it with compelling evidence (The University of Texas at El Paso, 2008).

Reflection 4.5

Reflect back on your writing assignments in high school experience.

a) What was the longest paper you wrote?

b) What types of thinking were you usually asked to demonstrate in your writing assignments (e.g., summarize, analyze, or criticize)?

Writing lengthy papers almost always take more time than you think it will; it's a multistage process that cannot be completed in one night. Breaking down the writing task into separate stages and completing these stages in advance of the paper's due date is an effective way to strengthen the quality of your final product (Boice, 1994). These stages include:

- Knowing your writing goal or purpose
- Generating ideas to write about
- Organizing your ideas into major categories
- Ordering your categories of ideas into a logical sequence

Dividing large writing assignments into smaller, manageable steps can reduce late-night frustration and the risk of permanent computer damage.

- Expressing your ideas in the form of well-written sentences and paragraphs
- Revising your writing after editing and proofreading

What follows is a systematic, 10-step process for completing these stages. Following this stepwise process should make your writing of papers and reports more manageable, less stressful, and more successful.

1. **Know the purpose of the writing assignment.** The critical first step in the process of writing an effective paper is having a clear understanding of its purpose or goal. This will help you stay on track and moving in the right direction. It also helps you get going in the first place, because one of the major causes of writer's block and writer procrastination is uncertainty about the goal or purpose of the writing task (Knaus, 2010).

    Before you start writing anything, be sure you have a clear understanding of your instructor's expectations. You can do this by asking yourself these three questions about the writing assignment:

    - What is the major objective or intended outcome of this assignment?
    - What type of thinking am I being asked to demonstrate?
    - What criteria (standards) will my instructor use to evaluate and grade my performance?

2. **Focus first on generating ideas.** In the initial stages of the writing process, the only thing you should be concerned about is getting ideas you have in your head out of your head and on to paper. Don't worry about how well the ideas are written. Writing scholars refer to this process as *focused freewriting*—you write freely for a

> "Begin with the end in mind."
> —*Stephen Covey*, The Seven Habits of Highly Effective People

certain period just to come up with ideas—not to write complete, eloquent, and grammatically correct sentences (Bean, 2011). Beginning first by just generating ideas can jump-start the writing process and enables you to overcome writer's block (Zinsser, 1993). The simple act of writing down your thoughts can, in itself, stimulate additional thoughts. If you're not sure what ideas you have, start writing because it will activate ideas, which, in turn, will lead to new ideas. (Sometimes, changing your writing environment or format can also stimulate production of new ideas, such as shifting to a new location or shifting from writing ideas in pen or pencil to typing them on your computer.)

3. **Categorize your ideas.** After you've completed generating ideas, the next step is to sort them out and figure out how they can be pieced together. This organizational process involves two key sub-steps.

   - Group together ideas relating to the same point or concept. For instance, if your topic is terrorism and you find three ideas on your list referring to what motivates terrorists, group those ideas together under the category of "motivational causes." Similarly, if you find ideas on your list that relate to preventing or deterring terrorism, group those ideas under the category of "potential solutions." Consider recording separate ideas on sticky notes and placing sticky notes containing specific ideas relating to the same general category on separate index cards. You can then arrange and rearrange the cards until you find an order that works best—which will lead you to the step below.

   - Arrange your categories of ideas in an order that flows smoothly and logically from start to finish. Try to come up with a sequence that has a meaningful beginning, middle, and end. Index cards come in handy when trying to find the best progression of your major ideas because the cards can be arranged and rearranged easily until you discover an order that produces the smoothest, most logical sequence. Your sequence of index cards can also be used to create an outline for your paper that contains all its major categories of ideas and the order in which they'll appear in your paper.

   Another effective way to organize and sequence ideas is by arranging them in a drawing or diagram. When ideas are laid out in such a visual-spatial format, the product is referred to as a "concept map" or "graphic organizer." **Figure 4.1** illustrates a concept map that organizes the main ideas related to higher-level thinking—a topic covered in Chapter 8. This type of concept map is known as a "clock map" because its main ideas are organized like the numbers of a clock that begins at the top and moves sequentially in a clockwise direction. Concept maps can be created in any pattern that works well for the material you're trying to organize and sequence. (To see a variety of concept-mapping formats and apps, go to: *www.graphic.org/concept.html*)

FIGURE 4.1: Concept Map Used to Organize and Sequence Major Ideas Relating to Higher-Level Thinking

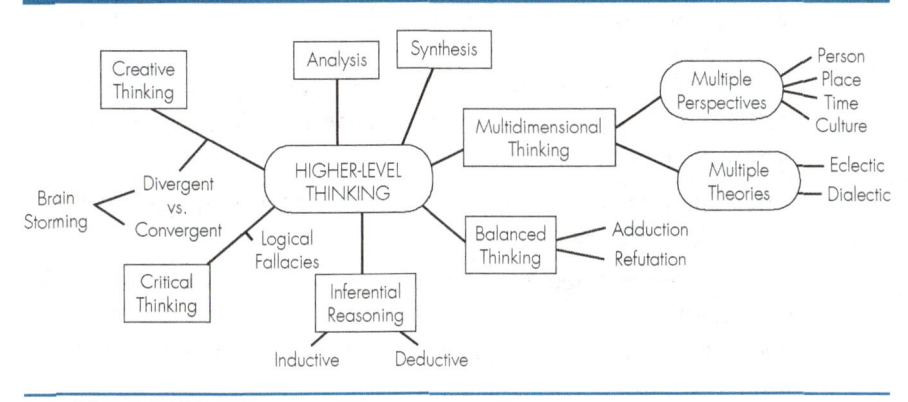

```
                    Analysis    Synthesis
                                                       Person
        Creative                              Multiple  Place
        Thinking                            Perspectives Time
                                                       Culture
                           Multidimensional
                               Thinking
  Brain   Divergent  HIGHER-LEVEL           Multiple   Eclectic
Storming    vs.       THINKING              Theories   Dialectic
          Convergent
                    Logical       Balanced   Adduction
                    Fallacies     Thinking   Refutation
        Critical
        Thinking   Inferential
                   Reasoning
                  Inductive  Deductive
```

©Kendall Hunt Publishing Company

4. **Write a first draft of your paper that focuses on expressing your main ideas in a logical sequence of paragraphs.** The previous steps in the writing process are often referred to as *prewriting* because they focus on generating and organizing ideas before they're put into complete sentences (Murray, 2004). In your *first draft*, you begin the actual writing process by converting your major ideas into sentences. The purpose of this first draft is to simply "talk through" your key ideas on paper. In later drafts, you will convert this informal writing into more formal and polished prose.

Your first draft should transform your major ideas into paragraphs that are arranged in a smooth and logical sequence. Here are some strategies for doing so.

- Use the first section of the paper to provide a meaningful introduction, overview, or preview of the major points you'll make in the remainder (body) of the paper. Your opening paragraph is critical because it shapes the reader's first impression and sets the stage for what will follow. Your opening paragraph should include a *thesis statement*—a short summary (one to three sentences) of the key point you intend to make or the central question you will answer in the body of your paper. In short, a thesis statement answers the following question about your paper: "What's your point?" It's the compass that guides your thinking and guides the reader's thinking throughout the paper, keeping you both on the same page and moving in the right direction toward the same destination (your conclusion).
- Keep ideas relating to different points in different paragraphs. A paragraph should represent a chain of sentences that are linked to the same thought or idea. If you shift to a new idea, shift to a new paragraph.
- Whenever possible, start new paragraphs with a *topic sentence* that introduces the new idea you're about to make and connects it to

the major point being made in your paper—your thesis statement. Topic sentences help bring coherence to your paper by showing the reader how separate paragraphs relate to your central idea (your thesis).

- Use the final paragraph (or two) of your paper to "tie it altogether" and finish strong; drive home your key point with the major evidence you've gathered to support it.

After all your paragraphs have been written, your paper should have three identifiable parts:

a) *Introduction*—an opening section that includes your thesis statement.
b) *Body*—a series of paragraphs that follows and flows from your introduction.
c) *Conclusion*—a final section that summarizes your major points and relates them to the thesis statement in your introduction.

5. **Write more than one draft.** Don't expect to write a perfect draft of your paper on the first try. Even professional writers report that it takes them more than one draft (often three or four) before they produce their final draft. Although the final product of award-winning writers may seem impeccably written, what preceded it was a messy process that included lots of revisions between the first try and the final product (Bean, 2011). Just as actors and actresses need multiple takes (take 2, take 3, etc.) to get their spoken lines right, so do writers need multiple takes (drafts) to get their written lines right.

After you've completed your first draft, step away from it for a while. Return to it later with a fresh mind and new eyes that look to improve your product in the next draft. In particular, review your thesis statement to be sure that it still serves as an accurate compass for the direction your paper has taken. It's okay to go back and tweak your original thesis statement to more closely match the conclusion in your final draft (Bean, 2011). However, if you find yourself radically changing your thesis statement, this suggests you strayed too far from it and may need to replace it with one that aligns more directly with the body of your paper, or make changes in the body of the paper so it aligns more closely with your original thesis statement.

6. **Critically review your own writing.** After you have completed at least two drafts of your paper and created what looks like a final product, take a look at it from a different perspective—as reader and editor, rather than writer. It's noteworthy that the term "revision" literally means to re-vision (view again). At this stage in the process, you're re-viewing your writing as if the words were written by someone else and your role now is to be a critic. If you find words and sentences that aren't clearly capturing or reflecting what you intended to say, this is the stage in the writing process to make major revisions. (Make sure your paper is double-spaced so that you have enough room for making changes and additions.)

When critiquing and editing your paper, use the same criteria (judgment standards) your instructor is likely to use. If your instructor has shared these criteria with the class, use them to critique and improve your paper. Your paper will probably be evaluated with respect to the following features, so keep them in mind when critiquing your work.

- **Documentation.** Are all of your paper's major points and final conclusions supported by evidence—such as:
  a) direct quotes from authoritative sources,
  b) specific examples,
  c) statistical data,
  d) scientific research findings, or
  e) firsthand experiences?
- **Overall Organization.** Take a panoramic or aerial view of your paper to see if you can clearly identify its three major parts: the beginning (introduction), the middle (body), and the end (conclusion). Do these three parts unite to form a connected whole? Also, check to be sure there's *continuity* from one paragraph to the next throughout your paper: Does your train of thought stay on track from start to finish? If you find yourself getting off track at certain points in your paper, eliminate that information or rewrite it in a way that re-routes your thoughts back onto its main track (your thesis statement).
- **Sentence Structure.** Refine and fine tune your sentences. Keep an eye out for *sentence fragments*—"sentences" missing either a noun or a verb—and *run-on sentences*—two sentences that are not separated by a period or conjunction (e.g., "and" or "but").

  Check for sentences that are too long—rambling sentences that go on and on without any punctuation, leaving readers without time to pause and catch their breath. If you find long-winded sentences, (a) punctuate them with a comma to give the reader a short pause, (b) punctuate them with a semicolon (;) to provide a longer pause than a comma (but not as long as a period), or (c) divide them into two shorter sentences (separated by a period).

  Also, check for *choppy sentences* that "chop up" what you've written into such short segments that it disrupts the natural rhythm of reading, forcing the reader to stop and restart. If you find choppy sentences in your writing, combine them to form larger sentence, and, if necessary, punctuate them with a comma or semicolon—instead of a period.

  A good strategy for helping you determine if your sentences flow smoothly is to read them aloud. Note the places where you naturally tend to pause and where you tend to keep going. Your natural pauses may serve as cues for places where your sentences need punctuation, and your natural runs may indicate sentences that are flowing smoothly and should be left alone.

- **Word Selection.** Are certain words or terms showing up so frequently in your paper that they sound repetitious? If you find any, replace the redundancy with variety by substituting words that have the same or similar meaning. This substitution process can be made easier by using a thesaurus, which may be conveniently available on your computer's word processing program.

7. **Seek feedback on your writing from a trusted peer or writing professional.** You should be the first reader of your paper, but you don't have to be the only reader before it's formally submitted and graded. No matter how honest or objective we try to be about our own writing, we may still be blind to its weaknesses. We all have a tendency to see what we hope or want to see in our work, especially after we've put a great deal of time, effort, and energy into the process of creating it. Consider getting a second opinion on your paper by seeking feedback from a trusted friend or a tutor in the Writing or Learning Center. This isn't cheating or plagiarism—as long as it's you who makes the changes and does the re-writing in response to the feedback you've received.

    You can seek feedback at any stage of the writing process—whether it be for help with understanding the assignment, brainstorming ideas, writing a first draft, or reviewing your final draft. Seeking help from the Writing or Learning Center is not just for students experiencing writing problems or writer's block. If you're already a good writer, the quality of your written work can get even better by seeking and receiving feedback from others. Even professional writers share their drafts with other writers to obtain feedback at different stages in the writing process (Leahy, 1990).

    Consider pairing up with a writing partner to exchange and assess each other's papers by using the same criteria your instructor will use to evaluate and grade your work. Studies show that when students at all levels of writing ability receive feedback from others prior to submitting a paper, the quality of their writing improves, as does their grade on the writing assignment (Patchan, Charney, & Schunn, 2009; Thompson, 1981).

8. **In your final draft, be sure that your conclusion and introduction are connected or aligned.** The most important component of your conclusion involves revisiting or restating your initial thesis and answering the question you originally posed in your introduction. Connecting your thesis statement and concluding statement provides a pair of meaningful bookends to your paper, anchoring it at its two most pivotal points: beginning and end. Making this connection ensures you've ended up at the destination you planned to reach when you started out. It also enables you to maximize the power of the two most important impressions your paper can make on the reader: the *first* impression and the *last* impression.

9. **Carefully proofread your paper for clerical and technical mistakes before submitting it.** Proofreading is the critical last step in

the editorial process. It's a step that's essential for catching small, technical errors that were likely overlooked during earlier stages of the writing process—when your attention was focused on the paper's content and organization. Proofreading may be viewed as a micro form of editing, during which you shift the focus of your editorial attention to minute mechanics related to referencing, grammar, punctuation, and spelling.

Don't forget that your computer's spell-checker may not catch words that are actually incorrectly spelled in the context you're using them. For instance, a spell-checker wouldn't detect the fact that there are five "correctly" spelled words that are actually misspellings in the context of the following sentence: "*Where* you're high-*heal* shoes when we *meat* for the executive *bored* meeting." (A career counselor once reported that a student forgot to proofread her job application before submitting it; her roommate read it and laughingly noticed that she mistakenly applied for a job in "pubic service" instead of public service [Brooks, 2009].)

> "Spell checkers aren't always reliable, so ask someone for suggestions or read papers out loud to yourself."
>
> —Advice to first-year students from a college sophomore

Note
Careful proofreading represents the last important step in the process of writing a high-quality paper. To skip this simple, final step and lose points on something you spent so much time creating would be a crying shame.

10. **After your paper is graded and returned to you, carefully review your instructor's written comments.** Some things you can only learn *after* receiving feedback about your performance. Use your instructor's comments as constructive feedback to improve your performance on future assignments. If the instructor didn't provide sufficient feedback and you're still unclear about what to do to improve your work, make an appointment for an office visit. If your instructor is willing to meet with you during office hours and review your paper with you, take full advantage of this opportunity. Besides receiving personalized feedback that can improve your future writing, your office visit sends a clear message to the instructor that you're a student who is serious about learning and achieving academic excellence.

Public Speaking: Making Oral Presentations and Delivering Speeches

The Importance of Oral Communication

In addition to writing, the second major channel you'll use in college to communicate your ideas and knowledge is speaking—whether it be raising your hand and speaking up in class, participating in small group discussions, or making formal presentations individually or as part of a group presentation. When graduating seniors at Harvard University were asked about what specific strategies they would recommend to first-year students for overcoming shyness and developing social self-confidence, their most frequent recommendation was to take classes in which you are expected to speak up (Light, 1992).

Developing your ability to speak in a clear, concise, and confident manner will strengthen your academic performance in college and your career performance after college. The oral communication skills you display during job interviews will likely play a pivotal role in determining whether you're initially hired. Speaking skills will also increase your prospects for career advancement by strengthening your professional presentations and performance at meetings. Research repeatedly shows that employers place a high value on oral communication skills and rank them among the top characteristics they seek in prospective employees (AAC&U, 2013; National Association of Colleges & Employers, 2014).

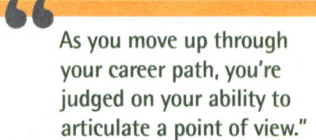

> "As you move up through your career path, you're judged on your ability to articulate a point of view."
>
> —Donald Keogh, former president of the Coca-Cola Company

Reflection 4.6

How many times have you made an oral presentation or delivered a speech?

Does your college require a course in speech or public speaking? If yes, when do you plan to take it? If no, would you consider taking an elective course in public speaking? (Why?)

(To assess your verbal skills, complete Exercise 4.5 at the end of this chapter.)

Strategies for Making Effective Oral Presentations

Listed below are strategies for delivering oral presentations and speeches. Since speaking and writing both involve communicating thoughts verbally, you'll find that many of the strategies suggested here for improving oral reports are similar to those for improving written reports. Thus, you'll be able to "double dip" by using the following oral presentation strategies to strengthen your written presentations and vice versa.

1. **Know the purpose of your presentation.** Oral presentations usually fall into one of the following two categories, depending on their purpose or objective:
    a) *informative* presentations—intended to provide the audience with accurate information to increase their knowledge or supply them with practical information they can use, or
    b) *persuasive* (expository) presentations—intended to persuade (convince) the audience to agree with a particular position or buy into a certain viewpoint.

    Be sure you're clear about what you're expected to accomplish and keep that objective in mind as you develop your presentation.

When deciding on what specific information to include, always ask yourself: Is this information relevant to the intended purpose of my presentation?

In college, most of your oral presentations will likely fall into the persuasive category, which means that you will search for information, draw conclusions about your research, and document your conclusions with evidence. Similar to writing research papers, persuasive presentations usually require you to think at a higher level, cite sources, and demonstrate academic integrity.

2. **Select a topic that matters to you and you're passionate about.** If you're given a choice about the topic of your presentation, seize this opportunity to pursue a subject that captures your interest and enthusiasm. By doing so, your interest and enthusiasm will show through in your delivery, which will increase your audience's attention, your self-confidence, and the overall quality of your presentation.

3. **Create an outline of your major ideas.** Get your major points down on index cards or PowerPoint slides and arrange them in an order that provides the best sequence or flow of your ideas from start to finish. Use the major points you've recorded on separate index cards or slides as memory "cue cards" to trigger your recall of specific details relating to each of your major points.

4. **Rehearse and revise.** Just as you should write several drafts of a paper before turning it in, an oral presentation should be rehearsed and revised before delivering it. Rehearsal will help ensure that your presentation isn't interrupted by long pauses, stops and starts, and distracting "fillers" (e.g., "uh," "umm," "like," "you know," "whatever"). Rehearsal will also help reduce your level of speech anxiety. Studies show that fear of public speaking is often really a fear of failure—fear of being negatively evaluated by the audience (Finn, Sawyer, & Behnke, 2009). If your oral presentation is well prepared and well rehearsed, your fear of receiving a negative evaluation should decrease, along with your level of speech anxiety.

> "The only time I get nervous is when I am not very familiar with my topic or if I'm winging my assignment and I'm not prepared."
> —First-year student commenting on her previous oral presentations

When rehearsing your presentation, pay special attention to the following parts:

- The *introduction*. This part of your speech should be particularly well-rehearsed because it provides the audience with a sense of direction and positive anticipation for what's to come. Like a well-designed written report, the introduction to your oral report should include a thesis statement—a statement about *why* you're speaking about this topic and what you intend to accomplish by the end of your presentation. It should also "hook" the audience and stimulate their interest in what you're about to say.

- *Transition statements* that signal you're moving from one major idea to another. These statements serve to highlight the key components of your presentation and show how its separate parts are connected.

> "One important key to success is self-confidence. An important key to self-confidence is preparation."
> —Arthur Ashe, former world number 1 professional tennis player and first black player ever selected to the United States Davis Cup team

- The *conclusion*. This is your chance to finish strong and create a powerful last impression that drives home your presentation's most important points. Your conclusion should include a statement that refers back to, and reinforces, your original thesis statement, thereby connecting your ending with your beginning.

    Lastly, when you rehearse your presentation, be aware of the total time it takes to complete it. Be sure it falls within the time range set by your instructor and that it's neither too short nor too long.

5. **Get feedback on your presentation before officially delivering it.** Ask a friend or group of friends to listen to your presentation and request their input. Not only can peers provide valuable feedback, they can provide you with a "live audience" for your rehearsal. This makes your rehearsal more realistic and effective because your practice environment closely matches your performance environment.

    Another way to obtain feedback prior to your presentation is to have a friend make a video recording of your rehearsed presentation. This will enable you to step outside of yourself and observe your presentation as the audience would. This "out-of-body experience" can dramatically increase awareness of your nonverbal communication (body language) habits.

    When you first see how you look and hear how you sound on videotape, you may be quite surprised (or shocked), but that's a normal reaction. After a while, the initial shock will fade and you'll feel more comfortable viewing, reviewing, and improving your presentation.

6. **Observe presentations made by other students and learn from them.** Note the things that effective speakers seem to do when delivering their speeches and use them as clues to improve the quality of your own presentations.

7. **During delivery of your speech, maximize eye contact with your audience.** You can occasionally look at your notes and slides during your presentation and use them as cue cards to help you recall the key points you intend to make; however, they shouldn't be used as a script that you read verbatim. PowerPoint presentations have the potential to become deadly boring when the speaker's "presentation" involves looking at and reading slides off a screen, rather than looking at and speaking to the audience. (See **Box 4.3** for tips on using, not abusing, PowerPoint.)

Effective oral presentations should not be written out entirely in advance and read (or memorized) word for word (Luotto, Stoll, & Hoglund-Ketttmann, 2001), nor should they be impromptu presentations delivered off the top of the speaker's head. Instead, they should be *extemporaneous* presentations, which fall between "winging it" and reading or memorizing it word-by-word. Extemporaneous speaking

Box 4.3

Tips for Using (Not Abusing) PowerPoint

- List information on your slides as bulleted points, not complete sentences. The more words included on your slides, the more time your audience will spend reading the slides rather than listening to you. You can help keep the focus on *you* (not your slides) by showing only one point on your slide at a time. This will keep the audience members focused on the point you're discussing and prevent them from reading ahead.

Note *Your PowerPoint slides are not your presentation; they're merely cue cards that trigger the ideas you will discuss in relation to the slides.*

> "A presentation is about explaining things to people that go above and beyond what they get in the slides. If it weren't, they might just as well get your slides and read them in the comfort of their own office, home, boat, or bathroom."
>
> —Jesper Johansson, senior security strategist for Microsoft and author of Death by PowerPoint *(personal blog) (2005)*

- List only three to five points on each slide. Research indicates that humans can retain only about four points or bits of information in their short-term memory (Cowan, 2001).
- Use the titles of slides as general headings or categories for your major ideas.
- Use a font size of at least 18 points to ensure that people in the back of the room can read what's printed on each slide.
- Don't use color just for decoration (which can be a source of distraction), but as a visual aid to highlight how points are organized on a slide. For example, a dark or bold blue heading could be used to highlight the title of the slide—to represent a major point, and sub-points could be listed as bullets in a lighter shade of blue.
- Incorporate visual images into your presentation. Don't hesitate to use pictures, graphs, cartoons, and objects or artifacts that relate to and reinforce your major points.

Note *The true power of PowerPoint may be that it allows you to illustrate visually what you're discussing verbally. Take advantage of this PowerPoint feature to display images and pictures that relate to your spoken words.*

- If you include words or images on a slide that are not your own work, demonstrate academic integrity by noting its source at the bottom of the slide.
- Before going public with your slides, proofread them with the same care as you would a written paper.

Sources: Hedges (2014); Johansson (2005); *The Ten Commandments of PowerPoint Presentations* (2015)

---

includes advanced preparation and the use of notes or slides as memory retrieval cues, but allows you some freedom to ad lib or improvise. If you happen to forget the exact words you planned to use, you can freely substitute different words to make the same point—without stumbling or stressing out—and without your audience even noticing you made any substitutions. The key to extemporaneous speaking is to rehearse and remember your major points, not the exact words you will use to express each and every point. This will ensure your presentation comes across as natural and authentic, rather than mechanical or robotic.

Managing Speech Anxiety

If you're uncomfortable about public speaking, you're certainly not alone. It's such a common feeling, it should be considered "normal." National surveys show that fear of public speaking affects people of all ages, including adolescents and young adults (Brewer, 2001; Croston, 2012). A significant number of college students also experience *classroom communication apprehension*—anxiety about speaking in classroom settings (Wrench, McCroskey, & Richmond, 2008).

Keep in mind that it's natural to experience at least some anxiety in any performance situation. This isn't necessarily a bad thing, because if your stress is kept at a moderate level, it can actually increase your energy, concentration, and memory (Rosenfield, 1988; Sapolsky, 2004). However, if it reaches the level of fear, leaving you unwilling or unable to stand up in front of a group to make an oral presentation, you may be experiencing speech anxiety or "stage fright." Listed below are strategies for controlling speech anxiety and keeping it at a moderate and productive level.

1. **In the minutes just prior to your speech, focus on relaxation.** Take deep breaths, or use any stress management strategy that works well for you.
2. **Avoid consuming caffeine or other "energy drinks" prior to speaking.** These substances will elevate your level of physiological arousal during your speech, which, in turn, can elevate your level of psychological arousal (anxiety).
3. **Come to your speech with a positive mindset.** Simply stated, positive thoughts trigger positive emotions (Ellis, 2000). Here are some strategies for putting yourself in a positive frame of mind:
   - Adopt the mindset that your speech is nothing more than a formal conversation with a group of friends. To help get you into this conversational mindset, make eye contact with small sections of the audience while delivering your speech. When you shift to a new idea or part of your speech, shift your focus of attention to a different section of the audience. This strategy will help relax you by making the audience seem smaller, and it will ensure that you make periodic eye contact with different sections of the audience.
   - Expect to give a good speech, but not a perfect speech. Don't think you're going to deliver a presentation like a TV reporter who is smoothly delivering (actually reading) the nightly news. A few verbal mistakes or lapses of memory are common during speeches, just as they are during normal conversations. You can still receive an excellent grade on an oral presentation without delivering a flawless performance.
   - Keep in mind that the audience to whom you are speaking is not made up of expert speakers. Most of them have no more public speaking experience than you do, nor are they experienced

critics. These are your peers and they know that standing up in front of class and delivering a formal speech isn't an easy thing to do. They're likely to be very accepting of any mistakes you make, as they hope you'll do for them when it's their turn to stand and deliver.

4. **During delivery of your speech, focus on the *message* (your ideas), not the *messenger* (yourself).** By keeping your attention on the ideas you're communicating, you'll be less self-conscious and anxious about the impression you're making on the audience or the audience's impression (evaluation) of you.

Like any fear, fear of public speaking tends to subside after getting your "feet wet" and doing it for the first time. The anticipation of the experience is often worse than the experience itself. Anxious feelings experienced before and during a speech are often replaced by feelings of accomplishment, pride, and self-confidence after the speech is completed.

> "I was really nervous during the entire thing, but I felt so relieved and proud afterwards."
>
> —First-year college student commenting on her first public speech

Chapter Summary and Highlights

This chapter began with a question about what you thought was the difference between acquiring factual knowledge and learning a transferable skill. You may have known the difference before reading this chapter, or discovered it while reading the chapter. Either way, you know now that a transferable skill has more flexibility and versatility than factual knowledge because it can be transferred and applied to a wide variety of situations throughout life. The transferable skills discussed in this chapter—research (information literacy), writing, and speaking—are powerful, durable skills that can be applied across different academic subjects you encounter in college and different career positions you hold after college.

Research, writing, and speaking are also complementary skills that can be used together to achieve educational and professional success. Research skills enable you to acquire high-quality information generated by others. Writing and speaking skills actively engage you with the ideas you acquire through research, and enable you to effectively communicate your interpretation of those ideas as well as your own ideas. Said in another way, *research* skills enable you to locate, evaluate, and integrate information, while *writing* and *speaking* skills enable you to comprehend, communicate, and demonstrate your mastery of that information to others. These three skills have always been important for achieving educational and professional success, but they've become even more important in the current information and communication age, and are more highly valued by today's employers than perhaps at any other time in history.

Work hard at developing the transferable skills discussed in this chapter and take full advantage of the campus resources designed to help you develop these skills. The time and energy you invest in developing your research, writing, and speaking skills will supply you with lifelong benefits.

Learning More through the World Wide Web: Internet-Based Resources

For additional information on research, writing, and oral communication skills, see the following websites:

Information Literacy (Information Search) Strategies:
https://liblearn.osu.edu/tutor/rightstuff.html

Writing Strategies:
www.enhancemywriting.com
http://writingcenter.fas.harvard.edu/pages/strategies-essay-writing

Academic Integrity and Character:
http://www.academicintegrity.org/icai/integrity-1.php
http://www.calea.org/calea-update-magazine/issue-100/who-s-watching-character-and-integrity-21st-century

Public Speaking Skills:
www.public-speaking.org/public-speaking-articles.htm
https://www.hamilton.edu/oralcommunication/tips-for-effective-delivery

References

Academic Integrity at Princeton. (2011). *Examples of plagiarism*. Retrieved from www.princeton.edu/pr/pub/integrity/.

AAC&U (Association of American Colleges and Universities). (2013). *It takes more than a major: Employer priorities for college learning and success*. Washington, DC: Author.

Bean, J. C. (2011). *Engaging ideas: The professor's guide to integrating writing, critical thinking and active learning in the classroom* (2nd ed.). San Francisco: Jossey-Bass.

Boice, R. (1994). *How writers journey to comfort and fluency: psychological adventure*. Westport, CT: Greenwood.

Brewer, G. (2001, March 19). "Snakes top list of Americans' fears: Public speaking, heights and being closed in small spaces also create fear in many Americans." *Gallup News Service*. Retrieved from www.gallup.com/poll/1891/snakes-top-list-americans-fears.aspx.

Brooks, K. (2009). *You majored in what? Mapping your path from chaos to career*. New York: Penguin.

Cairncross, F. C. (2001). *The death of distance: How the communication revolution is changing our lives*. Cambridge, MA: Harvard Business School Press.

Cowan, N. (2001). The magical number 4 in short-term memory: A reconsideration of mental storage capacity. *Behavioral and Brain Sciences, 24*, 87–114.

Croston, G. (2012). The thing we fear more than death. *Psychology Today*. Retrieved from https://www.psychologytoday.com/blog/the-real-story-risk/201211/the-thing-we-fear-more-death.

Ellis, A. (2000). *How to control your anxiety before it controls you*. New York: Citadel Press/Kensington Publishing.

Finn, A. N., Sawyer, C. R., & Behnke, R. R. (2009). A model of anxious arousal for public speaking. *Communication Education, 58*, 417–432.

Friedman, T. L. (2005). *The world is flat: A brief history of the twenty-first century*. New York: Farrar, Straus & Giroux.

Hacker, D., & Fister, B. (2014). *Research and documentation in the electronic age* (6th ed.). Boston: Bedford/St. Martin's.

Hedges, K. (2014). *Six ways to avoid death by PowerPoint*. Retrieved from http://www.forbes.com/sites/work-in-progress/2014/11/14/six-ways-to-avoid-death-by-powerpoint/.

Johansson, J. (2005). *Death by PowerPoint*. Retrieved from http://articles.tech.republic.com5100-22_11-5875608.html.

Knaus, B. (2010). Ten top tips to end writer's procrastination. *Psychology Today* (June 18). Retrieved from https://www.psychologytoday.com/blog/science-and-sensibility/201006/ten-top-tips-end-writer-s-block-procrastination.

Leahy, R. (1990). What the college writing center is—and isn't. *College Teaching, 38*(2), 43–48.

Light, R. L. (1992). *The Harvard assessment seminars, second report*. Cambridge, MA: Harvard University Press.

Light, R. L. (2001). *Making the most of college: Students speak their minds*. Cambridge, MA: Harvard University Press.

Luotto, J. A., Stoll, E. L., & Hoglund-Ketttmann, N. (2001). *Communication skills for collaborative learning* (2nd ed.). Dubuque, IA: Kendall/Hunt.

Murray, D. M. (2004). *Write to learn* (8th ed.). Fort Worth: Harcourt Brace.

National Association of Colleges & Employers. (2014). *Job outlook 2014 survey*. Bethlehem, PA: Author.

National Forum on Information Literacy. (2015). *Information literacy skills*. Retrieved from http://infolit.org/information-literacy-projects-and-programs.

Patchan, M. M., Charney, D., & Schunn, C. D. (2009). A validation study of students' end comments: Comparing comments by students, a writing instructor, and a content instructor. *Journal of Writing Research, 1*(2) 124–152.

Purdue University Online Writing Lab. (2015). *Avoiding plagiarism*. Retrieved from https://owl.english.purdue.edu/owl/resource/589/01/.

Rosenfield, I. (1988). *The invention of memory: A new view of the brain*. New York: Basic Books.

Sapolsky, R. (2004). *Why zebras don't get ulcers*. New York: W. H. Freeman.

The Ten Commandments of PowerPoint Presentations. (2015). Retrieved from http://avalaunchmedia.com/blog/using-power-point-for-presentations.

The University of Texas at El Paso. (2008). *High school writing v. college writing*. Retrieved from http://utminers.utep.edu/omwilliamson/univ1301/high_school_writing_vs.htm.

Thompson, R. F. (1981). Peer grading: Some promising advantages for composition research and the classroom. *Research in the Teaching of English, 15*(2), 172–174.

Wrench, J. S., McCroskey, J. C., & Richmond, V. P. (2008). *Human communication in everyday life: Explanations and applications*. Boston, MA: Allyn & Bacon.

Zinsser, W. (1993). *Writing to learn*. New York: HarperCollins.

Chapter 4 Exercises

4.1 Quote Reflections

Review the sidebar quotes contained in this chapter and select two that were especially meaningful or inspirational to you.

For each quote, provide a three- to five-sentence explanation of why you chose it.

4.2 Reality Bite

Crime and Punishment: Plagiarism and Its Consequences

In an article that appeared in an Ohio newspaper, titled "Plagiarism persists in classrooms," an English professor is quoted as saying: "Technology has made it easier to plagiarize because students can download papers and exchange information and papers through their computers. But technology has also made it easier to catch students who plagiarize." This professor works at a college that subscribes to a website that matches the content of students' papers with content from books and online sources. Many professors now require students to submit their papers through this website. If students are caught plagiarizing, for a first offense, they typically receive an F for the assignment or the course. A second offense can result in dismissal or expulsion from college, which has already happened to a few students.

Reflection and Discussion Questions

1. What do you suspect are the primary motives or reasons why students plagiarize from the web?
2. What would you say is a fair or just penalty for those found guilty of a first plagiarism violation? What do you think would be fair penalty for a second violation?
3. How might web-based plagiarism be minimized or prevented from happening in the first place?

4.3 Internet Research

Go to *www.itools.com/search*. This website allows you to conveniently access multiple search engines, web directories, and newsgroups. Type in the name of a subject or topic you'd like to research and select three of the multiple search engines listed at this site.

1. What differences did you find in the type of information generated by the three search engines?
2. Did any of these search engines locate better or more comprehensive information than the others?
3. Would you return to this website again to help you with future research?

4.4 Is It or Is It Not Plagiarism?

The following four incidents were brought to a judicial review board to determine if plagiarism had occurred and, if so, what the penalty should be. After reading each case, answer the questions listed below it.

CASE 1. A student turned in an essay that included substantial material copied from a published source. The student admitted that he didn't cite the sources properly, but argued that it was because he misunderstood the directions, not because he was attempting to steal someone else's ideas.

Is this plagiarism?

How severe is it? (Rate it on a scale from 1 = low to 5 = high)

What should the consequence or penalty be?

How could the accusation of plagiarism been avoided?

CASE 2. A student turned in a paper that was identical to a paper submitted by another student for a different course.

Is this plagiarism?

How severe is it? (Rate it on a scale from 1 = low to 5 = high)

What should the consequence or penalty be?

How could the accusation of plagiarism been avoided?

CASE 3. A student submitted a paper he wrote in a previous course as an extra credit paper for a course.

Is this plagiarism?

How severe is it? (Rate it on a scale from 1 = low to 5 = high)

What should the consequence or penalty be?

How could the accusation of plagiarism been avoided?

CASE 4. A student submitted a paper in an art history class that contained some ideas from art critics she read about and whose ideas she agreed with. The student didn't cite the critics as sources, but claimed it wasn't plagiarism because their ideas were merely their own subjective judgments or opinions, not facts or findings; furthermore, they were opinions she agreed with.

Is this plagiarism?

How severe is it? (Rate it on a scale from 1 = low to 5 = high)

What should the consequence or penalty be?

How could the accusation of plagiarism been avoided?

Look back at these four cases. Which of them do you think represents the most severe and least severe violation of academic integrity? Why?

4.5 Assessing Your Linguistic Intelligence

1. Complete the MI (Multiple Intelligence) Advantage self-assessment and review your results.
2. What does your report say about your linguistic intelligence?
3. What strengths does the report point out? What areas of development does it suggest?

Survival

A Simulation Game

Name: _____

You and your companions have just survived the crash of a small plane. Both the pilot and co-pilot were killed in the crash. It is mid-January, and you are in Northern Canada. The daily temperature is 25 below zero, and the night time temperature is 40 below zero. There is snow on the ground, and the countryside is wooded with several creeks crisscrossing the area. The nearest town is 20 miles away. You are all dressed in city clothes appropriate for a business meeting. Your group of survivors managed to salvage the following items:

A ball of steel wool
A small ax
A loaded .45-caliber pistol
Can of Crisco shortening
Newspapers (one per person)
Cigarette lighter (without fluid)
Extra shirt and pants for each survivor
20 x 20 ft. piece of heavy-duty canvas
A sectional air map made of plastic
One quart of 100-proof whiskey
A compass
Family-size chocolate bars (one per person)

Your task as a group is to list the above 12 items in order of importance for your survival. List the uses for each. You MUST come to agreement as a group.

Would you go for help or stay with the group?

Explanation

Mid-January is the coldest time of year in Northern Canada. The first problem the survivors face is the preservation of body heat and the protection against its loss. This problem can be solved by building a fire, minimizing movement and exertion, using as much insulation as possible, and constructing a shelter.

The participants have just crash-landed. Many individuals tend to overlook the enormous shock reaction this has on the human body and the deaths of the pilot and co-pilot increases the shock. Decision-making under such circumstances is extremely difficult. Such a situation requires a strong emphasis on the use of reasoning for making decisions and for reducing fear and panic. Shock would be shown in the survivors by feelings of helplessness, loneliness, hopelessness, and fear. These feelings have brought about more fatalities than perhaps any other cause in survival situations. Certainly the state of shock means the movement of the survivors should be at a minimum, and that an attempt to calm them should be made.

Before taking off, a pilot has to file a flight plan which contains vital information such as the course, speed, estimated time of arrival, type of aircraft, and number of passengers. Search-and-rescue operations begin shortly after the failure of a plane to appear at its destination at the estimated time of arrival.

The 20 miles to the nearest town is a long walk under even ideal conditions, particularly if one is not used to walking such distances. In this situation, the walk is even more difficult due to shock, snow, dress, and water barriers. It would mean almost certain death from freezing and exhaustion. At temperatures of minus 25 to minus 40, the loss of body heat through exertion is a very serious matter.

Once the survivors have found ways to keep warm, their next task is to attract the attention of search planes. Thus, all the items the group has salvaged must be assessed for their value in signaling the group's whereabouts.

Rankings

1. Cigarette lighter (without fluid)

The gravest danger facing the group is exposure to cold. The greatest need is for a source of warmth and the second greatest need is for signaling devices. This makes building a fire the first order of business. Without matches, something is needed to produce sparks, and even without fluid, a cigarette lighter can do that.

2. Ball of steel wool

To make a fire, the survivors need a means of catching the sparks made by the cigarette lighter. This is the best substance for catching a spark and supporting a flame, even if the steel wool is a little wet.

3. Extra shirt and pants for each survivor

Besides adding warmth to the body, clothes can also be used for shelter, signaling, bedding, bandages, string (when unraveled), and fuel for the fire.

4. Can of Crisco shortening

This has many uses. A mirror-like signaling device can be made from the lid. After shining the lid with steel wool, it will reflect sunlight and generate 5 to 7 million candlepower. This is bright enough to be seen beyond the horizon. While this could be limited somewhat by the trees, a member of the group could climb a tree and use the mirrored lid to signal search planes. If they had no other means of signaling than this, they would have a better than 80% chance of being rescued within the first day.

There are other uses for this item. It can be rubbed on exposed skin for protection against the cold. When melted into an oil, the shortening is helpful as fuel. When soaked into a piece of cloth, melted shortening will act like a candle. The empty can is useful in melting snow for drinking water. It is much safer to drink warmed water than to eat snow, since warm water will help retain body heat. Water is important because dehydration will affect decision-making. The can is also useful as a cup.

5. 20 x 20 foot piece of canvas

The cold makes shelter necessary, and canvas would protect against wind and snow (canvas is used in making tents). Spread on a frame made of trees, it could be used as a tent or a wind screen. It might also be used as a ground cover to keep the survivors dry. Its shape, when contrasted with the surrounding terrain, makes it a signaling device.

6. Small ax

Survivors need a constant supply of wood in order to maintain the fire. The ax could be used for this as well as for clearing a sheltered campsite, cutting tree branches for ground insulation, and constructing a frame for the canvas tent.

7. Family size chocolate bars (one per person)

Chocolate will provide some food energy. Since it contains mostly carbohydrates, it supplies the energy without making digestive demands on the body.

8. Newspapers (one per person)

These are useful in starting a fire. They can also be used as insulation under clothing when rolled up and placed around a person's arms and legs. A newspaper can also be used as a verbal signaling device when rolled up in a megaphone-shape. It could also provide reading material for recreation.

9. Loaded .45-caliber pistol

The pistol provides a sound-signaling device. (The international distress signal is 3 shots fired in rapid succession). There have been numerous cases of survivors going undetected because they were too weak to make a loud enough noise to attract attention. The butt of the pistol could be used as a hammer, and the powder from the shells will assist in fire building. By placing a small bit of cloth in a cartridge emptied of its bullet, one can start a fire by firing the gun at dry wood on the ground. The pistol also has some serious disadvantages. Anger, frustration, impatience, irritability, and lapses of rationality may increase as the group awaits rescue. The availability of a lethal weapon is a danger to the group under these conditions. Although a pistol could be used in hunting, it would take an expert marksman to kill an animal with it. Then the animal would have to be transported to the crash site, which could prove difficult to impossible depending on its size.

10. Quart of 100 proof whiskey

The only uses of whiskey are as an aid in fire building and as a fuel for a torch (made by soaking a piece of clothing in the whiskey and attaching it to a tree branch). The empty bottle could be used for storing water. The danger of whiskey is that someone might drink it, thinking it would bring warmth. Alcohol takes on the temperature it is exposed to, and a drink of minus 30 degrees Fahrenheit whiskey would freeze a person's esophagus and stomach. Alcohol also dilates the blood vessels in the skin, resulting in chilled blood belong carried back to the heart, resulting in a rapid loss of body heat. Thus, a drunken person is more likely to get hypothermia than a sober person is.

11. Compass

Because a compass might encourage someone to try to walk to the nearest town, it is a dangerous item. Its only redeeming feature is that it could be used as a reflector of sunlight (due to its glass top).

12. Sectional air map made of plastic

This is also among the least desirable of the items because it will encourage individuals to try to walk to the nearest town. It's only useful feature is as a ground cover to keep someone dry.

How to score

Each team should list its top 5 choices in order prior to seeing the answer sheet. To award points, look at the ranking numbers on this answer sheet. Award points to each team's top choices according to the numbers here. For example, the map would earn 12 points, while the steel wool would earn 2 points. Lowest score wins (and survives).

Chapter 5

Diversity

Learning about and from Human Differences

Chapter Preview

This chapter clarifies what "diversity" really means and demonstrates how experiencing diversity can deepen learning, promote critical and creative thinking, and contribute to your personal and professional development. Strategies are provided for overcoming cultural barriers and biases that block the development of rewarding relationships with diverse people and learning from others whose cultural backgrounds differ from our own. Simply stated, we learn more from people that are different from us than we do from people similar to us. There's more diversity among college students today than at any other time in history. This chapter will help you capitalize on this learning opportunity.

Learning Goal

Gain greater appreciation of human differences and develop skills for making the most of diversity in college and beyond.

Integrate your Faith

God's justice is rooted in His love; God's forgiveness toward us is based on Christ accepting the judgment for our unloving actions. How do you think stereotypes and prejudices affect our willingness to forgive wrongs done to us by others?

Ignite Your Thinking

Reflection 5.1

Complete the following sentence:

When I hear the word *diversity*, the first thing that comes to my mind is . . .

From *Thriving in College and Beyond: Research-Based Strategies for Academic Success and Personal Development*, Fourth Edition by Joseph B. Cuseo, Aaron Thompson, Michele Campagna, and Viki S. Fecas. Copyright © 2016 Kendall Hunt Publishing Company. Reprinted by permission.

What Is Diversity?

Literally translated, the word "diversity" derives from the Latin root *diversus*, meaning "various" or "variety." Thus, human diversity refers to the variety that exists in humanity (the human species). The relationship between humanity and diversity may be compared to the relationship between sunlight and the variety of colors that make up the visual spectrum. Similar to how sunlight passing through a prism disperses into the variety of colors that comprise the visual spectrum, the human species on planet earth is dispersed into a variety of different groups that comprise the human spectrum (humanity). **Figure 5.1** illustrates this metaphorical relationship between diversity and humanity.

As depicted in the figure below, human diversity is manifested in a multiplicity of ways, including differences in physical features, national origins, cultural backgrounds, and sexual orientations. Some dimensions of diversity are easily detectable, others are very subtle, and some are invisible.

FIGURE 5.1: Humanity and Diversity

"We are all brothers and sisters. Each face in the rainbow of color that populates our world is precious and special. Each adds to the rich treasure of humanity."

—Morris Dees, civil rights leader and cofounder of the Southern Poverty Law Center

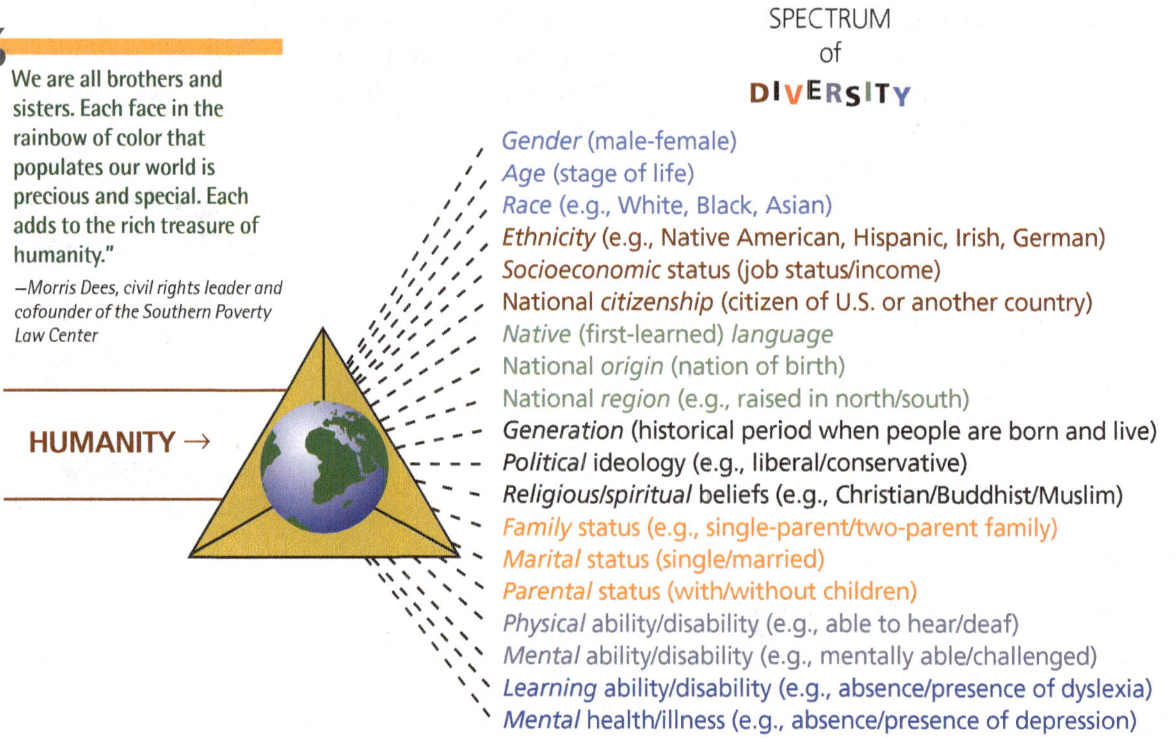

HUMANITY →

SPECTRUM of DIVERSITY

Gender (male-female)
Age (stage of life)
Race (e.g., White, Black, Asian)
Ethnicity (e.g., Native American, Hispanic, Irish, German)
Socioeconomic status (job status/income)
National *citizenship* (citizen of U.S. or another country)
Native (first-learned) *language*
National *origin* (nation of birth)
National *region* (e.g., raised in north/south)
Generation (historical period when people are born and live)
Political ideology (e.g., liberal/conservative)
Religious/spiritual beliefs (e.g., Christian/Buddhist/Muslim)
Family status (e.g., single-parent/two-parent family)
Marital status (single/married)
Parental status (with/without children)
Physical ability/disability (e.g., able to hear/deaf)
Mental ability/disability (e.g., mentally able/challenged)
Learning ability/disability (e.g., absence/presence of dyslexia)
Mental health/illness (e.g., absence/presence of depression)

_ _ _ _ _ _ = dimension of diversity

*This list represents some of the major dimensions of human diversity; it does not constitute a complete list of all possible forms of human diversity. Also, disagreement exists about certain dimensions of diversity (e.g., whether certain groups should be considered races or ethnic groups).

©Kendall Hunt Publishing Company

Reflection 5.2

Look at the diversity spectrum in **Figure 5.1** and look over the list of groups that make up the spectrum. Do you notice any groups missing from the list that should be added, either because they have distinctive backgrounds or because they've been targets of prejudice and discrimination?

Diversity includes discussion of equal rights and social justice for minority groups, but it's a broader concept that involves much more than political issues. In a national survey of American voters, the vast majority of respondents agreed that diversity is more than just "political correctness" (National Survey of Women Voters, 1998). Diversity is also an *educational* issue—an integral element of a college education that contributes to the learning, personal development, and career preparation of *all* students. It enhances the quality of the college experience by bringing multiple perspectives and alternative approaches to *what* is being learned (the content) and *how* it's being learned (the process).

> "Ethnic and cultural diversity is an integral, natural, and normal component of educational experiences for all students."
> —*National Council for Social Studies*

Note

Diversity is a human issue that embraces and benefits all people; it's not a code word for "some" people. Although one major goal of diversity is to promote appreciation and equitable treatment of particular groups of people who've experienced discrimination, it's also a learning experience that strengthens the quality of a college education, career preparation, and leadership potential.

What Is Racial Diversity?

A *racial group (race)* is a group of people who share distinctive physical traits, such as skin color or facial characteristics. The variation in skin color we now see among humans is largely due to biological adaptations that have evolved over thousands of years among groups of humans who migrated to different climatic regions of the world. Currently, the most widely accepted explanation of the geographic origin of modern humans is the "Out of Africa" theory. Genetic studies and fossil evidence indicate that all Homo sapiens inhabited Africa 150,000–250,000 years ago; over time, some migrated from Africa to other parts of the world (Mendez, et al., 2013; Meredith, 2011; Reid & Hetherington, 2010). Darker skin tones developed among humans who inhabited and reproduced in hotter geographical regions nearer the equator (e.g., Africans). Their darker skin color helped them adapt and survive by providing them with better protection from the potentially damaging effects of intense sunlight (Bridgeman, 2003). In contrast, lighter skin tones developed over time among humans inhabiting colder climates that were farther from the equator (e.g., Scandinavia). Their lighter skin color enabled them to absorb greater amounts of vitamin D supplied by sunlight, which was in shorter supply in those regions of the world.

Currently, the U.S. Census Bureau has identified five races (U.S. Census Bureau, 2013b):

White: a person whose lineage may be traced to the original people inhabiting Europe, the Middle East, or North Africa.

Black or African American: a person whose lineage may be traced to the original people inhabiting Africa.

American Indian or Alaska Native: a person whose lineage may be traced to the original people inhabiting North and South America (including Central America), and who continue to maintain their tribal affiliation or attachment.

Asian: a person whose lineage may be traced to the original people inhabiting the Far East, Southeast Asia, or the Indian subcontinent, including: Cambodia, China, India, Japan, Korea, Malaysia, Pakistan, the Philippine Islands, Thailand, and Vietnam.

Native Hawaiian or Other Pacific Islander: a person whose lineage may be traced to the original people inhabiting Hawaii, Guam, Samoa, or other Pacific islands.

It's important to keep in mind that racial categories are not based on scientific evidence; they merely represent group classifications constructed by society (Anderson & Fienberg, 2000). No identifiable set of genes distinguishes one race from another; in fact, there continues to be disagreement among scholars about what groups of people constitute a human race or whether distinctive races actually exist (Wheelright, 2005). In other words, you can't do a blood test or some type of internal genetic test to determine a person's race. Humans have simply decided to categorize themselves into races on the basis of certain external differences in their physical appearance, particularly the color of their outer layer of skin. The U.S. Census Bureau could have decided to divide people into "racial" categories based on other physical characteristics, such as eye color (blue, brown, and green), hair color (brown, black, blonde, or red), or body length (tall, short, or mid-sized).

While humans may display diversity in the color or tone of their external layer of skin, the reality is that all members of the human species are remarkably similar at an internal biological level. More than 98% of the genes of all humans are exactly the same, regardless of what their particular race may be (Bronfenbrenner, 2005). This large amount of genetic overlap accounts for our distinctively "human" appearance, which clearly distinguishes us from all other living species. All humans have internal organs that are similar in structure and function, and despite variations in the color of our outer layer of skin, when it's cut, all humans bleed in the same color.

Categorizing people into distinct racial or ethnic groups is becoming even more difficult because members of different ethnic and racial groups are increasingly forming cross-ethnic and interracial families. By 2050, the number of Americans who identify themselves as being of two or more races is projected to more than triple, growing from 7.5 million to 26.7 million (U.S. Census Bureau, 2013a).

Reflection 5.3

What race(s) do you consider yourself to be?

Would you say you identify strongly with your racial identity, or are you rarely conscious of it? Why?

What Is Cultural Diversity?

"Culture" may be defined as a distinctive pattern of beliefs and values learned by a group of people who share the same social heritage and traditions. In short, culture is the whole way in which a group of people has learned to live (Peoples & Bailey, 2011); it includes their style of speaking (language), fashion, food, art and music, as well as their beliefs and values. **Box 5.1** contains a summary of key components of culture that a group may share.

Box 5.1

Key Components of Culture

Language: How members of the culture communicate through written or spoken words; their particular dialect; and their distinctive style of nonverbal communication (body language).

Space: How cultural members arrange themselves with respect to social–spatial distance (e.g., how closely they stand next to each other when having a conversation).

Time: How the culture conceives of, divides, and uses time (e.g., the speed or pace at which they conduct business).

Aesthetics: How cultural members appreciate and express artistic beauty and creativity (e.g., their style of visual art, culinary art, music, theater, literature, and dance).

Family: The culture's attitudes and habits with respect to interacting with family members (e.g., customary styles of parenting their children and caring for their elderly).

Economics: How the culture meets its members' material needs, and its customary ways of acquiring and distributing wealth (e.g., general level of wealth and gap between the very rich and very poor).

Gender Roles: The culture's expectations for "appropriate" male and female behavior (e.g., whether or not women are able to hold the same leadership positions as men).

Box 5.1 (continued)

Politics: How decision-making power is exercised in the culture (e.g., democratically or autocratically).

Science and Technology: The culture's attitude toward and use of science or technology (e.g., the degree to which the culture is technologically "advanced").

Philosophy: The culture's ideas or views on wisdom, goodness, truth, and social values

(e.g., whether they place greater value on individual competition or collective collaboration).

Spirituality and Religion: Cultural beliefs about a supreme being and an afterlife (e.g., its predominant faith-based views and belief systems about the supernatural).

Reflection 5.4

Look at the components of culture cited in the previous list. Add another aspect of culture to the list that you think is important or influential. Explain why you think this is an important element of culture.

What Is an Ethnic Group?

A group of people who share the same culture is referred to as an *ethnic group*. Thus, "culture" refers to *what* an ethnic group shares in common (e.g., language and traditions) and "ethnic group" refers to the *people* who share the same culture that's been *learned* through common social experiences. Members of the same racial group—whose shared physical characteristics have been *inherited*—may be members of different ethnic groups. For instance, white Americans belong to the same racial group, but differ in terms of their ethnic group (e.g., French, German, Irish) and Asian Americans belong to the same racial group, but are members of different ethnic groups (e.g., Japanese, Chinese, Korean).

Currently, the major cultural (ethnic) groups in the United States include:

- Native Americans (American Indians)
  - Cherokee, Navaho, Hopi, Alaskan natives, Blackfoot, etc.
- European Americans (Whites)
  - Descendents from Western Europe (e.g., United Kingdom, Ireland, Netherlands), Eastern Europe (e.g., Hungary, Romania, Bulgaria), Southern Europe (e.g., Italy, Greece, Portugal), and Northern Europe or Scandinavia (e.g., Denmark, Sweden, Norway)

- African Americans (Blacks)
  - Americans whose cultural roots lie in the continent of Africa (e.g., Ethiopia, Kenya, Nigeria) and the Caribbean Islands (e.g., Bahamas, Cuba, Jamaica)
- Hispanic Americans (Latinos)
  - Americans with cultural roots in Mexico, Puerto Rico, Central America (e.g., El Salvador, Guatemala, Nicaragua), and South America (e.g., Brazil, Columbia, Venezuela)
- Asian Americans
  - Americans whose cultural roots lie in East Asia (e.g., Japan, China, Korea), Southeast Asia (e.g., Vietnam, Thailand, Cambodia), and South Asia (e.g., India, Pakistan, Bangladesh)
- Middle Eastern Americans
  - Americans with cultural roots in Iraq, Iran, Israel, etc.

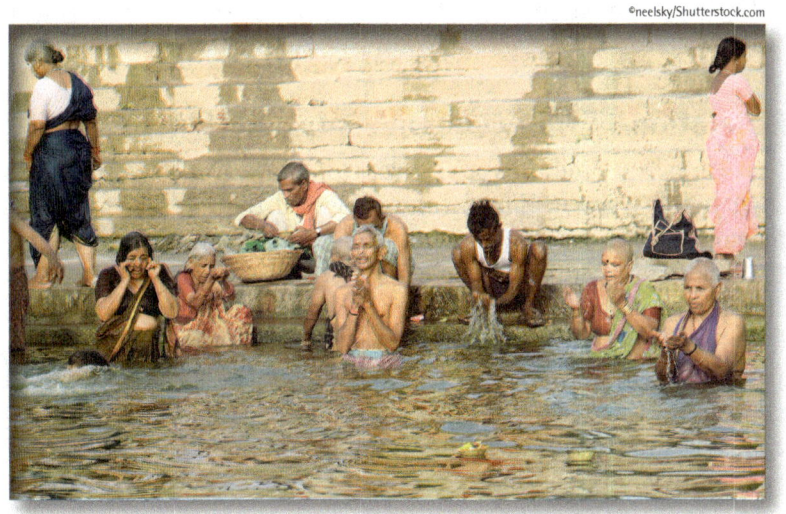

Culture is a distinctive pattern of beliefs and values that develops among a group of people who share the same social heritage and traditions.

Reflection 5.5

What ethnic group(s) are you a member of, or do you identify with? What would you say are the key cultural values shared by your ethnic group(s)?

European Americans are still the majority ethnic group in the United States; they account for more than 50% of the American population.

Native Americans, African Americans, Hispanic Americans, and Asian Americans are considered to be *minority* ethnic groups because each of these groups represents less than 50% of the American population (U.S. Census Bureau, 2015).

As with racial grouping, classifying humans into different ethnic groups can be very arbitrary and subject to debate. Currently, the U.S. Census Bureau classifies Hispanics as an ethnic group rather than a race. However, among Americans who checked "some other race" in the 2000 Census, 97% were Hispanic. This finding suggests that Hispanic Americans consider themselves to be a racial group, probably because that's how they're perceived and treated by non-Hispanics (Cianciotto, 2005). It's noteworthy that the American media used the term "racial profiling" (rather than ethnic profiling) to describe Arizona's controversial 2010 law that allowed police to target Hispanics who "look" like illegal aliens from Mexico, Central America, and South America. Once again, this illustrates how race and ethnicity are subjective, socially constructed concepts that reflect how people perceive and treat different social groups, which, in turn, affects how members of these groups perceive themselves.

> "I'm the only person from my race in class."
> —Hispanic student commenting on why he felt uncomfortable in his class on race, ethnicity, and gender

The Relationship between Diversity and Humanity

As previously noted, diversity represents variations on the same theme: being human. Thus, humanity and diversity are interdependent, complementary concepts. To understand human diversity is to understand both our differences and *similarities*. Diversity appreciation includes appreciating both the unique perspectives of different cultural groups as well as universal aspects of the human experience that are common to all groups—whatever their particular cultural background happens to be. Members of all racial and ethnic groups live in communities, develop personal relationships, have emotional needs, and undergo life experiences that affect their self-esteem and personal identity. Humans of all races and ethnicities experience similar emotions and reveal those emotions with similar facial expressions (see **Figure 5.2**).

Other characteristics that anthropologists have found to be shared by all humans in every corner of the world include: storytelling, poetry, adornment of the body, dance, music, decoration with artifacts, families, socialization of children by elders, a sense of right and wrong, supernatural beliefs, and mourning of the dead (Pinker, 2000). Although different cultural groups may express these shared experiences in different ways, they are universal experiences common to all human cultures.

Chapter 5 Diversity   161

FIGURE 5.2

Humans all over the world display the same facial expressions when experiencing and expressing different emotions. See if you can detect the emotions being expressed in the following faces. (To find the answers, turn your book upside down.)

Answers: The emotions shown. Top, left to right: anger, fear, and sadness. Bottom, left to right: disgust, happiness, and surprise.

All images ©JupiterImages Corporation.

Reflection 5.6

In addition to those already mentioned, can you think of another important human experience that is universal—that is experienced by all humans?

> "We are all the same, and we are all unique."
>
> —Georgia Dunston, African American biologist and research specialist in human genetics

> "We have become not a melting pot but a beautiful mosaic."
>
> —Jimmy Carter, 39th president of the United States and winner of the Nobel Peace Prize

You may have heard the question: "We're all human, aren't we?" The answer to this important question is "yes and no." Yes, we are all the same, but not in the same way. A good metaphor for understanding this apparent contradiction is to visualize humanity as a quilt in which we're all united by the common thread of humanity—the universal bond of being human (much like the quilt below). The different patches comprising the quilt represent diversity—the distinctive or unique cultures that comprise our shared humanity. The quilt metaphor acknowledges the identity and beauty of all cultures. It differs from the old American "melting pot" metaphor, which viewed cultural differences as something to be melted down and eliminated. It also differs from the old "salad bowl" metaphor that depicted America as a hodgepodge or mishmash of cultures thrown together without any common connection. In contrast, the quilt metaphor suggests that the unique cultures of different human groups should be preserved, recognized, and valued; at the same time, these cultural differences join together to form a seamless, unified whole. This blending of diversity and unity is captured in the Latin expression *E pluribus unum* ("Out of many, one")—the motto of the United States—which you'll find printed on all its currency.

Note

When we appreciate diversity in the context of humanity, we capitalize on the variety and versatility of human differences while preserving the collective strength and synergy of human unity.

What Is Individuality?

It's important to keep in mind that there are individual differences among members of any racial or ethnic group that are greater than the average difference between groups. Said in another way, there's more variability (individuality) within groups than between groups. For example, among members of the same racial group, individual differences in their physical attributes (e.g., height and weight) and psychological characteristics (e.g., temperament and personality) are greater than any average difference that may exist between their racial group and other racial groups (Caplan & Caplan, 2008).

Note
While it's valuable to learn about differences between different human groups, there are substantial individual differences among people within the same racial or ethnic group that should neither be ignored nor overlooked. Don't assume that individuals with the same racial or ethnic characteristics share the same personal characteristics.

As you proceed through your college experience, keep the following key distinctions in mind:

- **Humanity.** All humans are members of the *same group*—the human species.
- **Diversity.** All humans are members of *different groups*—such as, different racial and ethnic groups.
- **Individuality.** Each human is a *unique individual* who differs from all other members of any group to which he or she may belong.

> "I realize that I'm black, but I like to be viewed as a person, and this is everybody's wish."
> —Michael Jordan, Hall of Fame basketball player

> "Every human is, at the same time, like all other humans, like some humans, and like no other human."
> —Clyde Kluckhohn, American anthropologist

Major Forms or Types of Diversity in Today's World

Ethnic and Racial Diversity

America is rapidly becoming a more racially and ethnically diverse nation. Minorities now account for almost 37% of the total population—an all-time high; in 2011, for the first time in U.S. history, racial and ethnic minorities made up more than half (50.4%) of all children born in America (Nhan, 2012). By the middle of the 21st century, minority groups are expected to comprise 57% of the American population and more than 60% of the nation's children will be members of minority groups (U.S. Census Bureau, 2015).

More specifically, by 2050 the American population is projected to be more than 29% Hispanic (up from 15% in 2008), 15% Black (up from 13% in 2008), 9.6% Asian (up from 5.3% in 2008), and 2% Native Americans (up from 1.6% in 2008). The Native Hawaiian and Pacific Islander population is expected to more than double between 2008 and 2050. During this same timeframe, the percentage of white Americans will decline from 66% (2008) to 46% (2050). As a result of these demographic trends, today's ethnic and racial minorities will become the "new majority" of Americans by the middle of the 21st century (U.S. Census Bureau, 2015) (see **Figure 5.3**).

The growing racial and ethnic diversity of America's population is reflected in the growing diversity of students enrolled in its colleges and universities. In 1960, whites made up almost 95% of the total college population; in 2010, that percentage had decreased to 61.5%. Between 1976 and 2010, the percentage of ethnic minority students in higher education increased from 17% to 40% (National Center for

Chapter 5 Diversity

FIGURE 5.3: The "New Majority"

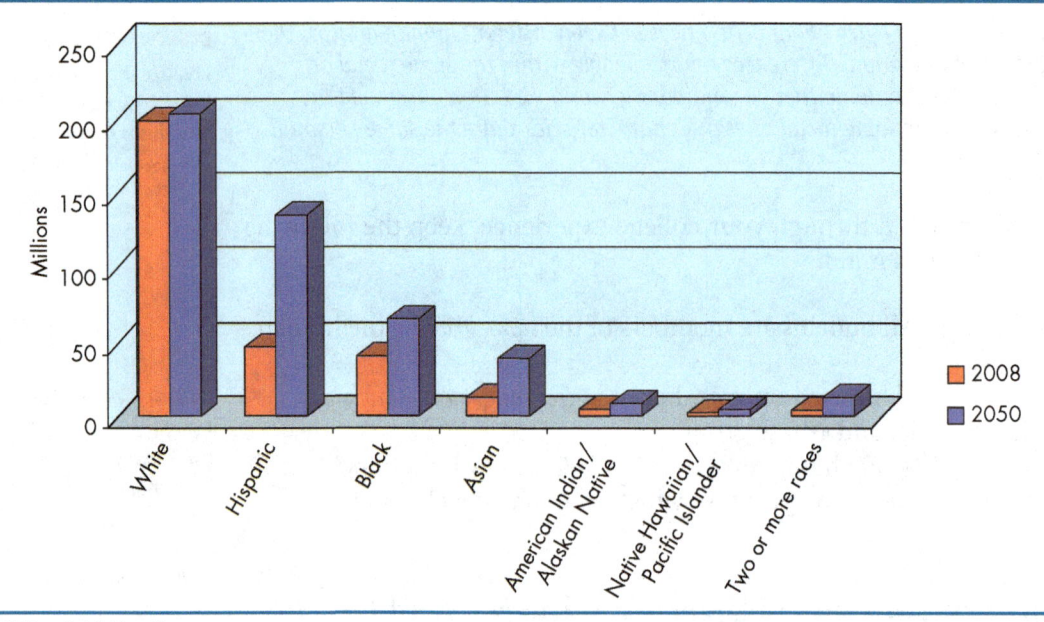

©Kendall Hunt Publishing Company

Education Statistics, 2011). This rise in ethnic and racial diversity on American campuses is particularly noteworthy when viewed in light of the historical treatment of minority groups in the United States. In the early 19th century, education was not a right, but a privilege available only to those who could afford to attend private schools, which was experienced largely by Protestants of European descent (Luhman, 2007).

Reflection 5.7

1. What diverse groups do you see represented on your campus?

2. Are there groups on campus you didn't expect to see or to see in such large numbers?

3. Are there groups on campus you expected to see but don't see or, see in smaller numbers than you expected?

Socioeconomic Diversity

Human diversity also exists among groups of people in terms of their socioeconomic status (SES), which is determined by their level of education, level of income, and the occupational prestige of the jobs they hold. Groups are stratified (divided) into lower, middle, or upper classes, and groups occupying lower social strata have less economic resources and social privileges (Feagin & Feagin, 2007).

Young adults from high-income families are more than seven times likely to have earned a college degree and hold a prestigious job than those from low-income families (Olson, 2007). Sharp discrepancies also exist in income level among different racial, ethnic, and gender groups. In 2012, the median income for non-Hispanic white households was $57,009, compared to $39,005 for Hispanics and $33,321 for African Americans (DeNavas-Walt, Proctor, & Smith, 2013). From 2005 to 2009, household wealth fell by 66% for Hispanics, 53% for blacks, and 16% for whites, largely due to the housing and mortgage collapse—which had a more damaging effect on lower-income families (Kochlar, Fry, & Taylor, 2011).

Despite its overall wealth, the United States is one of the most impoverished of all developed countries in the world (Shah, 2008). The poverty rate in the United States is almost twice the rate of other economically developed countries around the world (Gould & Wething, 2013). In 2012, more than 16% of the American population, and almost 20% of American children, lived below the poverty line ($23,050 yearly income for a family of four) (U.S. Census Bureau, 2013b).

Reflection 5.8

What do you think is the factor that's most responsible for poverty in:

a) the United States?

b) the world?

> "Being born in the elite in the U.S. gives you a constellation of privileges that very few people in the world have ever experienced. Being born poor in the U.S. gives you disadvantages unlike anything in Western Europe, Japan and Canada."
>
> —David I. Levine, economist and social mobility researcher

International Diversity

If it were possible to reduce the world's population to a village of precisely 100 people, with all existing human ratios remaining about the same, the demographics of this world village would look something like this:

61 would be Asians; 13 would be Africans; 12 would be Europeans; 9 would be Latin Americans; and 5 would be North Americans (citizens of the United States and Canada)

50 would be male, 50 would be female
75 would be non-white; 25 white
67 would be non-Christian; 33 would be Christian
80 would live in substandard housing
16 would be unable to read or write
50 would be malnourished and 1 would be dying of starvation
33 would be without access to a safe water supply
39 would lack access to modern sanitation
24 would have no electricity (and of the 76 who have electricity, most would only use it for light at night)
8 people would have access to the Internet
1 would have a college education
1 would have HIV
2 would be near birth; 1 near death
5 would control 32% of the entire world's wealth; all 5 would be U.S. citizens
48 would live on less than $2 a day
20 would live on less than $1 a day (Family Care Foundation, 2015).

In this world village, English would not be the most common language spoken; it would be third, following Chinese and Spanish (Lewis, Paul, & Fennig, 2014).

The need for American college students to develop an appreciation of international diversity is highlighted by a study conducted by an anthropologist who went "undercover" to pose as a student in a university residence hall. She found that the biggest complaint international students had about American students was their lack of knowledge of other countries and the misconceptions they held about people from different nations (Nathan, 2005). When you take the time to learn about other countries and the cultures of people who inhabit them, you move beyond being just a citizen of your own nation, you become *cosmopolitan*—a citizen of the world.

Generational Diversity

Humans are also diverse with respect to the historical time period in which they grew up. The term "generation" refers to a cohort (group) of individuals born during the same period in history whose attitudes, values, and habits have been shaped by events that took place in the world during their formative years of development. People growing up in different generations are likely to develop different attitudes and beliefs because of the different historical events they experienced during their upbringing.

Box 5.2 contains a brief summary of different generations, the key historical events they experienced, and the personal characteristics commonly associated with each generational group (Lancaster, Stillman, & Williams, 2002).

Box 5.2

Generational Diversity: A Snapshot Summary

- **The Traditional Generation (a.k.a. "Silent Generation")** (born 1922–1945). This generation was influenced by events such as the Great Depression and World Wars I and II. Characteristics associated with people growing up at this time include loyalty, patriotism, respect for authority, and conservatism.
- **The Baby Boomer Generation** (born 1946–1964). This generation was influenced by events such as the Vietnam War, Watergate, and the civil rights movement. Characteristics associated with people growing up at this time include idealism, emphasis on self-fulfillment, and concern for social justice and equal rights.
- **Generation X** (born 1965–1980). This generation was influenced by Sesame Street, the creation of MTV, AIDS, and soaring divorce rates. They were the first "latchkey children"—youngsters who used their own key to let themselves into their home after school—because their mother (or single mother) was working outside the home. Characteristics associated with people growing up at this time include self-reliance, resourcefulness, and ability to adapt to change.
- **Generation Y (a.k.a. "Millennials")** (born 1981–2002). This generation was influenced by the September 11, 2001, terrorist attack on the United States, the shooting of students at Columbine High School, and the collapse of the Enron Corporation. Characteristics associated with people growing up at this time include a preference for working and playing in groups, familiarity with technology, and willingness to engage in volunteer service in their community (the "civic generation"). This is also the most ethnically diverse generation, which may explain why they're more open to diversity than previous generations and are more likely to view diversity positively.

> "You guys [in the media] have to get used to it. This is a new day and age, and for my generation that's a very common word. It's like saying 'bro.' That's how we address our friends. That's how we talk."
>
> —Matt Barnes, 33-year-old, biracial professional basketball player, explaining to reporters after being fined for using the word "niggas" in a tweet to some of his African American teammates

- **Generation Z (a.k.a. "The iGeneration")** (born 1994–present). This generation includes the latter half of Generation Y. They grew up during the wars in Afghanistan and Iraq, terrorism, the global recession and climate change. Consequently, they have less trust in political systems and industrial corporations than previous generations. During their formative years, the world wide web was in place, so they're quite comfortable with technology and rely heavily on the Internet, Wikipedia, Google, Twitter, MySpace, Facebook, Instant Messaging, image boards, and YouTube. They expect immediate gratification through technology and accept the lack of privacy associated with social networking. For these reasons, they're also referred to as the "digital generation."

Reflection 5.9

Look back at the characteristics associated with your generation. Which of these characteristics accurately reflect your personal characteristics and those of your closest friends? Which do not?

The Benefits of Experiencing Diversity

Thus far, this chapter has focused on *what* diversity is; we now turn to *why* diversity is worth experiencing. National surveys show that by the end of their first year in college, almost two-thirds of students report "stronger" or "much stronger" knowledge of people from different races and cultures than they had when they first began college, and the majority of them became more open to diverse cultures, viewpoints and values (HERI, 2013, 2014). Students who develop more openness to and knowledge of diversity are likely to experience the following benefits.

Diversity Increases Self-Awareness and Self-Knowledge

Interacting with people from diverse backgrounds increases self-knowledge and self-awareness by enabling you to compare your life experiences with others whose experiences may differ sharply from your own. When you step outside yourself to contrast your experiences with others from different backgrounds, you move beyond ethnocentrism and gain a *comparative perspective*—a reference point that positions you to see how your particular cultural background has shaped the person you are today.

A comparative perspective also enables us to learn how our cultural background has advantaged or disadvantaged us. For instance, learning about cross-cultural differences in education makes us aware of the limited opportunities people in other countries have to attend college and how advantaged we are in America—where a college education is available to everyone, regardless of their race, gender, age, or prior academic history.

> "It is difficult to see the picture when you are inside the frame."
> —An old saying (author unknown)

Note
The more you learn from people who are different than yourself, the more you learn about yourself.

Diversity Deepens Learning

Research consistently shows that we learn more from people who differ from us than we do from people similar to us (Pascarella, 2001; Pascarella & Terenzini, 2005). Learning about different cultures and interacting with people from diverse cultural groups provides our brain with more varied routes or pathways through which to connect (learn) new ideas. Experiencing diversity "stretches" the brain beyond its normal "comfort zone," requiring it to work harder to assimilate something unfamiliar. When we encounter the unfamiliar, the brain has to engage in extra effort to understand it by comparing and contrasting it to something we already know (Acredolo & O'Connor, 1991; Nagda, Gurin, & Johnson, 2005). This added expenditure of mental energy results in the brain forming neurological connections that are deeper and more durable (Willis, 2006). Simply stated, humans learn more from diversity than they do from similarity or familiarity. In contrast, when we restrict the diversity of people with whom we interact (out of habit or prejudice), we limit the breadth and depth of our learning.

Diversity Promotes Critical Thinking

Studies show that students who experience high levels of exposure to various forms of diversity while in college—such as participating in multicultural courses and campus events and interacting with peers from different ethnic backgrounds—report the greatest gains in:

- thinking *complexly*—ability to think about all parts and sides of an issue (Association of American Colleges & Universities, 2004; Gurin, 1999),
- *reflective* thinking—ability to think deeply about personal and global issues (Kitchener, Wood, & Jensen, 2000), and
- *critical* thinking—ability to evaluate the validity of their own reasoning and the reasoning of others (Gorski, 1995–2009; Pascarella, et al., 2001).

These findings are likely explained by the fact that when we're exposed to perspectives that differ from our own, we experience "cognitive dissonance"—a state of cognitive (mental) disequilibrium or imbalance that "forces" our mind to consider multiple perspectives simultaneously; this makes our thinking less simplistic, more complex, and more comprehensive (Brookfield, 1987; Gorski, 1995–2009).

> "When the only tool you have is a hammer, you tend to see every problem as a nail."
>
> —Abraham Maslow, humanistic psychologist, best known for his self-actualization theory of human motivation

Diversity Stimulates Creative Thinking

Cross-cultural knowledge and experiences enhance personal creativity (Leung, et al., 2008; Maddux & Galinsky, 2009). When we have diverse perspectives at our disposal, we have more opportunities to shift perspectives and discover "multiple partial solutions" to problems (Kelly, 1994). Furthermore, ideas acquired from diverse people and cultures can "cross-fertilize," giving birth to new ideas for tackling old problems (Harris, 2010). Research shows that when ideas are generated freely and exchanged openly in groups comprised of people from diverse backgrounds, powerful "cross-stimulation" effects can occur, whereby ideas from one

> "What I look for in musicians is generosity. There is so much to learn from each other and about each other's culture. Great creativity begins with tolerance."
>
> —Yo-Yo Ma, French-born, Chinese-American virtuoso cellist, composer, and winner of multiple Grammy Awards

group member trigger new ideas among other group members (Brown, Dane, & Durham, 1998). Research also indicates that seeking out diverse alternatives, perspectives, and viewpoints enhances our ability to reach personal goals (Stoltz, 2014).

Note
By drawing on ideas generated by people from diverse backgrounds and bouncing your ideas off them, divergent or expansive thinking is stimulated; this leads to synergy *(multiplication of ideas) and* serendipity *(unexpected discoveries).*

In contrast, when different cultural perspectives are neither sought nor valued, the variety of lenses available to us for viewing problems is reduced, which, in turn, reduces our capacity to think creatively. Ideas are less likely to diverge (go in different directions); instead, they're more likely to converge and merge into the same cultural channel—the one shared by the homogeneous group of people doing the thinking.

Diversity Enhances Career Preparation and Career Success

Whatever line of work you decide to pursue, you're likely to find yourself working with employers, coworkers, customers, and clients from diverse cultural backgrounds. America's workforce is now more diverse than at any other time in history and will grow ever more diverse throughout the 21st century; by 2050, the proportion of American workers from minority ethnic and racial groups will jump to 55% (U.S. Census Bureau, 2008).

National surveys reveal that policymakers, business leaders, and employers seek college graduates who are more than just "aware" of or "tolerant" of diversity. They want graduates who have actual *experience* with diversity (Education Commission of the States, 1995) and are able to collaborate with diverse coworkers, clients, and customers (Association of American Colleges & Universities, 2002; Hart Research Associates, 2013). Over 90% of employers agree that all students should have experiences in college that teach them how to solve problems with people whose views differ from their own (Hart Research Associates, 2013).

The current "global economy" also requires skills relating to international diversity. Today's work world is characterized by economic interdependence among nations, international trading (imports/exports), multinational corporations, international travel, and almost instantaneous worldwide communication—due to rapid advances in the world wide web (Dryden & Vos, 1999; Friedman, 2005). Even smaller companies and corporations have become increasingly international in nature (Brooks, 2009). As a result, employers in all sectors of the economy now seek job candidates who possess the following skills and attributes: sensitivity to human differences, ability to understand and relate to people from different cultural backgrounds, international knowledge, and ability to communicate in a second language (Fixman, 1990; National

> "When all men think alike, no one thinks very much."
> —Walter Lippmann, distinguished journalist and originator of the term "stereotype"

> "The benefits that accrue to college students who are exposed to racial and ethnic diversity during their education carry over in the work environment. The improved ability to think critically, to understand issues from different points of view, and to collaborate harmoniously with co-workers from a range of cultural backgrounds all enhance a graduate's ability to contribute to his or her company's growth and productivity."
> —Business/Higher Education Forum

Association of Colleges & Employers, 2014; Office of Research, 1994; Hart Research Associates, 2013).

As a result of these domestic and international trends, *intercultural competence* has become an essential skill for success in the 21st century (Thompson & Cuseo, 2014). Intercultural competence may be defined as the ability to appreciate and learn from human differences and to interact effectively with people from diverse cultural backgrounds. It includes "knowledge of cultures and cultural practices (one's own and others), complex cognitive skills for decision making in intercultural contexts, social skills to function effectively in diverse groups, and personal attributes that include flexibility and openness to new ideas" (Wabash National Study of Liberal Arts Education, 2007).

> "Technology and advanced communications have transformed the world into a global community, with business colleagues and competitors as likely to live in India as in Indianapolis. In this environment, people need a deeper understanding of the thinking, motivations, and actions of different cultures, countries and regions."
>
> —The Partnership for 21st Century Skills

Reflection 5.10

What intercultural skills do you think you already possess?

What intercultural skills do you think you need to develop?

Note

The wealth of diversity on college campuses today represents an unprecedented educational opportunity. You may never again be a member of a community with so many people from such a wide variety of backgrounds. Seize this opportunity to strengthen your education and career preparation.

Overcoming Barriers to Diversity

Before we can capitalize on the benefits of diversity, we need to overcome obstacles that have long impeded our ability to appreciate and seek out diversity. These major impediments are discussed below.

Ethnocentrism

A major advantage of culture is that it builds group solidarity, binding its members into a supportive, tight-knit community. Unfortunately, culture not only binds us, it can also blind us from taking different cultural perspectives. Since culture shapes thought and perception, people from the same ethnic (cultural) group run the risk of becoming *ethnocentric*—centered on their own culture to such a degree they view the world solely through their own cultural lens (frame of reference) and fail to consider or appreciate other cultural perspectives (Colombo, Cullen, & Lisle, 2013).

Optical illusions are a good example of how our particular cultural perspective can influence (and distort) our perceptions. Compare the lengths of the two lines in **Figure 5.4**. If you perceive the line on the right

FIGURE 5.4:
Optical Illusion

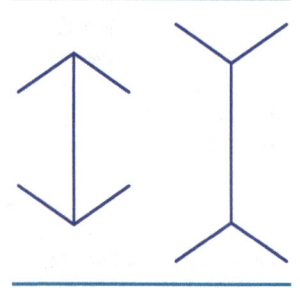

©Kendall Hunt Publishing Company

People whose cultural experiences involve living and working in circular structures would not be fooled by the optical illusion in Figure 5.4.

to be longer than the one on the left, your perception has been shaped by Western culture. People from Western cultures, such as Americans, perceive the line on the right to be longer. However, both lines are actually equal in length. (If you don't believe it, take out a ruler and measure them.) Interestingly, this perceptual error isn't made by people from non-Western cultures—whose living spaces and architectural structures are predominantly circular (e.g., huts or igloos)—in contrast to rectangular-shaped buildings with angled corners that typify Western cultures.

The optical illusion depicted in Figure 5.4 is just one of a number of illusions experienced by people in certain cultures, but not others (Shiraev & Levy, 2013). Cross-cultural differences in susceptibility to optical illusions illustrate how strongly our cultural experiences can influence and sometimes misinform our perception of reality. People think they are seeing things objectively (as they actually are) but they're really seeing things subjectively—as viewed from their particular cultural perspective.

If our cultural experience can influence our perception of the physical world, it can certainly shape our perception of social events and political issues. Research in psychology indicates that the more exposure humans have to somebody or something, the more familiar it becomes and the more likely it will be perceived positively and judged favorably. The effect of familiarity is so prevalent and powerful that social psychologists have come to call it the "familiarity principle"—that is, what is familiar is perceived as better or more acceptable (Zajonc, 1968, 1970, 2001). Thus, we need to be mindful that the familiarity of our cultural experiences can bias us toward seeing our culture as normal or better. By remaining open to the viewpoints of people who perceive the world from different cultural vantage points, we minimize our cultural blind spots, expand our range of perception, and position ourselves to perceive the world with greater clarity and cultural sensitivity.

Stereotyping

"Stereotype" derives from two different roots: *stereo*—to look at in a fixed way—and *type*—to categorize or group together, as in the word "typical." Thus, to stereotype is to view individuals of the same type (group) in the same (fixed) way.

Stereotyping overlooks or disregards individuality; all people sharing the same group characteristic (e.g., race or gender) are viewed as having the same personal characteristics—as in the expression: "You know how they are; they're all alike." Stereotypes can also involve *bias*—literally meaning "slant"—a slant that can tilt toward the positive or the negative. Positive bias results in favorable stereotypes (e.g., "Asians are great in science and math"); negative bias leads to unfavorable stereotypes (e.g., "Asians are nerds who do nothing but study"). Here are some other examples of negative stereotypes:

- Muslims are religious terrorists.
- Whites can't jump (or dance).
- Blacks are lazy.
- Jews are cheap.
- Women are weak.

While few people would agree with these crass stereotypes, overgeneralizations are often made about members of certain groups. Such negative overgeneralizations malign the group's reputation, rob group members of their individuality, and can weaken their self-esteem and self-confidence (as illustrated by the following experience).

©Kendall Hunt Publishing Company

Whether you are male or female, don't let gender stereotypes limit your career options.

Reflection 5.11

1. Have you ever been stereotyped based on your appearance or group membership? If so, what was the stereotype and how did it make you feel?

2. Have you ever unintentionally perceived or treated a person in terms of a group stereotype rather than as an individual? What assumptions did you make about that person? Was that person aware of, or affected by, your stereotyping?

Prejudice

If all members of a stereotyped group are judged and evaluated in a negative way, the result is *prejudice*. The word "prejudice" literally means to "pre-judge." Typically, the prejudgment is negative and involves *stigmatizing*—ascribing inferior or unfavorable traits to people who belong to the same group. Thus, prejudice may be defined as a negative stereotype held about a group of people that's formed before the facts are known.

People who hold a group prejudice typically avoid contact with members of that group. This enables the prejudice to continue unchallenged because there's little opportunity for the prejudiced person to have a positive experience with members of the stigmatized group that could contradict or disprove the prejudice. Thus, a vicious cycle is established in which the prejudiced person continues to avoid contact with individuals from the stigmatized group; this, in turn, continues to maintain and reinforce the prejudice.

Once prejudice has been formed, it often remains intact and resistant to change through the psychological process of *selective perception*—the tendency for biased (prejudiced) people to see what they *expect* to see and fail to see what contradicts their bias (Hugenberg & Bodenhausen, 2003). Have you ever noticed how fans rooting for their favorite sports team tend to focus on and "see" the calls of referees that go against their own team, but don't seem to react (or even notice) the calls that go against the opposing team? This is a classic example of selective perception. In effect, selective perception transforms the old adage, "seeing is believing," into "believing is seeing." This can lead prejudiced people to focus their attention on information that's consistent with their prejudgment, causing them to "see" what supports or reinforces it and fail to see information that contradicts it.

Making matters worse, selective perception is often accompanied by *selective memory*—the tendency to remember information that's consistent with one's prejudicial belief and to forget information that's inconsistent with it or contradicts it (Judd, Ryan, & Parke, 1991). The mental processes of selective perception and selective memory often work together

> "See that man over there? Yes. Well, I hate him. But you don't know him. That's why I hate him."
> —Gordon Allport, influential social psychologist and author of The Nature of Prejudice

> "We see what is behind our eyes."
> —Chinese proverb

and often work *unconsciously*. As a result, prejudiced people may not even be aware they're using these biased mental processes or realize how these processes are keeping their prejudice permanently intact (Baron, Byrne, & Brauscombe, 2008).

Reflection 5.12

Have you witnessed selective perception or selective memory—people seeing or recalling what they believe is true (due to bias), rather than what's actually true? What happened and why do you think it happened?

Discrimination

Literally translated, the term *discrimination* means "division" or "separation." Whereas prejudice involves a belief, attitude or opinion, discrimination involves an *act* or *behavior*. Technically, discrimination can be either positive or negative. A discriminating eater may only eat healthy foods, which is a positive quality. However, discrimination is most often associated with a harmful act that results in a prejudiced person treating another individual, or group of individuals, in an unfair manner. Thus, it could be said that discrimination is prejudice put into action. For instance, to fire or not hire people on the basis of their race or gender is an act of discrimination.

Box 5.3 below contains a summary of the major forms of discrimination, prejudice, and stereotypes that have plagued humanity. As you read through the following list, place a check mark next to any item that you, a friend, or family member has experienced.

Box 5.3

Stereotypes, Prejudices, and Forms of Discrimination: A Snapshot Summary

- **Ethnocentrism**: viewing one's own culture or ethnic group as "central" or "normal," while viewing different cultures as "deficient" or "inferior."

    Example: Viewing another culture as "abnormal" or "uncivilized" because its members eat animals our culture views as unacceptable to eat, although we eat animals their culture views as unacceptable to eat.

- **Stereotyping**: viewing all (or virtually all) members of the same group in the same way—as having the same personal qualities or characteristics.

    Example: "If you're Italian, you must be in the Mafia, or have a family member who is."

- **Prejudice**: negative prejudgment about another group of people.

    Example: Women can't be effective leaders because they're too emotional.

- **Discrimination**: unequal and unfair treatment of a person or group of people—prejudice put into action.

Box 5.3 (continued)

Example: Paying women less than men for performing the same job, even though they have the same level of education and job qualifications.

- **Segregation:** intentional decision made by a group to separate itself (socially or physically) from another group.

  Example: "White flight"—white people moving out of neighborhoods when people of color move in.

- **Racism:** belief that one's racial group is superior to another group and expressing that belief in attitude (prejudice) or action (discrimination).

  Example: Confiscating land from American Indians based on the unfounded belief that they are "uncivilized" or "savages."

> "Let us all hope that the dark clouds of racial prejudice will soon pass away and ... in some not too distant tomorrow the radiant stars of love and brotherhood will shine over our great nation."
> —Martin Luther King, Jr., Civil rights leader, humanitarian, and youngest recipient of the Nobel Peace Prize

- **Institutional Racism:** racial discrimination rooted in organizational policies and practices that disadvantage certain racial groups.

  Example: Race-based discrimination in mortgage lending, housing, and bank loans.

- **Racial Profiling:** investigating or arresting someone solely on the basis of the person's race, ethnicity, or national origin—without witnessing actual criminal behavior or possessing incriminating evidence.

  Example: Police making a traffic stop or conducting a personal search based solely on an individual's racial features.

- **Slavery:** forced labor in which people are considered to be property, held against their will, and deprived of the right to receive wages.

  Example: Enslavement of Blacks, which was legal in the United States until 1865.

- **"Jim Crow" Laws:** formal and informal laws created by whites to segregate Blacks after the abolition of slavery.

  Example: Laws in certain parts of the United States that once required Blacks to use separate bathrooms and be educated in separate schools.

- **Apartheid:** an institutionalized system of "legal racism" supported by a nation's government. (Apartheid derives from a word in the Afrikaan language, meaning "apartness.")

  Example: South Africa's national system of racial segregation and discrimination that was in place from 1948 to 1994.

> "Never, never, and never again shall it be that this beautiful land will again experience the oppression of one by another."
> —Nelson Mandela, anti-apartheid revolutionary, first Black president of South Africa after apartheid, and winner of the Nobel Peace Prize

- **Hate Crimes:** criminal action motivated solely by prejudice toward the crime victim.

  Example: Acts of vandalism or assault aimed at members of a particular ethnic group or gender.

- **Hate Groups:** organizations whose primary purpose is to stimulate prejudice, discrimination, or aggression toward certain groups of people based on their ethnicity, race, religion, etc.

  Example: The Ku Klux Klan—an American terrorist group that perpetrates hatred toward all non-white races.

- **Genocide:** mass murdering of a particular ethnic or racial group.

  Example: The Holocaust, in which millions of Jews were systematically murdered during World War II. Other examples include the murdering of Cambodians under the Khmer Rouge regime, the murdering of Bosnian Muslims in the former country of Yugoslavia, and the slaughter of the Tutsi minority by the Hutu majority in Rwanda.

Box 5.3 (continued)

- **Classism:** prejudice or discrimination based on social class, particularly toward people of lower socioeconomic status.

  Example: Acknowledging the contributions made by politicians and wealthy industrialists to America, while ignoring the contributions of poor immigrants, farmers, slaves, and pioneer women.

- **Religious Intolerance:** denying the fundamental human right of people to hold religious beliefs, or to hold religious beliefs that differ from one's own.

  Example: An atheist who forces nonreligious (secular) beliefs on others, or a member of a religious group who believes that people who hold different religious beliefs are infidels or "sinners" whose souls will not be saved.

> "Rivers, ponds, lakes and streams—they all have different names, but they all contain water. Just as religions do—
> they all contain truths."
> —Muhammad Ali, three-time world heavyweight boxing champion, member of the International Boxing Hall of Fame, and recipient of the Spirit of America Award as the most recognized American in the world

- **Anti-Semitism:** prejudice or discrimination toward Jews or people who practice the religion of Judaism.

  Example: Disliking Jews because they're the ones who "killed Christ."

- **Xenophobia:** fear or hatred of foreigners, outsiders, or strangers.

  Example: Believing that immigrants should be banned from entering the country because they'll undermine our economy and increase our crime rate.

- **Regional Bias:** prejudice or discrimination based on the geographical region in which an individual is born and raised.

  Example: A northerner thinking that all southerners are racists.

- **Jingoism:** excessive interest and belief in the superiority of one's own nation—without acknowledging its mistakes or weaknesses—often accompanied by an aggressive foreign policy that neglects the needs of other nations or the common needs of all nations.

  Example: "Blind patriotism"—failure to see the shortcomings of one's own nation and viewing any questioning or criticism of one's own nation as being disloyal or "unpatriotic." (As in the slogan, "America: right or wrong" or "America: love it or leave it!")

> "Above all nations is humanity."
> —Motto of the University of Hawaii

- **Terrorism:** intentional acts of violence committed against civilians that are motivated by political or religious prejudice.

  Example: The September 11, 2001, attacks on the United States.

- **Sexism:** prejudice or discrimination based on sex or gender.

  Example: Believing that women should not pursue careers in fields traditionally filled only by men (e.g., engineering or politics) because they lack the innate qualities or natural skills to do so.

- **Ageism:** prejudice or discrimination toward certain age groups, particularly toward the elderly.

  Example: Believing that all "old" people have dementia and shouldn't be allowed to drive or make important decisions.

- **Ableism:** prejudice or discrimination toward people who are disabled or handicapped (physically, mentally, or emotionally).

  Example: Intentionally avoiding social contact with people in wheelchairs.

Reflection 5.13

As you read through the above list, did you, a friend, or family member experience any of the form(s) of prejudice listed?

If yes, what happened and why do you think it happened?

> "I grew up in a very racist family. Even just a year ago, I could honestly say 'I hate Asians' with a straight face and mean it. My senior AP language teacher tried hard to teach me not to be judgmental. He got me to be open to others, so much so that my current boyfriend is half Chinese."
>
> —First-year college student

> "Stop judging by mere appearances, and make a right judgment."
>
> —Bible, John 7:24

> "You can't judge a book by the cover."
>
> —1962 hit song by Elias Bates, a.k.a. Bo Diddley (Note: a "bo diddley" is a one-stringed African guitar)

Strategies for Overcoming Stereotypes and Prejudices

We may hold prejudices, stereotypes, or subtle biases that bubble beneath the surface of our conscious awareness. The following practices and strategies can help us become more aware of our unconscious biases and relate more effectively to individuals from diverse groups.

Consciously avoid preoccupation with physical appearances. Remember the old proverb: "It's what inside that counts." Judge others by the quality of their inner qualities, not by the familiarity of their outer features. Get beneath the superficial surface of appearances and relate to people not in terms of how they look but who they are and how they act.

Form impressions of others on a person-to-person basis, not on the basis of their group membership. This may seem like an obvious and easy thing to do, but research shows that humans have a natural tendency to perceive individuals from unfamiliar groups as being more alike (or all alike) than members of their own group (Taylor, Peplau, & Sears, 2006). Thus, we need to remain mindful of this tendency and make a conscious effort to perceive and treat individuals of diverse groups as unique human beings, not according to some general (stereotypical) rule of thumb.

Note

It's valuable to learn about different cultures and the common characteristics shared by members of the same culture; however, this shouldn't be done while ignoring individual differences. Don't assume that all individuals who share the same cultural background share the same personal characteristics.

Reflection 5.14

Your comfort level while interacting with people from diverse groups is likely to depend on how much prior experience you've had with members of those groups. Rate the amount or variety of diversity you have experienced in the following settings:

> "I am very happy with the diversity here, but it also frightens me. I have never been in a situation where I have met people who are Jewish, Muslim, atheist, born-again, and many more."
>
> —First-year student (quoted in Erickson, Peters, & Strommer, 2006)

1. The high school you attended	high	moderate	low
2. The college or university you now attend	high	moderate	low
3. The neighborhood in which you grew up	high	moderate	low
4. Places where you have been employed	high	moderate	low

Which setting had the most and the least diversity?

What do you think accounted for this difference?

(Review your results from the My MI Advantage Inventory. How might the recommendations you received about your interpersonal skills enable you to become more adept at connecting with people from cultural backgrounds that are different from your own?)

> "Empirical evidence shows that the actual effects on student development of emphasizing diversity and of student participation in diversity activities are overwhelmingly positive."
> —Alexander Astin, What Matters in College

> "The classroom can provide a 'public place' where community can be practiced."
> —Susanne Morse, Renewing Civic Capacity: Preparing College Students for Service and Citizenship

Box 5.4

Tips for Teamwork: Creating Diverse and Effective Learning Teams

1. **Intentionally form learning teams with students who have different cultural backgrounds and life experiences.** Teaming up only with friends or classmates whose backgrounds and experiences are similar to yours can actually impair your team's performance because teammates can get off track and onto topics that have nothing to do with the learning task (e.g., what they did last weekend or what they're planning to do next weekend).

2. **Before jumping into group work, take some time to interact informally with your teammates.** When team members have some social "warm up" time (e.g., time to learn each other's names and learn something about each other), they feel more comfortable expressing their ideas and are more likely to develop a stronger sense of team identity. This feeling of group solidarity can create a foundation of trust among group members, enabling them to work together as a team, particularly if they come from diverse (and unfamiliar) cultural backgrounds.

    The context in which a group interacts can influence the openness and harmony of their interaction. Group members are more likely to interact openly and collaboratively when they work in a friendly, informal environment that's conducive to relationship building. A living room or a lounge area provides a warmer and friendlier team-learning atmosphere than a sterile classroom.

3. **Have teammates work together to complete a single work product.** One jointly created product serves to highlight the team's collaborative effort and collective achievement (e.g., a completed sheet of answers to questions, or a comprehensive list of ideas). Creating a common final product helps keep individuals thinking in terms of "we" (not "me") and keeps the team moving in the same direction toward the same goal.

Box 5.4 *(continued)*

4. **Group members should work interdependently—they should depend on each other to reach their common goal and each member should have equal opportunity to contribute to the team's final product.** Each teammate should take responsibility for making an indispensable contribution to the team's end product, such as contributing: (a) a different piece of *information* (e.g., a specific chapter from the textbook or a particular section of class notes), (b) a particular form of *thinking* to the learning task (e.g., analysis, synthesis, or application), or (c) a different *perspective* (e.g., national, international, or global). Said in another way, each group member should assume personal responsibility for a piece that's needed to complete the whole puzzle.

    Similar to a sports team, each member of a learning team should have a specific role to play. For instance, each teammate could perform one of the following roles:

    - manager—whose role is to assure that the team stays on track and keeps moving toward its goal;
    - moderator—whose role is to ensure that all teammates have equal opportunity to contribute;
    - summarizer—whose role is to monitor the team's progress, identifying what has been accomplished and what still needs to be done;
    - recorder—whose role is to keep a written record of the team's ideas.

5. **After concluding work in diverse learning teams, take time to reflect on the experience.** The final step in any learning process, whether it be learning from a lecture or learning from a group discussion, is to step back from the process and thoughtfully review it. Deep learning requires not only effortful action but also thoughtful reflection (Bligh, 2000; Roediger, Dudai, & Fitzpatrick, 2007). You can reflect on your experiences with diverse learning groups by asking yourself questions that prompt you to process the ideas shared by members of your group and the impact those ideas had on you. For instance, ask yourself (and your teammates) the following questions:

    - What major similarities in viewpoints did all group members share? (What were the common themes?)
    - What major differences of opinion were expressed by diverse members of our group? (What were the variations on the themes?)
    - Were there particular topics or issues raised during the discussion that provoked intense reactions or emotional responses from certain members of our group?
    - Did the group discussion lead any individuals to change their mind about an idea or position they originally held?

    When contact among people from diverse groups takes place under the five conditions described in this box, group work is transformed into *teamwork* and promotes higher levels of thinking and deeper appreciation of diversity. A win–win scenario is created: Learning and thinking are strengthened while bias and prejudice are weakened (Allport, 1979; Amir, 1969; Aronson, Wilson, & Akert, 2013; Cook, 1984; Sherif, et al., 1961).

Reflection 5.15

Have you had an experience with a member of an unfamiliar racial or cultural group that caused you to change your attitude or viewpoint toward that group?

Take a stand against prejudice or discrimination by constructively disagreeing with students who make stereotypical statements and prejudicial remarks. By saying nothing, you may avoid conflict, but your silence may be perceived by others to mean that you agree with the person who made the prejudicial remark. Studies show that when members of the same group observe another member of their own group making prejudicial comments, prejudice tends to increase among all group members—probably due to peer pressure of group conformity (Stangor, Sechrist, & Jost, 2001). In contrast, if a person's prejudicial remark is challenged by a member of one's own group, particularly a fellow member who is liked and respected, that person's prejudice decreases along with similar prejudices held by other members of the group (Baron, et al., 2008). Thus, by taking a leadership role and challenging peers who make prejudicial remarks, you're likely to reduce that person's prejudice as well as the prejudice of others who hear the remark. In addition, you help create a campus climate in which students experience greater satisfaction with their college experience and are more likely to complete their college degree. Studies show that a campus climate which is hostile toward students from minority groups lowers students' level of college satisfaction and college completion rates of both minority and majority students (Cabrera, et al., 1999; Eimers & Pike, 1997; Nora & Cabrera, 1996).

Note

By actively opposing prejudice on campus, you demonstrate diversity leadership and moral character. You become a role model whose actions send a clear message that valuing diversity is not only the smart thing to do, it's the right *thing to do.*

Reflection 5.16

If you heard another student telling an insulting racial or gender joke, do you think you would do anything about it? Why?

Chapter Summary and Highlights

Diversity refers to the variety of groups that comprise humanity (the human species). Humans differ from one another in multiple ways, including physical features, religious beliefs, mental and physical abilities, national origins, social backgrounds, and gender. Diversity involves the important political issue of securing equal rights and social justice for all people; however, it's also an important *educational* issue—an integral element of the college experience that enriches learning, personal development, and career preparation.

When a group of people share the same traditions and customs, it creates a culture that serves to bind people into a supportive, tight-knit community. However, culture can also lead its members to view the world solely through their own cultural lens (known as ethnocentrism), which can blind them to other cultural perspectives. Ethnocentrism can contribute to stereotyping—viewing individual members of another cultural group in the same (fixed) way, in which they're seen as having similar personal characteristics.

Stereotyping can result in prejudice—a biased prejudgment about another person or group of people that's formed before the facts are known. Stereotyping and prejudice often go hand in hand because if the stereotype is negative, members of the stereotyped group are then judged negatively. Discrimination takes prejudice one step further by converting the negative prejudgment into behavior that results in unfair treatment of others. Thus, discrimination is prejudice put into action.

Once stereotyping and prejudice are overcome, we are positioned to experience diversity and reap its multiple benefits—which include sharper self-awareness, deeper learning, higher-level thinking, and better career preparation.

The increasing diversity of students on campus, combined with the wealth of diversity-related educational experiences found in the college curriculum and co-curriculum, presents you with an unprecedented opportunity to infuse diversity into your college experience. Seize this opportunity and capitalize on the power of diversity to increase the quality of your college education and your prospects for success in the 21st century.

Learning More through the World Wide Web: Internet-Based Resources

For additional information on diversity, see the following websites:

Stereotyping:
ReducingStereotypeThreat.org at www.reducingstereotypethreat.org

Prejudice and Discrimination:
Southern Poverty Law Center at www.splcenter.org/

Human Rights:
Amnesty International at www.amnesty.org/en/discrimination
Center for Economic & Social Justice at www.cesj.org

Sexism in the Media:
"Killing Us Softly" at www.youtube.com/watch?v=PTlmho_RovY

References

Acredolo, C., & O'Connor, J. (1991). On the difficulty of detecting cognitive uncertainty. *Human Development, 34*, 204–223.

Allport, G. W. (1979). *The nature of prejudice* (3rd ed.). Reading, MA: Addison-Wesley.

Amir, Y. (1969). Contact hypothesis in ethnic relations. *Psychological Bulletin, 71*, 319–342.

Anderson, M., & Fienberg, S. (2000). Race and ethnicity and the controversy over the US Census. *Current Sociology, 48*(3), 87–110.

Aronson, E., Wilson, T. D., & Akert, R. M. (2013). *Social psychology* (8th ed.). Upper Saddle River, NJ: Pearson/Prentice Hall.

Association of American Colleges & Universities (AAC&U). (2002). *Greater expectations: A new vision for learning as a nation goes to college*. Washington, DC: Author.

Association of American Colleges & Universities (AAC&U). (2004). *Our students' best work*. Washington, DC: Author.

Baron, R. A., Branscombe, N. R., Byrne, D. R. (2008). *Social psychology* (12th ed). Boston, MA: Allyn & Bacon.

Bligh, D. A. (2000). *What's the use of lectures?* San Francisco: Jossey Bass.

Bridgeman, B. (2003). *Psychology and evolution: The origins of mind*. Thousand Oaks, CA: Sage Publications.

Bronfenbrenner, U. (Ed.). (2005). *Making human beings human: Bioecological perspectives on human development*. Thousand Oaks, CA: Sage.

Brookfield, S. D. (1987). *Developing critical thinkers*. San Francisco, CA: Jossey-Bass.

Brooks, I. (2009). *Organisational behaviour* (4th ed.). Englewood Cliffs, NJ: Prentice Hall.

Brown, T. D., Dane, F. C., & Durham, M. D. (1998). Perception of race and ethnicity. *Journal of Social Behavior and Personality, 13*(2), 295–306.

Cabrera, A., Nora, A., Terenzini, P., Pascarella, E., & Hagedorn, L. S. (1999). Campus racial climate and the adjustment of students to college: A comparison between White students and African American students. *The Journal of Higher Education, 70*(2), 134–160.

Caplan, P. J., & Caplan, J. B. (2008). *Thinking critically about research on sex and gender* (3rd ed.). New York: HarperCollins College Publishers.

Cianciotto, J. (2005). *Hispanic and Latino same-sex couple households in the United States: A report from the 2000 Census*. New York: The National Gay and Lesbian Task Force Policy Institute and the National Latino/a Coalition for Justice.

Colombo, G., Cullen, R., & Lisle, B. (2013). *Rereading America: Cultural contexts for critical thinking and writing* (9th ed.). Boston, MA: Bedford Books of St. Martin's Press.

Cook, S. W. (1984). Cooperative interaction in multiethnic contexts. In N. Miller & M. B. Brewer (Eds.), *Groups in contact: The psychology of desegregation* (pp. 291–302). New York: Academic Press.

DeNavas-Walt, C., Proctor, B. D., & Smith, J. C. (2013). *Income, poverty, and health insurance coverage in the United States, 2012*. U.S. Census Bureau, Current Population Reports, P60-245, Washington, DC: U.S. Government Printing Office.

Donald, J. G. (2002). *Learning to think: Disciplinary perspectives*. San Francisco: Jossey-Bass.

Dryden, G., & Vos, J. (1999). *The learning revolution: To change the way the world learns*. Torrance, CA and Auckland, New Zealand: The Learning Web.

Education Commission of the States. (1995). *Making quality count in undergraduate education*. Denver, CO: ECS Distribution Center.

Education Commission of the States. (1996). *Bridging the gap between neuroscience and education*. Denver, CO: Author.

Eimers, M. T., & Pike, G. R. (1997). Minority and nonminority adjustment to college: Differences or similarities. *Research in Higher Education, 38*(1), 77–97.

Erickson, B. L., Peters, C. B., & Strommer, D. W. (2006). *Teaching first-year college students*. San Francisco: Jossey-Bass.

Family Care Foundation. (2015). *If the world were a village of 100 people*. Retrieved from http://www.familycare.org/special-interest/if-the-world-were-a-village-of-100-people/.

Feagin, J. R., & Feagin, C. B. (2007). *Racial and ethnic relations* (8th ed.). Englewood Cliffs, NJ: Prentice Hall.

Fixman, C. S. (1990). The foreign language needs of U.S. based corporations. *Annals of the American Academy of Political and Social Science, 511*, 25–46.

Friedman, T. L. (2005). *The world is flat: A brief history of the twenty-first century: Revitalizing the civic mission of schools*. Alexandria, VA: Farrar, Strauss & Giroux.

Gorski, P. C. (1995–2009). *Key characteristics of a multicultural curriculum*. Critical Multicultural Pavilion: Multicultural Curriculum Reform (An EdChange Project). Retrieved from www.edchange.org/multicultural/curriculum/characteristics.html.

Gould, E. & Wething, H. (2013). Health care, the market and consumer choice. *Inquiry, 50*(1), 85–86.

Gurin, P. (1999). New research on the benefits of diversity in college and beyond: An empirical analysis. *Diversity Digest* (spring). Retrieved from http://www.diversityweb.org/Digest/Sp99/benefits.html.

Harris, A. (2010). Leading system transformation. *School Leadership and Management, 30* (July).

Hart Research Associates. (2013). *It takes more than a major: Employer priorities for college learning and student success*. Washington, DC: Author.

HERI (Higher Education Research Institute). (2013). *Your first college year survey 2012*. Los Angeles, CA: Cooperative Institutional Research Program, University of California-Los Angeles.

HERI (Higher Education Research Institute). (2014). *Your first college year survey 2014*. Los Angeles, CA: Cooperative Institutional Research Program, University of California-Los Angeles.

Hugenberg, K., & Bodenhausen, G. V. (2003). Facing prejudice: Implicit prejudice and the perception of facial threat. *Psychological Science, 14*, 640–643.

Jablonski, N. G., & Chaplin, G. (2002). Skin deep. *Scientific American, (October)*, 75–81.

Judd, C. M., Ryan, C. S., & Parke, B. (1991). Accuracy in the judgment of in-group and out-group variability. *Journal of Personality and Social Psychology, 61*, 366–379.

Kelly, K. (1994). *Out of control: The new biology of machines, social systems, and the economic world*. Reading, MA: Addison-Wesley.

Kitchener, K., Wood, P., & Jensen, L. (2000, August). *Curricular, co-curricular, and institutional influence on real-world problem-solving*. Paper presented at the annual meeting of the American Psychological Association, Boston.

Kochlar, R., Fry, R., & Taylor, P. (2011). Wealth gaps rise to record highs between Whites, Blacks, Hispanics, twenty-to-one. *Pew Research Social and Demographics Trends* (July). Retrieved from http://www.pewsocialtrends.org/2011/07/26/wealth-gaps-rise-to-record-highs-between-whites-blacks-hispanics/

Lancaster, L., et al. (2002). *When generations collide: Who they are. Why they clash*. New York: HarperCollins.

Leung, A. K., Maddux, W. W., Galinsky, A. D., & Chie-yue, C. (2008). Multicultural experience enhances creativity: The when and how. *American Psychologist, 63*(3), 169–181.

Lewis, M., Paul, G. W., & Fennig, C. D. (Eds). (2014). *Ethnologue: Languages of the world* (17th ed.). Dallas, TX: SIL International. Online version: http://www.ethnologue.com.

Luhman, R. (2007). *The sociological outlook*. Lanham, MD: Rowman & Littlefield.

Maddux, W. W. & Galinsky, A. D. (2009). Cultural borders and mental barriers: the relationship between living abroad and creativity. *Journal of Personality and Social Psychology, 96*(5), 1047–1061.

Mendez, F., Krahn, T., Schrack, B., Krahn, A. M., Veeramah, K., Woerner, A., Fomine, F. L. M., Bradman, N., Thomas, M., Karafet, T., & Hammer, M. (2013). An African American paternal lineage adds an extremely ancient root to the human Y chromosome phylogenetic tree. *The American Journal of Human Genetics, 92*, 454–459.

Meredith, M. (2011). *Born in Africa: The quest for the origins of human life*. New York: Public Affairs.

Nagda, B. R., Gurin, P., & Johnson, S. M. (2005). Living, doing and thinking diversity: How does pre-college diversity experience affect first-year students' engagement with college diversity? In R. S. Feldman (Ed.), *Improving the first year of college: Research and practice* (pp. 73–110). Mahwah, NJ: Lawrence Erlbaum.

Nathan, R. (2005). *My freshman year: What a professor learned by becoming a student*. London: Penguin.

National Association of Colleges & Employers. (2014). *Job Outlook 2014 survey*. Bethlehem, PA: Author.

National Center for Education Statistics. (2011). *Digest of education statistics, table 237. Total fall enrollment in degree-granting institutions, by level of student, sex, attendance status, and race/ethnicity: Selected years, 1976 through 2010*. Alexandria, VA: U.S. Department of Education. Retrieved from http://neces.ed/gov/programs/digest/d11/tables/dt11_237.asp.

National Survey of Women Voters. (1998). *Autumn overview report conducted by DYG Inc*. Retrieved from http:www.diversityweb.org/research_and_trends/research_evaluation_impact_/campus_community_connections/ national_poll.cfm.

Nhan, D. (2012). "Census: Minorities constitute 37 percent of U.S. population." *National Journal: The Next America—Demographics 2012*. Retrieved from http:www.nationaljournal.com/thenextamerica/demographics/census-minorities-constitute-37-percent-of-u-s-population-20120517.

Nora, A., & Cabrera, A. (1996). The role of perceptions of prejudice and discrimination on the adjustment of minority college students. *The Journal of Higher Education, 67*(2), 119–148.

Office of Research. (1994). *What employers expect of college graduates: International knowledge and second language skills.* Washington, DC: Office of Educational Research and Improvement, U.S. Department of Education.

Olson, L. (2007). What does "ready" mean? *Education Week, 40,* 7–12.

Pascarella, E. T. (2001, November/December). Cognitive growth in college: Surprising and reassuring findings from the National Study of Student Learning. *Change,* 21–27.

Pascarella, E. T., & Terenzini, P. T. (2005). *How college affects students: A third decade of research* (Vol. 2). San Francisco, CA: Jossey-Bass.

Pascarella, E., Palmer, B., Moye, M., & Pierson, C. (2001). Do diversity experiences influence the development of critical thinking? *Journal of College Student Development, 42*(3), 257–291.

Peoples, J., & Bailey, G. (2011). *Humanity: An introduction to cultural anthropology.* Belmont, CA: Wadsworth, Cengage Learning. Retrieved from http://www.aacu.org/leap/documents/2009-employersurvey.pdf.

Pinker, S. (2000). *The language instinct: The new science of language and mind.* New York: Perennial.

Reid, G. B. R., & Hetherington, R. (2010). *The climate connection: Climate change and modern evolution.* Cambridge, UK: Cambridge University Press.

Roediger, H. L., Dudai, Y., & Fitzpatrick, S. M. (2007). *Science of memory: concepts.* New York, NY: Oxford University Press.

Shah, A. (2009). *Global issues: Poverty facts and stats.* Retrieved from http://www.globalissues.org/artoc;e/26/poverty-facts-and-stats.

Sherif, M., Harvey, D. J., White, B. J., Hood, W. R., & Sherif, C. W. (1961). *The Robbers' cave experiment.* Norman, OK: Institute of Group Relations.

Shiraev, E. D., & Levy, D. (2013). *Cross-cultural psychology: Critical thinking and contemporary applications* (5th ed.). Upper Saddle River, NJ: Pearson Education.

Stangor, C., Sechrist, G. B., & Jost, J. T. (2001). Changing racial beliefs by providing consensus information. *Personality and Social Psychology Bulletin, 27,* 484–494.

Stoltz, P. G. (2014). *Grit: The new science of what it takes to persevere, flourish, succeed.* San Luis Obispo: Climb Strong Press.

Taylor, S. E., Peplau, L. A., & Sears, D. O. (2006). *Social psychology* (12th ed.). Upper Saddle River, NJ: Pearson/Prentice-Hall.

Thompson, A., & Cuseo, J. (2014). *Diversity and the college experience.* Dubuque, IA: Kendall Hunt.

U.S. Census Bureau. (2008). *Bureau of Labor Statistics.* Washington, DC: Author.

United States Census Bureau. (2013a, July 8). *About race.* Retrieved from http://www.census.gov/topics/population/race/about.html.

U.S. Census Bureau. (2013b). *Poverty.* Retrieved from https://www.census.gov/hhes/www/poverty/data/threshld/.

United States Census Bureau. (2015, March). *Projections of the size and composition of the U.S. population: 2014 to 2060.* Retrieved from http://www.census.gov/content/dam/Census/library/publications/2015/demo/p25-1143.pdf.

Wabash National Study of Liberal Arts Education. (2007). *Liberal arts outcomes.* Retrieved from http:www.liberalarts.wabash.edu/ study-overview/.

Wheelright, J. (2005, March). Human, study thyself. *Discover,* 39–45.

Willis, J. (2006). *Research-based strategies to ignite student learning: Insights from a neurologist and classroom teacher.* Alexandria, VA: ASCD.

Zajonc, R. B. (1968). Attitudinal effects of mere exposure. *Journal of Personality and Social Psychology, 9,* Monograph Supplement, No. 2, Part 2.

Zajonc, R. B. (1970). Brainwash: Familiarity breeds comfort. *Psychology Today,* (February), 32–35, 60–62.

Zajonc, R. B. (2001). Mere exposure: A gateway to the subliminal. *Current Directions in Psychological Science, 10,* 224–228.

Chapter 5 Exercises

5.1 Quote Reflections

Review the sidebar quotes contained in this chapter and select two that were especially meaningful or inspirational to you.

For each quote, provide a three- to five-sentence explanation why you chose it.

5.2 Reality Bite

Hate Crime: A Racially Motivated Murder

Jasper County, Texas, has a population of approximately 31,000 people. In this county, 80% of the people are White, 18% are Black, and 2% are of other races. The county's poverty rate is considerably higher than the national average, and its average household income is significantly lower. In 1998, the mayor, the president of the Chamber of Commerce, and two councilmen were Black. From the outside, Jasper appeared to be a town with racial harmony, and its Black and White leaders were quick to state that there was no racial tension in Jasper.

However, one day, James Byrd Jr.—a 49-year-old African American man—was walking home along a road one evening and was offered a ride by three White males. Rather than taking Byrd home, Lawrence Brewer (age 31), John King (age 23), and Shawn Berry (age 23), three men linked to White-supremacist groups, took Byrd to an isolated area and began beating him. They then dropped his pants to his ankles, painted his face black, chained Byrd to their truck, and dragged him for approximately three miles. The truck was driven in a zigzag fashion to inflict maximum pain on the victim. Byrd was decapitated after his body collided with a culvert in a ditch alongside the road. His skin, arms, and other body parts were strewn along the road, while his torso was found dumped in front of a Black cemetery. Medical examiners testified that Byrd was alive for much of the dragging incident.

When they were brought to trial, the bodies of Brewer and King were covered with racist tattoos; they were eventually sentenced to death. As a result of the murder, Byrd's family created the James Byrd Foundation for Racial Healing. A wrought iron fence that separated Black and White graves for more than 150 years in Jasper Cemetery was removed in a special unity service. Members of the racist Ku Klux Klan have since visited the gravesite of Byrd several times, leaving racist stickers and other marks that angered the Jasper community and Byrd's family.

Source: *Louisiana Weekly* (February 3, 2003).

Reflection Questions

1. What factors do you think were responsible for this incident?
2. Could this incident have been prevented? If yes, how? If no, why not?
3. How likely do you think an incident like this could take place in your hometown or near your college campus?
4. If this event happened to take place in your hometown, how do you think members of your community would react?

5.3 Gaining Awareness of Your Group Identities

We are members of multiple groups at the same time and our membership in these overlapping groups can influence our personal development and identity. In the following figure, consider the shaded center circle to be yourself and the six unshaded circles to be six different groups you belong to and have influenced your development.

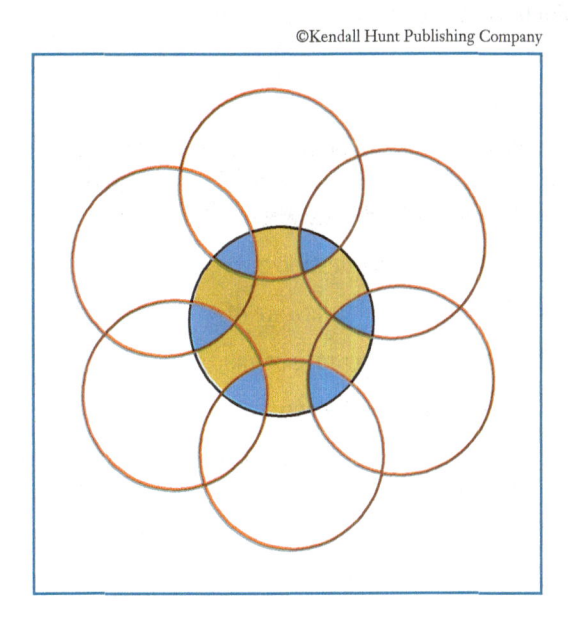

©Kendall Hunt Publishing Company

Fill in the unshaded circles with the names of groups to which you think you belong that have had the most influence on your personal development and identity. You can use the diversity spectrum to help you identify different groups to which you may be a member. Don't feel you have to fill in all six circles. What's more important is to identify those groups that you think have had a significant influence on your personal development or identity.

Reflection Questions

1. Which one of your groups has had the greatest influence on your personal development or identity? Why?
2. Have you ever felt limited or disadvantaged by being a member of any group(s) to which you belong? Why?
3. Have you ever felt advantaged or privileged by your membership in any group(s)? Why?

5.4 Intercultural Interview

1. Identify a person on your campus who is a member of an ethnic or racial group that you've had little previous contact. Ask that person for an interview, and during the interview, include the following questions:

   - What does "diversity" mean to you?
   - What prior experiences have affected your current viewpoints or attitudes about diversity?
   - What would you say have been the major influences and turning points in your life?
   - Who would you cite as your positive role models, heroes, or sources of inspiration?
   - What societal contributions made by your ethnic or racial group would you like others to be aware of and acknowledge?
   - What do you hope will never again be said about your ethnic or racial group?

2. If you were the interviewee instead of the interviewer, how would you have answered the above questions?

3. What do you think accounts for the differences (and similarities) between your answers to the above questions and those provided by the person you interviewed?

5.5 Hidden Bias Test

Go to https://www.tolerance.org/professional-development/test-yourself-for-hidden-bias and take one or more of the hidden bias tests on this website. These tests assess subtle bias with respect to gender, age, ethnic minority groups, religious denominations, disabilities, and body weight.

After completing the test, answer the following questions:

1. Did the results reveal any bias(es) you weren't unaware of?
2. Did you think the assessment results were accurate or valid?
3. What do you think best accounts for or explains your results?
4. If your closest family member and best friend took the test, how do you think their results would compare with yours?

Cross-Cultural Curiosity

Write down (in question form) one thing you have always wondered about, or would like to know more about, the following groups of people.

- Native American (American Indians)
- Hispanic Americans (Latinos)
- African Americans
- Asian Americans
- Elderly (Senior Citizens)

Would you feel comfortable approaching a member of each of these groups to ask your questions about their culture? Why or why not?

DIVERSITY BINGO–Find 1 person in the room who the statement is true for, may not use anyone twice

Has relatives in another country	Owns an iphone	Comes from a family of three or more children	Loves Chinese food	Owns at least two dogs	Is bilingual	Has experienced being stereotyped
Has visited a foreign country	Has a friend or relative who is disabled	Is an only child	Is 30 years or older	Loves to dance	Favorite color is purple	Is a fan of the Twilight movies
Is left handed	Has blue eyes	Owns a cat	Plays an instrument	Does volunteer work	Has dated someone of another race	Is a shopaholic
Has a fear of clowns	Was raised by a single parent	Has a best friend of another race	Is a vegetarian	Hates feet	Was raised by grandparents	Belongs to a social networking site, (facebook, myspace)
Was born in Kentucky	Prefers white chocolate	Loves country music		Is adopted	Hates chocolate	Has bungee jumped
Loves sports	Knows someone with autism	Prefers Pepsi	Has never eaten Mexican food	Knows someone who is famous	Never misses an episode of "The Bachelor"	Is addicted to video games

CHAPTER 6

Health and Wellness

BODY, MIND, AND SPIRIT

Chapter Preview

Humans cannot reach their full potential without attending to their physical well-being. Sustaining health and attaining peak levels of performance depend on how well we treat our *body*—what we put into it (healthy food), what we keep out of it (unhealthy substances), what we do with it (exercise), and how well we rejuvenate it (sleep). This chapter examines strategies for maximizing wellness by maintaining a balanced diet, attaining quality sleep, promoting total fitness, and avoiding risky behaviors that jeopardize our health and impair our performance.

Learning Goal

Acquire wellness strategies that can be immediately practiced in the first year of college and beyond.

Integrate Your Faith

How do you think the way in which you (personally) live your life is a reflection of your relationship with God?

Ignite Your Thinking

Reflection 6.1

What would you say are the three most important things that college students could do to preserve their health and promote peak performance?

1.

2.

3.

From *Thriving in College and Beyond: Research-Based Strategies for Academic Success and Personal Development*, Fourth Edition by Joseph B. Cuseo, Aaron Thompson, Michele Campagna, and Viki S. Fecas. Copyright © 2016 Kendall Hunt Publishing Company. Reprinted by permission.

> "Wellness is a multidimensional state of being describing the existence of positive health in an individual as exemplified by quality of life and a sense of well-being."
> —Charles Corbin and Robert Pangrazi, President's Council on Physical Fitness and Sports

What Is Wellness?

Wellness may be defined as a high-quality state of health in which our risk of illness is minimized and the quality of our physical and mental performance is maximized. Research indicates that people who attend to multiple dimensions of self-development and live a well-rounded, well-balanced life are more likely to be healthy (physically and mentally) and successful (personally and professionally) (Covey, 2004; Goleman, 1995; Heath, 1977).

There's still some debate about the exact number and nature of the components that define the "whole self" (Miller & Foster, 2010; President's Council on Physical Fitness and Sports, 2001). However, the following seven dimensions of personal development are commonly cited as the key elements of the "wellness wheel"; they provide the foundation for a well-rounded life.

> "Wellness is an integrated method of functioning, which is oriented toward maximizing the potential of the individual."
> —H. Joseph Dunn, originator of the term, "wellness"

1. *Physical* Wellness: adopting a healthy lifestyle (e.g., balanced diet and regular exercise) and avoiding health-threatening habits (e.g., smoking and drug abuse).
2. *Intellectual* Wellness: openness to new ideas, learning from new experiences, and willingness to continue learning throughout life.
3. *Emotional* Wellness: being aware of personal feelings, effectively expressing feelings, and handling stress in a productive manner.
4. *Social* Wellness: interacting effectively with others and maintaining healthy relationships with family, friends, and romantic partners.
5. *Occupational (Vocational)* Wellness: finding personal fulfillment in a job or career and having positive, productive experiences with employers and coworkers.
6. *Environmental* Wellness: preserving the quality of key elements of the surrounding world that humans depend on for their health (i.e., air, land, and water).
7. *Spiritual* Wellness: finding meaning, purpose, and peace in life.

> "May the sun bring you new energy by day; may the moon restore you by night. May the rain wash away your worries; may the breeze blow strength into your being."
> —Apache Indian blessing

These elements of wellness correspond closely to the components of holistic ("whole person") development, which is a primary goal of a college education. One of the multiple advantages of the college experience is that college graduates are more likely to live longer, healthier lives and experience higher levels of psychological well-being. Apparently, students learn something important about wellness in college that improves the overall quality of their lives.

Physical Wellness

The physical component of wellness is the primary focus of this chapter. It could be said that physical health is a precondition or prerequisite that enables all other elements of wellness to be experienced. It's hard to grow intellectually and professionally if you're not well physically, and it's hard to become wealthy and wise without first being healthy.

> "Buono salute é la vera ricchezza" ("Good health is true wealth.")
> —Italian proverb

Promoting physical wellness involves more than treating illness or disease after it occurs. Instead, it's engaging in health-promoting behaviors that proactively prevent illness from happening in the first place (Corbin, Pangrazi, & Franks, 2000). Wellness puts into practice two classic proverbs: "Prevention is the best medicine" and "An ounce of prevention is worth a pound of cure."

> "Health is a state of complete well-being, and not merely the absence of disease or infirmity."
>
> —World Health Organization

As depicted in **Figure 6.1**, there are three potential interception points for preventing illness, preserving health, and promoting peak performance; they range from reactive (after illness) to proactive (before illness). Wellness goes beyond maintaining physical health to attaining a higher quality of life that includes vitality (energy and vigor), longevity (longer life span), and life satisfaction (happiness).

FIGURE 6.1: **Potential Points for Preventing Illness, Preserving Health, and Promoting Peak Performance**

Proactive		Reactive
1. Feeling great and attaining peak levels of performance	2. Not sick, but could be feeling better and performing at a higher level	3. Sick, unable to perform, and trying to regain health

©Kendall Hunt Publishing Company

During any major life transition, such as the transition to college, unhealthy habits add to the level of transitional stress (Khoshaba & Maddi, 2005). In contrast, engaging in healthy habits is one way to manage and reduce stress at all stages of life—especially during stages of transition.

Reflection 6.2

If you could single out one thing about your physical health right now that you'd like to improve or learn more about, what would it be?

Essential Elements of Physical Wellness

A healthy physical lifestyle includes three key components:

1. Supplying our body with effective fuel (nutrition) and transforming that fuel into bodily energy (exercise)
2. Giving our body adequate rest (sleep) so that it can recover and replenish the energy it has expended
3. Avoiding risky substances (alcohol and drugs) and risky behaviors that can threaten personal health and safety.

> "Tell me what you eat and I'll tell you what you are."
>
> —Anthelme Brillat-Savarin, French lawyer, gastronomist, and founder of the low-carbohydrate diet

> "If we are what we eat, then I'm cheap, fast, and easy."
>
> —Steven Wright, award-winning comedian

Nutrition

Similar to the way in which high-performance fuel improves the performance of an automobile, a high-quality (nutritious) diet improves the performance of the human body and mind, enabling each to operate at peak capacity. Unfortunately, we frequently pay more attention to the quality of fuel we put in our cars than to the quality of food we put into our bodies. We often eat without any intentional plan about what they should eat. We eat at places where we can get food fast and conveniently without having to step out of our car (or off of our butts). America has become a "fast food nation"; we have grown accustomed to consuming food that can be accessed quickly, conveniently, cheaply, and in large (super-sized) portions (Schlosser, 2005). National surveys reveal that less than 40% of American college students report that they maintain a healthy diet (Sax, et al., 2004).

Reflection 6.3

Have your eating habits changed since you've begun college? If yes, in what ways?

We should eat in a thoughtful, nutritionally conscious way, rather than solely out of convenience, habit, or pursuit of what's most pleasing to our taste buds. We should also "eat to win" by consuming the types of food that will best equip us to defeat disease and enable us to reach peak levels of physical and mental performance. The following nutrition management strategies may be used to enhance your body's ability to stay well and perform well.

Nutrition Management Strategies

1. **Develop a nutrition management plan that ensures your diet has variety and balance.** Planning what we eat is an essential step toward ensuring we eat what best preserves health and promotes wellness. If we don't plan in advance to obtain food we should eat, we're more likely to eat food that can be accessed conveniently and doesn't require advanced preparation. Unfortunately, the types of foods that are readily available, easily accessible, and immediately consumable are usually fast foods and prepackaged or processed foods, which are often the least healthy options. If we are serious about eating in a way that's best for our health and performance, we need to do more advanced planning.

    Figure 6.2 depicts the *The MyPlate* chart; this is the new version of the former Food Guide Pyramid created by the Academy of Nutrition and Dietetics. Since foods vary in terms of the nature of nutrients they contain, no single food group can supply all the nutrients our body needs. Therefore, our diet should contain a balanced blend of all food groups, albeit in different proportions or percentages.

FIGURE 6.2: MyPlate

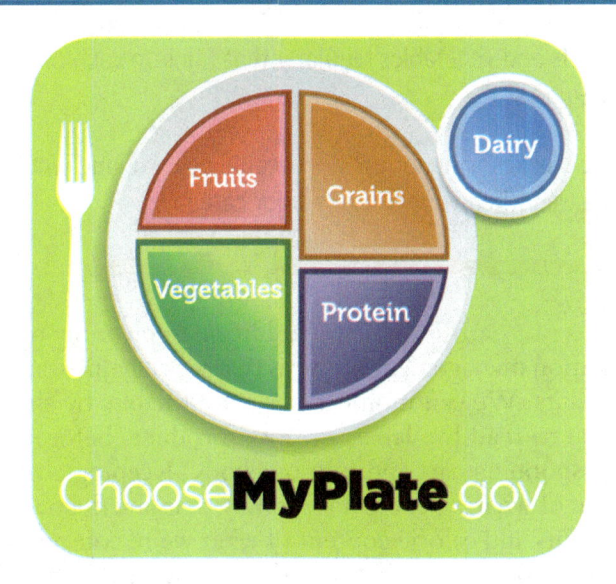

Source: USDA

To find the daily amount of food that should be consumed from each of the major food groups for your age and gender, go to *www.ChooseMyPlate.gov* or *www.cnpp.usda.gov/dietaryguideilines*. You can use these guidelines to create a personal dietary plan that ensures you consume each of these food groups every day, which will result in a balanced diet that minimizes your risk of nutritional deficiencies and disorders, and maximizes your health and performance.

"Eating the rainbow" is a phrase used by nutritionists to help people remember that including a variety of colorful fruits and vegetables in our diet is a simple way to get an ample amount of vitamins, minerals, and disease-fighting nutrients. The colors of certain fruits and vegetables can serve as indicators of the specific nutrients contained within them. For instance, fruits and vegetables that are:

- Orange and yellow (e.g., carrots, squash, melons): contain high amounts of vitamins A and C as well as nutrients that prevent cataracts and other types of eye disease
- Green (e.g., spinach, broccoli, avocado): contain high levels of vitamins B, E, and K as well as anticancer agents
- Red (e.g., tomatoes, strawberries, cherries): contain an antioxidant that reduces the risk of cancer and heart disease.
- Purple and blue (e.g., grapes, eggplant, red cabbage): contain abundant amounts of vitamins C and K as well as antioxidants that reduce the risk of cancer and cardiovascular disease
- Brown and white (e.g., cauliflower, mushrooms, bananas): contain chemicals that reduce the risk of infectious diseases by attacking viruses and bacteria (Nutrition Australia, 2015).

Reflection 6.4

Do you eat fruits and vegetables regularly that fall into each of the above five color categories?

What are your weakest categories? What could you eat, and would be willing to eat, to strengthen your weakest color category?

2. **Monitor your eating habits.** In addition to planning our diet, effective nutrition management requires that we remain aware of our daily eating habits. We can monitor our eating habits by simply taking a little time to read the labels on food products before we put them into our shopping cart and into our body. Keeping a nutritional log or journal of what we eat in a typical week is an effective way to track the nutrients and caloric content of what we're consuming.

   When choosing our diet, you should also be mindful of your family history. Are there members of your immediate and extended family who have shown tendencies toward heart disease, diabetes, or cancer? If so, intentionally adopt a diet that reduces your risk for developing the types of illnesses that you may have genetic tendencies to develop. (For regularly updated information on dietary strategies for reducing the risk of common diseases, see the following website: https://fnic.nal.usda.gov/diet-and-disease).

Reflection 6.5

Are you aware of any disease or illness that tends to run in your family?

If yes, are you aware of how you may reduce your risk of experiencing this disease or illness through your diet?

Eating Disorders

While some students experience the "freshman 15"—a 15-pound weight gain during the first year of college (Levitsky, et al., 2006)—others experience eating disorders related to weight loss and losing control of their eating habits. These disorders are more common among females (National Institute of Mental Health, 2014), largely because Western cultures place more emphasis and pressure on females to maintain lighter body weight and body size. Studies show that approximately one of every three college females reports worrying about her weight, body image, or eating habits (Leavy, Gnong, & Ross, 2009).

Box 6.1 provides a short summary of the major eating disorders experienced by college students. These disorders are often accompanied by emotional issues (e.g., depression and anxiety) that are serious enough to require professional treatment (National Institute of Mental Health, 2014). The earlier these disorders are identified and treated, the better the prognosis or probability of complete and permanent recovery.

Box 6.1

Major Eating Disorders

Anorexia Nervosa

Individuals experiencing anorexia nervosa are dangerously thin, yet they see themselves as overweight and have an intense fear of gaining weight. Anorexics typically deny that they're severely underweight; even if their weight drops to the point where they may look like walking skeletons, they may continue to be obsessed with losing weight, eating infrequently, and eating extremely small portions. Anorexics may also use other methods to lose weight, such as compulsive exercise, diet pills, laxatives, diuretics, or enemas.

Bulimia Nervosa

This eating disorder is characterized by repeated episodes of "binge eating"—consuming excessive amounts of food within a limited period of time. Bulimics tend to lose self-control during their binges and then try to compensate for overeating by engaging in behavior to purge their guilt and prevent weight gain. They may purge themselves by self-induced vomiting, consuming excessive amounts of laxatives or diuretics, using enemas, or fasting. The binge–purge pattern typically takes place at least twice a week and continues for three or more months.

> I had a friend who took pride in her ability to lose 30 lbs. in one summer by not eating and working out excessively. I know girls that find pleasure in getting ill so that they throw up, can't eat, and lose weight."
>
> —Comments written in a first-year student's journal

Unlike anorexics, bulimics are harder to detect because their binges and purges typically take place secretly and their body weight looks about normal for their age and height. However, similar to anorexics, bulimics fear gaining weight, aren't happy with their body, and have an intense desire to lose weight.

Binge-Eating Disorder

Like bulimia, binge-eating disorder involves repeated, out-of-control episodes of consuming large amounts of food. However, unlike bulimics, binge eaters don't purge after binging episodes.

Those suffering from binge-eating disorder demonstrate at least three of the following symptoms, two or more times per week, for several months:

1. Eating at an extremely rapid rate
2. Eating until becoming uncomfortably full
3. Eating large amounts of food when not physically hungry
4. Eating alone because of embarrassment about others seeing how much they eat
5. Feeling guilty, disgusted, or depressed after overeating.

Sources: American Psychiatric Association (2015); National Institute of Mental Health (2014).

Exercise and Fitness

Wellness depends not only on fueling the body but using that fuel to move the body. We know that eating natural (unprocessed) foods is better for our health because those were the foods eaten by our ancient human ancestors, which has contributed to the survival of our species. Similarly, exercise is another "natural" health-promoting activity that contributed to the health and survival of the human species (World Health Organization, 2012). Our ancient ancestors didn't have the luxury of motorized vehicles to transport them from point A to point B, nor could they stroll up leisurely to grocery stores and buy food or have food served to them while seated in restaurants. Instead, they had to roam and rummage for fruit, nuts, and vegetables, or chase down animals for meat to eat. Thus, exercise was part of their daily routine.

The benefits of physical exercise for improving the longevity and quality of human life are simply extraordinary. If done regularly, exercise may well be the most effective "medicine" available to humans for preventing disease and preserving lifelong health. The major health-promoting benefits of exercise are described below.

> "If exercise could be packaged into a pill, it would be the single most widely prescribed and beneficial medicine in the nation."
>
> —Robert N. Butler, former director of the National Institute of Aging

Benefits of Exercise for the Body

1. **Exercise promotes cardiovascular health.** Simply stated, exercise makes the heart stronger. Since the heart is a muscle, like any other muscle in the body, its size and strength are increased by exercise. A bigger and stronger heart pumps more blood per beat, reducing the risk for heart disease and stroke (loss of oxygen to the brain) by increasing circulation of oxygen-carrying blood and increasing the body's ability to dissolve blood clots (Khoshaba & Maddi, 2005).

    Exercise further reduces the risk of cardiovascular disease by: (a) decrease the levels of triglycerides (clot-forming fats) in the blood, (b) increasing the levels of "good" cholesterol (high-density lipoproteins), and (c) preventing "bad" cholesterol (low-density lipoproteins) from sticking to and clogging up blood vessels.

2. **Exercise stimulates the immune system.** Exercise enables us to better fight off infectious diseases (e.g., colds and the flu) for the following reasons:

    - It reduces stress—which normally weakens the immune system.
    - It increases blood flow throughout the body, which increases circulation of antibodies that flush germs out of our system.
    - It increases body temperature, which helps kill germs in a way similar to how a low-grade fever kills germs when we're sick (Walsh, et al., 2011).

3. **Exercise strengthens muscles and bones.** Exercise reduces muscle tension, which helps prevent muscle strain and pain; for example, strengthening abdominal muscles reduces the risk of developing lower back pain. Exercise also maintains bone density and reduces

the risk of osteoporosis (brittle bones that bend and break easily). It's noteworthy that our bone density before age 20 affects the bone density we will have for the remainder of life. Thus, by engaging in regular exercise early in life, we minimize risk of bone deterioration throughout life.

Reflection 6.6

Have your exercise habits changed (for better or worse) since you've begun college?

If yes, why has this change taken place?

> "I'm less active now than before college because I'm having trouble learning how to manage my time."
> —First-year student

4. **Exercise promotes weight loss and weight management.** In a study of 188 countries, the highest proportion of overweight and obese people live in the United States, and the rate is increasing (Ng & Associates, 2014). The national increase in overweight Americans is due not only to our consuming more calories but also to our lower levels of physical activity (NIDDK, 2010). We're now playing double jeopardy with our health by eating more and moving less. Much of our reduced level of physical activity has resulted from the emergence of modern technological conveniences that make it easier for us to go about our daily business without exerting ourselves in the slightest. TVs now come with remote controls; we don't have to move to change channels, change volume, or turn the TV on and off. We now have instant access to video games that can be played virtually without actually running, jumping, or even getting on our feet.

Intentional exercise is our best antidote to all the inactivity that characterizes modern life. As a weight-control strategy, it's superior to dieting in one key respect: It raises the body's rate of metabolism—the rate at which consumed calories are burned as energy rather than stored as fat. In contrast, dieting lowers the body's rate of metabolism and the rate at which calories are burned (Agus, et al., 2000; Leibel, Rosenbaum, & Hirsch, 1995). After two to three weeks of low-calorie dieting without exercising, the body "thinks" it's starving, so it compensates by conserving more calories as fat so that the fat can be used for future energy (Mayo Clinic, 2014). In contrast, exercise speeds up basal metabolism—the body's rate of metabolism when it's resting. Thus, in addition to burning fat directly while exercising, exercise burns fat by continuing to keep the body's metabolic rate higher after we stop exercising.

Benefits of Exercise for the Mind

In addition to its multiple benefits for the body, exercise benefits the mind. Here's a summary of the powerful effects that physical exercise has on our mental health and mental performance.

1. **Exercise increases mental energy and improves mental performance.** Have you noticed how red our face gets when we engage in strenuous physical activity? This rosy complexion occurs because physical activity pumps enormous amounts of blood into our head region and more oxygen into our brain. Exercise increases blood flow to all parts of the body, but since the brain uses more oxygen than any other organ of the body, it's the organ that benefits most from exercise. Moreover, aerobic exercise (exercise that increases respiratory rate and circulates oxygen throughout the body) has been found to: (a) enlarge the frontal lobe—the part of the brain responsible for higher-level thinking (Colcombe, et al., 2006; Kramer & Erickson, 2007) and (b) increase production of brain chemicals that enable neurological connections to form between brain cells (Howard, 2014; Ratey, 2013). As noted in Chapter 5, these are the connections that provide the biological basis of learning and memory. One well-designed study of more than 250 college students discovered that students who regularly engaged in vigorous physical activity had higher GPAs (Parker-Pope, 2010).

   Furthermore, exercise is a stimulant whose stimulating effects are similar to those provided by popular energy drinks (e.g., Red Bull, Full Throttle, and Monster). However, exercise delivers these stimulating effects without the sugar, caffeine, and negative side effects of energy drinks—such as nervousness, irritability, increased blood pressure, and a sharp drop in energy ("crash") after the drink's stimulating effects wear off (Malinauskas, et al., 2007).

2. **Exercise elevates mood.** Exercise stimulates release of: (a) endorphins—morphine-like chemicals found in the brain that produce a natural high; and (b) serotonin—a mellowing brain chemical that reduces feelings of tension, anxiety, and depression. It is for these reasons that psychotherapists often prescribe exercise for patients experiencing mild cases of anxiety and depression (Johnsgard, 2004). Studies show that people who exercise regularly report feeling happier (Myers, 1993; National Institutes of Health, 2012).

3. **Exercise improves self-esteem.** Exercise can enhance our sense of self-worth by providing us with a feeling of accomplishment and improving our physical self-image (e.g., better weight control, muscle tone, and skin tone).

4. **Exercise deepens and enriches the quality of sleep.** Sleep research indicates that if we engage in exercise at least three hours before bedtime, it helps us fall asleep, stay asleep, and sleep more deeply (Youngstedt, 2005). This is why exercise is a common component of treatment programs for people suffering from insomnia (Dement & Vaughan, 2000).

> "To keep the body in good health is a duty, otherwise we shall not be able to keep our mind strong and clear."
> —Buddha, founder of Buddhism

> "It is exercise alone that supports the spirits, and keeps the mind in vigor."
> —Marcus Cicero, ancient Roman orator and philosopher

Guidelines and Strategies for Maximizing the Effectiveness of Exercise

Although specific types of exercises benefit the body and mind in different ways, there are general guidelines that can be followed to maximize the positive impact of any exercise routine or personal fitness program. These guidelines are discussed below.

1. **Warm up before exercising and cool down after exercising.** Start with a 10-minute warm up of low-intensity movements similar to the ones you'll be using during the actual exercise. This will increase circulation of blood to the muscles you'll be exercising, which will reduce muscle soreness and risk of muscle pulls.

   Finish your exercise routine with a 10-minute cool down that involves stretching the muscles you used while exercising. Stretch the muscle until it burns a little bit, and then release it. By cooling down after exercise, you improve circulation to the muscles you exercised, enabling them to return more gradually to a tension-free state; this minimizes the risk of muscle tightness, cramps, pulls, and tears.

2. **Engage in cross-training to attain total body fitness.** A balanced, comprehensive fitness program includes cross-training—a combination of different exercises to achieve total-body fitness. We should strive to combine exercises that enable us to achieve all of the following physical benefits:
   - Endurance and weight control (e.g., running, cycling, or swimming);
   - Muscle strength and tone (e.g., weight training, push-ups, or sit-ups); and
   - Flexibility (e.g., yoga, Pilates, or tai chi).

   Cross-training also entails exercising different muscle groups on a rotational basis (e.g., upper body muscles one day, lower body muscles the next). This gives different sets of muscle tissue extra time to rest, repair, and recover before they're exercised again.

3. **Include *interval training* as part of your exercise plan.** Interval training involves interspersing high-intensity exercise workouts with low-intensity exercise or short rest periods (Roxburgh, et al., 2014), such as interspersing walking with short bursts of running. Research indicates that alternating between higher- and lower-intensity exercises effectively strengthens the heart muscle and increases its oxygen-carrying capacity; it also burns calories faster and enables you to exercise longer and at more intense levels (Mayo Clinic, 2015; Mazurek, et al., 2014).

4. **Exercise regularly, allowing strength and stamina to increase gradually.** The key to attaining fitness and avoiding injury is body training, not body straining. One strategy for ensuring you're not straining your body is to see if you can talk while you're exercising.

If you can't continue speaking without stopping to catch your breath, this may indicate you're overdoing it. Drop the intensity level and allow your body to adapt or adjust to a less strenuous level. After continuing at this lower level for a while, try again at the higher level and try to talk simultaneously. If you can do both, you're ready to continue at that level for some time. Continue to use this strategy and gradually increase the intensity, frequency, or duration of your exercise routine to a level that produces maximum benefits with minimal post-exercise discomfort.

5. **Take advantage of exercise and fitness resources on your campus.** Your college tuition pays for use of the campus gym or recreation center so take advantage of it. Also, consider taking physical education courses offered by your college. They count toward your college degree, and typically they carry one unit of credit so that they can be easily added to your course schedule. If exercise groups or clubs meet on campus, join them; they can provide you with a motivational support group that converts exercise from a solitary routine into a social experience. (It's also a good way to meet people.)

6. **Take advantage of natural opportunities for physical activity that present themselves during the day.** Exercise can take place in places beyond a gym or fitness center and outside scheduled workout times. Opportunities for exercise are available to us as we go about our daily activities. If you can walk or ride your bike to class, do that instead of driving a car or riding a bus. If you can climb some stairs instead of taking an elevator, take the route that requires more bodily activity.

Reflection 6.7

Do you have a regular exercise routine?

If yes, what do you do and how often do you do it? If no, why not?

What more could you do to improve your:

a) Endurance?

b) Strength?

c) Flexibility?

Rest and Sleep

Sleep experts agree that humans in today's information-loaded, multitasking world aren't getting the quantity and quality of sleep needed to perform at peak levels (Centers for Disease Control and Prevention, 2015).

We often underestimate the power of sleep and think we can cut down on the time we spend sleeping without compromising the quality of our lives. However, as discussed below, the amount of sleep we get plays a pivotal role for preserving our health and enhancing our performance.

The Value and Purpose of Sleep

Resting and reenergizing the body are the most obvious purposes of sleep. Listed below are other benefits of sleep that are less well known but equally important (Dement & Vaughan, 2000; National Institutes of Health, 2012).

> "Sleep deprivation is a major epidemic in our society. Americans spend so much time and energy chasing the American dream that they don't have much time left for actual dreaming."
>
> —William Dement, pioneering sleep researcher and founder of the American Sleep Disorders Association

1. **Sleep restores and preserves the power of the immune system.** Studies show that when humans and other animals lose sleep, it lowers their production of disease-fighting antibodies, making them more susceptible to illness, such as common colds and the flu (Bryant, Trinder, & Curtis, 2004).

2. **Sleep helps us cope with daily stress.** Sleep research shows that when we're experiencing stress, we spend more time in the REM (rapid eye movement) stage of sleep, which is the stage when most dreaming takes place (Suchecki, Tiba, & Machado, 2012). This suggests that dreaming is our brain's natural way of coping with stress. When we lose dream sleep, emotional problems—such as anxiety and depression—worsen (Voelker, 2004). It's thought that the biochemical changes that take place in our brain during dream sleep help restore imbalances in brain chemistry that occur when we experience anxiety or depression. Thus, getting high-quality sleep (especially high-quality dream sleep) helps us maintain our emotional stability and keeps us in a positive frame of mind. Indeed, surveys reveal that people who report sleeping well also report feeling happier (Myers, 1993).

3. **Sleep helps the brain form and retain memories.** When we're sleeping, our brain isn't bombarded with sensory input from the outside world. This allows the brain—particularly during dream sleep—to devote more of its energy (metabolism) to processing and storing information taken in during the day (Willis, 2006). Studies show that loss of dream sleep at night results in poorer memory for information learned during the day (Greer, 2004). For instance, teenagers who get less than adequate amounts of sleep have more difficulty retaining information they learn in school (Wolfson & Carskadon, 2003). Studies also show that increasing sleep time from six or fewer hours per night to eight hours can increase memory by as much as 25% (Frank, Issa, & Stryker, 2001). Additional research indicates that when students study before going to bed and stop studying when they begin to feel drowsy (rather than trying to continue studying after drowsiness sets in), their memory for the studied material is superior (Willis, 2006).

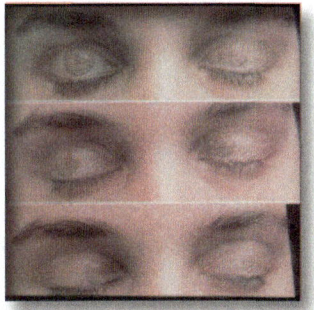

Studies show that dreaming during the REM stage of sleep helps us cope with stress and retain memories.

The Importance of Sleep for College Students

College students tend to have poorer sleep habits and experience more sleep problems than the general population. Heavier academic workloads, more opportunities for late-night socializing, and more frequent late-night (or all-night) study sessions often lead to more irregular sleep schedules and more sleep deprivation among college students. It's estimated that 60% of college students get an insufficient amount of sleep—a rate twice that of the general population (Kingkade, 2014).

How much sleep do we need and should we get? The answer lies in our genes and varies from person to person. On average, adults need seven to eight hours of sleep each day and teenagers need slightly more—about nine hours (Ohayon, et al., 2004). Research shows that college students get an average of less than seven hours of sleep per night (Gaultney, 2010), which means they're not getting the amount of sleep needed for optimal academic performance.

Attempting to train our body to sleep less is likely to be an exercise in futility because it's attempting to make our body do something it's not naturally (genetically) "hard-wired" to do. When our body is deprived of the amount of sleep it's genetically designed to receive, it accumulates "sleep debt," which, like financial debt, must be paid back (Dement & Vaughan, 2000; National Institutes of Health, 2015). If our sleep debt isn't repaid, it catches up to us and we pay for it by experiencing lower energy, lower mood, poorer health, and poorer performance (Van Dongen, et al., 2003). For example, studies show that the negative effects of sleep loss on driving an automobile are similar to the effects of drinking alcohol (Arnedt, et al., 2001; Fletcher, et al., 2003). Studies of sleep-deprived college students indicate that their academic performance is poorer than students who get sufficient sleep (Spinweber, cited in Zimbardo, Johnson, & McCann, 2012).

The best way to open up more time for sleep is by using our time more effectively and efficiently to get things done during the day that are cutting into our sleep time at night. (For time management strategies, see Chapter 4 and Chapter 7.)

> "I'm not getting enough sleep. I've been getting roughly 6–7 hours of sleep on weekdays. In high school, I would get 8–9 hours of sleep."
> —First-year student

> "First of all, you should probably know that your body will not function without sleep. I learned that the hard way."
> —Words written by a first-year student in a letter of advice to incoming college students

Reflection 6.8

How much sleep do you think you need to perform at a peak level?

How many nights per week do you typically get this amount of sleep?

If you're not getting this optimal amount of sleep each night, what's preventing you from doing so?

Adjusting Academic Work Tasks to Your Biological Rhythms

Attaining peak performance in college requires attention to both time management and energy management. Listed below are strategies for connecting these two forms of self-management to maximize your academic performance.

When planning your daily work schedule, be aware of your "biological rhythms"—that is, your natural *peak periods* and *down times*. Studies show that humans vary in terms of when they naturally prefer to fall asleep and wake up; some are "early birds" who prefer to go to sleep early and wake up early; others are "night owls" who prefer to stay up late at night and get up late in the morning (Smolensky & Lamberg, 2001). As a result of these differences in sleep patterns, individuals vary with respect to the time of day when they experience their highest and lowest levels of energy. Naturally, early birds are more likely to be "morning people" whose peak energy period takes place before noon; night owls are likely to be more productive in the late afternoon and evening. Most people, whether they're night owls or early birds, tend to experience a "post-lunch dip" in energy in the early afternoon (Monk, 2005).

Become aware of your most productive hours of the day and schedule your highest priority work and most challenging tasks at times when you tend to work at peak effectiveness. For instance, schedule out-of-class academic work so that you tackle tasks requiring intense thinking (e.g., technical writing or complex problem-solving) at times of the day when you tend to be most productive; schedule lighter work (e.g., light reading or routine tasks) at times when your energy level tends to be lower.

Also, when scheduling your courses, be mindful of your natural peak and down times. Try to arrange your schedule in such a way that you're sitting in your most challenging courses at times of the day when your body and mind are most ready to tackle those challenges.

(Take Self-Assessment Exercise 6.4 at the end of this chapter to identify your peak performance times.)

Strategies for Improving Sleep Quality

Since sleep has such powerful benefits for both the body and mind, if you can improve the quality of your sleep, you can improve your physical and mental well-being. Listed below are specific strategies for improving sleep quality, which, in turn, should improve your health and performance.

1. **Become more aware of your sleep habits by keeping a sleep log or sleep journal.** Make note of what you did before going to bed on nights when you slept well or poorly. Tracking your sleep experiences in a journal may enable you to detect a pattern or relationship between certain things you do (or don't do) during the day on those

nights when you sleep well. If you discover a pattern, you may have found yourself a routine to follow that gets you a good night's sleep on a consistent basis.

2. **Try to get into a regular sleep schedule by going to sleep and getting up at about the same time each day.** The human body functions best when it's on a biological rhythm of set cycles. If you can get your body on a regular sleep cycle, you can get into a biological rhythm that makes it easier for you to fall asleep, stay asleep, and wake up naturally from sleep—according to your body's own "internal alarm clock."

   Establishing a stable sleep schedule is particularly important around midterms and finals. Unfortunately, however, these are the times during the term when just the opposite happens. Normal sleep cycles are disrupted by cramming in last-minute studying, staying up later, getting up earlier, or pulling all-nighters and not sleeping at all. Sleep research shows that if students want to be at their physical and mental best for upcoming exams, they should get themselves on a regular sleep schedule of going to bed about the same time and getting up about the same time for at least one week before exams are to be taken (Dement & Vaughan, 1999). To help you get into this pattern, use the "distributed" practice strategies and the "part-to-whole" study method. (See Chapter 5 for a discussion of these techniques.)

3. **Attempt to get into a relaxing pre-bedtime ritual each night.** Taking a hot bath or shower, consuming a hot (noncaffeinated) beverage, or listening to relaxing music are bedtime rituals that can get you into a worry-free state before sleep and help you fall asleep sooner. Also, making a list of things you intend to do the next day before going to bed may help you relax and fall asleep because you know you're organized and ready to handle the following day's tasks.

   A light review of class notes or reading highlights just before bedtime can be a good nighttime ritual because sleep helps you retain what you experienced just before falling asleep. Many years of research indicate that the best thing you can do after attempting to learn information is to "sleep on it," probably because your brain can focus on processing and storing that information without interference from external stimulation or outside distractions (Kuriyama, et al., 2008; National Institutes of Health, 2013).

Reflection 6.9

What do you do on most nights immediately before going to bed? Do you think this helps or hinders the quality of your sleep?

4. **Avoid intense mental activity just before going to bed.** Light mental work may serve as a relaxing pre-sleep ritual, but cramming frantically for a difficult exam or doing intensive writing before bedtime will put you in a state of mental arousal, which can interfere with your ability to wind down and fall asleep (National Institutes of Health, 2012).
5. **Avoid intense physical exercise before bedtime.** Physical exercise elevates muscle tension and increases oxygen flow to the brain, both of which will hinder your ability to fall asleep. If you like to exercise in the evening, it should be done at least three hours before bedtime (Epstein & Mardon, 2007).
6. **Avoid consuming sleep-interfering foods, beverages, or drugs in the late afternoon or evening.** In particular, avoid the following substances near bedtime:
    - **Caffeine.** It's a stimulant drug; for most people, it will stimulate their nervous system and keep them awake.
    - **Nicotine.** Another stimulant drug that's also likely to reduce the depth and quality of your sleep. (Note: Smoking hookah through a water pipe delivers the same amount of nicotine as a cigarette.)
    - **Alcohol.** It's a depressant (sedative) that makes you feel sleepy in larger doses; however, in smaller doses, it can have a stimulating effect. Furthermore, alcohol in any amount disrupts the quality of sleep by reducing the amount of time we spend in dream-stage sleep.
    - **High-fat foods.** Eating just before bedtime (or during the night) increases digestive activity in the stomach. This "internal noise" is likely to interfere with the soundness of our sleep. Peanuts, beans, fruits, raw vegetables, and high-fat snacks should especially be avoided because these are harder-to-digest foods.

Note

Substances that make us feel sleepy or cause us to fall asleep (e.g., alcohol and marijuana) typically reduce the quality of our sleep by interfering with dream sleep.

7. **Make sure the temperature in the room where you're sleeping is not warmer than 70 degrees (Fahrenheit).** Warm temperatures often make us feel sleepy, but they usually don't help us stay asleep or sleep deeply. This is why people have trouble sleeping on hot summer evenings. High-quality, uninterrupted sleep is more likely to take place at room temperatures around 65 degrees (Lack, et al., 2008).

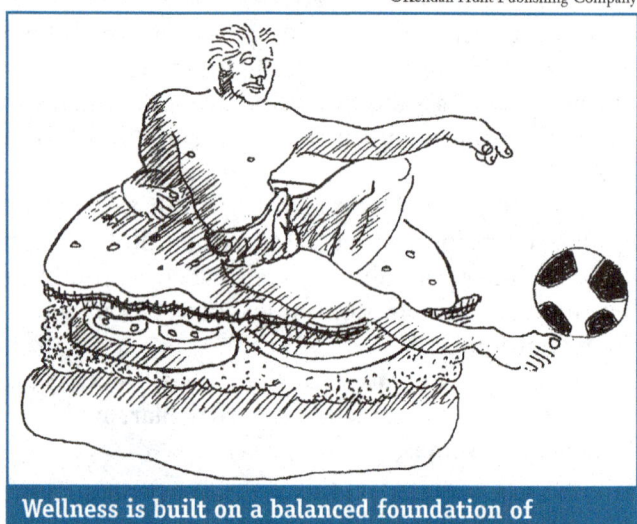

Wellness is built on a balanced foundation of nutrition, exercise, and rest.

Campus Safety

College campuses are generally safe and no more prone to crime than other locations or organizations. However, crimes do occur on campuses and one element of wellness is reducing your risk of being victimized by crimes, particularly crimes that threaten your physical well-being. Listed below are some top tips on doing so.

- After dark, don't walk alone; use a buddy system.
- At night or when walking alone, don't get so absorbed in texting or listening to iTunes that you tune out or block out what's going on around you.
- If you're carrying valuable electronics, keep them concealed.
- Check if your campus has an escort service at night; if it does, take advantage of it.
- Call ahead for campus shuttles and escort services to reduce the amount of time you're waiting for a ride.
- Have your keys out and ready before entering your building or your car, and double-check to be sure the door locks behind you.
- Know the phone number and location of the office for campus safety.
- Be aware of the location of emergency phones in academic buildings.
- Put emergency numbers in your cell phone.

Sources: Lucler, 2015; "Staying Safe on Campus," 2012.

Mobile apps are also available to promote your safety. For instance, "Circle of 6" (www.circleof6app.com/) is a free mobile map that allows you to choose a network of six friends whom you can contact with emergency text messages, such as: "Call me immediately," "Come and get me," or "I need help getting home safely." When you text a message, your GPS location is included. This app was a co-winner of the national "Apps Against Abuse Challenge" sponsored by the White House (Rivera, 2015).

"ArcAngel" (www.patrocinium.com/arcangel) is another mobile safety app that notifies you within seconds of an emergency or if you're near danger (e.g., a crime scene, fire, or flood); it also provides ongoing status reports throughout the emergency and recommends evacuation routes as needed. If you need help, you can click a button that informs local authorities, campus security teams, and family members of your exact location.

Take advantage of these new safety technologies to lower your risk of being victimized by crime and avoiding dangerous situations.

Chapter Summary and Highlights

Wellness is a state of high-quality health and personal well-being that promotes peak physical and mental performance. It requires a healthy lifestyle that includes the following key elements: (a) supplying our body with effective fuel (nutrition) for optimal energy, (b) using energy to engage in heath-preserving exercise, and (c) giving our body adequate rest (sleep) so that it can recover and replenish the energy it has expended.

Research findings and recommendations from health care professionals indicate that physical wellness is most effectively promoted by adopting the following strategies:

- **Watch what we eat.** In particular, we should increase consumption of natural fruits, vegetables, legumes, whole grains, fish, and water and decrease consumption of processed foods, fatty foods, fried foods, fast foods, and foods purchased from vending machines. Although the expression, "you are what you eat" may be a bit of an exaggeration, it contains a kernel of truth because the food we consume does affect our health, our emotions, and our performance.
- **Become more physically active.** To counteract the sedentary lifestyle created by life in modern society and attain total fitness, we should engage in a balanced blend of exercises that build stamina, strength, and flexibility.
- **Don't cheat on sleep.** Humans typically do not get the amount of sleep they need to perform at peak levels. College students, in particular, need to get more sleep than they usually do and develop more regular (consistent) sleep habits.
- **Avoid unhealthy relationships that are abusive or violent.** If involved in such a relationship, don't tolerate it and allow it to escalate. Instead, escape it, or seek immediate help to address it.
- **Minimize the risk of being victimized by crime.** Be mindful of surroundings, particularly when alone and at night, use social support strategies and emerging technological tools (e.g., apps) to enhance personal safety.

The wellness-promoting strategies discussed in this chapter are effective ways to preserve health and promote peak performance, both in college and beyond.

Learning More through the World Wide Web: Internet-Based Resources

For additional information on health and wellness, see the following websites.

Nutrition:
www.eatright.org

Physical Activities and Fitness:
http://archive.ncppa.org/resources/coalitions/

Sleep:
www.sleepfoundation.org

Mental Health:
http://www.activeminds.org/issues-a-resources/mental-health-resources/student-resources

References

Agus M. S., Swain, J. F., Larson, C. L., Eckert, E. A., & Ludwig, D. S. (2000). Dietary composition and physiologic adaptations to energy restriction. *American Journal of Clinical Nutrition, 74*(4), 901–907.

American Psychiatric Association. (2015). *Diagnostic and statistical manual of mental disorders, DSM-IV-TR* (5th ed.). Washington, DC: Author.

Arnedt, J. T., Wilde, G. J. S., Munt, P. W., & MacLean, A. W. (2001). How do prolonged wakefulness and alcohol compare in the decrements they produce on a simulated driving task? *Accident Analysis and Prevention, 33,* 337–344.

Bryant, P. A., Trinder, J., & Curtis, N. (2004). Sick and tired: does sleep have a vital role in the immune system? *Nature Reviews Immunology, 4,* 457–467.

Centers for Disease Control & Prevention. (2015). *Insufficient sleep is a public health problem.* Retrieved from http://www.cdc.gov/features/dssleep/.

Colcombe, S. J., Erickson, K., Scalf, P. E., Kim, J. S., Prakash, R., & McAuley, E. (2006). Aerobic exercise training increases brain volume in aging humans. *Journal of Gerontology: Medical Sciences, 61A*(11), 1166–1170.

Corbin, C. B., Pangrazi, R. P., & Franks, B. D. (2000). Definitions: Health, fitness, and physical activity. *President's Council on Physical Fitness and Sports Research Digest, 3*(9), 1–8.

Covey, S. R. (2004). *Seven habits of highly effective people* (3rd ed.). New York: Fireside.

Dement, W. C., & Vaughan, C. (2000). *The promise of sleep: A pioneer in sleep medicine explores the vital connection between health, happiness, and a good night's sleep.* New York: Dell.

Epstein, L., & Mardon. S. (2007). *The Harvard medical school guide to a good night's sleep.* New York: McGraw Hill.

Fletcher, A., Lamond, N., van den Heuvel, C. J., & Dawson, D. (2003). Prediction of performance during sleep deprivation and alcohol intoxication using a quantitative model of work-related fatigue. *Sleep Research Online, 5,* 67–75.

Frank, M., Issa, N., & Stryker, M. (2001). Sleep enhances plasticity in the developing visual cortex. *Neuron, 30*(1), 275–297.

Gaultney, J. F. (2010). The prevalence of sleep disorders in college students: Impact on academic performance. *Journal of American College Health*, 59(2), 91–97.

Goleman, D. (1995). *Emotional intelligence: Why it can matter more than IQ*. New York: Random House.

Greer, M. (2004). Strengthen your brain by resting it. *American Psychological Association*, 35(7), 60.

Heath, H. (1977). *Maturity and competence: A transcultural view*. New York: Halsted Press.

Howard, P. J. (2014). *The owner's manual for the brain: Everyday applications of mind-brain research* (4th ed.). New York: HarperCollins.

Johnsgard, K. W. (2004). *Conquering depression and anxiety through exercise*. New York: Prometheus.

Khoshaba, D., & Maddi, S. R. (2005). *HardiTraining: Managing stressful change* (4th ed.). Newport Beach, CA: Hardiness Institute.

Kingkade, T. (2014, August 27). "Sleepy college students are worried about their stress levels." *The Huffington Post*. Retrieved from http://www.huffingtonpost.com/2014/08/27/college-students-sleep-stress_n_5723438.html.

Kramer, A. F., & Erickson, K. I. (2007). Capitalizing on cortical plasticity: Influence of physical activity on cognition and brain function. *Trends in Cognitive Sciences*, 11(8), 342–348.

Kuriyama, K., Mishima, K., Suzuki, H., Aritake, S., & Uchiyama, M. (2008). Sleep accelerates improvement in working memory performance. *The Journal of Neuroscience*, 28(4), 10145–10150.

Lack, L. C., Gradisar, M., Van Someren, E. J. W., Wright, H. R., & Lushington, K. (2008). The relationship between insomnia and body temperatures. *Sleep Medicine Reviews* 12(4), 307–317.

Leavy, P., Gnong, A., & Ross, L. S. (2009). Femininity, masculinity, and body image issues among college-age women: An in-depth and written interview study of the mind-body dichotomy. *The Qualitative Report*, 14(2), 261–292.

Leibel, R. L., Rosenbaum, M., & Hirsch, J. (1995). Changes in energy expenditure resulting from altered body weight. *New England Journal of Medicine*, 332, 621–628.

Levitsky, D. A., Garay, J., Nausbaum, M., Neighbors, L., & Dellavalle, D. M. (2006). Monitoring weight daily blocks the freshman weight gain: A model for combating the epidemic of obesity. *International Journal of Obesity*, 30(6), 1003–1010.

Lucler, K. L. (2015). "15 ways to stay safe while in college." Retrieved from http://collegelife.about.com/od/healthwellness/qt/SafetyTips.htm.

Malinauskas, B. M., Aeby, V. G., Overton, R. F., Carpenter-Aeby, T., & Barber-Heidal, K. (2007). A survey of energy drink consumption patterns among college students. *Nutrition Journal*, 6(1), 35.

Mayo Clinic. (2014, September 19). "Metabolism and weight loss: How you burn calories." Retrieved from http://www.mayoclinic.org/healthy-lifestyle/weight-loss/in-depth/metabolism/art-20046508?pg=1.

Mayo Clinic. (2015). "Rev up your workout with interval training: Interval training can help you get the most out of your workout." Retrieved from http://www.mayoclinic.org/healthy-living/fitness/in-depth/interval-training/art-20044588?pg=1.

Mazurek, K., Karwczyk, K., Zemijeeski, P., Norkoski, H., & Czajkowska, M. (2014). Effects of aerobic interval training versus continuous moderate exercise programme on aerobic and anaerobic capacity, somatic features and blood lipid profile in collegiate females. *Annals of Agricultural and Environmental Medicine*, 21(4), 844–849.

Miller, G. D., & Foster, L. T. (2010). *Critical synthesis of wellness literature*. Victoria: University of Victoria. Retrieved from http://www.geog.uvic.ca/wellness.

Monk, T. H. (2005). The post-lunch dip in performance. *Clinical Sports Medicine*, 24(2), 15–23.

Myers, D. G. (1993). *The pursuit of happiness: Who is happy—and why?* New York: Morrow.

National Institute of Mental Health. (2014). *What are eating disorders?* Washington, DC: U.S. Department of Health and Human Services. Retrieved from http://www.nimh.nih.gov/health/publications/eating-disorders-new-trifold/index.shtml.

National Institutes of Health. (2012). *Why is sleep important?* Retrieved from http://www.nhlbi.nih.gov/health/health-topics/topics/sdd/why.

National Institutes of Health. (2013). *Sleep on it: How snoozing strengthens memories*. Retrieved from https://newsinhealth.nih.gov/issue/apr2013/feature2.

National Institutes of Health. (2015). *What are some myths about sleep?* Retrieved from https://www.nichd.nih.gov/health/topics/sleep/conditioninfo/Pages/sleep-myths.aspx.

Ng, M., & Associates. (2014). Global, regional, and national prevalence of overweight and obesity in children and adults during 1980–2013: A systematic analysis for the Global Burden of Disease Study 2013. *The Lancet*, 384 (No. 9945), 766–781.

NIDDK (National Institute of Diabetes & Digestive Kidney Diseases). (2010). *Overweight and obesity statistics*. Washington, DC: U.S. Department of Health and Human Services.

Nutrition Australia. (2015). *Eat a rainbow*. Retrieved from http://www.nutritionaustralia.org/national/resource/eat-rainbow.

Ohayon, M. M., Carskadon, M. A., Guilleminault, C., & Vitiello, M. V. (2004). Meta-analysis of quantitative sleep parameters from childhood to old age in healthy individuals: developing normative sleep values across the human lifespan. *Sleep, 27*, 1255–1273.

Parker-Pope, T. (2010). "Vigorous exercise linked with better grades." Retrieved from http://query.nytimes.com/gst/fullpage.html?res=9A03EEDE103EF93BA35755C0A9669D8B63.

President's Council on Physical Fitness and Sports. (2001). Toward a uniform definition of wellness: A commentary. *Research Digest, 3*(15), 1–8.

Ratey, J. J. (2013). *Spark: The revolutionary new science of exercise and the brain*. New York: Little, Brown & Company.

Rivera, C. (2015, July 1). "College safety gets a tech boost." *Los Angeles Times*, p. B2.

Roxburgh, et al. (2014). Is moderate intensity exercise training combined with high intensity interval training more effective at improving cardiorespiratory fitness than moderate intensity exercise training alone? *Journal of Sports Science and Medicine, 13*(3), 702–707.

Sax, L. J., Bryant, A. N., & Gilmartin, S. K. (2004). A longitudinal investigation of emotional health among male and female first-year college students. *Journal of the First-Year Experience and Students in Transition, 16*(2), 29–65.

Schlosser, E. (2005). *Fast food nation: The dark side of the all-American meal*. New York: Harper Perennial.

Smolensky, M., & Lamberg, L. (2001*). The body clock guide to better health: How to use your body's natural clock to fight illness and achieve maximum health*. New York: Henry Holt.

"Staying Safe on Campus". (2012 July 20). Retrieved from http://www.nytimes.com/2012/07/20/education/edlife/students-fear-venturing-out-alone-at-night-on-campus.html?pagewanted=all.

Suchecki, D., Tiba, P. A., & Machado, R. B. (2012). REM sleep rebound as an adaptive response to stressful situations. *Frontiers in Neurology, 3*, 41.

Van Dongen, H. P. A., Maislin, G., Mullington, J. M., & Dinges, D. F. (2003). The cumulative cost of additional wakefulness: Dose—response effects on neurobehavioral functions and sleep physiology from chronic sleep restriction and total sleep deprivation. *Sleep, 26*, 117–126.

Voelker, R. (2004). Stress, sleep loss, and substance abuse create potent recipe for college depression. *Journal of the American Medical Association, 291*, 2177–2179.

Walsh, N. P., Gleeson, M., Shephard, R. J., Woods, J. A., Bishop, N. C., Fleshner, M., Green, C., Pedersen, B. K., Hoffman-Goetz, L., Rogers, C. J., Northoff, H., Abbasi, A., & Simon. P. (2011). Position statement. Part one: Immune function and exercise. *Exercise Immunology Review, 17*, 6–63.

Willis, J. (2006). *Research-based strategies to ignite student learning: Insights from a neurologist and classroom teacher*. Alexandria, VA: ASCD.

Wolfson, A. R., & Carskadon, M. A. (2003). Understanding adolescents' sleep patterns and school performance: A critical appraisal. *Sleep Medicine Reviews, 7*(6), 491–506.

World Health Organization. (2012). *Obesity and overweight*. Retrieved from http://www.who.int/entity/mediacentre/factsheets/fs311/en/index.html.

Youngstedt, S. D. (2005). Effects of exercise on sleep. *Clinical Sports Medicine, 24*(2), 355–365.

Zimbardo, P. G., Johnson, R. L., & McCann, V. (2012). *Psychology: Core concepts* (7th ed.). Boston: Pearson.

Chapter 6 Exercises

6.1 Quote Reflections

Review the sidebar quotes contained in this chapter and select two that were especially meaningful or inspirational to you.

For each quote, provide a three- to five-sentence explanation why you chose it.

6.2 Wellness Self-Assessment for Self-Improvement

For each aspect of wellness listed below, rate yourself in terms of how close you are to doing what you should be doing (1 = furthest from the ideal, 5 = closest to the ideal).

	Nowhere Close to What I Should Be Doing 1	2	Not Bad but Should Be Better 3	4	Right Where I Should Be 5
Nutrition	1	2	3	4	5
Exercise	1	2	3	4	5
Sleep	1	2	3	4	5
Alcohol and Drugs	1	2	3	4	5

For each area in which there's a gap between where you are now and where you should be, identify the best action you could take to reduce or eliminate the gap.

6.3 Nutritional Self-Assessment and Self-Improvement

1. Go to: *www.ChooseMyPlate.gov*.
2. For each of the five food groups listed below, record in the first column the amount you *should* be consuming daily; in the second column, estimate the amount you *do* consume daily.

Basic Food Type	Amount Recommended	Amount Consumed
Fruits		
Vegetables		
Grains		
Protein Foods		
Dairy		

Chapter 6 Health and Wellness

3. For any food group that you're consuming less than the recommended amounts, use the website to find foods that would enable you to meet the recommended daily amount. Write down those food items, and answer the following questions about each of them:

   (a) How likely is it that you'll actually add these food items to your regular diet?

   Very Likely   Possibly   Very Unlikely

   (b) For those food items you identified as "very unlikely," why would you be very unlikely to add these items to your regular diet?

6.4 Identifying Your Peak Performance Times

Refer to your results from the *My PEPS Learning Style Inventory*, under the section Time of Day Preference.

What do the results suggest about times during the day when you're at your best and when it would be best to schedule your most challenging academic work?

How could you set up a study schedule that allows you to make the best use of the time when you're most productive while still balancing your other responsibilities?

FYE Health Habits

Name: _____

Section: _____

List four healthy behaviors you practice in your everyday life:
1.
2.
3.
4.

List four unhealthy behaviors you currently practice:
1.
2.
3.
4.

Why do you partake in these unhealthy behaviors?

How do these unhealthy behaviors negatively impact your success in College?

What can you do to improve upon your unhealthy behaviors?

CHAPTER 7

Time Management

PRIORITIZING TASKS, PREVENTING PROCRASTINATION, AND PROMOTING PRODUCTIVITY

Chapter Preview

Time is a valuable personal resource—if you gain greater control of it, you gain greater control of your life. Time managed well not only enables you to get work done in a timely manner; it also enables you to set and attain personal priorities and maintain balance in your life. This chapter offers a comprehensive set of strategies for managing time, combating procrastination, and ensuring that you spend time in a way that aligns with your educational goals and priorities.

Learning Goal

Equip you with a powerful set of strategies for setting priorities, planning time, and completing tasks in a timely and productive manner.

Integrate Your Faith

We should have our ears open to hearing when those around us are in need. Using the talents and blessings God has given you, what are some ways that you could fit some time into your schedule to meet the need of others?

Ignite Your Thinking

Reflection 7.1

Complete the following sentence with the first thought that comes to your mind:

For me, time is . . .

The Importance of Time Management

To have any realistic chance of attaining our goals, we need an intentional and strategic plan for spending our time in a way that aligns with our goals and enables us to make steady progress toward them. Thus, setting goals, reaching goals, and managing time are interrelated skills.

"The major difference [between high school and college] is time. You have so much free time on your hands that you don't know what to do for most of the time."

—*First-year college student (Erickson & Strommer,* Teaching College Freshmen*)*

From *Thriving in College and Beyond: Research-Based Strategies for Academic Success and Personal Development*, Fourth Edition by Joseph B. Cuseo, Aaron Thompson, Michele Campagna, and Viki S. Fecas. Copyright © 2016 Kendall Hunt Publishing Company. Reprinted by permission.

> "I cannot stress enough that you need to intelligently budget your time."
>
> —Advice to new college students from a student finishing his first year in college

Most college students struggle to at least some extent with time management, particularly first-year students who are transitioning from the lockstep schedules of high school to the more unstructured time associated with college course schedules. National surveys indicate that almost 50% of first-year college students report difficulty managing their time effectively (HERI, 2014). In college, time-management skills grow in importance because students' time is less structured or controlled by school authorities or family members and more responsibility is placed on students to make their own decisions about how their time will be spent. Furthermore, the academic calendar and class scheduling patterns in college differ radically from high school. There's less "seat time" in class each week and college students are expected to do much more academic work on their courses outside of class time, which this leaves them with a lot more "free time" to manage.

Simply stated, college students who have difficulty managing their time have difficulty managing college. One study compared college sophomores who had an outstanding first year (both academically and personally) with sophomores who struggled in their first year. Interviews with both groups revealed there was one key difference between them: sophomores who experienced a successful first year repeatedly brought up the topic of time during the interviews. The successful students said they had to think carefully about how they spent their time and that they needed to budget their time. In contrast, sophomores who experienced difficulty in their first year of college hardly talked about the topic of time during their interviews, even when they were specifically asked about it (Light, 2001).

Studies also indicate that people of all ages report time management to be a critical element of their life. Working adults report that setting priorities and balancing multiple responsibilities (e.g., work and family) can be a stressful juggling act (Harriott & Ferrari, 1996). For them, time management and stress management are interrelated. These findings suggest that time management is more than just a college success skill; it's also a life management and life success skill that benefits both our family life and work life (Gupta, Hershey, & Gaur, 2012). When we gain greater control of our time, we gain greater control and a greater sense of satisfaction with all areas of our life. In fact, studies show that people who manage their time well report feeling happier (Myers, 1993, 2000).

Strategies for Managing Time and Tasks

Effectively managing our time and our tasks involves three key processes:

1. **Analysis**—breaking down time to see how much of it we have and what we're spending it on;
2. **Itemizing**—identifying and listing the tasks that we need to complete and when we need to complete them; and

3. **Prioritizing**—ranking our tasks in terms of their importance and attacking them in order of their importance.

The following strategies can be used to implement these three processes and should help you open up more time in your schedule, enabling you to discover new ways to use your time more productively.

Become more aware of how your time is spent by breaking it into smaller units. How often have you heard someone say, "Where did all the time go?" or "I just can't seem to find the time!" One way to find out where all our time goes and find more time to get things done is by doing a *time analysis*—a detailed examination of how much total time we have and where we're spending it—including patches of wasted time when we get little done and nothing accomplished. This time analysis only has to be done for a week or two to give us a pretty good idea of where our time is going and to find better ways to use our time productively.

(Complete the online Exercise 7.5 at the end of this chapter to gain insights into how you organize your time and the approach you take to completing tasks.)

Identify *what* specific tasks you need to accomplish and *when* you need to accomplish them. When we want to remember items we need to buy at the grocery store or people we want to invite to a party, we make a list. This same list-making strategy can be used for tasks we need to complete so we don't forget about them, or forget to do them on time. One characteristic of successful people is that they are list makers; they make lists for things they want to accomplish each day (Covey, 2004).

Take advantage of time-planning and task-management tools, such as the following:

- *Small, portable planner.* You can use this device to list all your major assignments and exams for the term, along with their due dates. By pulling together all work tasks required in each of your courses and getting them in one place, it will be much easier to keep track of what you have to do and when you have to do it throughout the entire term. It will also sync with the same calendar programs available on your desktop or laptop.
- *Large, stable calendar.* In the calendar's date boxes, record your major assignments for the term. The calendar should be posted in a place you can see it every day (e.g., bedroom or refrigerator). If you repeatedly see the things you have to do, you're less likely to overlook them, forget about them, or subconsciously push them out of your mind because you'd really prefer not to do them.
- *Smartphone.* This device can be used for more than checking social networking sites and sending or receiving text messages. It can be used as a calendar tool to record due dates and set up alert functions to remind

Using a calendar is an effective way to itemize your academic commitments.

you of deadlines. Many smartphones also allow you to set up task or "to-do" lists and set priorities for each item entered. A variety of apps are now available for planning tasks and tracking time spent on tasks (for example, see: http://www.rememberthemilk.com). Take advantage of these cutting-edge tools, but at the same time, keep in mind that planners don't plan time, people do. Effectively planning time and tasks flows from a clear vision of your goals and priorities.

Prioritize: rank tasks in order of their importance. After you itemize your work tasks by identifying and listing them, the next step is to *prioritize* them—determine the order or sequence in which they get done. Prioritizing basically involves ranking tasks in terms of their importance, with the highest-priority tasks placed at the top of the list to ensure they're tackled first.

How do you decide on what tasks are to be ranked highest and tackled first? Here are two key criteria (standards of judgment) for determining your highest-priority tasks:

- **Urgency.** Tasks that are closest to their deadline or due date should receive highest priority. Finishing an assignment that's due tomorrow should receive higher priority than starting an assignment that's due next month.
- **Gravity.** Tasks that carry the greatest weight (count the most) should receive highest priority. If an assignment worth 100 points and an assignment worth 10 points are due at the same time, the 100-point task should receive higher priority. We want to be sure to invest our work time on tasks that matter most. Similar to investing money, we should invest our time on tasks that yield the greatest pay-off.

> **Note**
>
> *Put first things first: Plan your work by identifying your most important and most urgent tasks, and work your plan by attacking these tasks first.*

An effective strategy for prioritizing tasks is to divide them into "A," "B," and "C" lists (Lakein, 1973; Morgenstern, 2004). The "A" list is reserved for *essential* (nonnegotiable) tasks—those that that *must* be done now. The "B" list is for *important* tasks—those that *should* be done soon. The "C" list is for *optional* tasks—those that *could* or *might* be done if there's time remaining after the more important tasks on lists A and B have been completed. Organizing tasks and time in this fashion helps you decide how to divide your labor in a way that ensures you "put first things first." You shouldn't waste time doing unimportant things to deceive yourself into thinking that you're "getting stuff done"—when, in reality, all you're doing is "keeping busy" and

> "Things that matter most must never be at the mercy of things that matter least."
> —Johann Wolfgang von Goethe, German poet, dramatist, and author of the epic *Faust*

> "When I have lots of homework to do, I suddenly go through this urge to clean up and organize the house. I'm thinking, 'I'm not wasting my time. I'm cleaning up the house and that's something I have to do.' But all I'm really doing is avoiding school work."
> —College sophomore

distracting yourself (and subtracting time) from doing the things that should be done.

Note
Developing awareness of how our time is spent is more than a brainless, clerical activity. When it's done well, it becomes an exercise in self-awareness and values clarification—how we spend our time is a true test of who we are and what we really value.

Create a Time-Management Plan

You may have heard of the old proverb, "A stitch in time saves nine." Planning your time represents the "stitch" (unit of time) that saves you nine additional stitches (units of time). Similar to successful chess players, successful time managers plan ahead and anticipate their next moves.

Don't buy into the myth that taking time to plan takes time away from getting started and getting things done. Time-management experts estimate that the amount of time planning your total work actually reduces your total work time by a factor of three: for every one unit of time you spend planning, you save three units of time working (Goldsmith, 2010; Lakein, 1973). For example, 5 minutes of planning time will typically save you 15 minutes of total work time, and 10 minutes of planning time will save you 30 minutes of work time.

Planning your time saves you time because it ensures you start off in the right direction. If you have a plan of attack, you're less vulnerable to "false starts"—starting your work and then discovering you're not on the right track or not doing things in the right sequence, which forces you to retreat and start all over again.

> "If you fail to plan, you are planning to fail."
> —Benjamin Franklin, renowned author, inventor, civic activist, and a founding father of the United States

Once you have accepted the idea that taking time to plan your time will save you time in the long run, you're ready to create a plan for effectively managing time. Listed below are specific strategies for doing so.

Take *portable work* with you during the day that you can work at any place at any time. This will enable you to take advantage of "dead time" such as time spent sitting and waiting for appointments or transportation. Portable work allows you to resurrect dead time and transform it into productive work time. Not only is this a good time-management strategy, it's a good stress-management strategy because you replace the frustration and boredom associated with having no control over "wait time" with a sense of accomplishment.

Make good use of your *free time between classes* by working on assignments and studying in advance for upcoming exams. See **Box 7.1** for a summary of how you can use your out-of-class time to improve your academic performance and course grades.

Box 7.1

Making Productive Use of "Free Time" Outside the Classroom

Students' class schedules in college differ radically from high school. College students are often pleasantly surprised by how much "free time" they have because they're spending much less time in class. However, students are expected to spend two or more hours outside of class for every hour they spend in class. Thus, using out-of-class time strategically and productively is critical to ensuring college success.

Compared to high school, "homework" in college typically doesn't involve turning in assignments on a daily or weekly basis. Academic work done outside the college classroom may not even be collected and graded. Instead, it's often assigned for your own benefit to help you prepare for upcoming exams and complete written reports (e.g., assigned reading and assigned problems in math and science). Rather than formally assigning and collecting this work as homework, your professors expect that you will do this work on your own and without supervision.

> " In high school we were given a homework assignment every day. Now we have a large task assigned to be done at a certain time. No one tells [us] when to start or what to do each day."
> —First-year college student

Listed in this box are strategies for working independently and in advance of college exams and assignments. By building time for each of these activities into your regular schedule, you'll make more productive use of out-of-class time, decrease your level of stress, and strengthen your academic performance.

Doing Out-of-Class Work in Advance of Exams

- **Complete reading assignments** relating to lecture topics *before* the topic is discussed in class. This will make lectures easier to understand and enable you to participate intelligently in class (e.g., by asking meaningful questions and making informed comments during class discussions).

- **Review class notes** from your last class before the next class to build a mental bridge from one class to the next. Many students don't look at their class notes until they study them right before an exam. Don't be one of those students; instead, review your notes before the next class. Rewrite any class notes that may have been sloppily written the first time. If you find notes related to the same point all over the place, reorganize them into the same section. Lastly, if you find any information gaps or confusing points in your notes, seek out the course instructor or a trusted classmate to clear them up before the next class takes place.

  By reviewing your class notes on a regular basis, you will improve your ability to understand each upcoming lecture and reduce the total time you'll need to spend studying your notes the night before an exam.

- **Review your reading notes and highlights** to improve retention of important material. If you find certain points in your reading to be confusing, discuss them with your course instructor during office hours or with a fellow classmate outside of class.

- **Integrate class material with reading material.** Connect related information from your lecture notes and reading notes and get them in the same place (e.g., on the same index card).

- **Use a "part-to-whole" study method** whereby you study material from your class notes and assigned reading in small pieces (parts) during short, separate study sessions in advance of the exam; then make your last study session before the exam a longer review session during which you restudy all the small parts (the whole) at the

Box 7.1 (continued)

same time. Don't buy into the myth that studying in advance is a waste of time because you'll forget everything you studied by test time. As will be fully explained in Chapter 5, material studied in advance of an exam remains in your brain and is still there when you later review it. Even if it doesn't immediately come back to mind when you first start reviewing it, you'll relearn it much faster than you did the first time.

Doing Out-of-Class Work in Advance of Term Papers and Research Reports

Work on large, long-range assignments due at the end of the term by breaking them into smaller, short-term tasks completed at separate times during the term. For instance, a large term paper may be broken up into the following smaller tasks and completed in separate installments.

1. Search for and decide on a topic.
2. Locate sources of information on the topic.
3. Organize information obtained from your sources into categories.
4. Develop an outline of your paper's major points and the order or sequence in which you plan to present them.
5. Construct a first draft of your paper (and, if necessary, a second or third draft).
6. Write a final draft of your paper.
7. Proofread your final draft for spelling and grammatical errors before turning it in.

Reflection 7.2

Do you have time gaps between your classes this term? If you do, what have you been doing during these "free" periods between classes?

What would you say is your greatest between-class time waster?

Do you see a need to stop or eliminate it?

If yes, what could you do to convert your wasted time into productive time?

A good time-management plan transforms intention into action. Once you've planned the work, the next step is to work the plan. A time-management plan turns into an action plan when you: (a) preview what you intend to do, (b) review whether you actually did what you intended to do, and (c) close the gap between your intentions and actions. The action plan begins with your *daily to-do list*, bringing that list with you as the day begins, and checking off items on the list as they're completed during the day. At the end of the day, the list is reviewed to determine what got done and what still needs to be done. The uncompleted tasks then become high priorities on the following day's to-do list.

A good time-management plan includes reserving time for the unexpected. Always hope for the best, but prepare for the worst. Your plan should include a buffer zone or safety net that contains extra time in case you encounter unforeseen developments or unexpected emergencies. Just as you should plan to have extra funds in your account to pay for unexpected expenses (e.g., auto repair), you should plan to have extra time in your schedule for unexpected events (e.g., personal illness or family emergency).

A good time-management plan should also contain time for work and play. Your plan shouldn't consist solely of a daunting list of work tasks you have to do; it should also include fun things you like to do. Plan time to relax, refuel, and recharge. Your overall time-management plan shouldn't turn you into an obsessive-compulsive workaholic. Instead, it should represent a balanced blend of work and play, including activities that promote your mental and physical wellness—such as recreation and reflection. Consider following the daily "8-8-8 rule"—eight hours for sleep, eight hours for school, and eight hours for other activities.

If you schedule things you like to do, you're more likely do to the things you have to do. You're much more likely to faithfully execute your plan if play time is scheduled along with work time, and if you use play as a reward for completing your work.

A good time-management plan has some flexibility. A time-management plan shouldn't enslave you to a rigid work schedule. The plan should be flexible enough to allow you to occasionally bend it without breaking it. Just as work commitments and family responsibilities can crop up unexpectedly, so, too, can opportunities for fun and enjoyable activities. Your plan should allow you the freedom to modify your schedule to take advantage of these enjoyable opportunities and experiences. However, you should plan to make up the work time you lost. In other words, you can borrow or trade work time for play time, but don't "steal" it; plan to pay back the work time you borrowed by substituting it for play time that was planned for another time. If you decide not to do work you planned, the next best thing to do is re-plan when you'll do it.

Dealing with Procrastination

A major enemy of effective time management is procrastination. Procrastinators don't abide by the proverb: "Why put off till tomorrow what can be done today?" Instead, their philosophy is just the opposite: "Why do today what can be put off till tomorrow?" Adopting this philosophy promotes a perpetual pattern of postponing what needs to be done until the last possible moment, forcing the procrastinator to rush frantically to finish work on time and turn in work that's inferior or incomplete (or not turn in anything at all).

> **Murphy's Laws:**
> 1. Nothing is as simple as it looks.
> 2. Everything takes longer than it should.
> 3. If anything can go wrong, it will.
>
> —Author unknown (Murphy's Laws were named after Captain Edward Murphy, a naval engineer)

> **List of Things To Do Today**
> 1. Write Paper
> 2. Study for Math Test
> 3. Prepare Speech
>
> **List of Things Due Today**
> 1. Turn in Paper
> 2. Take Math Test
> 3. Deliver Speech
>
> Next time I'll start sooner!

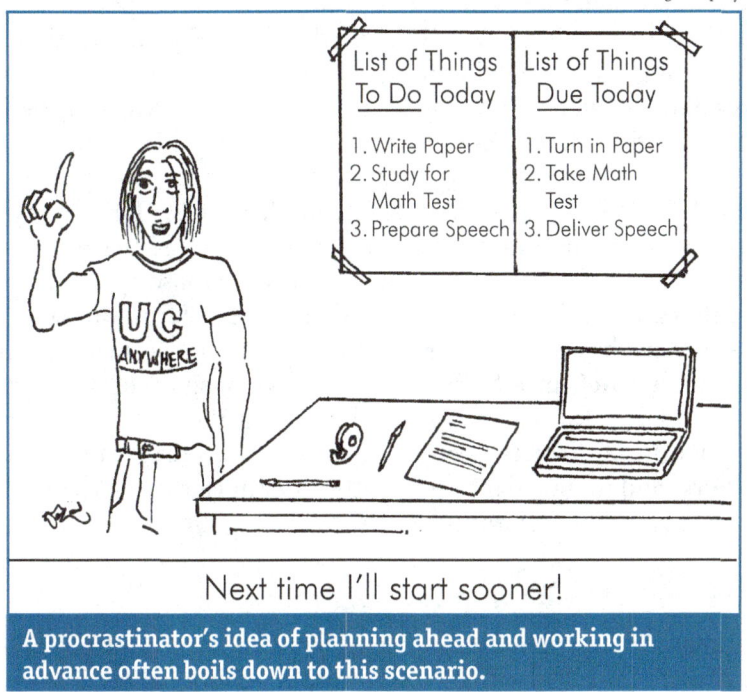

A procrastinator's idea of planning ahead and working in advance often boils down to this scenario.

Research shows that 80% to 95% of college students procrastinate (Steel, 2007) and almost 50% report that they procrastinate consistently (Onwuegbuzie, 2000). Procrastination is such a serious issue for college students that some campuses have opened "procrastination centers" to help them (Burka & Yuen, 2008).

Myths That Promote Procrastination

To have any hope of putting a stop to procrastination, procrastinators need to let go of two popular myths or misconceptions about time and performance.

Myth 1. "I work better under pressure" (e.g., on the day or night before something is due). Procrastinators often confuse desperation with motivation. Their belief that they work better under pressure is usually a rationalization to justify the fact that they *only* work under pressure—when they have to work because they've run out of time and are under the gun of a looming deadline.

It's true that when people are under pressure, they will start working and work with frantic energy, but that doesn't mean they're working more *effectively* and producing work of better *quality*. Because procrastinators are playing "beat the clock," they focus less on doing the job well and more on beating the buzzer. This typically results in a work product that's incomplete or inferior to what could have been produced if they had begun the work process sooner.

> Haste makes waste."
> —Benjamin Franklin

Myth 2. "Studying in advance is a waste of time because you will forget it all by test time." This myth is used by procrastinators to justify putting off all studying until the night before an exam. As will be discussed in Chapter 5, studying that's distributed (spread out) over time is more effective than massed (crammed) studying all at one time. Furthermore, last minute studying before exams often involves pulling "late-nighters" or "all-nighters" that result in sleep loss. This fly-by-night strategy deprives the brain of dream sleep (a.k.a. REM sleep), which it needs to retain information and manage stress (Hobson, 1988; Voelker, 2004). Research indicates that procrastinators suffer from higher rates of stress-related physical disorders, such as insomnia, stomach problems, colds, and flu (McCance & Pychyl, 2003). Working under time pressure also increases performance pressure by leaving the procrastinators with (a) no margin of error to correct mistakes, (b) no time to seek help on their work, and (c) no chance to handle random catastrophes or setbacks that may arise at the last minute.

Psychological Causes of Procrastination

Sometimes, procrastination has deeper psychological roots. People may procrastinate for reasons that relate more to emotional issues than poor time-management habits. Studies show that some people procrastinate as a psychological strategy to protect their self-esteem. Referred to as *self-handicapping* (Rhodewalt & Vohs, 2005), this strategy is used by some procrastinators, often unconsciously, to give themselves a "handicap" or disadvantage. By starting their work at the last possible moment, if their performance turns out to be less than spectacular, they can always conclude (rationalize) that it was because they were performing under a handicap—lack of time rather than lack of ability (Chu & Cho, 2005).

For example, if they receive a low grade on a test or paper, they can "save face" (self-esteem) by concluding that it was because they waited until the last minute and didn't put much time or effort into it. In other words, they had enough ability or intelligence to earn a high grade; they just didn't put in enough time. Better yet, if they happen to get a good grade—despite their last-minute, last-ditch effort—it proves just how smart they are. It shows they were able to earn a high grade, even without putting in much time at all. Thus, self-handicapping creates a fail-safe or win-win scenario that always protects the procrastinators' self-image.

In addition to self-handicapping, other psychological factors have been found to contribute to procrastination, including the following:

- **Fear of failure.** The procrastinator feels better about not turning in work than turning it in and getting negative feedback (Burka & Yuen, 2008; Solomon & Rothblum, 1984);

- **Perfectionism.** The procrastinator has unrealistically high personal standards or expectations, which leads to the belief that it's better to postpone work or not do it than to risk doing it less than perfectly (Kachgal, Hansel, & Nuter, 2001);
- **Fear of success.** The procrastinator fears that doing well will show others that he has the ability to achieve success, leading others to expect him to maintain those high standards in the future (Beck, Koons, & Milgram, 2000; Ellis & Knaus, 2002);
- **Indecisiveness.** The procrastinator has difficulty making decisions, including decisions about what to do first, when to do it, or whether to do it (Anderson, 2003; Steel, 2007), so they delay doing it or don't do it at all; and
- **Thrill seeking.** The procrastinator is hooked on the adrenaline rush triggered by rushing around to get things done just before a deadline (Szalavitz, 2003).

If these psychological issues are at the root of procrastination, they must be uprooted and dealt with before the problem can be solved. This may take some time and assistance from a counseling psychologist (either on or off campus) who is professionally trained to deal with emotional issues, including those that underlie procrastination.

Strategies for Preventing and Overcoming Procrastination

Consistently use effective time-management strategies. When effective time-management practices (such as those cited in this chapter) are implemented consistently, they turn into regular habits. Research indicates that procrastinators are less likely to procrastinate when they convert their intentions or vows ("I swear I'm going to start tomorrow") into concrete action plans (Gollwitzer, 1999; Gollwitzer & Sheeran, 2006). When they repeatedly practice effective time-management strategies with respect to tasks they tend to procrastinate on, their bad procrastination habits gradually fade and are replaced by good time-management habits (Ainslie, 1992; Baumeister, Heatherton, & Tice, 1994).

> "We are what we repeatedly do. Excellence, then, is not an act, but a habit."
> —Aristotle, influential Ancient Greek philosopher

Make the start of work as inviting or appealing as possible. Starting work—getting off the starting blocks—is often the major stumbling block for procrastinators. It's common for procrastinators to experience what's known as "start-up stress"—when they're about to start a task, they start having negative feelings about it—expecting it to be difficult, stressful, or boring (Burka & Yuen, 2008).

If you have trouble starting your work, sequence your work tasks in a way that allows you to start on tasks you find more interesting or are more likely to do well. Beginning with these tasks can give you a "jump start," enabling you to overcome inertia and create momentum. You can

> "The secret to getting ahead is getting started."
> —Mark Twain (Samuel Clemens), American humorist and author of the Adventures of Huckleberry Finn (1885), a.k.a. "the Great American Novel"

ride this initial momentum to motivate you to attack less appealing or more daunting work tasks that come later in your work sequence, which often turn out not to be as unpleasant or time-consuming as you thought they would be. Like many events in life, anticipation of the event turns out to be worse than the event itself. In one study of college students who didn't start a project until just before its due date, it was found that that they experienced anxiety and guilt while they were procrastinating, but once they began working, these negative emotions subsided and were replaced by more positive feelings of progress and accomplishment (McCance & Pychyl, 2003).

> "Did you ever dread doing something, then it turned out to take only about 20 minutes to do?"
>
> —Conversation between two college students overheard in a coffee shop

You can also reduce start-up stress by beginning your work in an environment you find pleasant and relaxing (e.g., working in your favorite coffee shop while sipping your favorite beverage). In other words, if you have trouble starting work, start it in a place you enjoy while doing something you enjoy.

Organization matters. Research indicates that disorganization is a factor that contributes to procrastination (Steel, 2007). How well you organize your workplace and manage your work materials can reduce your tendency to procrastinate. Having the right materials in the right place at the right time can make it easier to get started. Once you decide to start working, you don't want to delay acting on that decision by looking for the tools you need to work with. If you're a procrastinator, this slight delay may provide the time (and excuse) to change your mind and not start working.

Note
The less time and effort it takes to start working, the more likely the work will be started.

One simple, yet effective way to organize academic materials is to develop your own file system. Start by filing (storing) materials from different courses in different colored folders or notebooks. This not only enables you to keep all materials related to the same course in the same place, it also gives you immediate access to them when you need them. A file system helps get you organized, gets rid of the stress associated with having things all over the place, and reduces your risk of procrastinating by reducing the time and effort it takes to get started.

Location matters. *Where* you choose to work can influence *whether* your work gets done. Research indicates that distractions promote procrastination (Steel, 2007). Thus, working in an environment that minimizes distraction and maximizes concentration will reduce the risk of procrastination.

Arrange your work environment in a way that minimizes social distractions (e.g., people nearby who are not working), and media distractions (e.g., cell phones, e-mails, text messages, music, and TV). Remove everything from your work site that's not relevant or directly related to the work you're doing.

Your concentration will also improve if you work in an environment that allows you easy access to (a) work-support materials (e.g., class notes, textbooks, and a dictionary), and (b) social-support networks (e.g., working with a group of motivated students who help you stay focused, on task, and on track toward completing your work).

If you have difficulty maintaining or sustaining commitment to your work until it's finished, schedule easier and more interesting work tasks *in the middle or toward the end* **of your planned work time.** Some procrastinators have difficulty starting work, others have trouble continuing and completing the work they've started (Pierro, et al., 2011). As previously mentioned, if you have trouble starting work, it might be best for you to start with tasks you find most interesting or easiest. In contrast, if you tend to experience procrastination by not completing your work once you've started, it might be better to schedule tasks of greater interest and ease at later points during your work session. Doing so can restore or revive your interest and energy. Tackling enjoyable and easier tasks last can also provide you with an incentive or reward for completing your less enjoyable and more difficult tasks first. (Take a look at the Persistence Preference results of your My PEPS Learning Inventory. What do the results say about your inclination to finish tasks and activities?)

> "I'm very good at starting things but often have trouble keeping a sustained effort."
> —*First-year college student*

If you're close to completing a task, "go for the kill"—finish it then and there—rather than stopping and completing it later. Completing a task that's almost done allows you to build on the momentum you've already generated. In contrast, postponing work on a task that's near completion means that you have to overcome inertia and regenerate momentum all over again. As the old saying goes, "There's no time like the present."

Furthermore, finishing a task gives you a sense of *closure*—the feeling of personal accomplishment and self-satisfaction that comes from knowing you've "closed the deal." Checking off a completed task can motivate you to keep going and complete the unfinished tasks ahead of you.

> "Just do it."
> —*Commercial slogan of Nike, athletic equipment company named after the Greek goddess of victory*

Divide large work tasks into smaller, bite-sized pieces. Work becomes less overwhelming and stressful when it's handled in small chunks or segments. You can conquer procrastination for large tasks by using a "divide and conquer" strategy: divide the large task into smaller, more manageable subtasks; then tackle and complete these subtasks one at a time.

Don't underestimate the power of short work sessions. They're often more effective than longer sessions because it's easier to maintain concentration and momentum for shorter periods of time. By dividing work into short sessions, you can take quick jabs at a tall task, poke holes in it, and shrink its overall size with each successive jab. This reduces the pressure of having to deliver one, big knockout punch right before the final bell (deadline date).

> "To eat an elephant, first cut it into small pieces."
> —*Author unknown*

Chapter Summary and Highlights

Effective goal-setting gets you going, but effective time management gets things done. To manage time effectively, we need to

- *Analyze* it. Break down time and become aware of how we spend it;
- *Itemize* it. Identify the tasks we need to accomplish and their due dates; and
- *Prioritize* it. Tackle our tasks in order of their importance.

Developing a comprehensive time-management plan for academic work involves long-, mid-, and short-range steps that involve:

- Planning the total term (long-range steps);
- Planning your week (mid-range steps); and
- Planning your day (short-range steps).

A good time-management plan includes the following features:

- It transforms intention to action.
- It includes time to take care of unexpected developments.
- It contains time for work and play.
- It gives you the flexibility to accommodate unforeseen opportunities.

The enemy of effective time management is procrastination. Overcoming it involves letting go of two major myths:

- Better work is produced "under pressure"—on the day or night before it's due.
- Studying in advance is a waste of time—because you'll forget it all by test time.

Effective strategies for beating the procrastination habit include the following:

- Organize your work materials to make it easy and convenient for you to start working.
- Organize your work place or space so that you work in a location that minimizes distractions and temptations not to work.
- Intentionally arrange your work schedule so that you are working on more enjoyable or stimulating tasks at times when you're less vulnerable to procrastination.
- If you're close to finishing a task, finish it, because it's often harder to restart a task than to complete one that's already been started.
- Divide large tasks into smaller, more manageable units and tackle them in separate work sessions.

> "Doesn't thou love life? Then do not squander time, for that is the stuff life is made of."
>
> —Benjamin Franklin, 18th-century inventor, newspaper writer, and cosigner of the Declaration of Independence

Mastering the skill of managing time is critical for success in college and beyond. Time is one of our most powerful personal resources; the better we manage it, the more likely we are to achieve our goals and gain control of our life.

Learning More through the World Wide Web: Internet-Based Resources

For additional information on managing time, and preventing procrastination, see the following websites:

Time-Management Strategies for All Students:
www.studygs.net/timman.htm

www.pennstatelearning.psu.edu/resources/study-tips/time-mgt

Time-Management Strategies for Adult Students:
www.essortment.com/lifestyle/timemanagement_sjmu.htm

Beating Procrastination:
www.mindtools.com/pages/article/newHTE_96.htm

http://success.oregonstate.edu/learning-corner/time-management/managing-procrastination

References

Ainslie, G. (1992). Specious reward: A behavioral theory of impulsiveness and impulse control. *Psychological Bulletin, 82*, 463–496.

Anderson, C. J. (2003). The psychology of doing nothing: Forms of decision avoidance result from reason and emotion. *Psychological Bulletin, 129*, 139–167.

Baumeister, R. F., Heatherton, T. F., & Tice, D. M. (1994). *Losing control: How and why people fail at self-regulation*. San Diego, CA: Academic Press.

Beck, B. L., Koons, S. R., & Milgram, D. L. (2000). Correlates and consequences of behavioural procrastination: The effects of academic procrastination, self-consciousness, self-esteem and self-handicapping. [Special issue], *Journal of Social Behaviour & Personality, 15*(5), 3–13.

Burka, J. B., & Yuen, L. M. (2008). *Procrastination: Why you do it, what to do about it now*. Cambridge, MA: De Capo Press.

Chu, A. H. C., & Cho, J. N. (2005). Rethinking procrastination: Positive effects of "active" procrastination behavior on attitudes and performance. *The Journal of Social Psychology, 145*(3), 245–264.

Covey, S. R. (2004). *Seven habits of highly effective people* (3rd ed.). New York: Fireside.

Ellis, A., & Knaus, W. J. (2002). *Overcoming procrastination* (Rev. ed.). New York: New American Library.

Goldsmith, E. B. (2010). *Resource management for individuals and families* (4th ed.). Upper Saddle River, NJ: Prentice Hall.

Gollwitzer, P. M. (1999). Implementation intentions: Strong effects of simple plans. *American Psychologist, 54*(7), 493–503.

Gollwitzer, P. M., & Sheeran, P. (2006). Implementation intentions and goal achievement: A meta-analysis of effects and processes. *Advances in Experimental Social Psychology, 38*, 69–119.

Gupta, R., Hershey, D. A., & Gaur, J. (2012). Time perspective and procrastination in the workplace: An empirical investigation. *Current Psychology, 31*(2), 195–211.

Harriot, J., & Ferrari, J. R. (1996). Prevalence of procrastination among samples of adults. *Psychological Reports, 78*, 611–616.

HERI (Higher Education Research Institute). (2014). *Your first college year survey 2014*. Los Angeles, CA:

Cooperative Institutional Research Program, University of California—Los Angeles.

Hobson, J. A. (1988). *The dreaming brain*. New York: Basic Books.

Kachgal, M. M., Hansen, L. S., & Nutter, K. T. (2001). Academic procrastination prevention/intervention: Strategies and recommendations. *Journal of Developmental Education, 25*(1), 2–12.

Lakein, A. (1973). *How to get control of your time and your life*. New York: New American Library.

Light, R. J. (2001). *Making the most of college: Students speak their minds*. Cambridge, MA: Harvard University Press.

McCance, N., & Pychyl, T. A. (2003, August). *From task avoidance to action: An experience sampling study of undergraduate students' thoughts, feelings and coping strategies in relation to academic procrastination*. Paper presented at the Third Annual Conference for Counseling Procrastinators in the Academic Context, University of Ohio, Columbus.

Morgenstern, J. (2004). *Time management from the inside out: The foolproof system for taking control of your schedule—and your life* (2nd ed.). New York: Henry Holt & Co.

Myers, D. G. (1993). *The pursuit of happiness: Who is happy—and why?* New York: Morrow.

Myers, D. G. (2000). *The American paradox: Spiritual hunger in an age of plenty*. New Haven, CT: Yale University Press.

Onwuegbuzie, A. J. (2000). Academic procrastinators and perfectionistic tendencies among graduate students. *Journal of Social Behavior and Personality, 15*, 103–109.

Pierro, A., Giacomantonio, M., Pica, G., Kruglanski, A. W., & Higgins, E. T. (2011). On the psychology of time in action: regulatory mode orientations and procrastination. *Journal of Personality and Social Psychology, 101*(6), 1317–1331.

Rhodewalt, F., & Vohs, K. D. (2005). Defensive strategies, motivation, and the self. In A. Elliot & C. Dweck (Eds.). *Handbook of competence and motivation* (pp. 548–565). New York: Guilford Press.

Solomon, L. J., & Rothblum, E. D. (1984). Academic procrastination: Frequency and cognitive-behavioral correlates. *Journal of Counseling Psychology, 31*(4), 503–509.

Steel, P. (2007). The nature of procrastination: A meta-analytic and theoretical review of quintessential self-regulatory failure. *Psychological Bulletin, 133*(1), 65–94.

Szalavitz, M. (2003, July/August). Tapping potential: Stand and deliver. *Psychology Today*, 50–54.

Voelker, R. (2004). Stress, sleep loss, and substance abuse create potent recipe for college depression. *Journal of the American Medical Association, 291*, 2177–2179.

Chapter 7 Exercises

7.1 Quote Reflections

Review the sidebar quotes contained in this chapter and select two that were especially meaningful or inspirational to you.

For each quote, provide a three- to five-sentence explanation why you chose it.

7.2 Reality Bite

Procrastination: The Vicious Cycle

Delayla has a major paper due at the end of the term. It's now past midterm and she still hasn't started to work on it. She keeps telling herself, "I should have started sooner," but she continues to postpone her work and is becoming increasingly anxious and guilty. To relieve her growing anxiety and guilt, Delayla starts doing other tasks instead, such as cleaning her room and returning e-mails. This makes her feel a little better because these tasks keep her busy, take her mind off the term paper, and give her the feeling that at least she's getting something accomplished. Time continues to pass; the deadline for the paper grows dangerously close. Delayla now finds herself in the position of having lots of work to do and little time in which to do it.

Adapted from *Procrastination: Why You Do It, and What to do about It* (Burka & Yuen, 2008).

Reflection and Discussion Questions

1. What do you expect Delayla will do at this point? Why?
2. What grade do you think she'll end up receiving on her paper?
3. Other than simply starting sooner, what else could Delayla (and other procrastinators like her) do to break the cycle
   of procrastination?
4. Can you relate to this student's predicament, or do you know other students who often find themselves in this predicament?

7.3 Procrastination Self-Assessment

Look at the results of your My PEPS Learning Style Inventory, under the section of Persistence Preference.

What did you learn about your inclination to finish tasks and activities?

How likely are you to procrastinate?

How could you incorporate some of the suggestions offered to you increase your persistence?

7.4 Developing a Task-Management Plan for Your First Term in College

1. Review the *course syllabus (course outline)* for each class you are enrolled in this term and highlight all major exams, tests, quizzes, assignments, and papers and the dates on which they are due.

2. Obtain a *large calendar* for the academic term (available at your campus bookstore or learning center) and record all the highlighted information for your exams and assignments for all your courses in the calendar boxes that represent their due dates. To fit this information within the calendar boxes, use creative abbreviations to represent different tasks, such as RA for reading assignment, E for exam, and TP for term paper. When you're done, you'll have a detailed chart or map of deadline dates and a master schedule for the entire term.

3. Activate the calendar and task lists functions on your smartphone. Enter your schedule, important dates, deadlines, and set alert reminders. By carrying your phone with you regularly, you will always have this information at your fingertips.

Reflections

1. Is your overall workload what you expected? Are your surprised by the amount of work time you will need to devote to your courses?

2. At this point in the term, what course is demanding the greatest amount of out-of-class work time? Have you been able to put in this time?

3. What adjustments or changes (if any) could you make to your personal schedule this term to create more time to handle your academic workload?

7.5 Time Management Self-Awareness

Take the online *My PEPS Learning Style Inventory* tool that accompanies this text.

Did the results provide you with helpful insights on how you organize your time and the approach you take to completing tasks? If yes, why? If no, why not?

7.6 Time Analysis Inventory

1. Go to the following website: http://tutorials.istudy.psu.edu/timemanagement/TimeEstimator.html

2. Complete the time management exercise at this site. The exercise asks you to estimate the hours per day or week that you engage in various activities (e.g., sleeping, employment, and commuting). When you enter the amount of time devoted to each activity, this website will automatically compute the total number of remaining hours you have available in the week for academic work.

3. After completing your entries, answer the following questions (or provide your best estimate).
   a) How many hours per week do you have available for academic work?
   b) Do you have two hours available for academic work outside of class for each hour you spend in class? If you don't, what activities could be eliminated or reduced to create more time for academic work outside of class?

7.7 Developing a Time-Management Plan for Your First Term in College

Keep in mind the task-management plan you developed in Exercise 7.4, use the following *Week-at-a-Glance Grid* to map out your typical or average week for this term. Start by recording what you usually do on these days, including the times you're in class, when you work, and when you relax or recreate. You can use abbreviations (e.g., CT for class time, HW for homework, J for job, and R&R for rest and relaxation). List the abbreviations you created at the bottom of the page so that your instructor can follow them.

If you're a *full-time* student, plan for 25 *hours* in your week for homework (HW). (If you're a *part-time* student, find 2 *hours* you could devote to homework *for every hour* you're in class—for example, if you're in class 9 hours per week, find 18 hours of homework time).

> The amount of free time you have in college is much more than in high school. Always have a weekly study schedule to go by. Otherwise, time slips away and you will not be able to account for it."
>
> —Advice to new college students from a first-year student (Rhoads, 2005)

These homework hours could take place at any time during the week, including weekends. If you combine 25 hours per week of out-of-class school work with the amount of time you spend in class each week, you'll end up with a 40-hour academic workweek—comparable to a full-time job—which is how college should be viewed.

Week-at-a-Glance Grid

	Sunday	Monday	Tuesday	Wednesday	Thursday	Friday	Saturday
7:00 a.m.							
8:00 a.m.							
9:00 a.m.							
10:00 a.m.							
11:00 a.m.							
12:00 p.m.							
1:00 p.m.							
2:00 p.m.							
3:00 p.m.							
4:00 p.m.							
5:00 p.m.							
6:00 p.m.							
7:00 p.m.							
8:00 p.m.							
9:00 p.m.							
10:00 p.m.							
11:00 p.m.							

Reflections

1. How likely are you to put this time-management plan into practice?
   Circle one: Definitely   Probably   Unlikely

2. What would *promote or encourage* you to put this plan into practice?

3. What would *prevent or discourage* you from putting this plan into practice?

4. How do you think other students would answer the above-three questions?

Time Management Ball Activity

Teacher/Classroom Preparation: 5 small balls and 1 plastic spider, lizard, etc. Balls can be purchased from Oriental Trading Company or at a Dollartree Store. You need a space without any obstacles in the middle. Move desks to the edge of the room to have a large open space.

Length of Time: 15 minutes

Group Size: As few as 6 and as many as 20 people. I have completed this activity with more than 20, but it takes longer and is harder to keep everyone focused. If there are more than 20 participants, it would be best to divide them into two groups. A facilitator is needed for each group.

I introduce the activity as a way to learn names or as an ice breaker. I go around the circle to introduce everyone with first names. The students are to say the name of the person they will be throwing to before they throw the ball. The person receiving the ball must say "Thank you" and the person's name who threw the ball. Thus the students will learn at least the names of two people during this activity.

The group and facilitator stand in a circle facing one another. The facilitator tosses one ball to someone in the circle. Each person then tosses to another (across from them) until each person has received the ball once. The facilitator is the last one to receive the ball. The group is told to pass the ball in this sequence without dropping it. Practice this order until the process is smooth, and the ball is not dropped. Then repeat the exercise, but after the first ball is tossed, the facilitator adds the other balls and the spider to the sequence without warning. The added balls and the spider must be passed in the same sequence as the first ball. The group must decide how to manage these items in the same order without dropping a ball or spider.

Debriefing: When the facilitator stops the activity, a debriefing should occur. Through questions, the facilitator will help the students discover the connection between this activity and time management. Ask the students to think of this in terms of time management. What would the balls represent? What do we try to do with all our activities when we are trying to manage our time? What happens when we over-schedule ourselves? What does the spider or lizard represent?

This activity is a great way to help students learn some names of others in the class, to help them realize the class may actually be fun and offer some good tips for studying, and it helps them to develop community within the group.

Time Management
Prioritzing Tasks, Preventing Procrastination, & Promoting Productivity

Possible Classroom Exercises & Out-of Class Assignments

In addition to, or instead of the exercises included at the end of the chapter, the following may be used as exercises/assignments relating to content covered in Chapter 4.

Master Schedule Jigsaw
Steps:
1. Ask students to form four-member teams.
2. Ask the team to divide into pairs. One pair takes on the task of compiling a list of key *academic* dates and deadlines for the remainder of the year (e.g., last day to drop classes, to register for next-term classes, etc.), and the other pair does the same for *co-curricular* events (e.g., on-campus workshops, guest speakers, social events).
3. After the pairs have completed their respective assignments, ask them to reconvene as a quartet and integrate the work they did in pairs to create a master calendar which contains all major academic and co-curricular events that will take place during their first year of college.

Procrastination Self-Assessment
Steps:
1. As a course assignment, have your students take a free procrastination self-assessment test at either of the following websites:
   https://www.xing.com/communities/posts/are-you-a-procrastinator-take-the-test-1002299347
   http://discoveryhealth.queendom.com/procrastination_short_access.html
2. Have students submit their scores to you individually.
3. Form groups of three (triads) composed of one student who scored among the lowest one-third of students in class (least procrastination), a student who scored in the highest third (most procrastination), and one whose score has about average.
4. Have the triads brainstorm strategies for combating procrastination.
5. Ask a student volunteer in each group to report their team's suggestions for beating procrastination and record them on the board.
6. After the groups report back their strategies, ask the members in each group who had the lowest procrastination score to stand. Ask them if they use any of the strategies listed on the board that may account for their low procrastination score and to add any strategies they use that aren't on the board.

Name: _____   Date: _____   Section: _____

Procrastination Quotient

Complete the following survey by reading each statement and indicting which column most applies to you. Add up the total number of responses in each column in the last row.

Statement	Strongly Agree	Mildly Agree	Mildly Disagree	Strongly Disagree
I usually find reasons for not acting immediately on a difficult assignment.				
I know what I have to do but frequently find that I have done something else instead.				
I carry my books/work assignments with me to various places but do not open them or get them out.				
I work best at the "last minute" when the pressure is really on.				
There are too many interruptions that interfere with my accomplishing my top priorities.				
I avoid giving direct and honest answers when pressed to make an unpleasant decision.				
I take half measures which will avoid or delay unpleasant decisions.				
I have found myself to be too tired, nervous or upset to do the difficult task that faced me.				
I like to get my room in a good order before starting a difficult task.				
I find myself waiting for inspirations before becoming involved on most important study/work tasks.				
Total Number of Responses				
Weight	x 4	x 3	x 2	x 1
SCORE				
TOTAL =				

Below 20 = Occasional Procrastinator
21–30 = Chronic Procrastinator
Above 30 = Severe Procrastinator

240 Chapter 7 Time Management

Rocks, Sand, & Water: An Exercise for Prioritizing Time & Values

(Adapted from Covey, S., Merrill, A. R., & Merrill, R. R. (1994) *First Things First: To Live, to Love, to Learn, to Leave a Legacy.* New York: Simon and Schuster, 1994.)

Materials Needed:
1) Empty vase or a wide-mouth Mason jar
2) Enough small rocks to fill the vase or jar
3) Small bucket of sand or gravel
4) Small pitcher of water.

Steps:
1. Tell students to clear their desk because they're going to take a pop quiz on time management.
2. Pull out the jar or vase and place it on a table in front of the class and tell your students that it represents the amount of time they have each week.
3. Put the rocks into the jar, one by one, until you can't fit in any more. Ask the class: "Would you say that this jar is full?" (Typically, they'll say "yes.")
4. Pull out the bucket of sand or gravel and dump some of it in the jar, allowing it to seep through the spaces between the rocks. Ask the class: "Would you say that this jar is full? (Typically, they'll respond more tentatively this time, saying something like: "Maybe not.")
5. Grab the pitcher of water and pour it into the jar until it fills to the brim. Ask the class: "What do you think is the point of this demonstration?"
6. After giving students the opportunity to offer their hypotheses about the message behind the demonstration, tell them that the message is this: The big rocks represent the highest priorities in their life (e.g., their life goals, their education, their family and friends). If they don't puts the big rock in first, they'll never fit them in—i.e., they'll never make room or find time for their top priorities).

Note: A final (7th) step may be added to this procedure that asks students to explicitly identify what the "big rocks" are in their life (i.e., what they'd put into their "jar" first).

FYE Time Management Group Activity Strategize and Prioritize

Groups will have **10 minutes** to collect as many points as possible
One participant in each group will keep track of points earned
Groups must be safe and stay in the room
Group with the highest point total wins a prize

1. Walk one lap around the room (5 points)
2. Create something for the instructor to wear, such as a hat or tie (10 points; bonus 5 points if the instructor actually wears it)
3. Find out something unique about each person on the team (5 points)
4. Sing a song together (15 points)
5. Make a paper airplane and throw it from one end of the room to another (10 points)
6. Get everyone in the room to sign a single piece of paper (5 points)

7. Count the number of pets owned by your group (20 points)
8. Assign a nickname to each member of the team (5 points)
9. Create name cards for each team member (5 points; bonus 5 points if you use your team nicknames)
10. Make a tower out of the materials owned by your group (10 points)
11. Convince a member of another team to join you (20 points)
12. Name your team and come up with a slogan (5 points for the name, 5 points for the slogan)
13. Re-create the sounds of the Amazon rainforest with the sounds of your voices (10 points)
14. Form a conga line and conga from one end of the room to another (5 points; bonus 10 points if anyone joins you)

Time Management Problem/Position Gallery
Steps:
1. Have students form 3- or 4-member groups and brainstorm what they think are the major time wasters that interfere with effective time management.
2. Ask students to record their ideas on a large poster or chart post on a nearby wall.
3. Ask the groups to mill around the room and observe ideas generated by other groups, noting time wasters that weren't on their own poster.
4. Have student reconvene in their original groups and identify strategies for preventing the time wasters from happening in the first place, and/or for converting the wasted time into productive time.

Note: A 4th step could be added to this exercise, whereby each group passes their solution strategies clockwise to another group that records what they think is the best idea found in the notes they've received. This clockwise rotation continues until each group has received and recorded the best idea they found in the notes received from all other groups in class.

CHAPTER 8

Educational Planning and Academic Decision-Making

MAKING WISE CHOICES ABOUT COLLEGE COURSES AND A COLLEGE MAJOR

Chapter Preview

Making strategic choices about your courses and your major is essential to reaching your educational goals. You want to be sure your choice of major is compatible with your personal interests, talents, and values. You should also have a strategic plan in mind (and in hand) that enables you to strike a healthy balance between exploring your major options and making a final commitment. This chapter will help you strike this balance and make educational decisions that put you in the best position to reach your long-term goals.

Learning Goal

Equip you with effective strategies for choosing courses wisely and pursuing an educational path that's compatible with your personal interests, talents, and goals.

Integrate Your Faith

God has equipped each of us with special skills, talents, and yearnings. What do you think are your unique skills and talents? How could you use these to show Gods love to others?

Ignite Your Thinking

Reflection 8.1

At this point in your college experience, are you decided or undecided about a major?

1. If you're undecided, what subjects are you considering as possible majors?

2. If you're decided:

    a) What's your choice?

    b) What led you to this choice?

From *Thriving in College and Beyond: Research-Based Strategies for Academic Success and Personal Development*, Fourth Edition by Joseph B. Cuseo, Aaron Thompson, Michele Campagna, and Viki S. Fecas. Copyright © 2016 Kendall Hunt Publishing Company. Reprinted by permission.

c) How sure are you about this choice? (Circle one.)

absolutely sure   fairly sure   not too sure   likely to change

To Be or Not to Be Decided: What Research Shows about Students' Choice of a College Major

"What's your major?" is a question that students are asked over and over again—even before they've stepped foot on a college campus. You probably also saw this question on every one of your college applications and you're likely to hear it again during your very first term in college. Family members are also likely to ask you the same question, particularly if they're paying or helping to pay the high cost of a college education. They want to be sure that their investment will pay off and they're more likely to feel assured if they know you're committed to a major and are on your way to a self-supporting career.

Studies of student decisions about a college major show that:

- Fewer than 10% of new college students feel they know a great deal about the field they intend to major in;
- As students proceed through the first year of college, they grow more uncertain about the major they chose when they entered college;
- More than one-third of new students change their mind about their major during their first year of college; and
- Only one in three college seniors eventually major in the same field they had in mind when they began college (Cuseo, 2005; HERI, 2014).

These findings demonstrate that the vast majority of first-year students are uncertain about their academic specialization. Typically, they don't make a final decision about their major *before* starting college; instead, they reach that decision *during* their college experience.

> "All who wander are not lost."
> —J. R. R. Tolkien, author of Lord of the Rings

Thus, being initially undecided about a major isn't something you should be worried or embarrassed about; it doesn't mean you're clueless. It may just mean you're open-minded. In fact, studies show that new students are often undecided for very good reasons. Some are undecided because they have multiple interests; this is a healthy form of indecision indicating they have a wide range of interests and a high level of intellectual curiosity. Students may also be undecided because they are reflective and deliberate decision-makers who prefer to explore their options carefully before making a firm and final commitment. In a national study of students who were undecided about a major at the start of college, 43% of them had some majors in mind but weren't quite ready to make a final commitment to one of them (Gordon & Steele, 2003).

For new students to be at least somewhat uncertain about their educational goals at the start of their college experience is only natural because they haven't yet experienced the variety of subjects included in the college curriculum. One goal of general education courses is to help new students develop the critical thinking skills needed to make wise choices and well-informed decisions, including their decision about a college major.

The college curriculum will introduce you to new fields of study, some of which you never experienced before and all of which represent possible choices for a college major. A key benefit of experiencing the variety of courses in the general education curriculum is that they help you become more aware of the range of academic disciplines and subject areas available to you as potential majors, while at the same time, helping you become more aware of yourself. As you gain experience with the college curriculum, you will gain greater self-insight into your academic interests, strengths, and weaknesses. Take this self-knowledge into consideration when choosing a major because you want to pursue a field that capitalizes on your intellectual curiosity, abilities, and talents.

It's true that some students can take too long to choose a major or procrastinate about making important decisions. However, it's also true that some students make decisions too quickly, resulting in premature choices made without sufficient reflection and careful consideration of their options. Judging from the large number of students who end up changing their major, it's probably safe to say that more students make the mistake of reaching a decision about a major too quickly rather than waiting too long.

If you're currently feeling pressure to make an early decision, we encourage you to respectfully resist it until you've gained more self-knowledge and more experience with the college curriculum and co-curriculum. As a first-year student, you can still make steady progress toward your destination (a college degree) by taking general education courses that will count toward a college degree in any major you eventually declare.

If you think you're certain about a major right now, be sure to take a course or two in the major to test it out and confirm whether it's a "good fit" for your personal interests, talents, and values. If you discover that your first choice wasn't a good choice, don't think you're "locked" into that major and your only option is to stick with it or drop out of college. You still have time to change your mind without falling far behind. Changing your original educational plans is not necessarily a bad thing. It may mean that your first choice wasn't the best choice for you and that you've discovered another field that's more compatible with your personal interests and talents.

The only drawback to delaying your choice of a major, or changing your original major, is *waiting too long* to make your first choice or to change your mind about your first choice. Prolonged delay in initially choosing a major or late changing of a major can lengthen your time to college graduation. It can also increase the cost of your college education because you may need to complete additional courses for your newly chosen major—particularly if it's in a very different field than your original choice. The key to preventing this late-change scenario from happening to you is by engaging in long-range educational planning *early* in your college experience—beginning now.

> You have brains in your head. You have feet in your shoes. You can steer yourself any direction you choose.
>
> —Theodore Seuss Giesel (a.k.a. Dr. Seuss), Oh the Places You'll Go

> I see so many people switch [their] major like 4 or 5 times; they end up having to take loads of summer school just to catch up because they invest time and money in classes for a major that they end up not majoring in anyway."
>
> —College sophomore

> Changing your major this close to graduation will add to the time it takes for you to earn your college degree; it will also add to the cost of your college education.

Note

When students are required to declare a major varies across different campuses and different fields of study. As a general rule, you should reach a firm and final decision about your major during your second (sophomore) year in college. However, no matter how much time you're allowed to make this decision, the process of planning for your major should start now—during your first term in college.

Reflection 8.2

Have you decided on a major?

If yes, how sure are you about your decision? What led you to this decision?

If no, what major(s) are you considering? Why?

The Importance of Long-Range Educational Planning

If you haven't declared a major, it doesn't mean you're indecisive or a hopeless procrastinator. However, it also doesn't mean you can put all thoughts about your major on the back burner and simply drift along until you're forced to make a choice. Being undecided doesn't mean you have no plan; your plan is to find out what your major will be. Now is the time to start the major selection process by testing your interests and narrowing down your choices.

Similarly, if you've already chosen a major, this doesn't mean you'll never have to give any more thought to that decision. Instead, you should continue the exploration process by carefully testing your first choice, making sure it's a choice that is compatible with your abilities and interests. Take the approach that this is your *current* choice; whether it becomes your firm and *final* choice will depend on how well you perform (and how interested you are) in the first courses you take in the field.

Developing a long-range educational plan enables you to take a *proactive* approach to your education—you take charge of it by taking early and preemptive action that anticipates your future. Rather than waiting and passively letting your educational future happen *to* you, advanced planning makes it happen *for* you.

> "Some people make things happen, while others watch things happen or wonder what has happened."
> —Author unknown

Don't take the avoidance and denial approach to planning your educational future.

By looking beyond your first year of college and engaging in long-range educational planning, you're able to get a sneak preview and "big picture" overview of your entire college experience. In contrast, looking at and scheduling your classes one term at a time—just before each registration period—carves up your college experience into a choppy series of small, separate snapshots that leaves you with little sense of continuity, connection, and direction. On pp. 299–306, you will find directions and guidelines on how to develop a long-range educational plan. We strongly encourage you to complete this exercise. It's an opportunity for you to begin steering your educational future in a direction that has meaning and purpose for you.

Note

Keep in mind that a long-range educational plan isn't something set in stone. As you gain more educational experience, your specific academic and career interests may change and so may the specifics of your long-range plan. The purpose of a plan is not to tie you up or pin you down, but provide you with a roadmap that keeps you on course and moving in the right direction.

Factors to Consider When Choosing a Major

Self-awareness is the critical first step in the process of making any effective personal decision or choice. You need to know yourself well before knowing what major is best for you. When choosing a major, self-awareness should include awareness of your:

- Mental abilities and talents
- Learning styles and tendencies
- Personal interests and curiosities

As illustrated in **Figure 8.1**, these three pillars provide a solid foundation on which to base your decision about a college major.

FIGURE 8.1: Three Key Personal Characteristics to Consider when Choosing a College Major

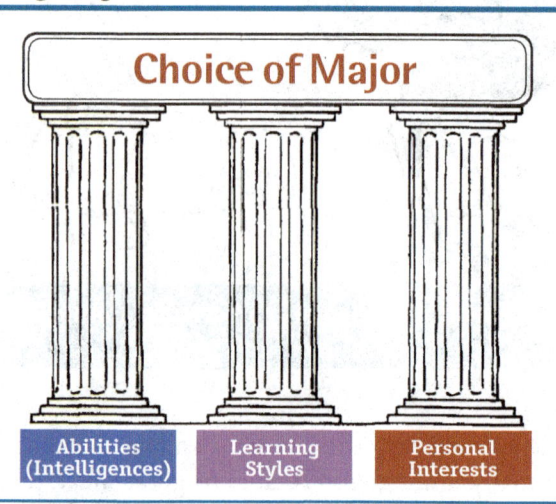

©Kendall Hunt Publishing Company

Research indicates that students who choose majors that are compatible with their personal characteristics are more likely to be academically successful in college and complete their degree (Leuwerke, et al., 2004; Pascarella & Terenzini, 2005).

Multiple Intelligences: Becoming Aware of Your Mental Abilities and Talents

One personal characteristic you should be aware of when choosing a major is your mental strengths, abilities, and talents. Intelligence was once considered to be a single, general trait that could be identified by one intelligence test score. Scholars have since discovered that intelligence doesn't come conveniently wrapped in a one-size-fits-all package. The singular word "intelligence" has been replaced by the plural word "intelligences" to reflect the fact that humans display intelligence (mental ability) in a variety of forms other than that measured by their score on an IQ or SAT test.

Based on studies of gifted and talented individuals, experts in different lines of work, and research on the human brain, psychologist Howard Gardner (1993, 1999, 2006) has identified the multiple forms of intelligence listed in **Box 8.1**. Keep these forms of intelligence in mind when you're choosing a college major because different majors emphasize different intellectual skills (Brooks, 2009). Ideally, you want to pursue an academic field that allows you to utilize your strongest mental attributes and talents. If you do, you're likely to master the concepts and skills required by your major more efficiently and more deeply, excel in courses required by your major, and experience a higher level of academic self-confidence and motivation to continue your education.

> "Exceptional individuals have a special talent for identifying their own strengths and weaknesses."
>
> —*Howard Gardner*, Extraordinary Minds

Box 8.1

Multiple Forms of Intelligence

As you read through the following forms of intelligence, place a checkmark next to the type that you think represents your strongest ability or talent. (You can possess more than one type.)

1. *Linguistic* Intelligence: ability to comprehend the meaning of words and communicate through language (e.g., verbal skills relating to speaking, writing, listening, and learning foreign languages).

2. *Logical-Mathematical* Intelligence: aptitude for understanding logical patterns (e.g., making and following logical arguments) and solving mathematical problems (e.g., working well with numbers and quantitative calculations).

3. *Spatial* Intelligence: aptitude for visualizing relationships among objects arranged in different spatial positions and ability to perceive or create visual images (e.g., forming mental images of three-dimensional objects; detecting detail in objects or drawings; drawing, painting, sculpting, and graphic design; strong sense of direction and capacity to navigate unfamiliar places).

4. *Musical* Intelligence: ability to appreciate or create rhythmical and melodic sounds (e.g., playing, writing, or arranging music).

5. *Interpersonal (Social)* Intelligence: ability to relate to others and accurately identify their needs, motivations, or emotional states; effective at expressing emotions and feelings to others (e.g., interpersonal communication skills, ability to accurately "read" the feelings of others and meet their emotional needs).

6. *Intrapersonal (Self)* Intelligence: ability to introspect and understand your own thoughts, feelings, and behaviors (e.g., capacity for personal

Box 8.1 *(continued)*

reflection; emotional self-awareness; self-insight into personal strengths and weaknesses).

7. *Bodily–Kinesthetic (Psychomotor)* Intelligence: ability to control one's own body skillfully and learn through bodily sensations or movements; skilled at tasks involving physical coordination, working well with hands, operating machinery, building models, assembling things, and using technology.

> "I used to operate a printing press. In about two weeks I knew how to run it and soon after I could take the machine apart in my head and analyze what each part does, how it functioned, and why it was shaped that way."
>
> —*Response of college sophomore to the questions: "What are you really good at? What comes easily or naturally to you?"*

8. *Naturalist* Intelligence: ability to carefully observe and appreciate features of the natural environment; keen awareness of nature or natural surroundings; ability to understand causes and consequences of events occurring in the natural world.

9. *Existential* Intelligence: ability to conceptualize phenomena and ponder experiences that go beyond sensory or physical evidence, such as questions involving the origin of human life and the meaning of human existence.

Source: Gardner (1993, 1999, 2006).

Reflection 8.3

Look back at the nine forms of intelligence listed in **Box 8.1**.

Which of these types of intelligence do you think represents your strongest talent(s)?

Which college major(s) do you think may best match your natural talents?

Learning Styles: Becoming Aware of Your Learning Preferences and Tendencies

Another personal characteristic you should be aware of when choosing a major is your learning style. It refers to the way in which you prefer to *perceive* information (receive or take it in) and *process* information (deal with it after taking it in). For instance, students may differ in terms of whether they prefer to take in information by reading about it, listening to it, seeing an image or diagram of it, or physically touching and manipulating it. Individuals may also vary in terms of whether they like to receive information in a structured, orderly format or in an unstructured formats that allows them the freedom to explore, play with, and restructure it in their own way. Individuals may also differ in terms of how they prefer to process (deal with) information after it's been received. Some may like to think about it on their own, while others prefer to discuss it with someone else; some may like to outline it, while others prefer to map it out or draw it.

There are tests specially designed to assess your learning style. (If you're interested in taking one, the Learning Center and Career Center are two places on campus where you may be able to do so.) Probably the most frequently used learning styles test is the *Myers-Briggs Type Indicator (MBTI)*—a test based on the personality theory of psychologist Carl Jung. It assesses how people vary along a scale (low to high) on each of four sets of opposing traits, which are illustrated in **Figure 8.2**.

As you read through these pairs of opposite traits, place a mark along the line where you think you fall with respect to each set. Place a mark toward the far left or far right if you think you lean strongly toward that end of the scale; place a mark in the middle of the line if you think you don't lean strongly toward either end of the scale.

FIGURE 8.2: **Traits and Learning Styles Measured by the Myers-Briggs Type Indicator (MBTI)**

Extraversion	*Introversion*
Prefer to focus on the "outer" world of persons, actions, or objects	Prefer to focus on the "inner" world of thoughts and ideas
Sensing	*Intuition*
Prefer interacting with the world directly through concrete, sensory experiences	Prefer dealing with symbolic meanings and imagining possibilities
Thinking	*Feeling*
Prefer to rely on logic and rational thinking when making decisions	Prefer to rely on human needs and feelings when making decisions
Judging	*Perceiving*
Prefer to plan for and control events	Prefer flexibility and spontaneity

Reflection 8.4

For each of the following four sets of opposing traits, make a note about where you fall—low, middle, or high.

MBTI Personality Traits	Low	Middle	High
Extraversion–Introversion			
Sensing–Intuition			
Thinking–Feeling			
Judging–Perceiving			

What majors or fields of study do you think are most compatible with your personality traits?

Research indicates that college students who score high on the introversion scale of the MBTI are more likely to stay engaged and attentive when performing mental tasks that require repetition and involve little external stimulation (Bodanovich, Wallace, & Kass, 2005). This suggests that students may differ in terms of the academic tasks they prefer to perform. For instance, it's been found that students who score differently on the MBTI prefer different writing styles and writing assignments (Jensen & Tiberio, cited in Bean, 2001). These differences are summarized below.

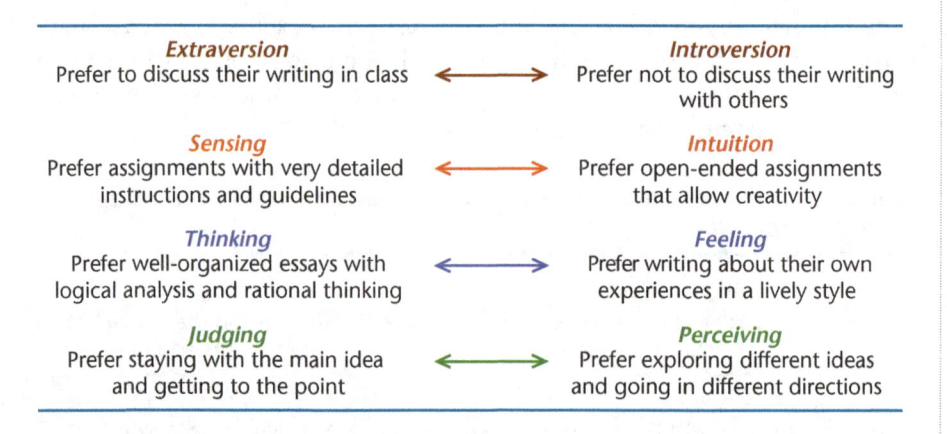

Extraversion Prefer to discuss their writing in class	*Introversion* Prefer not to discuss their writing with others
Sensing Prefer assignments with very detailed instructions and guidelines	*Intuition* Prefer open-ended assignments that allow creativity
Thinking Prefer well-organized essays with logical analysis and rational thinking	*Feeling* Prefer writing about their own experiences in a lively style
Judging Prefer staying with the main idea and getting to the point	*Perceiving* Prefer exploring different ideas and going in different directions

Keep your learning style in mind when choosing your major because different academic fields emphasize different styles of learning. Some fields place heavy emphasis on structured, tightly focused writing (e.g., science and business), while other fields encourage writing with personal style, flair, and creativity (e.g., English). How your writing style meshes with the style emphasized by different academic fields is one factor to consider when choosing a college major.

Another popular learning styles test is the *Learning Styles Inventory* (Dunn, Dunn, & Price, 1990), originally developed by David Kolb, a professor of philosophy (Kolb, 1976, 1985). It's based on how individuals differ with respect to the following two dimensions of the learning process:

How Information Is *Perceived* (Taken in)

Concrete Experience Learning through direct involvement or personal experience	*Reflective Observation* Learning by watching or observing

How Information Is *Processed* (Dealt with after it has been taken in)

Abstract Conceptualization Learning by thinking about things and drawing logical conclusions	*Active Experimentation* Learning by taking chances and trying things out

When these two dimensions are crisscrossed, four sectors (areas) are created, each of which represents a different learning style—as illustrated in **Figure 8.3**. As you read the characteristics associated with each of the four areas (styles), circle the style that you think reflects your most preferred way of learning.

FIGURE 8.3: **Learning Styles Measured by the Learning Styles Inventory (LSI)**

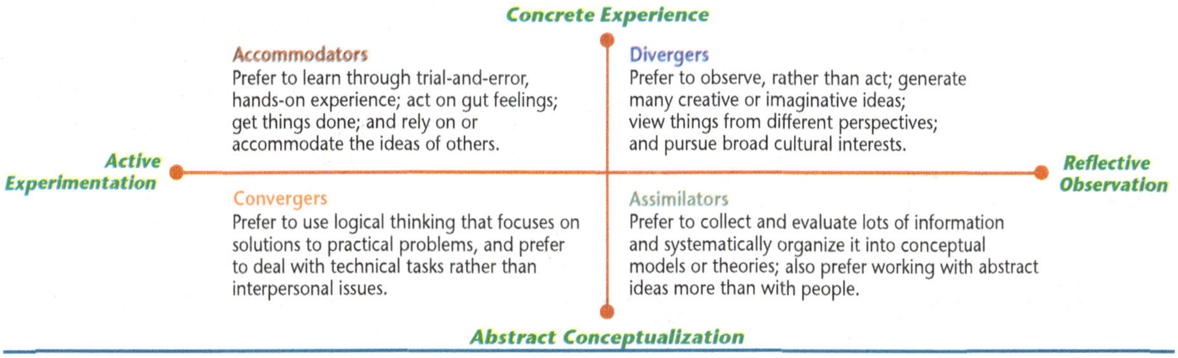

Concrete Experience

Accommodators
Prefer to learn through trial-and-error, hands-on experience; act on gut feelings; get things done; and rely on or accommodate the ideas of others.

Divergers
Prefer to observe, rather than act; generate many creative or imaginative ideas; view things from different perspectives; and pursue broad cultural interests.

Active Experimentation ← → *Reflective Observation*

Convergers
Prefer to use logical thinking that focuses on solutions to practical problems, and prefer to deal with technical tasks rather than interpersonal issues.

Assimilators
Prefer to collect and evaluate lots of information and systematically organize it into conceptual models or theories; also prefer working with abstract ideas more than with people.

Abstract Conceptualization

Reflection 8.5

Which one of the four learning styles appears to most closely match yours? (Check one of the following boxes.)

☐ Accommodator

☐ Diverger

☐ Converger

☐ Assimilator

What majors or fields of study appear to be a good match for your learning style?

Research indicates that students who display differences in these four learning styles tend to major in different fields (Svinicki, 2004; Svinicki & Dixon, 1987). "Assimilators" are more often found majoring in mathematics and natural sciences (e.g., chemistry and physics), probably because these subjects emphasize reflection and abstract thinking. In contrast, "accommodators" tend to be more commonly found majoring in business, accounting and law, perhaps because these fields involve taking practical action and making concrete decisions. "Divergers" are more often attracted to majors in the fine arts (e.g., music, art, and drama), humanities (e.g., history and literature), or social sciences (e.g., psychology and

©Kendall Hunt Publishing Company

Engineering and humanities majors settle their learning style differences in the fine arts quad!

political science), possibly because these fields emphasize accommodating multiple (divergent) viewpoints and perspectives. In contrast, "convergers" are more often found majoring in fields such as accounting, engineering, medicine, and nursing, probably because these subjects require students to focus in on (converge on) finding a specific answer to a specific problem (Kolb, 1976). When college instructors were asked to classify academic fields in terms of the type of learning style emphasized by the field, this same pattern of preferences was discovered (Biglan, 1973; Schommer-Aikins, Duell, & Barker, 2003).

Since students have different learning styles and academic fields emphasize different styles of learning, it's important to consider how your learning style meshes with the style of learning emphasized by the field you're considering as a major. If the styles match or are closely compatible, the marriage could be one that leads to a very satisfying and successful learning experience.

We recommend taking a trip to the Learning Center or Career Development Center on your campus to take a learning styles test, or take the learning styles inventory that accompanies this text (see the inside of the front cover for details). Even if the test doesn't help you choose a major, it will at least help you become more aware of your learning style. This alone could contribute to your academic success because studies show that when college students gain greater self-awareness of their learning style, their academic performance tends to improve (Claxton & Murrell, 1987; Hendry, et al., 2005).

Reflection 8.6

In addition to taking formal tests to assess your learning style, you can gain awareness of your learning styles through some simple self-reflection. Take a moment to reflect on your learning style by completing the following statements:

I learn best if . . .

I learn most from . . .

I enjoy learning when …

Do you see any pattern in your answers that may suggest that certain majors would be compatible with your learning style?

(Complete Exercise 8.3 at the end of the chapter to see if your learning style and personality traits are a good match for the major you've chosen or are considering.)

Discovering a Major that's Compatible with Your Personal Interests and Talents

In addition to knowing your intellectual strengths and learning styles, another key factor to factor into your decisions about a college major are your *interests*. Here are some specific strategies for exploring and confirming whether a major is compatible with your educational interests.

Reflect on past learning experiences you found stimulating and were productive. Think about previous classes that piqued your curiosity and in which you produced your best work. The subjects of these courses may be major fields of study that match up well with your interests, talents, and learning style.

At the website *www.mymajors.com*, you can enter information about your academic performance in high school courses. Your inputted information will be analyzed and you'll receive a report on what college majors appear to be a good match for you. You can do the same analysis for the first courses you complete in college.

Take a look at introductory textbooks in the field you're considering as a major. Review the table of contents and read a few pages of the text to get some sense of the writing style used in the field and whether the topics are compatible with your educational interests. You should be able to conveniently find introductory textbooks for different fields of study in your college bookstore.

Seek out students majoring in the subject you're considering and ask them about their experiences. Talk to several students to get a different and balanced perspective on what the field is like. You can find these students by visiting student clubs on campus related to the major (e.g., psychology club or history club). You could also check the class schedule to see when and where classes in that major are meeting. Go there and speak with students about the major, either before or after class. The following questions may be good ones to ask students in a major you're considering:

- What attracted you to this major?
- What would you say are the advantages and disadvantages of majoring in this field?

- Knowing what you know now, would you choose the same major again?

Also, ask students about the quality of teaching and advising in the department offering the major. Studies show that different departments within the same college or university can vary greatly in terms of the quality of teaching as well as their educational philosophy and attitude toward students (Pascarella & Terenzini, 1991, 2005).

Sit in on some classes in the field you're considering as a major. If the class you'd like to visit is large, you may be able to just slip into the back row and listen. If the class is small, ask the instructor for permission. When visiting a class, focus on the content or ideas being covered rather than the instructor's personality or teaching style. Remember: you're trying to decide whether to major in the subject, not the teacher.

Discuss the major you're considering with an academic advisor. To get unbiased feedback about the pros and cons of majoring in a particular field, it's probably best to speak with an academic advisor who works with students from a variety of majors. If you're still interested, you can follow up by getting more detailed information by consulting with an advisor who works primarily with students in that particular major.

Speak with faculty members in the department. Consider asking them the following questions:

- What academic skills or qualities are needed for a student to be successful in your field?
- What are the greatest challenges faced by students majoring in your field?
- What can students do with a major in your field after graduation?
- What types of graduate programs or professional schools would a student in your major be well prepared to enter?

Surf the website of the professional organization associated with the field you're considering as a major. These websites often contain useful information for students interested in pursuing a major in the field. To locate the professional website for a field you would like to explore as a major, ask a faculty member in that field or complete a search on the web by simply entering the name of the field followed by the word "association." For example, if you're thinking about becoming an anthropology major, check out the website of the American Anthropological Association. If you're considering history as a major, take a look at the website of the American Historical Association. The website of the American Philosophical Association contains information about nonacademic careers for philosophy majors, and the American

Sociological Association's website identifies various careers that sociology majors are qualified to pursue.

Visit your Career Development Center to inquire about what college graduates have gone on to do with the major you're considering. Ask if the Center has information about the type of careers the major has led to and what graduate or professional school programs students have entered after completing the major.

Be sure you're aware of all courses required for the major that you've chosen or are considering. You can find this information in your college catalog, university bulletin, or campus website. If you're in doubt, seek assistance from an academic advisor.

Sometimes college majors require courses you never expect would be required. For example, students interested in majoring in the field of forensics are often surprised by the number of science courses for this major. Keep in mind that college majors can require courses in fields outside of the major that are designed to support the major. For instance, psychology majors are often required to take at least one course in biology, and business majors are often required to take calculus.

If you're interested in majoring in a particular field, be sure you are fully aware of such outside requirements and are comfortable with them. Once you've accurately identified all courses required for the major you're considering, ask yourself the following two questions:

1. Do the course titles and descriptions appeal to my interests and values?
2. Do I have the abilities or skills needed to do well in these courses?

Be sure you know if certain academic standards must be met to be admitted to the major. Some college majors may be "impacted" or "oversubscribed," meaning that more students are interested in majoring in these fields than there are openings for students to major in them. Majors that are often most likely to be oversubscribed are pre-professional fields that lead directly to a particular career (e.g., engineering, premed, nursing, or physical therapy). On some campuses, these majors are called "restricted" majors, meaning that departments control their enrollment by restricting the number of students admitted to the major. Admission may be limited to students who earn a GPA of 3.0 or higher in certain introductory courses required by the major, or the department may rank students who apply for the major according to their overall GPA and go down the list until the maximum number of openings has been filled.

If you intend to major in a restricted field of study, be sure to keep track of whether you're meeting the acceptance standards of the major as you continue to complete courses and earn grades. If you're falling short of the academic standards of the major you hope to enter—despite working at your maximum level of effort and regularly using the learning assistance services available on campus—consult with an academic advisor about the possibility of finding an alternative field of study that may be closely related to the restricted major you were hoping to enter.

Use your elective courses to test your interest in subjects that you might major in. As its name implies, "elective" courses are those you elect or choose to take. They come in two forms: free electives and restricted electives. *Free electives* are any courses you take that count toward your college degree but aren't required for general education or a major. *Restricted electives* are courses you must take, but you get to choose them from a restricted list (menu) of possible courses that have been specified by your college to fulfill a requirement in general education or a major. For example, your campus may have a general education requirement in the social or behavioral sciences that stipulates you must take two courses in this field, but you choose what those two courses are from a list of options (e.g., anthropology, economics, political science, psychology, or sociology). If you're considering one of these fields as a possible major, you can take an introductory course in that subject to test your interest in the subject while simultaneously fulfilling a general education requirement needed for graduation. This strategy allows you to use general education as the main highway for travel toward your final destination (a college degree) while using your restricted electives to explore side roads (potential majors) along the way. You can use the same strategy with your free electives.

Naturally, you don't have to use all your electives to explore majors. Up to one-third of your courses in college may be electives. This leaves you with a significant amount of freedom to shape your college experience in a way that best meets your educational and personal goals. Box 8.2 contains suggestions for making the best use of your free electives.

> " I took it (Biology) to satisfy the distribution requirement and I ended up majoring in it."
>
> —Pediatrician (quoted in Brooks, 2009)

Box 8.2

Top Ten Suggestions for Making the Most of Your College Electives

Elective courses give you the academic freedom to take personal control over your coursework. Exercise this freedom responsibly by making strategic selections of electives that allow you to make the most of your college experience and college degree.

Listed below are ten recommendations for making effective use of your college electives. As you read them, note three strategies that appeal most to you and you're most likely to put into practice.

You can make strategic use of your elective to:

1. **Complete a minor or build an area of concentration.** Electives can be used to pursue a field of personal interest that complements and strengthens your major.
2. **Help you choose a career path.** Just as you can use electives to test your interest in a college

Box 8.2 *(continued)*

major, you can use them to test your interest in a career. For instance, you could enroll in:
- career planning or career development courses; and
- courses that include internships or service learning experiences in a field you're considering as a possible career (e.g., health, education, or business).

3. **Strengthen your skills in areas that may appeal to future employers.** For instance, courses in foreign language, leadership development, and persuasive communication can develop skills attractive to current employers. (See Chapter 2 for skills sought by today's employers.)

4. **Develop practical life skills.** Courses in managing personal finances, marriage and family, or child development can help you manage your money and your family relationships.

5. **Seek balance in your life and develop yourself as a whole person.** You can use your electives intentionally to cover all key dimensions of self-development. Electives may be used to promote your emotional development (e.g., stress management), social development (e.g., social psychology), intellectual development (e.g., critical thinking), physical development (e.g., nutrition or self-defense), and spiritual development (e.g., world religions or death and dying).

> " I discovered an unknown talent and lifelong stress-reducing hobby."
>
> —An attorney talking about an elective ceramics course taken in college (quoted in Brooks, 2009)

6. **Make connections between different academic disciplines (subject areas).** *Interdisciplinary* courses are courses designed specifically to integrate two or more academic disciplines. For instance, psychobiology is an interdisciplinary course that integrates the fields of psychology (focusing on the mind) and biology (focusing on the body), enabling you to see how the mind influences the body and vice versa.

    Making connections across subjects and seeing how they can be combined to create a more complete understanding of personal or societal issues can be a stimulating intellectual experience. Furthermore, the presence of interdisciplinary courses on your college transcript may be attractive to future employers because "real world" work responsibilities and challenges cannot be handled through the lens of a single major; they require the ability to integrate skills acquired from different fields of study (Colby, et al., 2011).

7. **Help you develop broader perspectives on the human condition and the surrounding world.** You can intentionally take electives that progressively widen your world perspectives, such as courses that provide a societal perspective (sociology), a national perspective (political science), an international perspective (world geography), a global perspective (ecology), and a cosmological perspective (astronomy).

8. **Appreciate different cultural viewpoints and enhance your ability to communicate with people from diverse cultural backgrounds.** You could take electives that focus on cultural differences across nations (e.g., international relations) or courses related to cultural differences within America (e.g., race and ethnicity).

9. **Stretch yourself beyond your customary learning style to experience different ways of learning and acquire new skills.** You'll find courses in the college curriculum you never took before (or even knew existed) that supply you with knowledge and skills you've never had a previous opportunity to acquire or develop. These courses will stretch your mind, allowing you to explore new ideas and expand your skill set in a way that's consistent with a key characteristic of successful people—"growth mindset."

Box 8.2 (continued)

10. **Learn something you were always curious about.** If you've always wondered how members of the other sex think and feel, you could take a course on the psychology of men and women. Or, if you've heard about a particular professor who teaches a course that students find especially interesting, take that course and find out why it's so interesting.

Your college catalog (bulletin) contains descriptions of all courses offered on your campus. Take time to review these course descriptions carefully and explore all the elective options available to you.

Note

Your elective courses give you the opportunity to shape and create an academic experience that's uniquely your own. Seize this opportunity to exercise your academic freedom responsibly. Don't make elective choices randomly or merely on the basis of scheduling convenience (e.g., choosing electives to create a schedule with no early morning or late afternoon classes and no classes on Friday). Instead, make course selections strategically so that they contribute most to your educational, personal, and professional development.

©Kendall Hunt Publishing Company

Choosing courses that best enable you to achieve your long-term educational and personal goals should take precedence over creating a schedule that leaves your Fridays free for three-day weekends.

Consider the possibility of completing a college minor in a field that complements your major. A college minor usually requires about half the number of credits (units) required for a major. Most campuses allow you the option of completing a minor along with your major. Check your course catalog or consult with an academic advisor for college minors that may interest you.

If you have a strong interest in two different fields, a minor will allow you to major in one of these fields while minoring in the other. Thus, you're able to pursue two fields of interest without having to sacrifice one for the other. Another advantage of a minor is that it can usually be completed with a major without delaying your time to graduation. In contrast, a double major is likely to lengthen your time to graduation because it requires completing all requirements for both majors.

Another way to complete a second field of study without increasing your time to graduation is by completing a "concentration" or "cognate area"—an academic specialization that requires fewer courses to complete than a minor (e.g., four to five courses vs. seven to eight courses). A concentration area may have even fewer requirements (only three to four courses).

Taking a cluster of courses in a field outside your major can be an effective way to strengthen your resume and your employment prospects; it demonstrates your versatility and ability to acquire knowledge and skills in areas that may be missing or underemphasized in your major. For example, by taking a cluster of courses in fields such as mathematics (e.g., statistics), technology (e.g., computer science), and business (e.g., economics), students majoring in the fine arts (e.g., music or theater) or humanities (e.g., English or history) can acquire knowledge and skills in areas not strongly emphasized by their major, thereby increasing their prospects for employment after graduation.

Myths about the Relationship between Majors and Careers

Reflection 8.7

Consider the following statement: "Choosing a major is a life-changing decision because it will determine what you will do for the rest of your life."

Would you agree or disagree?

Why?

Numerous misconceptions exist about the relationship between college majors and careers, some of which can lead students to make uninformed or unrealistic decisions about a major. Here are four common myths about the major—career relationship you should be aware of and factor into your decision about a college major.

Myth 1. When you choose your major, you're choosing your career.

While some majors lead directly to a specific career, most do not. Majors leading directly to specialized careers are often called preprofessional or pre-vocational majors; they include such fields as accounting, engineering, and nursing. However, the relationship between most college majors and future careers is often not direct or linear; you don't travel on a monorail straight from your major to a single career that's directly connected to your major. For instance, all physics majors don't become physicists, all philosophy majors don't become philosophers, all history majors don't become historians, and all English majors don't become Englishmen (or Englishwomen). Instead, the same major typically leads you to a variety of career options.

The truth is that for most college students the journey from college major to future career(s) is less like scaling a vertical pole and more like climbing a tree. As illustrated in **Figure 8.4**, you begin with the tree's trunk (the foundation provided by general education (the liberal arts); this leads to separate limbs (choices for college majors), which, in turn, lead to different branches (different career paths or occupational options). Note that different sets of branches (careers) grow from the same limb (major).

> "Linear thinking can keep you from thinking broadly about your options and being open-minded to new opportunities."
> —*Katharine Brooks, author,* You Majored in What?

FIGURE 8.4: The Relationship between General Education (Liberal Arts), College Majors, and Careers

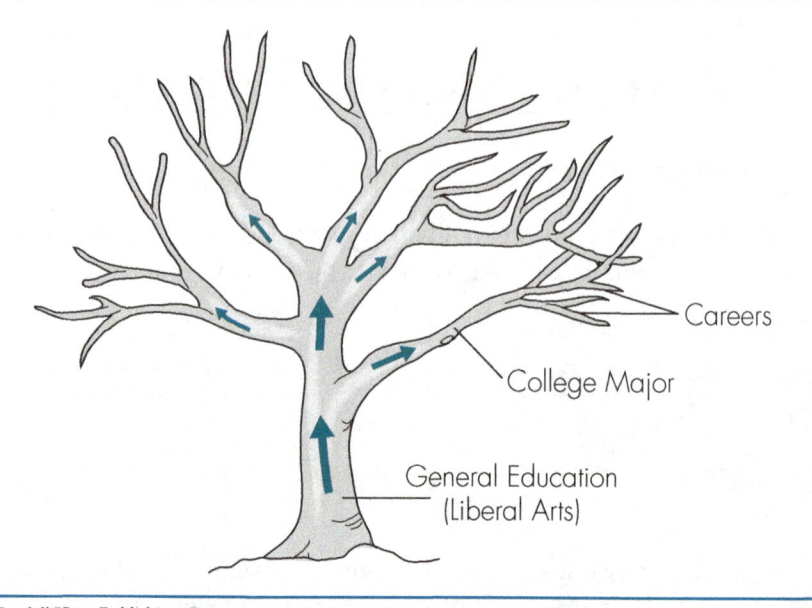

©Kendall Hunt Publishing Company

Similarly, different career clusters or "career families" grow from the same major. An English major can lead to a variety of careers that involve writing (e.g., editing, journalism, or publishing), and a major in Art can lead to different careers that involve visual media (e.g., illustration, graphic design, or art therapy).

Furthermore, different majors can lead to the same career. For instance, a variety of majors can lead a student to law school and a career as a lawyer; in fact, there's really no such thing as a "law major" or "pre-law major." Students with a variety of majors (or minors) can also enter medical school as long as they have a solid set of foundational courses in biology and chemistry and score well on the medical college admissions test.

Studies show that today's workers change jobs 10 times in the two decades following college and the job-changing rate is highest for younger workers (AAC&U, 2007). Research also indicates that only half of new college graduates expect to be working in the same field in which they're currently employed (Hart Research Associates, 2006); they frequently change positions during their first two decades of employment following college completion, and the further along they proceed in their career path, the more likely they are to be working in a field that's unrelated to their college major (Millard, 2004).

So, don't assume that your major *is* your career, or that your major automatically turns into your lifelong career. It's this belief that can result in some students procrastinating about choosing a major; they think they're making a lifelong decision and fear that if they make the "wrong" choice, they'll be stuck doing something they hate for the rest of their life. Although it's important to think about how your choice of a college major will affect your career path, for most college students—particularly those not majoring in preprofessional fields—choice of a major and choice of a career are not identical decisions made at the same time. Choosing a specific major is a decision that should be made by your sophomore year; choosing a career is a decision that can be made later.

> "I intend on becoming a corporate lawyer. I am an English major. The reason I chose this major is because while I was researching the educational backgrounds of some corporate attorneys, I found that a lot were English majors. It helps with writing and delivering cases."
> —College sophomore

> "Things like picking majors and careers really scare me a lot! I don't know exactly what I want to do with my life."
> —First-year student

Note

Don't assume that choosing your college major means you're choosing what you'll be doing for the remainder of your working life. Deciding on a major and deciding on a career are not identical decisions that must be made simultaneously.

Myth 2. If you want to continue your education after college graduation, you must continue in the same field as your college major.

After graduating with a four-year (baccalaureate) degree, you have two primary paths available to you: (a) enter the workforce immediately, and/or (b) continue your education in graduate school or professional school. (See **Figure 8.5** for a visual map of the stages and milestones in the college experience and the paths available to you after college.)

FIGURE 8.5: A Snapshot of the College Experience and Beyond

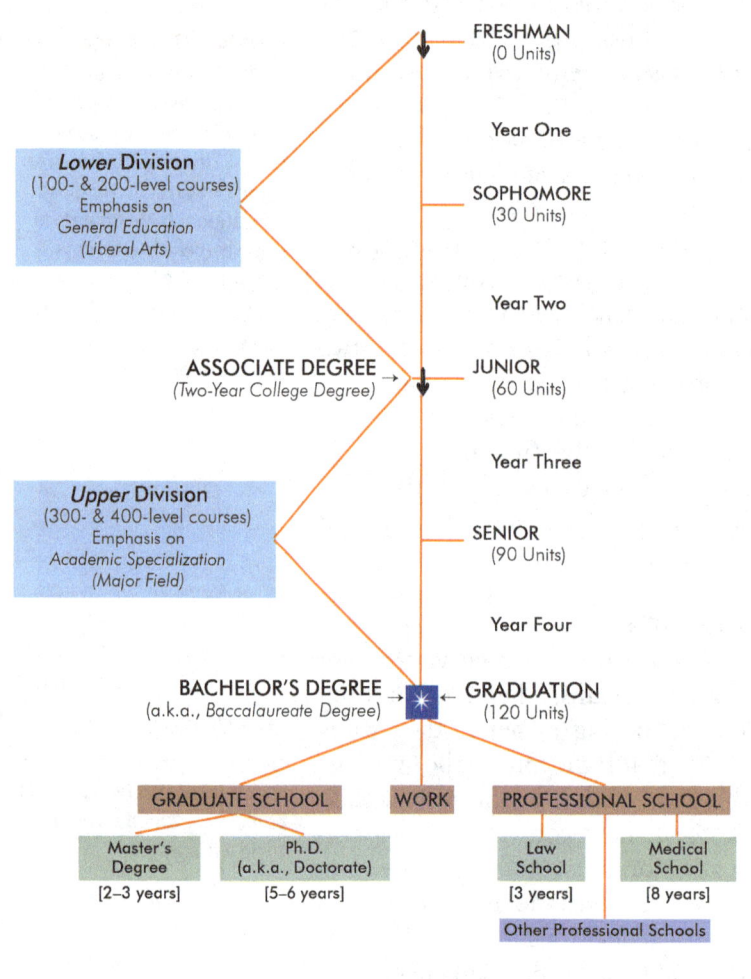

Lower Division (100- & 200-level courses) Emphasis on General Education (Liberal Arts)

Upper Division (300- & 400-level courses) Emphasis on Academic Specialization (Major Field)

- FRESHMAN (0 Units) — Year One
- SOPHOMORE (30 Units) — Year Two
- ASSOCIATE DEGREE (Two-Year College Degree) → JUNIOR (60 Units) — Year Three
- SENIOR (90 Units) — Year Four
- BACHELOR'S DEGREE (a.k.a., *Baccalaureate* Degree) → GRADUATION (120 Units)

After graduation:
- **GRADUATE SCHOOL**
  - Master's Degree [2–3 years]
  - Ph.D. (a.k.a., Doctorate) [5–6 years]
- **WORK**
- **PROFESSIONAL SCHOOL**
  - Law School [3 years]
  - Medical School [8 years]
  - Other Professional Schools

Notes

1. On average, about one-third of the courses required for a college degree are general education courses selected from the liberal arts curriculum. However, the number of required general education courses varies from campus to campus and can vary at the same campus depending on the student's major.
2. The word "freshman" originated in England in 1596, when every college student was a "fresh" (new) "man." Today, the term "freshman" is frequently being replaced by "first-year student" because this is a more gender-neutral term.
3. The term "baccalaureate" derives from "Bacchus"—the Greek god of wine and festive celebration, and "laurel"—a wreath made from the laurel plant that ancient Greeks draped around the neck of Olympic champions.
4. It often takes college students longer than four years to graduate due to a variety of reasons, such as working part-time and taking fewer courses per term, needing to repeat courses that were failed or dropped, or making a late change to a different major and needing to fulfill additional requirements for the new major.
5. Graduate and professional schools are options for continuing to higher levels of education after completion of an undergraduate (college) education.
6. Students going to graduate school on a full-time basis can sometimes support themselves financially by working part-time as a teaching assistant (TA) or research assistant (RA). It's also possible to enroll in some graduate or professional school programs on a part-time basis while holding a full-time job.
7. The term "Ph.D." refers to "Doctor of Philosophy," respecting the fact that the first scholars were the ancient Greek philosophers (e.g., Socrates, Plato, and Aristotle). However, a Ph.D. can be earned in many different academic fields (Mathematics, Music, Economic, etc.).
8. Compared to graduate school, professional school involves advanced education in more "applied" professions (e.g., pharmacy or public administration).

©Kendall Hunt Publishing Company

Once you earn a college diploma, you can continue your education in a field that's not directly related to your college major. This is particularly true for students majoring in liberal arts fields that don't lead directly to a specific career after graduation (Pascarella & Terenzini, 1991, 2005). For example, an English major can go to graduate school in a subject other than English, or go to law school, or get a master's degree in business administration. In fact, most students who attend graduate school in the field of business (e.g., MBA programs) were not business majors when they were in college (Zlomek, 2012).

Myth 3. Since most college graduates are employed in business organizations or corporations, you should major in business.

Most college graduates are employed in business settings, so students (and their parents) often conclude that if students are going to work for a business, they better major in business. This belief likely explains why business is the most popular major among college students (National Center for Education Statistics, 2011). However, college graduates now working in business settings have majored in variety of fields besides business, and many CEOs of today's most profitable companies did not major in business. Certainly, if you have an interest in and passion for majoring in business, by all means major in business; however, don't choose a business major because you think it's the only major that will qualify you to work for and succeed in a business organization after graduation.

Myth 4. If you major in a liberal arts field, the only career available to you is teaching.

A commonly held myth is that all you can do with a major in a liberal arts subject is to teach the subject you majored in (e.g., math majors become math teachers; history majors become history teachers). The truth is that students majoring in different liberal arts fields go on to enter, advance, and prosper in a wide variety of careers. College graduates with degrees in the liberal arts who went on to achieve professional success in careers other than teaching include:

- Jill Barad (English major), CEO, Mattel Toys
- Willie Brown (liberal studies major), Mayor of San Francisco
- Ken Chenault (History major), CEO, American Express
- Christopher Connor (Sociology major), CEO, Sherwin Williams
- Robert Iger (Communications major), CEO, Walt Disney Company

Significant numbers of liberal arts majors are also employed in positions relating to marketing, human resources, and public affairs (Bok, 2006; Useem, 1989). An experienced career counselor once tracked the majors of college graduates working in the insurance industry. She found an art history major working at a major insurance firm whose job was to value oriental carpets and art holdings. She found a geology major working for an insurance company whose job was to evaluate beach properties and determine the odds of hurricanes or other natural phenomena causing property damage. This former geology major spent much of her work time traveling to beachfront communities to review new developments and assessing damages after hurricanes or other tragic events (Brooks, 2009).

> "The first week of law school, one of my professors stressed the importance of 'researching, analyzing and writing.' I thought this was an interesting thing to say, because English majors learn and practice these skills in every class."
>
> —English major attending law school

> "They asked me during my interview why I was right for the job and I told them because I can read well, write well and I can think. They really liked that because those were the skills they were looking for."
>
> —English major hired by a public relations firm

Research also reveals that the career mobility and career advancement of liberal arts majors working in the corporate world are comparable to business majors. For example, liberal arts majors are just as likely to advance to the highest levels of corporate leadership as majors in such preprofessional fields as business and engineering (Pascarella & Terenzini, 2005). The point we're making here is that if you have a passion for and talent in a liberal arts field, don't dismiss it as being "impractical," and don't be dismayed or discouraged by those who challenge your choice by asking: "What are you going to do with a degree in that major?" (Brooks, 2009).

Reflection 8.8

Look back at the four myths about the relationships between majors and careers. Which of these four myths did you know were false? Which myths did you previously think were true?

Chapter Summary and Highlights

Studies show that the vast majority of students entering college are uncertain about their academic specialization. Most students do not reach a final decision about their major before starting college; typically, they make that decision during their college experience.

As a new student, it's only natural to be at least somewhat uncertain about educational goals at the early stages of your college experience because you haven't experienced the variety of subjects and academic programs that comprise the college curriculum. The general education curriculum will introduce you to new fields of study, some of which you've never experienced before and all of which represent possible choices for a college major. A key benefit of experiencing the variety of courses that make up the general education curriculum is that they enable you to become more aware of yourself, and at the same time, enable you to become more aware of the academic fields available to you as potential majors. As you gain experience with the college curriculum, you will gain greater self-insight into your academic interests, strengths, and weaknesses. Take this self-knowledge into consideration when choosing a major to help you select a field that capitalizes on your personal interests, abilities, and talents.

You can use your elective courses strategically to help you explore or confirm your choice of a college major as well as to:

- Acquire a minor that complements and augments your major
- Broaden your perspectives on the world around you
- Become a more balanced, well-rounded person

- Handle the practical life tasks that face you now and in the future
- Strengthen your career development and employment prospects after graduation

Compared to high school, higher education allows you more freedom of academic choice and a greater opportunity to determine your own educational path. Enjoy this freedom and employ it responsibly to make the most of your college experience and college degree.

To make a well-informed choice of a college major, there are several myths you should be aware of:

- **Myth 1. When you choose your major, you're choosing your career.** While some majors lead directly to a specific career, most do not. The relationship between most college majors and careers is not direct or linear. Different career clusters or "career families" can grow from the same major. Furthermore, different majors can lead to the same career.
- **Myth 2. After you graduate with a college degree, any further education you pursue must be in the same field as your college major.** College graduates can continue their education in a field that's not directly related to their college major. This is particularly true for students majoring in liberal arts fields that do not funnel them directly into a specific career after graduation.
- **Myth 3. Since most college graduates work in business settings, you should major business.** Students (and their parents) see most college graduates employed in business settings and conclude that if students are going to work for a business, they better major in business. However, the majority of college graduates now working in business settings didn't major in business when they were in college.
- **Myth 4. If you major in a liberal arts subject, the only career available to you is teaching.** The truth is that students majoring in different fields of the liberal arts go on to enter, advance, and prosper in a wide variety of careers. If you have a passion for and talent in a liberal arts field, consider majoring in it; don't dismiss it as being impractical, and don't be dismayed or discouraged by those who may challenge your choice by asking: "What are you going to do with a degree in that major?"

Learning More through the World Wide Web: Internet-Based Resources

For additional information related to educational planning and choosing a major, see the following websites.

Identifying and Choosing College Majors:
www.mymajors.com
www.princetonreview.com/majors.aspx

Relationships between Majors and Careers:
http://uncw.edu/career/WhatCanIDoWithaMajorIn.html

Careers for Liberal Arts Majors:
Liberal Arts Career Network (www.liberalartscareers.org/)
"What can I do with my liberal arts degree?" (www.bls.gov/ooq/2007/winter/art.01pdf)

References

AAC&U (Association of American Colleges and Universities). (2007). *College learning for the new global century*. A report from the National Leadership Council for Liberal Education & America's Promise. Washington, DC: Association of American Colleges and Universities.

Bean, J. C. (2001). *Engaging ideas: The professor's guide to integrating writing, critical thinking and active learning in the classroom*. San Francisco: Jossey-Bass.

Biglan, A. (1973). The characteristics of subject matter in different academic areas. *Journal of Applied Psychology, 57*, 195–203.

Bodanovich, S. J., Wallace, J. C., & Kass, S. J. (2005). A confirmatory approach to the factor structure of the Boredom Proneness Scale: evidence for a two-factor short form. *Journal of Personality Assessment, 85*(3), 295–303.

Bok, D. (2006). *Our underachieving colleges*. Princeton, NJ: Princeton University Press.

Brooks, K. (2009). *You majored in what? Mapping your path from chaos to career*. New York: Penguin.

Claxton, C. S., & Murrell, P. H. (1987). *Learning styles: Implications for improving practice*. ASHE-ERIC Educational Report No. 4. Washington, DC: Association for the Study of Higher Education.

Colby, A., Ehrlich, T., Sullivan, W. M., & Dolle, J. R. (2011). *Rethinking undergraduate business education: Liberal learning for the profession*. The Carnegie Foundation for the Advancement of Teaching. San Francisco: Jossey-Bass.

Cuseo, J. B. (2005). "Decided," "undecided," and "in transition": Implications for academic advisement, career counseling, and student retention. In R.S. Feldman (Ed.), *Improving the first year of college: Research and patience* (pp. 27–50). Mahwah, NJ: Lawrence Erlbaum.

Dunn, R., Dunn, K., & Price, G. (1990). *Learning style inventory*. Lawrence, KS: Price Systems.

Gardner, H. (1993). *Frames of mind: The theory of multiple intelligences* (2nd ed.). New York: Basic Books.

Gardner, H. (1999). *Intelligence reframed: Multiple intelligences for the 21st century*. New York: Basic Books.

Gardner, H. (2006). *Changing minds. The art and science of changing our own and other people's minds*. Boston, MA: Harvard Business School Press.

Gordon, V. N., & Steele, G. E. (2003). Undecided first-year students: A 25-year longitudinal study. *Journal of the First-Year Experience and Students in Transition, 15*(1), 19–38.

Hart Research Associates. (2006). *How should colleges prepare students to succeed in today's global economy? Based on surveys among employers and recent college graduates*. Conducted on behalf of the Association of American Colleges and Universities. Washington, DC: Author.

Hendry, G., Heinrich, L. P., Barratt, A. L., Simpson, J. M., Hyde, S. J., Gonsalkorale, S., Hyde, M., & Mgaieth, S. (2005). Helping students understand their learning styles: Effects on study self-efficacy, preference for group work, and group climate. *Journal of Educational Psychology, 25*(4), 395–407.

HERI (Higher Education Research Institute). (2014). *Your first college year survey 2014*. Los Angeles, CA: Cooperative Institutional Research Program, University of California-Los Angeles.

Kolb, D. A. (1976). Management and learning process. *California Management Review, 18*(3), 21–31.

Kolb, D. A. (1985). *Learning styles inventory*. Boston: McBer.

Leuwerke, W. C., Robbins, S. B., Sawyer, R., & Hovland, M. (2004). Predicting engineering major status from mathematics achievement and interest congruence. *Journal of Career Assessment, 12*, 135–149.

Millard, B. (2004, November 7). *A purpose-based approach to navigating college transitions*. Preconference workshop presented at the Eleventh National Conference on Students in Transition, Nashville, Tennessee.

National Center for Education Statistics. (2011). U.S. Department of Education Institute of Education Sciences. https://nces.ed.gov/fastfacts/#.

Pascarella, E., & Terenzini, P. (1991). *How college affects students: Findings and insights from twenty years of research*. San Francisco: Jossey-Bass.

Pascarella, E., & Terenzini, P. (2005). *How college affects students: A third decade of research* (Vol. 2). San Francisco: Jossey-Bass.

Schommer-Aikins, M., Duell, O. K., & Barker, S. (2003). Epistemological beliefs across domains using Biglan's classification of academic disciplines. *Research in Higher Education, 44*(3), 347–366.

Svinicki, M. D. (2004). *Learning and motivation in the postsecondary classroom*. Bolton, MA: Anker.

Svinicki, M. D., & Dixon, N. M. (1987). The Kolb model modified for classroom activities. *College Teaching, 35*(4), 141–146.

Useem, M. (1989). *Liberal education and the corporation: The hiring and advancement of college graduates*. Piscataway, NJ: Aldine Transaction.

Zlomek, E. (2012, March 26). As MBA applicants, business majors face an uphill battle. *Bloomburg Business*. Retrieved from http://www.bloomberg.com/bw/articles/2012-03-26/as-mba-applicants-business-majors-face-an-uphill-battle.

Chapter 8 Exercises

8.1 Quote Reflections

Review the sidebar quotes contained in this chapter and select two that were especially meaningful or inspirational to you.

For each quote, provide a three- to five-sentence explanation for why you chose it.

8.2 Reality Bite

Whose Choice Is It Anyway?

Ursula, a first-year student, was in tears when she showed up at the Career Center. She had just returned from a weekend visit home, during which she informed her parents of her plans to major in art or theater. After Ursula's father heard about her plans, he exploded and insisted that she major in something "practical," like nursing or accounting, so that she could get a job after graduation. Ursula replied that she had no interest in these majors, nor did she feel she had the skills in science and math required by these majors. Her father shot back that he had no intention of "paying four years of college tuition for her to end up as a starving artist or unemployed actress!" He went on to say that if she wanted to major in art or theater she'd "have to figure out a way to pay for college herself."

Reflection and Discussion Questions

1. If Ursula were your friend, what would you suggest she do?
2. Do you see any way(s) in which Ursula might pursue a major that's compatible with her interests and talents, while at the same time, ease her father's concern that she'll end up jobless after college graduation?
3. Can you relate to this student's predicament, or know any other students in a similar situation?

8.3 Learning Styles Self-Assessment and Choice of Major

1. Complete the *My PEPS Learning Styles Inventory* that accompanies this book.
    a) Review the results from the report on your preferred modes for learning and working.
    b) Do you think that your learning style preferences are a good match for the major or major(s) you're considering? If yes, why? If no, why not?
2. Complete the *Do What You Are* inventory that provides you with a personality report as well as a list of suggested majors and careers.
    a) How do the suggested majors align with your strengths?
    b) Is your current major or the major you are considering on the list? If it is, explain how the major is a good fit for you. If it's not on the list, explain why you still think it's a good fit or why you think it's not.

8.4 Faculty Interview

Identify a faculty member on campus in a field you've chosen or are considering as a college major. Make an appointment to speak with the faculty member during office hours to learn about that field of study. Let the faculty member know the purpose of your visit. Use the following interview questions, to get to know the faculty member and give you a better understanding of the field.

1. What initially *attracted* you to your academic field?
2. *When* did you decide to pursue a career in your academic field? Was it your *first* choice, or did you *change* to it from another academic area? (If you changed your original major, *why* did you change?)
3. What would you say is the most *enjoyable, exciting,* or *stimulating* aspect of your field of study?
4. Are there any *unexpected* requirements in your academic field that prove to be particularly *challenging* for students?
5. What *careers* are related to your academic field? (Or, what types of careers does a major in your field prepare students to pursue?)
6. What particular *skills, abilities,* or *talents* do you think are needed for *success* in your field of study?
7. What personality *traits* or personal *interests* do you think would *"match up"* well with the type of work required in your academic field?
8. What particular *courses* or *out-of-class experiences* would you recommend to help students decide if your field is a good fit for them?

8.5 Developing a Long-Range Academic Plan for Your Course Work

This exercise is designed to help you design a detailed yet flexible, four-year academic plan. While it may seem a bit overwhelming to develop a long-range plan at this stage of your college experience, you will receive guidance from your course instructor and academic advisor. This is an opportunity to begin customizing your college experience and mapping your educational future. Remember: an educational plan isn't something set in stone; it can change depending on changes in your academic and career interests. As you create, shape, and follow your plan, consult frequently with your academic advisor.

Overview of Courses Comprising Your Plan

Your trip through the college curriculum will involve taking courses in the following three key categories:

1. *General education* courses required of all college graduates regardless of their major;
2. *Required* courses in your chosen *major*; and
3. *Elective* courses you choose to take from any listed in your college catalog.

What follows are planning directions for each of these types of courses. By building these three sets of courses into your educational plan, you can create a roadmap that guides your future coursework. Once you've reserved slots for these three key categories of courses you will have a blueprint to guide (not dictate) your educational future. If you later change your mind about a particular course you originally planned to take, you can do so without interfering with your educational progress by substituting another course from the same category. For instance, if your original plan was to take psychology to fulfill a general education requirement in the Social and

Behavioral Sciences, but you decide later to take anthropology instead, you have a space reserved in your plan to make the switch.

As you gain more educational experience, your specific academic and career interests are likely to change and so may the specifics of your long-range plan. The purpose of this plan is not to tie you up or pin you down, but to supply you with a map that keeps you on course and moving in the right direction. Since this is a flexible plan, it's probably best to complete it in pencil or electronically so you can make future changes as needed.

Once you've developed your plan, hold onto it, and keep an up-to-date copy of it throughout your time in college. Bring it with you when you meet with advisors and career development specialists, and come prepared to discuss your progress on the plan as well as any changes you would like to make to it.

Part A. Planning for General Education

Step 1. Use your course catalog (bulletin) to identify the general education requirements for graduation. You're likely to find these requirements organized into general divisions of knowledge (Humanities, Natural Sciences, etc.). Within each of these divisions, courses will be listed that you can take to fulfill the general education requirement(s) for that particular division. (Course catalogs can sometimes be tricky to navigate or interpret; if you run into any difficulty, seek help from your course instructor or an academic advisor.) You'll probably be able to choose courses from a list of different options. Use your freedom of choice to choose general education courses whose descriptions capture your curiosity and contribute to your personal development and career plans. You can use general education courses not only to fulfill general education requirements, but also to test your interest and talent in different fields—one of which may end up becoming your major (or minor).

Step 2. Identify courses in the catalog you plan to take to fulfill your general education requirements and list them on the following form. Some courses you're taking this term may be fulfilling general education requirements, so be sure to list them as well.

Planning Grid for *General Education* Courses

Course Title	Units	Course Title	Units

Total Number of Units Required for *General Education* = _____

Part B. Planning for a College Major

The point of this portion of your educational plan is not to force you to commit to a major right now, but to develop a flexible plan that will allow you to reach a well-informed decision about your major. If you have already chosen a major, this exercise will help you lay out exactly what's ahead of you and confirm whether the coursework required by your major is what you expected and "fits" well with your interests and talents.

Step 1. Go to your college catalog and locate the major you've chosen or are considering. If you're completely undecided, select a field that you might consider as a possibility. To help you identify possible majors, peruse your catalog or go online and answer the questions at *www.mymajors.com*.

Another way to identify a major for this exercise is to first identify a career you might be interested in and work backward to find a major that leads to this career. If you would like to use this strategy, the following website will guide you through the process: *http://uncw.edu/career/WhatCanIDoWithaMajorIn.html*.

Step 2. After you've selected a major, consult your college catalog to identify the courses required for that major. Your campus may also have "major planning sheets" that list the specific course requirements for each major. (To see if these major planning sheets are available, check with the Advising Center or the academic department that offers the major you've selected.)

A college major will require all students majoring in that field to complete specific courses. For instance, all business majors are required to take microeconomics. Other courses required for a major may be chosen from a menu or list of options (e.g., "choose any three courses from the following list of six courses"). Such courses are often called "major electives." For these major electives, read their course descriptions carefully and use your freedom of choice wisely to select courses that interest you and are most relevant to your future plans.

Note: You can "double dip" by taking courses that fulfill a major requirement and a general education requirement at the same time. For instance, if your major is psychology, you may be able to take a course in General or Introductory Psychology that counts simultaneously as a required major course and a required general education course in the area of Social and Behavioral Sciences.

Step 3. Identify courses you plan to take to fulfill your major requirements and major electives and list them on the following form. Courses you're taking this term may be fulfilling requirements in the major you've selected, so be sure to list them as well.

Planning Grid for Courses in Your *Major*

Course Title	Units	Course Title	Units

Total Number of Units Required for Your *Major* = _____

Plan C. Planning Your Free Electives

Now that you've built general education courses and major courses into your educational map, you're well positioned to plan your *free electives*—courses not required for general education or your major but that are needed to reach the minimum number of units required for a college degree. These are courses you are free to choose from any listed in the college catalog.

To determine how many free elective units you have, add up the number of course units you're taking to fulfill general education and major requirements, then subtract this number from the total number of units you need to graduate. The number of course units remaining represents your total number of free electives.

Planning Grid for Your *Free Electives*

Course Title	Units	Course Title	Units

Total Number of *Free Elective* Units = _____

Part D. Putting It Altogether: Developing a Comprehensive Graduation Plan

In the previous three sections, you built three key sets of college courses into your plan: general education courses, major courses, and free elective courses. Now you're positioned to tie these three sets of courses together and create a comprehensive graduation plan.

Using the "Long-Range Graduation Planning Form" enter the courses you selected to fulfill general education requirements, major requirements, and free electives. In the space provided next to each course, use the following shorthand notations to designate its category:

GE = *general education* course

M = *major* course

E = *elective* course

Notes:
1. If there are courses in your plan that fulfill two or more categories at the same time (e.g., a general education requirement and a major requirement), note both categories.
2. To complete a college degree in four years (approximately 120 units), you should plan to complete about 30 course credits each academic year. Keep in mind that you can take college courses in the summer as well as the fall and spring.

Note

Unlike high school, taking summer courses in college doesn't mean you've fallen behind or need to retake a course you failed during the "normal" school year (fall and spring terms). Instead, summer term can be used to get ahead and reduce your time to graduation. Adopt the mindset that summer term is a regular part of the college academic year; use it strategically to stay on track to complete your degree in a timely fashion.

3. Keep in mind that the number associated with a course indicates the year in the college experience when the course is usually taken. Courses numbered in the 100s (or below) are typically taken in the first year of college, 200-numbered courses in the sophomore year, 300-numbered courses in the junior year, and 400-numbered courses in the senior year.

4. If you haven't decided on a major, a good strategy is to focus on completing general education requirements during your first year of college. This first-year strategy will open more slots in your course schedule during your sophomore year—by that time, you may have a better idea of what you'll major in, so you can fill these open slots with courses required for the major you've chosen. (This first-year strategy will also allow you to use general education courses in different subjects to test your interest in majoring in one of these subjects.)

5. Be sure to check whether the course you're planning to take has any *prerequisites*—courses that need to be completed *before* you can enroll in the course you're planning to take. For example, before you can enroll in a literature course, you may need to complete at least one prerequisite course in writing or English composition.

6. Your campus may have a *degree audit program* that allows you to electronically track the courses you've completed and the courses you still need to complete a degree in your chosen major. If such a program is available, take advantage of it.

7. You're not locked into taking all your courses in the exact terms you originally placed them in your plan. You can trade terms if it turns out that the course isn't offered during the term you were planning to take it, or if it's offered at a time that conflicts with another course in your schedule.

8. Keep in mind that not all college courses are offered every term, every year. Typically, college catalogs do not contain information about when courses will be scheduled. If you're unsure when a course will be offered, check with an academic advisor. Some colleges develop *a projected plan of scheduled courses* that shows what academic term(s) courses will be offered for the next few years. If such a projected schedule of courses is available, take advantage of it. It will enable you to develop an educational plan that not only includes *what* courses you will take, but also *when* you will take them.

Long-Range Graduation Planning Form

FRESHMAN YEAR
Fall Term

Course Title	Course Type General Ed. (GE), Major (M), Elective (E)	Course Units

Total Units = _____

Spring Term

Course Title	Course Type General Ed. (GE), Major (M), Elective (E)	Course Units

Total Units = _____

Summer Term

Course Title	Course Type General Ed. (GE), Major (M), Elective (E)	Course Units

Total Units = _____

SOPHOMORE YEAR
Fall Term

Course Title	Course Type General Ed. (GE), Major (M), Elective (E)	Course Units

Total Units = _____

Spring Term

Course Title	Course Type General Ed. (GE), Major (M), Elective (E)	Course Units

Total Units = _____

Summer Term

Course Title	Course Type General Ed. (GE), Major (M), Elective (E)	Course Units

Total Units = _____

JUNIOR YEAR
Fall Term

Course Title	Course Type General Ed. (GE), Major (M), Elective (E)	Course Units

Total Units = _____

Spring Term

Course Title	Course Type General Ed. (GE), Major (M), Elective (E)	Course Units

Total Units = _____

Summer Term

Course Title	Course Type General Ed. (GE), Major (M), Elective (E)	Course Units

Total Units = _____

SENIOR YEAR
Fall Term

Course Title	Course Type General Ed. (GE), Major (M), Elective (E)	Course Units

Total Units = _____

Spring Term

Course Title	Course Type General Ed. (GE), Major (M), Elective (E)	Course Units

Total Units = _____

Reflection Questions

1. What is the total number of credits in your graduation plan? Does it equal or exceed the total number of credits needed to graduate from your college or university?

2. How many credits will you be taking in the following areas?
   a) General Education =
   b) Major =
   c) Free Electives =

3. Look over the course required for the major you selected:
   a) Are there required courses you were surprised to see or didn't expect would be required?
   b) Are you still interested in majoring in this field?
   c) How likely is it that you will change the major you selected?
   d) If you were to change your major, what would "Plan B" likely be?

4. Did completing this long-range graduation plan help you clarify your educational goals? Why or why not?

8.6 Developing a Co-Curricular Plan for Learning Experiences Outside the Classroom

Now that you've completed a curricular plan for your coursework, let's turn to devising a plan for the second key component of a college education: *experiential* learning—learning from "hands-on" experiences outside the classroom—either on campus (e.g., leadership positions) or off campus (e.g., service experiences, internships, or employment). Learning opportunities available to you beyond the curriculum are known collectively as the *co-curriculum*. Co-curricular experiences complement your coursework, enhance the quality of your education, and increase your employability. Keep in mind that co-curricular experiences are also resume-building experiences.

Ideally, by the time you graduate, you should have co-curricular experiences in each of the following areas:

- *Volunteer work* or *community service* that demonstrates social responsibility and allows you to gain "real world" experience
- *Leadership and mentoring* skills—for example, participating in leadership retreats, student government, peer mentoring, or serving as a student representative on college committees
- *Internships* or work experiences in a field related to your major or career goals
- Interacting and collaborating with members of *diverse racial and cultural groups*—for example, participating in multicultural clubs, organizations, or retreats
- *Study abroad* or *study travel* experiences that allow you to acquire international knowledge and a global perspective

Step 1. Consult your *Student Handbook* or check with professionals working in the offices of Student Life (Student Development) and Career Development to locate co-curricular experiences in each of the above areas.

Step 2. Identify one campus program or opportunity in each of these areas that interests you and note it on the planning form below.

Planning Grid for Co-Curricular Experiences

Volunteer Work/Community Service: _____

Leadership/Mentoring: _____

Diversity (Multicultural) Experience: _____

Study Abroad (International) Experience: _____

Internship or Work Experience Relating to Your Major or Career Goals: _____

Notes:

- Summer term is an excellent time of the year to build experiential learning into your educational plan without having to worry about conflicts with your scheduled classes or doing it while simultaneously handling all the academic work associated with a full load of courses.
- Keep track of the specific skills you develop while engaging in co-curricular experiences, and be sure to showcase them to future employers. Don't just accumulate extracurricular activities to list on your resume, reflect on your experiences and articulate what you learned from them. Identify the thinking processes you used as well as the transferable skills and personal qualities you developed while engaging in these experiences.

- Keep in mind that the professionals with whom you interact while participating in co-curricular experiences can serve as valuable references and sources of letters of recommendation to future employers, graduate schools, and professional schools.

Reflection Questions

1. What *challenges* or *obstacles* do you think might interfere with your ability to complete this co-curricular plan? What campus *resources* might help you deal with these challenges or obstacles?

2. What people on or off campus could you *network* with to help you successfully navigate your co-curricular plan?

3. As you pursue your plans for experiential learning outside the classroom, who might be a *mentor* for you, or serve as a personal source of *inspiration and motivation*?

Final Reminder:

Hold onto your curricular and co-curricular plans. Keep an up-to-date copy of them throughout your years in college. Bring these plans with you when you meet with your academic advisor and career development specialists, and come prepared to discuss your progress on these plans as well as any changes you would like to make.

Role Playing or Worksheet Scenarios for Effective Communication

Have students refer to the following definitions in the *Thriving in the Community College & Beyond* textbook:

- **Passive**-not standing up for your personal rights and allowing others to take advantage of you
- **Aggressive**-Stand up for your rights but also violate the rights of others by threatening, domination, humiliating, or bullying them
- **Passive-Aggressive**-You get back or even with the other person in an indirect and ineffective way by withholding or taking away something
- **Assertive**-Striking middle ground between aggression and passivity

Once students understand these concepts, break them into four groups representing each of these four methods. Use the scenarios on the back and have students role-play a response based on the method their group represents.

Effective (and Ineffective) Communication Response Scenarios

1. A family member asks to borrow your car to run an errand. You usually do not lend your car to anyone because it makes you very nervous and anxious.
2. You are at dinner at a very nice and expensive restaurant. You order your steak rare but when it comes to the table it is well-done.
3. You are at the mall with your family. You make a mistake and a family member notices and calls you out publicly. He/she is very persistent and harsh and won't let up about your mistake!
4. A relative calls and says they will be going out of town and know that you stay home all day with "nothing to do". They figure since you are not doing anything, you should watch their cat while they are away.

Name _____ Section _____

FYE Work Values Activity

The following list contains work values. This list and the following process may help you clarify your values (what is *important* to you) in relation to the world of work.

DIRECTIONS:

1. Read each definition and check the items you would like as part of your ideal job.
2. Review the items you have checked, and identify the 10 items you want most.
3. Review these 10 items and prioritize them (1 as most important, 10 as least important).

____ **Help Society**: Do something to contribute to the betterment of communities or the world.
____ **Help Others**: Be involved in helping people in a *direct* way, either individually or in a small group.
____ **Esthetics**: Make beautiful things and contribute to the beauty of the world.
____ **Creativity (general)**: Create new ideas, programs, products, organizational structures or anything else not following a format previously developed by others.
____ **Work Alone**: Do projects by myself, without any significant amount of contact with others.
____ **Public Contact**: Have a lot of day-to-day contact with people.
____ **Work With Associates**: Have close working relationships with a group; work as a team toward common goals.
____ **Friendships**: Develop close personal relationships with people as a result of my work activities, get along well with (perhaps even socialize off hours with) my colleagues.
____ **Competition**: Engage in activities that pit my abilities against others where there are clear "win" and "lose" outcomes.
____ **Knowledge**: Engage myself in the pursuit of knowledge, truth, and understanding for knowledge sake.
____ **Intellectual status**: Be regarded as a person of high intellectual powers or as one who is an acknowledged "expert" in a given field.
____ **Recognition**: Be recognized by others for my quality of work in some visible or public way.
____ **Achievement**: Have *personal* satisfaction and a feeling of accomplishment in my position.
____ **Supervisory Relationship**: Have a fair supervisor with whom I get along with well.
____ **Power and Authority**: Work which permits me to plan, layout, supervise, and be directly responsible for the work activities or (partially) the destinies of other people.
____ **Make Decisions**: Have the power to decide courses of action, policies, etc.
____ **Fast Pace**: Work in circumstances where there is a high pace of activity, work must be done rapidly.
____ **Excitement**: Experience a high degree of (or frequent) excitement in the course of my work.
____ **Adventure**: Have work duties that involve frequent risk-taking.
____ **Change and Variety**: Have work responsibilities that frequently change their content and setting.
____ **Independence**: Be able to determine the nature of my work and how I approach it without significant direction from others; do not have to do what others tell me to do.

____ **Time Freedom**: Have work responsibilities that I can fulfill according to my own schedule; no specific working hours required.

____ **Way of Life**: Position that allows me to maintain my own identity in the workplace in terms of dress, speech, decorating my office, listening to music, eating at my desk, etc.

____ **Location**: Find a place to live (town, geographical area) which is conducive to my lifestyle and affords me the opportunity to do the things I enjoy most.

____ **Surroundings**: Have an environment (physically) which appeals to me in terms of temperature, noise level, ability for privacy, view from office, cleanliness, newness of building, furniture, decorating, etc.

____ **Stability**: Have work routine and job duties that are largely predictable and not likely to change over a long period of time.

____ **Security**: Be assured of keeping my job and a reasonable financial reward.

____ **Profit/Gain**: Have a strong likelihood of accumulating large amounts of money or other material gain.

Adapted from: University of South Carolina 2012 Faculty Resource Manual 2.0 University 101 Programs
Variations of this inventory appear on multiple institutional web sites. Original source unknown.

CHAPTER 9
Goal Setting and Motivation

MOVING FROM INTENTION TO ACTION

The path to personal success begins with goals and finding the means (succession of steps) to reach those goals. People who set specific goals are more likely to succeed than people who simply tell themselves they're going to try hard and do their best. This chapter lays out the key steps involved in the process of setting effective goals, identifies key self-motivational strategies for staying on track and sustaining progress toward our goals, and describes how personal qualities such as self-efficacy, grit, and growth mindset are essential for achieving goals.

> "What keeps me going is goals."
> —Muhammad Ali, philanthropist, social activist, and Hall of Fame boxer crowned "Sportsman of the 20th Century" by Sports Illustrated

Chapter Preview

Help you set meaningful goals and maintain motivation to achieve your goals.

Learning Goal

Specifically, how can you display patience and perseverance to ensure you can accomplish your goals? What goals are you willing to set to show God's love to others?

Integrate Your Faith

Reflection 9.1

Complete the following sentence:

For me, success is . . .

> "Stopping a long pattern of bad decision-making and setting positive, productive priorities and goals."
> —College sophomore's answer to the question: "What does being successful mean to you?"

Ignite Your Thinking

From *Thriving in College and Beyond: Research-Based Strategies for Academic Success and Personal Development*, Fourth Edition by Joseph B. Cuseo, Aaron Thompson, Michele Campagna, and Viki S. Fecas. Copyright © 2016 Kendall Hunt Publishing Company. Reprinted by permission.

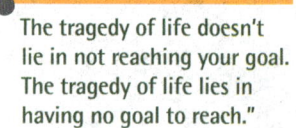

> "The tragedy of life doesn't lie in not reaching your goal. The tragedy of life lies in having no goal to reach."
> —Benjamin Mays, minister, scholar, activist, president of Morehouse College

The Relationship between Goal Setting and Success

Achieving success begins with setting goals. Research shows that people who set goals and develop plans to reach them are more likely to reach them (Halvorson, 2010), and successful people set goals on a regular basis (Locke & Latham, 1990). In fact, the word "success" derives from the Latin root "successus"—meaning "to follow or come after"—as in the word "successive." Thus, by definition, success involves a sequence of actions that leads to a desired outcome; the process starts with identifying an end (goal) and then finding a means (sequence of steps) to reach that goal.

Motivation begins with dreams and great intentions that get turned into realistic goals. Depending on the length of time it takes to reach them and the order in which they are to be achieved, goals may be classified into three general categories: long-range, mid-range, and short-range. Short-range goals need to be completed before a mid-range goal can be reached, and mid-range goals must be reached before a long-range goal can be achieved. For example, if your long-range goal is a successful career that requires a college degree, your mid-range goal is completing all the coursework required for a degree that will allow you entry into that career. To reach your mid-range goal of a college degree, you need to start by successfully completing the courses you're taking this term (your short-range goal).

This goal-setting process is called *means-end analysis*; it involves working backward from your long-range goal (the end) and identifying what mid-range and short-range subgoals (the means) must be reached in order to achieve your long-range goal (Brooks, 2009; Newell & Simon, 1959). Engaging in this means-end analysis doesn't mean you're locking yourself into a premature plan that will restrict your flexibility or options. It's just a process that gets you to: (a) think about where you want to go, (b) provides some sense of direction about how to get there, and (c) starts moving you in the right direction.

> "You've got to be careful if you don't know where you're going because you might not get there."
> —Yogi Berra, Hall of Fame baseball player

Characteristics of a Well-Designed Goal

Studies show that people who set specific, well-designed goals are more likely to succeed than are people who simply tell themselves they're going to try hard and do their very best (Halvorson, 2010; Latham & Locke, 2007). The acronym SMART is a well-known mnemonic device (memory strategy) for recalling all the key components of a well-designed goal (Meyer, 2003). **Box 9.1** describes the different components of a SMART goal.

Box 9.1

The *SMART* Method of Goal Setting

A *SMART* goal is one that's:

Specific—it states precisely what the goal is, targets exactly what needs to be done to achieve it, and provides a clear picture of what successfully reaching the goal looks like.

Example: By spending 25 hours per week on my coursework outside of class and by using the effective learning strategies (such as those

Box 9.1 *(continued)*

recommended in this book), I'll achieve at least a 3.0 grade point average this term. (Note that this is a much more specific goal than saying, "I'm really going to work hard this term.")

> "Dreams can be fulfilled only when they've been defined."
> —Ernest Boyer, former United States Commissioner of Education

*M*eaningful (and *M*easurable)—the goal really matters to you (not someone else) and the progress you're making toward the goal can be clearly measured (tracked).

Example: Achieving at least a 3.0 grade point average this term is important to me because it will enable me to get into the field I'd like to major in. I'll measure my progress toward this goal by calculating the grade I'm earning in each of my courses this semester at regular intervals throughout the term.

Note: At *www.futureme.org* you can set up a program to send future emails to yourself that remind you to check and reflect on whether you're making steady progress toward the goals you set.

*A*ctionable (i.e., *A*ction-Oriented)—the actions or behaviors that will be taken to reach your goal are clearly specified.

Example: I will achieve at least a 3.0 grade point average this term by (a) attending all classes, (b) taking detailed notes in all my classes, (c) completing all reading assignments before their due dates, and (d) avoiding cramming by studying in advance for all my major exams.

*R*ealistic—there is a good chance of reaching the goal, given the time, effort, and skills needed to get there.

Example: Achieving a 3.0 grade point average this term is a realistic goal because my course load is manageable, I will be working no more than 15 hours per week at my part-time job, and I'll be able to get help from campus support services for any academic skills or strategies I need to strengthen.

*T*ime-framed—the goal has a deadline plus a timeline or timetable that includes short-range (daily), mid-range (weekly), and long-range (monthly) steps.

Example: To achieve at least a 3.0 grade point average this term, first I'll acquire all the information I need to learn by taking complete notes in my classes and complete all reading assignments (short-range step). Second, I'll learn the information I've acquired from my notes and readings, break it into parts, and study the parts in separate sessions in advance of major exams (mid-range step). Third, on the day before exams, I'll review all the information I previously studied in parts so I avoid cramming and get a good night's sleep (long-range step).

Note: The SMART process can be used to set goals in any area of your life or dimension of personal development, such as:

- self-management (e.g., time-management and money-management goals),
- physical development (e.g., health and fitness goals),
- social development (e.g., relationship goals),
- emotional development (e.g., stress-management or anger-management goals),
- intellectual development (e.g., learning and critical thinking goals),
- career development (e.g., career exploration and preparation goals), or
- any other element of holistic (whole-person) development discussed in Chapter 2 (see p. 00).

In addition to the effective goal-setting properties associated with the SMART method, research reveals that the following goal-setting features characterize people who set and reach important goals.

1. Effective goal-setters set *improvement (get-better) goals* that emphasize progress and growth, rather than perfection (be-good) goals. Studies show that when people pursue get-better goals, they pursue them with greater interest and intensity, and they are more likely to enjoy the process (Halvorson, 2010). This is likely because get-better goals give us a sense of accomplishment about how far we've come—even when we still have a long way to go.

2. Effective goal-setters focus on outcomes they have *influence or control over*, not on outcomes that are beyond their control. For example, a controllable goal for an aspiring actress would be to improve her acting skills and opportunities, rather than to become a famous movie star—which will depend on factors that are beyond her control.

3. Effective goal-setters set goals that are *challenging and effortful*. Goals worth achieving require that we stretch ourselves and break a sweat; they require endurance, persistence, and resiliency. Studies of successful people in all occupations indicate that when they set goals that are attainable but also *challenging*, they pursue those goals more strategically, with more intensity, and with greater commitment (Locke & Latham, 2002; Latham & Locke, 2007). There's another advantage of setting challenging goals: Achieving them supplies us with a stronger sense of accomplishment, satisfaction, and self-esteem.

4. Effective goal-setters anticipate *obstacles* they may encounter along the path to their goal and have a plan in place for dealing with them. Successful people often imagine what things will be like if they don't reach their goals, which drives them to anticipate problems and setbacks before they arise (Gilbert, 2006; Harris, Griffin, & Murray, 2008). They're optimistic about succeeding, but they're not blind optimists; they realize the road will be tough and they have a realistic plan in place for dealing with the rough spots (Oettingen, 2000; Oettingen & Stephens, 2009). Thus a well-designed goal should not only include specific information about how the goal will be achieved, but also specific plans to handle anticipated impediments along the way—for example, identifying what resources and social support networks may be used to keep you on track and moving forward.

Capitalize on resources that can help you stay on track and moving toward your goal. Research indicates that success in college involves a combination of what students do for themselves (personal responsibility) and how they capitalize on resources available to them (Pascarella & Terenzini, 1991, 2005). Successful people are *resourceful*; they seek out and take advantage of resources to help them reach their goals. Use your campus (and community) resources to help you achieve your long-range goals (e.g., academic advising and career counseling).

> "Nothing ever comes that is worth having, except as a result of hard work."
>
> —Booker T. Washington, born-in-slavery Black educator, author, and advisor to Republican presidents

Don't forget that your peers can serve as a resource to help you reach your goals. Much has been said about the dangers of "peer pressure," but much less attention has been paid to the benefits of "peer power." The power of social support groups for helping people achieve personal goals is well documented by research in different fields (Brissette, Cohen, & Seeman, 2000; Ewell, 1997). There's also a long historical trail of research pointing to the power of peers for promoting the development and success of college students (Astin, 1993; Feldman & Newcomb, 1994; Pascarella & Terenzini, 2005). Be sure to ask yourself: Who can help me stick to my plan and complete the steps needed to reach my goal? You can harness the power of social support by surrounding yourself with peers who are committed to successfully achieve their educational goals and by avoiding "toxic" people who are likely to poison your plans or dampen your dreams.

Find motivated peers with whom you can make mutually supportive "pacts" to help one another reach your respective goals. These mutual support pacts may be viewed as "social contracts" signed by "co-witnesses" who help them stay on track and moving toward their long-range goals. Studies show that making a commitment to a goal in the presence of others increases our commitment to that goal because our successful pursuit of it is viewed not only through our own eyes, but through the eyes of others as well (Hollenbeck, Williams, & Klein, 1989; Locke, 2000).

Strategies for Maintaining Motivation and Progress toward Your Goals

The word "motivation" derives from the Latin *movere*, meaning "to move." Success comes to those who overcome inertia—they start moving toward their goal—then they maintain momentum until their goal is reached. Goal-setting only creates the potential for success; it takes motivation to turn this potential into reality by converting intention into action. We can have the best-designed goals and know the way to succeed, but if we don't have the *will* to succeed, there's no way we will succeed. Studies show that goal-setting is just the first step in the process; it must be accompanied by a strong commitment to achieve the goal that has been set (Locke, 2000; Locke & Latham, 1990).

> You can lead a horse to water, but you can't make him drink."
> —Author unknown

Reaching challenging goals requires that you maintain motivation and sustain effort over an extended period of time. Listed below are strategies for doing so.

Put your goals in writing and make them visible. Written goals can serve almost like a written contract that holds you accountable for following through on your commitments. By placing written goals where you can't help but see them on a daily basis (e.g., your laptop, refrigerator, and bathroom mirror), you're less likely to "lose sight" of them and more likely to continue pursuing them. What's kept in sight is kept in mind.

> **Note**
> *The next best thing to doing something you intend to do is to write down your intention to do it.*

Keep your eye on the prize. Visualize reaching your long-range goals; picture it by creating vivid mental images of your future success. For example, if your goal is to achieve a college degree, visualize a crowd of cheering family, friends, and faculty at your graduation. (You could even add musical accompaniment to your visualization by playing a motivational song in your head—e.g., "We are the Champions" by Queen). Imagine cherishing this proud memory for the rest of your life and being in a career your college degree enabled you to enter. Picture a typical workday going something like this: You wake up on a Monday morning and are excited about the upcoming workweek. When you're at work, time seems to fly by; before you know it, the day is over. When you go home after work and reflect on your day, you feel great about what you did and how well you did it.

Visualize completing the steps leading to your goal. For visualization to be really effective, you need to visualize not just the success itself (the end goal), but also the steps you'll take along the way. "Just picturing yourself crossing the finish line doesn't actually help you get there—but visualizing how you run the race (the strategies you will use, the choices you will make, the obstacles you will face) not only will give you greater confidence, but also leave you better prepared for the task ahead" (Halvorson, 2010, p. 000).

Thus, reaching a long-term goal requires focusing on the prize—your dream and *why* it's important to you; this "big picture" view provides the inspiration. At the same time, however, you have to focus on the little things—*what* it will take to get there—the nitty-gritty of due dates, to-do lists, and day-to-day tasks. This is the perspiration that transforms inspiration into action, enabling you to plug away and stay on track until your goal is achieved.

It could be said that successfully achieving a long-term goal requires two lenses, each of which provides you with a different focus point: (a) a wide-angle lens that gives you a big-picture view of a future that's far ahead of you (your ultimate goal), and (b) a narrow-angle lens that allows you to focus intently on the here and now—on the steps that lie immediately ahead of you. Alternating between these two perspectives allows you to view your small, short-term chores and challenges (e.g., completing an assignment that's due next week) in light of the larger, long-range picture (e.g., college graduation and a successful future).

Characteristics of Successful People

Achieving success involves effective use of goal-setting and motivational strategies, but it takes something more. Ultimately, success emerges from the inside out; it flows from personal qualities and attributes found within a person. Studies of successful people who achieve their goals reveal they possess the following personal characteristics. Keep these characteristics in mind as you set and pursue your goals.

Internal Locus of Control

Successful people have what psychologists call an "internal locus of control"; they believe that the locus (location or source) of control for events in their life is *internal*—"inside" them and within their control—rather than *external*—outside them and beyond their control. They believe that success is influenced more by attitude, effort, commitment, and preparation than by inherited ability, inborn intelligence, luck, chance, or fate (Rotter, 1966; Carlson, et al., 2009; Jernigan, 2004).

Research shows that individuals with a strong internal locus of control display the following positive qualities:

1. Greater independence and self-direction (Van Overwalle, Mervielde, & De Schuyer, 1995),
2. More accurate self-assessment of strengths and weaknesses (Hashaw, Hammond, & Rogers, 1990), and
3. Higher levels of learning and achievement (Wilhite, 1990).

Self-Efficacy

An internal locus of control contributes to the development of another positive trait that psychologists refer to as *self-efficacy*—the belief that you have power to produce a positive effect on the *outcomes* of your life (Bandura, 1994). People with low self-efficacy tend to feel helpless, powerless, and passive; they think (and allow) things to happen to them rather than taking charge and making things happen for them. College students with a strong sense of self-efficacy believe they're in control of their educational success and can shape their future, regardless of their past experience or current circumstances.

People with a strong sense of self-efficacy initiate action and exert effort. They believe success is something that's earned and the harder they work at it, the more likely they'll get it. If they encounter setbacks or bad breaks along the way, they don't give up or give in; they persevere and push on (Bandura, 1986, 1997).

Students with a strong sense of *academic self-efficacy* have been found to:

1. Put considerable effort into their studies;
2. Use active-learning strategies;
3. Capitalize on campus resources; and
4. Persist in the face of obstacles (Multon, Brown, & Lent, 1991; Zimmerman, 1995, 2000).

Students with a strong sense of self-efficacy also possess a strong sense of personal responsibility. As the breakdown of the word "responsible" implies, they are "response" "able"—they believe they're able to respond to personal challenges, including academic challenges.

> "I'm a great believer in luck, and I find the harder I work the more I have of it."
>
> —Thomas Jefferson, third president of the United States

Grit

When you expend significant effort, energy, and sacrifice over a sustained period of time to achieve a goal, you're demonstrating grit (Stoltz, 2014). People with grit have been found to possess the following qualities (Duckworth, et al., 2007).

Persistence. They hang in there and persevere until they reach their goals. When the going gets tough, they don't give up; they step it up. They have the fortitude to persist in the face of frustration and adversity.

Tenacity. They pursue their goals with relentless determination. If they encounter something along the way that's hard to do, they work harder to do it.

Resilience. They bounce back from setbacks and keep striving to reach their goals. They adopt the mindset that they'll bounce back from setbacks and turn them into comebacks. How you react mentally and emotionally to a setback affects what action you take in response to it. For instance, you can react to a poor test grade by knocking yourself down with self-putdowns ("I'm a loser") or by building yourself back up with positive self-talk ("I'm going to learn from my mistakes on this test and rebound with a stronger performance on the next one").

It's noteworthy that the word "problem" derives from the Greek root *proballein*, meaning "to throw forward." This suggests that a problem is an opportunity to move ahead. You can take this approach to problems by rewording or rephrasing the problem you're experiencing in terms of a positive goal statement. (For example, "I'm flunking math" can be reframed as: "My goal is to get a grade of C or better on the next exam to pull my overall course grade into passing territory.")

Similarly, the root of the word "failure" is *fallere*—meaning to trip or fall. Thus, failing at something doesn't mean we've been defeated; it just means we've stumbled and taken a temporary spill. Success can still be achieved after a fall if we don't give up, but get up and get back to taking the next step needed to reach our goal. By viewing poor academic performances and other setbacks (particularly those occurring early in your college experience) not as failures but as learning opportunities, you put yourself in a position to bounce back and transform your setbacks into comebacks. Here are some notable people who did so:

- Louis Pasteur, famous bacteriologist, failed his admission test to the University of Paris;
- Albert Einstein, Nobel Prize—winning physicist, failed math in elementary school;
- Thomas Edison, prolific inventor, once expelled from school as "uneducable";
- Johnny Unitas, Hall of Fame football player, cut twice from professional football teams early in his career; and
- Michael Jordan, Hall of Fame basketball player, cut from his high school team as a sophomore.

> "Grit is perseverance and passion for long-term goals. Sticking with your future day in, day out, not just for the week, not just for the month, but for years and working really hard to make that future a reality."
>
> —Angela Duckworth, psychologist, University of Pennsylvania

> "How smart you are will influence the extent to which you experience something as difficult (for example, how hard a math problem is), but it says nothing about how you will deal with difficulty when it happens. It says nothing about whether you will be persistent and determined or feel overwhelmed and helpless."
>
> —Heidi Grant Halvorson, social psychologist, and author of *Succeed: How We Can Reach Your Goals*

Note

Don't let early setbacks bring you down emotionally or motivationally. Reflect on them, learn from them, and make sure they don't happen again.

Reflection 9.2

What would you say is the biggest setback or obstacle you've overcome in your life thus far?

How did you overcome it? (What enabled you to get past it, or what did you do to prevent it from stopping you?)

Self-Discipline. People with grit have *self-control*—they keep their actions aligned with their goal, staying on course and moving in the right direction—despite distractions and temptations (Halvorson, 2010). They resist the impulse to pursue instant gratification and do what they feel like doing instead of what needs to be done to reach their goal. They're able to sacrifice immediate, short-sighted needs and desires to do what has to be done to get where they want to be in the long run.

Setting long-range goals is important but having the self-discipline to reach them is another matter. Each day, whether we're aware of it or not, we're tempted to make choices and decisions that interfere with our ability to reach our goals. We need to remain mindful about whether these choices are moving us in the direction of our goals or taking us off course.

> "Self-discipline is the ability to make yourself do the thing you have to do, when it ought be done, whether you like it or not."
>
> —Thomas Henry Huxley, 19th-century English biologist

Chapter Summary and Highlights

A key to success is challenging ourselves to set ambitious, yet realistic goals. Studies consistently show that goal-setting is a more effective self-motivational strategy than simply telling ourselves to "try hard" or "do our best." Achieving success begins with setting goals and successful people set goals on a regular basis.

The acronym "SMART" is a popular mnemonic device (memory strategy) for recalling all the key components of a well-designed goal. A *SMART* goal is one that is:

Specific—it states precisely what the goal is and what you will do to achieve it.
Meaningful (and **M**easurable)—it's a goal that really matters to you and your progress toward reaching it can be steadily measured or tracked.
Actionable (or **A**ction-Oriented)—it identifies concrete actions and specific behaviors you'll engage in to reach the goal.
Realistic—the goal is attainable and you're aware of the amount of time, effort, and skill it will take to attain it, as well as obstacles you'll need to overcome along the way.

*T*ime-framed—the goal has a deadline and a timeline that includes a sequence of short-range, mid-range, and long-range steps.

In addition to the effective goal-setting properties associated with the SMART method, research reveals that the following goal-setting features characterize people who set and reach important goals.

1. Effective goal-setters set *improvement (get-better) goals* that emphasize progress and growth, rather than *perfection (be-good) goals*.
2. Effective goal-setters focus on what outcomes can *influence or control*, not on outcomes that are beyond their control.
3. Effective goal-setters set goals that are *challenging and effortful*.
4. Effective goal-setters anticipate *obstacles* they may encounter along the path to their goal and have a plan in place for dealing with them.

Setting goals ignites motivation, but maintaining motivation after it's been ignited requires use of effective self-motivational strategies. You can maintain your motivation by using such strategies as:

- Visualizing reaching your long-range goals;
- Putting your goals in writing;
- Creating a visual map of your goals;
- Keeping a record of your progress toward your goals;
- Rewarding yourself for milestones you reach along the path to your goals;
- Converting setbacks into comebacks by learning from mistakes and maintaining positive expectations.

Studies of successful people who achieve their goals reveal they possess the following personal characteristics.

Internal Locus of Control. They believe that the locus (location or source) of control for events in their life is *internal*—"inside" them and within their control—rather than *external*—outside them and beyond their control.

Self-Efficacy. They believe they have power to produce a positive effect on the *outcomes* of their lives. They believe success is something that's earned and the harder they work at it, the more likely they'll get it.

Grit. They expend significant effort, energy, and sacrifice over an extended period of time to achieve their goals. People with grit have been found to possess the following qualities:

- *Persistence*—when the going gets tough, they don't give up, they step it up; they have the fortitude to persist in the face of frustration and adversity.
- *Tenacity*—they pursue their goals with relentless determination; if they encounter something along the way that's hard to do, they work harder to do it.

- *Resilience*—they bounce back from setbacks and turn them into comebacks.
- *Self-Discipline*—they have *self-control*—they resist the impulse to pursue instant gratification and do what they feel like doing instead of what should be done to reach their goal; they're able to sacrifice immediate, short-sighted needs and desires to do what has to be done to get where they want to be in the long run.

Note

Achieving success isn't a short sprint; it's a long-distance run that takes patience and perseverance. Goal-setting is the key that gets us off the starting blocks and motivation is the fuel that keeps us going until we cross the finish line.

Learning More through the World Wide Web: Internet-Based Resources

For additional information on goal-setting and motivation, see the following websites.

Goal Setting:
https://www.mindtools.com/page6.html

Self-Motivational Strategies:
www.selfmotivationstrategies.com

Self-Efficacy:
www.psychologytoday.com/blog/flourish/201002/if-you-think-you-can-t-think-again-the-sway-self-efficacy

Grit and Resilience:
https://undergrad.stanford.edu/resilience

Growth Mindset:
www.ted.com/talks/carol_dweck_the_power_of_believing_that_you_can_improve?language=en

References

Astin, A. W. (1993). *What matters in college?* San Francisco: Jossey-Bass.

Bandura, A. (1986). *Social foundations of thought and action: A social cognitive theory.* Englewood Cliffs, NJ: Prentice Hall.

Bandura, A. (1994). Self-efficacy. In V. S. Ramachaudran (Ed.), *Encyclopedia of human behavior* (Vol. 4, pp. 71–81). New York: Academic Press.

Bandura, A. (1997). *Self-efficacy: The exercise of control.* New York: Freeman.

Brissette, I., Cohen, S., & Seeman, T. E. (2000). Measuring social integration and social networks. In S. Cohen, L. G. Underwood, & B. H. Gottlieb (Eds.), *Social support measurement and intervention* (pp. 53–85). New York: Oxford University Press.

Brooks, K. (2009). *You majored in what? Mapping your path from chaos to career.* New York: Penguin.

Carlson, N. R., Miller, H., Heth, C. D., Donahoe, J. W., & Martin, G. N. (2009). *Psychology: The science of behaviour* (7th ed.). Toronto, ON: Pearson Education Canada.

Duckworth, A.L., Peterson, C., Matthews, M.D., & Kelly, D.R. (2007). Grit: Perseverance and passion for long-term goals. *Journal of Personality and Social Psychology, 92*(6), 1087–1101.

Ewell, P. T. (1997). Organizing for learning. *AAHE Bulletin, 50*(4), 3–6.

Feldman, K. A., & Newcomb, T. M. (1994). *The impact of college on students.* New Brunswick, NJ: Transaction Publishers. (Original work published 1969).

Gilbert, P. T. (2006). *Stumbling on happiness.* New York: Alfred A. Knopf.

Halvorson, H. G. (2010). *Succeed: How we can reach our goals.* New York: Plume.

Harris, P., Griffin, D., & Murray, S. (2008). Testing the limits of optimistic bias: Event and person moderators in a multilevel framework. *Journal of Personality and Social Psychology, 95*, 1225–1237.

Hashaw, R. M., Hammond, C. J., & Rogers, P. H. (1990). Academic locus of control and the collegiate experience. *Research & Teaching in Developmental Education, 7*(1), 45–54.

Hollenbeck, J. R., Williams, C. R., & Klein, H. J. (1989). An empirical examination of the antecedents of commitment to difficult goals. *Journal of Applied Psychology, 74*(1), 18–23.

Jernigan, C. G. (2004). What do students expect to learn? The role of learner expectancies, beliefs, and attributions for success and failure in student motivation. *Current Issues in Education* [On-line], 7(4). Retrieved from cie.asu.edu/ojs/index.php/cieatasu/article/download/824/250.

Latham, G., & Locke, E. (2007). New developments in and directions for goal-setting research. *European Psychologists, 12*, 290–300.

Locke, E. A. (2000). Motivation, cognition, and action: An analysis of studies of task goals and knowledge. *Applied Psychology: An International Review, 49*, 408–429.

Locke, E. A., & Latham, G. P. (1990). *A theory of goal setting and task performance.* Englewood Cliffs, NJ: Prentice Hall.

Locke, E. A., & Latham, G. P. (2002). Building a practically useful theory of goal setting and task motivation. *American Psychologist, 57*, 705–717.

Meyer, P. J. (2003). "What would you do if you knew you couldn't fail? Creating S.M.A.R.T. Goals." In *Attitude is everything: If you want to succeed above and beyond.* Meyer Resource Group, Incorporated.

Multon, K. D., Brown, S. D., & Lent, R. W. (1991). Relation of self-efficacy beliefs to academic outcomes: A meta-analytic investigation. *Journal of Counseling Psychology, 38*(1), 30–38.

Newell, A., & Simon, H. A. (1959). *The simulation of human thought.* Santa Monica, CA: Rand Corporation.

Oettingen, G. (2000). Expectancy effects on behavior depend on self-regulatory thought. *Social Cognition, 14*, 101–129.

Oettingen, G., & Stephens, E. (2009). Mental contrasting future and reality: A motivationally intelligent self-regulatory strategy. In G. Moskowitz & H. Grant (Eds.), *The psychology of goals.* New York: Guilford.

Pascarella, E., & Terenzini, P. (1991). *How college affects students: Findings and insights from twenty years of research.* San Francisco: Jossey-Bass.

Pascarella, E., & Terenzini, P. (2005). *How college affects students: A third decade of research* (Vol. 2). San Francisco: Jossey-Bass.

Rotter, J. (1966). Generalized expectancies for internal versus external controls of reinforcement. *Psychological Monographs: General and Applied, 80*(609), 1–28.

Stoltz, P. G. (2014). *Grit: The new science of what it takes to persevere, flourish, succeed.* San Luis Obispo: Climb Strong Press.

Van Overwalle, F. I., Mervielde, I., & De Schuyer, J. (1995). Structural modeling of the relationships between attributional dimensions, emotions, and performance of college freshmen. *Cognition and Emotion, 9*(1), 59–85.

Wilhite, S. (1990). Self-efficacy, locus of control, self-assessment of memory ability, and student activities as predictors of college course achievement. *Journal of Educational Psychology, 82*(4), 696–700.

Zimmerman, B. J. (1995). Self-efficacy and educational development. In A. Bandura (Ed.), *Self-efficacy in changing societies.* New York: Cambridge University Press.

Zimmerman, B. J. (2000). Self-efficacy: An essential motive to learn. *Contemporary Educational Psychology, 25*, 82–91.

Chapter 9 Exercises

9.1 Quote Reflections

Review the sidebar quotes contained in this chapter and select two that were especially meaningful or inspirational to you.

For each quote, write a three- to five-word sentence explaining why you chose it.

9.2 Reality Bite

No Goals, No Direction

Amy Aimless decided to go to college because it seemed like that's what she was expected to do. All of her closest friends were going and her parents have talked to her about going to college for as long as she can remember.

Now that she's in her first term, Amy isn't sure she made the right decision. She has no educational or career goals, nor does she have any idea about what her major might be. None of the subjects she took in high school and none of the courses she's taking during her first term in college have really sparked her interest. Since she has no goals or sense of purpose, she's beginning to think that being in college is a waste of her time and her parents' money, so she's considering withdrawing at the end of the term.

Reflection and Discussion Questions

1. Would you agree that Amy shouldn't have begun college in the first place? Why?
2. What suggestions do you have for Amy that might help her find some sense of educational purpose or direction?
3. Would you agree that Amy is currently wasting her time and her parents' money? Why?
4. Can you relate to Amy's story, or do you know other students who are in a similar predicament? (Briefly describe why or how.)

9.3 Clarifying Your Goals

Take a moment to answer the following questions as honestly as possible:

- What are my highest priorities?
- What competing needs and priorities do I need to keep in check?
- How will I maintain balance across different aspects of my life?
- What am I willing and able to give up in order to achieve my educational and personal goals?

- How can I maintain motivation on a day-to-day basis?
- Who can I collaborate with to reach my goals and what will that collaboration involve?

9.4 Reducing the Gap between Your Ideal Future and Your Current Reality

Think of an aspect of your life where there's a significant gap between what you'd like it to be (the ideal) and where you are (the reality).

Use the following form to identify a goal you could pursue to reduce this gap.

Goal: _____

What specific *actions* will be taken?

When will these actions be taken?

What *obstacles or roadblocks* do you anticipate?

What *resources* could you use to overcome your anticipated obstacles or roadblocks?

How will you *measure your progress*?

How will you know when you *reached or achieved* your goal?

9.5 Converting Setbacks into Comebacks: Transforming Pessimism into Optimism through Positive Self-Talk

In *Hamlet*, Shakespeare wrote: "There is nothing good or bad, but thinking makes it so." His point was that experiences have the potential to be positive or negative, depending on how people interpret them and react to them.

Listed below is a series of statements representing negative, motivation-destroying interpretations and reactions to a situation or experience:

a) "I'm just not good at this."
b) "There's nothing I can do about it."
c) "Nothing is going to change."
d) "This always happens to me."
e) "Everybody is going to think I'm a loser."

For each of the preceding statements, replace the negative statement with a statement that represents a more positive, self-motivating interpretation or reaction.

Goal Setting & Motivation
Moving from Intention to Action

Name: _____

Possible Classroom Exercises & Out-of Class Assignments

In addition to, or instead of the exercises included at the end of the chapter, the following may be used as exercises/assignments relating to content covered in Chapter 3.

Brainstorming Characteristics of Successful People

In small groups or as a whole class, ask students to brainstorm ideas in response to the question: "What makes people successful?" or "What personal qualities characterize successful people?" If students completed the reflection at the very beginning of Chapter 3 ("For me, success is . . ."), have them flash back to their answer and compare/contrast it with their answer to the current question about what personal qualities characterize successful people.

Assessing Motivation to Implement Key College-Success Principles and Practices

Ask students to assess their motivation for putting into practice the college-success principles and practices listed on the following checklist. Next to each practice, have them put a number (1–5) in the box, using the following scale:

5 = *Strongly Motivated* to Put into Practice

4 = *Somewhat Motivated* to Put into Practice

3 = Not Sure

2 = *Somewhat Unmotivated* to Put into Practice

1 = *Definitely Not Motivated* to Put into Practice

Checklist of College-Success Principles & Practices
1. **ACTIVE INVOLVEMENT**
   Inside the Classroom:
   - ☐ I will *not miss* class—I'll treat it like a job, showing up to class as consistently as I'd show up for work.
   - ☐ I will get *involved* in class—I'll come prepared, listen actively, take notes, and participate.

Outside the Classroom:
- ☐ I will *read actively*—I'll take notes while I read to increase my attention and retention.
- ☐ I will spend about two hours of time outside of class working on my courses for every one hour I spend in class, thus making it a 40-hour academic work week.

2. **UTILIZING CAMPUS RESOURCES**

   I will take advantage of the following *support services*:
   - ☐ Veterans Services
   - ☐ Math Lab
   - ☐ Learning Center
   - ☐ Writing Center
   - ☐ L Mendel Rivers Library
   - ☐ Faculty Academic Advisor
   - ☐ The Counseling Center

   I will capitalize on the following *experiential learning* opportunities:
   - ☐ Co-curricular experiences on campus
   - ☐ Volunteer experiences and internships off campus

3. **INTERPERSONAL INTERACTION & COLLABORATION**
   - ☐ I will *interact* with my *peers* by joining campus clubs and student organizations.

   I will *collaborate* with my peers by forming *learning teams* for the following purposes:
   - ☐ taking lecture notes
   - ☐ completing reading assignments
   - ☐ editing writing assignments
   - ☐ conducting library research
   - ☐ reviewing results of exams and course assignments.

   I will interact with:
   - ☐ *Faculty*—by connecting with my instructors immediately after class, in their offices, or via e-mail.
   - ☐ *Academic Advisors*—I will see them for more than just a signature to register; I'll find an advisor I can relate to and with whom I can develop an ongoing relationship.
   - ☐ *Mentors*—I will find an experienced person who can serve as a trusted guide and role model for me.

4. **SELF-REFLECTION & SELF-AWARENESS**
   - ☐ I will *self-monitor* my learning and remain aware of *how* I'm learning, *what* I'm learning, and *if* I'm learning it effectively.

☐ I will reflect on *feedback* that I've received from others about the quality of my performance and what specifically I can do to improve it.

☐ I will take *self-assessment* tests or inventories to gain greater awareness of my personal characteristics (e.g., my interests, values, abilities, learning habits, learning styles, self-concept, or personality traits) and use the results to help me explore or confirm my decision about a major and career.

☐ I will reflect on *my future* by taking time to project ahead, set long-term goals, and develop plans for exploring and deciding about my major, my career, and my future life.

Reflections on the Motivational Checklist

For each item you rated "1" or "2":
(a) *Why* are you weakly motivated or unmotivated to engage in this practice?
(b) *What* might help you develop the motivation needed to engage in this practice?

For each item you rated "4" or "5":
(a) Are you are already engaging in this practice?
(b) If not, when are you planning to do so?

Long-Term Goal Clarification

Either as an in-class exercise or take-home assignment, have your students respond to the 12 questions listed in the box below.

Identify a **long-term goal** that's most important to you— i.e., a goal that would take you at least two years to reach—and honestly answer the following 12 questions about your goal.

1. *Why* do you want to achieve this goal? (What's your primary reason or motive for choosing it?)
2. How *passionate* are you about reaching this goal? (How important is it for you to attain it?)
3. Will you need to really *stretch or push* yourself to reach this goal?
4. What *changes* (if any) in your attitude or behavior would you have to make in order to reach this goal?
5. What about yourself, or your current circumstances, *might interfere or hold you back* from reaching this goal?
6. What's likely to be the major *obstacle* you'll encounter on the path toward your goal, and how hard it will be for you to overcome this obstacle?
7. What do you think will be your most valuable *resource* for helping you reach your goal?
8. *Who* would you inform about your goal to hold you accountable for continuing to pursue it and not give up until you've achieved it?
9. When will you *start* (or when did you start) taking steps toward achieving your long-term goal?
10. What are the major *stepping stones* or *milestones* that need to be reached along the way to your long-term goal and what's your *timeline* for reaching them?
11. If you reach your goal, what *positive consequences and feelings* do you expect to experience?
12. If you don't reach your, what *negative consequences and feelings* are you likely to experience?

Motivational Recommendations for Next Year's Entering Class

Based on your successes and struggles thus far as a new college student, write a short letter or "tip sheet" of strategies that you'd recommend to next year's entering class of students about what they could do to get off to a fast start in college. Please include specific recommendations for each of the following aspects of the college experience:

(1) the classroom
(2) course assignments
(3) exams
(4) campus life outside the classroom.

Prioritizing Important Life Goals

Directions to Students:

1. Rank the following life goals order of their priority for you (1 = highest, 5 = lowest).
   ___ Emotional well-being
   ___ Spiritual growth
   ___ Physical health
   ___ Social relationships
   ___ Rewarding career

2. What were the primary reasons behind your first—and last-ranked choices?

3. Have you established any short—or mid-range goals for reaching your highest-ranked choice? If yes, what are they? If not, what could they be?

Quote Interpretations & Reactions

Ask students to provide their reaction, interpretation, or level of agreement with the following quotes:

(1) "You were born to win, but to be a winner you must plan to win, prepare to win, and expect to win."
—Zig Ziglar, author, salesperson and motivational speaker

(2) "Patience and tenacity of purpose are worth more than twice their weight in cleverness."
—Thomas Huxley, 19th-century English biologist

(3) "A man's errors are his portals of discovery."
—James Joyce, Irish writer and poet